From the Authors of *Handgun Stopping*

Evan P. Marshall · Edwin J. Sa

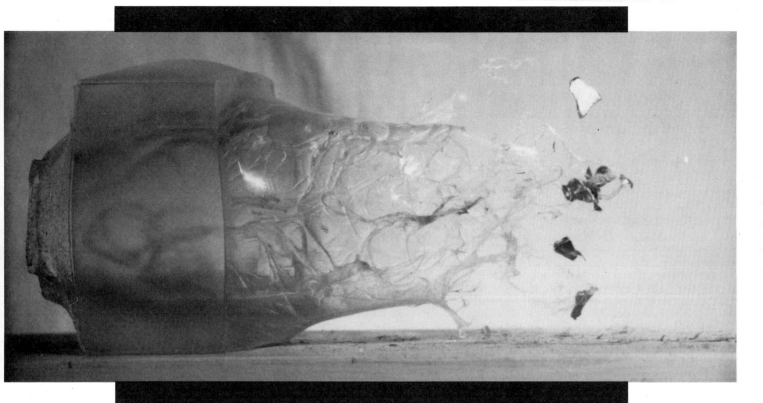

STREET STOPPERS

The Latest Handgun Stopping Power Street Results

Paladin Press · Boulder, Colorado

Also by Evan P. Marshall and Edwin J. Sanow:
Handgun Stopping Power: The Definitive Study
Stopping Power: A Practical Analysis of the Latest Handgun Ammunition

Street Stoppers: The Latest Handgun Stopping Power Street Results
by Evan P. Marshall and Edwin J. Sanow

Copyright © 1996 by Evan P. Marshall and Edwin J. Sanow

ISBN 0-87364-872-2
Printed in the United States of America

Published by Paladin Press, a division of
Paladin Enterprises, Inc.
Gunbarrel Tech Center
7077 Winchester Circle
Boulder, Colorado 80301 USA
+1.303.443.7250

Direct inquiries and/or orders to the above address.

Chapter 3, Neurogenic Shock, copyright © 1996 by Dennis Tobin

Chapter 7, Royal Canadian Mounted Police Ammo Tests, copyright ©
HER MAJESTY THE QUEEN IN RIGHT OF CANADA (1994)
as represented by the Solicitor General of Canada

Chapter 22, The History of Hydra-Shok, Starfire, and Quik-Shok
Ammunition, copyright © 1996 by Tom Burczynski

Cover photo courtesy of Tom Burczynski

Visit our Web site at www.paladin-press.com

Contents

Evan Marshall: This work is dedicated to my wife, Maryann, who has always believed in me, and to my children and their spouses: John and Marcia Marshall, Kelly and Melissa Wall, Gary and Sara Gudmundson, Mark Marshall, and Martha Marshall.

And to my grandchildren: Derek and Emily Wall.

And especially to Elder Matthew Marshall, Romania Bucharest Mission, The Church of Jesus Christ of Latter Day Saints; and Elder Evan J. Marshall, Taiwan Taipei Mission, The Church of Jesus Christ of Latter Day Saints.

"No success can compensate for failure in the home."
—David O. McKay

Ed Sanow: This book is also dedicated to my wife and best friend, Cindy Jo, who has supported my enthusiasm for the study of wound ballistics even to the extent of accepting the risks of law enforcement, and to Deputy Matt Rosenbarger, whose gunshot injury during a late-night vehicle stop served as a wake-up call to many in rural law enforcement.

Acknowledgements

No work such as this is possible without the help of others. The individuals and organizations listed below were critical to the success of this effort.

Peter Pi and Lynn Eichler of Cor-Bon Ammunition
Vince O'Neill, CLET, Oklahoma City, Oklahoma
Shep Kelly, Bob Kramer, Mike Larsen, and Dave Longren of
  Federal Cartridge Corporation
Ted Rowe, Mike Bussard, and Alan Newcomb of Sigarms
Bill Wohl, Greg Foster, Phil Birch, Sean Dwyer, John Chisnall,
  and Dave Schluckebier of Remington Arms Company
Mike Jordan, Alan Corzine, Dave Trowbridge, and Don Emde
  of Winchester-Olin Corporation
Massad Ayoob, Lethal Force Institute
John Farnam, Defense Training International
Col. Robert Young, USMC (Ret.)
John Klein, Sage International
John Hambrick, Waco, Texas, PD
Brian Felter, Beretta Arms
Dr. Tomas Mijares, South West Texas State University
Gerald Solai, Director of Public Safety, Centerline, Michigan
Jeff Hopkins, Central Florida Criminal Justice Institute
Sgt. Dave Spaulding, Montgomery County, Ohio, Sheriff
Cpl. Jim Horan, Howard County, Maryland, Sheriff

Deputy Nick Roberts, Salt Lake County, Utah, Sheriff
Deputy Leigh Kilpack, Salt Lake County, Utah, Sheriff
Gary Runyon, U.S. Border Patrol, Pennsylvania
Richard Davis, Second Chance Body Armor
Lt. Al Kulavitz, Cook County Sheriff, Illinois
Tom Burczynski, Experimental Research
C. Kurt Cannon, Glaser Safety Slug, Inc.
Allan Jones, Tom Saleen, and Darrell Inman of CCI-Speer/Blount, Inc.
Dr. Daniel Frank, NIJ Law Enforcement Standards Lab
Larry McGee, Rob Reiber, and Stan Isa of PMC-Eldorado Cartridge
Anthony Gregory, Tactical Training Associates
Jim Reinholt, Reinholt Firearms
Stan Robinson, Cook County, Illinois, Sheriff
Dennis Martin, CQB Services (England)
Gary Wesitrand, Kennedy Space Center
John Wiseman, 22nd SAS (Ret.), Hereford, England
Jan Libourel, *Handguns* magazine
David W. Arnold, *Handguns* magazine
Denny Hansen, *SWAT* magazine
Jim Shults, *Modern Guns* magazine
Frank Repass, Orlando, Florida, PD
Warren Buttler, FLETC, Georgia
Sid Swanson, Pathcor Corporation
Roy McGruder, Dale Johnston, Bob Wilson, Bernard Farr, David
   Pouch, and Paul Dragen, of the Detroit Police Crime Laboratory
Ed Lovette, Langley, Virginia
Dr. Dennis Tobin, Victoria, Texas
Col. Rex Applegate
Bob Taubert, FBI (Ret.)
Bert DuVernay and Tom Avini of the Smith & Wesson Academy
Dr. Ed Hancock, Mesa, Arizona
Dr. Pete Divasto, Albuquerque, New Mexico
Uzi Gal, Carlisle, Pennsylvania
Walt Farr, Los Angeles, California, Sheriff (Ret.)
Sgt. Joe Solomon, Detroit PD FTU
Norm Sieloff, Detroit PD (Ret.)
Joseph Piersante, University of Michigan Department of Public Safety
Marty and Gila May Hayes, Seattle, Washington
Scott Blackledge, New Mexico Department of Public Safety
Joe Viviano, U.S. Secret Service
Grace Matthews, Metro Dade PD
Clint Smith, Thunder Ranch
Donna Rogers, *Law Enforcement Technology* magazine

Bruce Cameron, *Law and Order* magazine
Charles Leslie Dees, *Police Marksman* magazine
Richard Fairburn, Lawman Group
Judy Hamilton, J's Custom Printing
Gene Coffing, Color Tech
Jimmy Cirillo, New York City PD, FLETC (Ret.)
Robert B. Lutz, U.S. Secret Service
Lt. Randy Davis, Indiana Law Enforcement Academy
Lt. Glenda Mercer, Indiana Law Enforcement Academy
Lt. Robert Black, Indiana Law Enforcement Academy
Sheriff Boston Pritchett, Benton County, Indiana, Sheriff
Capt. Dale Linville, Benton County, Indiana, Sheriff
Deputy Joe Salla, Benton County, Indiana, Sheriff
Deputy Matt Rosenbarger, Benton County, Indiana, Sheriff
Chief Tim Gordon, Fowler, Indiana, PD
Sgt. Terry Risner, Jasper County, Indiana, Sheriff
Sgt. Brian Stover, Los Angeles County, CA, Sheriff
Cpl. David Durant, Marion County, Indiana, Sheriff
Sgt. Mike Summerville, Illinois State Police
Dep. Insp. John Cerar, New York City PD
Det. Frank DiMario, New York City PD
Dr. Paul Whitesell, Ft. Wayne, Indiana, PD
Tpr. David Young, Indiana State Police
Lt. Ken Campbell, Boone County, Indiana, Sheriff
Officer Neill Yeaman, Zionsville, Indiana, PD
Lt. Steve Robertson, Indianapolis, Indiana, PD
Sgt. James Heath, Indianapolis, Indiana, PD
Lt. Jeff Belttari, Markleville, Indiana, PD
Lt. Col. Jeff Cooper, Gunsite (Ret.)
Sheriff Ern Hudson, Boone County, Indiana, Sheriff
Lt. Mike Russo, Marion County, Indiana, Sheriff
Sgt. Joey Cox, Arkansas State Police
Dan Watters, University of South Carolina
Fernando Coelho, Triton Cartridge
Richard Dixon, D&D Bullets
David Keen, Signature Products
Steve Hornady, Hornady Mfg.
Doug Engh, Hornady Mfg.
Joe Zambone, MagSafe Ammo Co.
Col. Billy Hancock, Crisp County, Georgia, Sheriff
Chief Deputy Joe Rupe, Johnson County, Indiana, Sheriff
Capt. Al Kasper, Pike Township, Indiana, PD
Dan Fair, U.S. Marshals Service

ACKNOWLEDGMENTS

Robert Gates II, Smith & Wesson
Frank DiNuzzio, Glock, Inc.
Paul Jannuzzo, Esq., Glock, Inc.
Sgt. Denny Reichard, Rochester, Indiana, PD
Curtis Shipley, Master Cartridge/Georgia Arms
Jeff Hoffman, Black Hills Ammo

In addition, there are those who contributed valuable information but for obvious reasons cannot be identified by name. They belong to the following organizations, and the authors want them to know we appreciate their contributions in spite of great personal risk:

The Strasbourg Study Staff
Federal Bureau of Investigation
FBI FTU, Quantico, Virginia
FBI Hostage Rescue Team
SEAL Team 5
SEAL Team 6
Marine Corp Force Recon
GSG9
GIGN
Royal Marines, England
Special Boat Squadron, England
Delta Force
DEA CLET
U.S. Secret Service CAT
Illinois State Police Academy
Medical examiners personnel in a variety of cities both in the
    United States and overseas
Harvard Medical School
University of Michigan Medical School
Wayne State University Medical School
U.S. Army-Mott Lake
Crane Lab, Indiana
U.S. Army Rangers
DEA, Lima, Peru
U.S. Marine Corp Special Ops, South America
Several veterans of Operations URGENT FURY, JUST CAUSE, DESERT
    STORM, and a couple of others that had best remain nameless
DIA
CIA
NIS
Maryland State Police

Detroit, Michigan, PD Homicide
Los Angeles, California, PD SWAT
Los Angeles, California, PD Homicide
Los Angeles Sheriff's Department Homicide
Los Angeles Sheriff's Department Special Enforcement Bureau
California Highway Patrol
New Jersey State Police
Las Vegas, Nevada, Metro PD
Anchorage, Alaska, PD
Washington, D.C., Homicide
Baltimore, Maryland, PD Homicide
San Francisco, California, PD
Los Angeles, California, PD Crime Lab
Dallas, Texas, PD
New Orleans, Louisiana, PD Homicide
Metro-Dade (Miami) PD
Atlanta, Georgia, PD
GBI
FLETC
U.S. Postal Inspectors
New York City PD Emergency Services Unit
DEA, Miami, Florida
U.S. Border Patrol
Chicago, Illinois, PD Narcotics
Long Beach, California, PD
Phoenix, Arizona, PD
Alaska Highway Patrol
Pasadena, California, PD
Newark, New Jersey, PD
Madison, Wisconsin, PD
Texas DPS
Seattle, Washington, PD
Oklahoma City, Oklahoma, PD
Jackson, Mississippi, PD
Houston, Texas, PD
Boston, Massachusetts, PD
Winston-Salem, North Carolina, PD
Austin, Texas, PD
San Diego, California, PD
Macon, Georgia, PD
State Department Security
and especially to "Scooter" and "Buzz Saw," who busted SCUDs
    prior to Desert Storm.

Foreword

by John Farnam

A number of years ago, I was asked to write the foreword for Evan Marshall's and Ed Sanow's first book on the subject of terminal handgun ballistic performance. That book, *Handgun Stopping Power: The Definitive Study*, is still an excellent work, and I commend it to your reading before you start this present volume.

Handgun Stopping Power was a blockbuster! It shattered hallowed fantasies and dear falsehoods from one end of the ballistic spectrum to the other. As a result, it and its authors have been embroiled in bitter controversy ever since its publication. It seems there were and are many vested interests in the ammunition and ballistic consulting industries, and many people were very unhappy with the book because it said unkind things about particular types of pistol ammunition which were (mistakenly) held in high esteem by many people. Many accusations and insults were hurled at Evan and Ed, but, being men of honor, they stuck to the facts and never responded in kind.

I've known Ev and Ed for many years, and they are two of the people in this business for which I have a great deal of respect. I remember seeing an embattled Ed Sanow deliver an address at an industry conference several years ago. His antagonists within the organization denounced and condemned him. They said he shouldn't even be allowed to speak! But speak he did! His consumate honesty and almost childlike devotion to the pursuit of the truth stunned the entire audience that night. He hammered home point after point. His statistical ducks were all in a row. His logic and conclusions were incontrovertible. His presentation was a marvel indeed.

The naysayers were rendered speechless. But Ed never once said anything harsh about any of his critics, even the viciously vocal ones. He never let it get personal. Ed Sanow made a lot of friends that night. Even his antagonists grudgingly admitted that he knew what he was talking about. Evan and Ed have passed "the test."

This new volume is a quantum leap above

the first. It contains never-before-published data. The conclusions and recommendations made herein are authoritative and thoroughly researched. It's not just academic speculation and conclusions gleaned from eggheads shooting at jello. It contains virtually all we know about terminal ballistics, including all the known and verifiable data from actual shootings.

These guys are the foremost authorities on this subject. They are worthy. They are men of honor. I'm not sure if even I agree with everything said herein, but there is solid data behind all of it.

In *Handgun Stopping Power*, I indicated that when these guys talk, I listen. Well, I'm still listening. You should too!

—*John Farnam*
Defense Training International

Introduction

Like its predecessor, *Handgun Stopping Power: The Definitive Study*, the goal of this book is to provide accurate and reliable information to good guys and gals to help them select handgun, submachine gun, rifle, and shotgun loads that will assist them in surviving attacks by committed, violent felons who are all too common these days.

All of us have been exposed to various theories that have been designed to "prove" that a particular type of load works better than others. Julian Hatcher argued that bigger was better, while the National Institute of Justice (NIJ) Computer Man study proposed that light and fast was always superior. The real world, however, has shown us that while some big-bore moderate-velocity loads work extremely well, others are dismal failures. Conversely, while some lightweight high-velocity loads have proven to be reliable street stoppers, others of similar velocity and bullet weight have been mediocre at best.

While assigned to the Crime Scene Investigation Unit of the Detroit Police Department, I responded to a number of shootings. Curious about which bullets were effective, I began to ask a lot of questions and received conflicting and confusing answers. I made a trip to the Wayne County Morgue, where I learned a number of valuable lessons. First, the high performance load of the day, Super Vel, did not turn internal organs to mush, as some uninformed individuals wanted us to believe. I found, in fact, that when examining wound channels in the human body, it was virtually impossible to tell the difference between the Detroit PD issue Federal .38 Special 158-grain round-nose lead load and the Super Vel 110-grain jacketed hollowpoint.

Since the Detroit Police Department allowed wide latitude in the choice of personal handguns, I carried a Smith & Wesson Model 58 .41 Magnum loaded with Remington 210-grain lead semiwadcutters. I had been exposed to Hatcher, and it made sense then. After all, my grandfather had preached the same approach for hunting rifles—bigger is always better. Later on, I began to realize that theory was not correlating with reality.

I can only claim that I had a good idea—if we could gather enough data about how a particular load had worked in actual shootings in the past, we might be able, with some degree of accuracy, to predict how the same load *might* work in the future. Beyond that, anyone could have collected the appropriate data, but no one did. Some thought such an approach anecdotal and unscientific, as if anecdotal was a bad word. But this work was aimed at cops and civilians concerned about survival, not scientists ensconsed in ivory towers thinking obtuse thoughts.

Coauthor Ed Sanow has been an invaluable partner whose incisive mind and strong streak of skepticism have made this work as valuable as it is. We don't always agree, but even when we agree to disagree, it is done cheerfully. Ed has been unfairly attacked because of his association with me, and it is sad that those who disagree with us cannot do so without resorting to character assassination and lies.

This work is our best effort to provide the reader with accurate, reliable information. The cold, hard fact is that those who have complained that all of this data is made up have had a decade to accumulate actual shooting data to refute these efforts. Does anyone honestly think the critics would not like to make me out as a fraud and liar? They have not, because they cannot. For those who do not believe that the 9mm 115-grain JHP +P+ works as well as indicated here, contact the Illinois State Police or U.S. Border Patrol. For those who think Hydra-Shok is a gimmick, talk to the FBI and Washington, D.C., Police Department. And so on and so on.

What follows, then, is not Marshall's or Sanow's Theory of Ballistic Supremacy but the results of actual handgun shootings and the first street-relevant formula to use 10-percent gelatin as a predictor of future performance. It is offered with affection to assist people in making this most critical of decisions.

Finally, it must be clearly understood that there is no substitute for bullet placement. Yet because the ability to place bullets with surgical precision becomes extremely difficult under high stress, the selection of rounds that have worked better in actual shootings can be important.

—Evan Marshall
Midland, Michigan
August 1995

1

Gunfights and Ammo: The Big Picture

by Keith Jones

One of the hardest things to get across to students of survival is that bullet performance is a very small part of an enormously large picture. You can't fault someone for wanting an edge on survival, but the fact remains: being on the wrong end of a homicidal assault is not a happy place to be.

Some years ago during an "officer safety" class, a police cadet raised his hand and asked the question that cut to the heart of what everyone else was thinking: "How do you keep from getting hurt in a gunfight?" The instructor, a veteran of several shooting incidents, quoted the late Elmer Keith: "The only way to keep from getting hurt in a gunfight is don't get in a gunfight."

There is no simple formula for surviving a gunfight. There are too many variables present for any single tool or technique to work for every person every time. The key to surviving is to control as many of those variables as you can before the fight even starts. Then use cover to buy time to deal with the variables you'll encounter during the fight. You've got to shoot straight and be flexible.

Gunfight survival is not just a study of bullets or velocities or anything else that can be replicated in a laboratory. It is a study of the dynamics of situations, situations that are so fluid, so unique unto themselves, that they resist being encompassed by any single philosophy. Opinions should never be so rigid that they rob you of your flexibility or cause you to place too much emphasis on the wrong thing. Your capabilities, and ultimately your survival, can be seriously impaired if your focus is too narrow or misplaced.

Debate is healthy and a vital hallmark of a free society. It provides a ready forum for the testing of ideas. It helps us define the middle ground by exposing us to the extremes of the spectrum. Most of all, it promotes an exchange of information and results in an alerted citizenry. Knowledge really is power.

But the power can be crippled if the knowledge isn't kept in perspective. A "fanatic" has been described as someone who redoubles his efforts after he has lost sight of his goal. Perspective keeps you from losing sight of your goal, which in this case is to survive a gunfight. To lose sight of the whole picture is to lose the ability to react quickly to the fluid variables of a life-threatening encounter.

Examples of what can happen when good people lose their sense of perspective can be found in any forum. In popular gun magazines, we've all seen the debates over "Weaver vs. Isosceles," "revolver vs. auto pistol," or "aimed fire vs. point shooting." The acrimony that has welled up in some of these disputes has been astonishing. We're talking about two "systems" here, folks. Why would anyone train with, or use, one to the exclusion of the other?

The selection of a handgun and ammunition is as good a test of your ability to compromise as can be found. It requires a realistic assessment of the type of trouble you might face and the type of scenario where you'll face it. It also requires an honest—and that means *honest*—appraisal of your ability to handle a weapon under stress. Remembering a few simple rules will help you keep things in perspective.

First, bear in mind that when you don't know what to do, you'll do what you know how to do. You have got to have a plan with several simple options, and you have to train ahead of time. The handgun you select must be reliable, accurate, and simple to operate under stress. Combat shooting has to be done with very little mental involvement, thus freeing your mind for tactical decision making.

Second, remember that any tool or technique you select must help you survive both the incident and the post-incident investigation. All incidents involving the use of deadly force must be investigated thoroughly in a free society, and they should be. Unfortunately, the post-incident investigation by the authorities and news media is sometimes nearly as traumatic as the incident itself.

While we all agree that "it's better to be tried by twelve than carried by six," the choice is rarely that extreme. At least it doesn't have to be. If you use your head and make some intelligent compromises, you will prevail when it all hits the proverbial fan.

Finally, never forget that nothing works 100

"You have to hit 'em to hurt 'em," instructs Keith Jones, four-time gunfight veteran and certified survival tactics instructor.

percent of the time. It goes beyond a mere acknowledgement of Murphy's Law. During a gunfight, things can go to pieces quicker and in more different directions than during anything you could imagine. Your tactical skills and, most importantly, your mind-set will be a much greater factor in your survival than your weapon and ammo combination. If there were a bullet, gun, or gadget that could guarantee your survival under all circumstances, it would have been invented, patented, and mass-produced long before any of us were born.

Many people seemingly cannot absorb this aspect of survival, including a lot of people who ought to know better. For them, survival readiness ends up being a frenzied search for the "ultimate weapon" or a "magic bullet." It actually gets to be an obsession for some people, but maybe that's not so surprising. Americans are a pretty gadget-oriented group, always seeking the newest or most high-tech tool for dealing with a problem.

But gunfights tend to be pretty low-tech affairs. Big city tactical cops will quickly tell you that a well-directed impact from a hard-wood nightstick or a 12-gauge rifled slug works about as well as anything else, neither of which is new or high-tech. These men, who literally do it for a living, often pay scant attention to the cutting-edge developments in weaponry that become a staple of conversation for the rest of us. In their line of work, success is largely measured by how often they *don't* shoot. They know that survival depends on mind-set, tactics, and marksmanship far more than slight differences in bullet performance. They know that, beyond a certain point, it doesn't matter what kind of ammo you stuff in your weapon.

That "certain point" may vary, depending on the type of weapon you use, your shooting skill, and the type of shooting scenarios that you might reasonably expect to encounter. The performance needs of, say, a VIP bodyguard in a crowded corridor might be a lot different from those of a state trooper stopping a suspect on a lonely highway. A shopkeeper who rarely practices with his weapon might need to make different choices than those made by a well-trained SWAT policeman.

One of the main purposes of this book and its predecessor, *Handgun Stopping Power*, is to assist you in deciding what that "certain point" is for you. Once you've made that decision, the authors hope to help you identify which loads in the various calibers will best meet your needs and, just as importantly, which ones will not.

The load you choose need not be the absolute king of its caliber on some performance list, at least not until you understand what that particular list maker's performance standards are. A quick survey of U.S. federal police agencies, for instance, would reveal that each has its own ideas when it comes to picking a top load in a given caliber. Does this indicate that some of them are right and others are wrong? Not at all. What it does indicate is that each of these agencies has a different mission within our framework of decentralized federal law enforcement.

Some federal officers are tasked with protecting lives in very densely populated scenarios such as airports, courtrooms, and parade routes. These are scenarios where "hard" targets are seldom a problem and target perforation is a great concern. Other federal agents collide with armed criminals under more haphazard circumstances, requiring ammunition that performs well over a wider range of applications. It all adds up to a thoughtful and responsible attempt to tailor ammo performance to the mission goals of each police agency.

Ammunition designers and manufacturers took up this challenge and eventually began producing handgun bullets that will perform predictably within some amazingly precise parameters. The competition is so keen among the various companies that there often isn't a lot of practical difference between their respective offerings in a particular caliber and weight class.

Your emphasis should be on seeking to identify the parameters within which you want your ammunition to do its best. Once you have that nailed down, find a load in the upper third of a well-documented performance list. Make sure that it functions reliably in your weapon and is priced right for your pocketbook. Cost, of course, is a big factor in how much practice you do, and your shooting skill depends on how much you practice.

You don't have expend a lot of ammunition in practice, you just have to practice frequently. In years past, police departments would require each officer to shoot a 60-round PPC-type qualification course twice a year and budgeted their ammo costs accordingly. A few innovative police agencies, however, began taking the same allotted 120-rounds-per-man and had their officers shoot 12 rounds 10 times a year. They soon noticed a significant improvement in gunfight hit ratios by their street cops for the same cash outlay. A simple change in perspective resulted in a tangible improvement in real-world performance.

So bullet performance is important, but it has to take a backseat to bullet placement. The time and money spent on searching for the ultimate bullet would be much better spent on improving your marksmanship with a better-than-average bullet. You certainly have to hurt people when you hit them, but you have got to hit 'em to hurt 'em.

Beyond that, there is not much to say about the practical aspects of bullet selection that counts. The good news is the hard work of gathering meaningful data has been done for us in on-going studies like the one in this book. What a bullet does on impact is no longer purely a matter of conjecture. The bad news is that a handgun is still a less-than-optimum choice as a tool for defending human life.

Nothing is perfect, of course, but at least we now have workable, reliable information regarding terminal bullet performance. This information, if kept in the proper perspective, can enable you to get the most that you reasonably can out of your humble sidearm. The time devoted to worrying and bickering about bullets can be better applied to a much more important task: finding ways to control the dynamics of a gunfight.

Winning a deadly encounter involves recognizing and doing your best to control the variables both before and during the fight. Too many variables exist to catalog in your head. You cannot be sure how they interrelate. Worst of all, they seem to be in a constant state of flux. This sort of situation is not static but constantly in motion, right up to the final gunshot.

How well you fare in an armed encounter depends, in very large measure, on how alert you were, and are, to what's going on around you. The color-coded "levels of awareness" developed and popularized by Col. Jeff Cooper, when used religiously, will allow you to remain safely alert for long periods without fatigue and without seeming paranoid to those around you. Alertness is a major key to your survival and is far more important than the type of weapon you have or your ammo, hol-ster, body armor, or any other accoutrement. Without Colonel Cooper's excellent tactical awareness scale and the vigilance it promotes, you will surely miss, or misinterpret, those little things that might well give you that edge you seek.

You've got to be alert if you hope to get a handle on the variables. There is just no other option. The variables themselves tend to group into three loose categories involving 1) your assailant's actions, 2) your own actions, and 3) the situational factors that affect both of you.

Your assailant's actions are what define the scope of the fight. It is his decision, his aggression, that initiates the attack and determines both the degree and duration of the violence. Criminal assaults themselves are generally a product of opportunity and impulse. Controlling a hoodlum's opportunities can be a fairly simple proposition. His impulses, though, can be another matter entirely. Criminals are dangerously unpredictable. This stems partly from their innate personal make-up. They don't call it the "criminal mentality" for nothing.

A large portion of this unpredictability is also due to our consistent failure to simply recognize criminals for who and what they really are. The rest of us ceaselessly try to fathom their motives and actions based on how we would think and act in similar circumstances. That is a major error on our part because it makes criminals seem unpredictable when, in a lot of respects, they're quite the opposite. This is not to say we should spend all our time looking for the worst in others. But we do need to trust our instincts and accept the fact that there are predators among us who must be dealt with when the need arises.

Dangerous criminals are capable of both predatory and defensive aggression. A basic understanding of the two is necessary because they have different characteristics that can have quite a bearing on the type and degree of danger you're facing. Knowing the practical differences between the two can sometimes give you an edge, both before and during the fight.

The goal of predatory aggression is pure and

simple conquest. Those of us who are socialized, as the psychologists put it, tend to channel our aggressions into socially acceptable pursuits. A lot of successful people got that way because of properly controlled aggression.

A criminal predator, however, doesn't subscribe to the system of values and morals the rest of us use to keep our aggressions in check. That is what makes him a criminal. It isn't that he doesn't know about our system of legal and moral standards. He just doesn't believe that they place any constraints on him. He pretty much looks on us as a crop to be harvested by him and his kind. Our standards of right and wrong are, to him, a pen for sheep that was built for the benefit of the wolves. This is what mental health professionals mean by unsocialized behavior or an antisocial personality.

Predatory aggression is a property of the thinking, calculating part of the human brain. It is directed and focused, usually incorporating a simple plan, a simple goal, and a headlong assault. Antisocial types characteristically do not like to delay the gratification of their desires and don't often set long-term goals. Like other predators, they tend to pick as victims those they perceive to be weaklings or strays. Also like many predators, criminals often use the principles of stealth, distance, and timing when launching an assault. Once it is launched, it's just as predictable, and just as dangerous, as a runaway locomotive. Until you act to forcibly derail things, you will have little or no control over how far it goes.

Defensive aggression, on the other hand, is a property of the emotional part of the brain, an area that harbors our primal responses to danger: fight, flee, or freeze. When an attack plan fails or meets unexpected resistance, or whenever confusion or fear take over, the defensive mode kicks in and further offensive aggression is, for the time being, no longer possible. The goal of defensive aggression is escape or, at best, the recapture of control. It is nonspecific, unplanned, and highly unpredictable. It doesn't mean that person is no longer dangerous, however; people can fight ferociously from the defensive mode. It's just

that they are temporarily incapable of further offensive aggression.

Criminals who are driven into the defensive mode very often drop it and run. However, it is best to avoid second-guessing someone who has a firearm plus an adrenaline dump—and who knows what else—in his bloodstream.

The second category of variables, the one that covers your own actions, is the area over which you have the most control. It deals with the stuff that you're bringing to the party, so to speak. This includes things like your physical and mental attributes, your weapon skills, and your ability to function well under extreme stress. It is an area that occupies a good deal of our time and thought simply because we are able to exert a lot of control over it. It might also explain the fixation some of us have on magic bullets or ultimate handguns.

Adults tend to think in pictures, and it is hard sometimes to envision the abstract concepts that writers and teachers are often forced to use. It is also hard to exert control over an intangible. You *can* measure velocities and cycle rates, however, so it is only natural to be drawn toward a solution that you can actually pick up and hold in your hands—a good weapon and the well-honed skills needed to use it. The trouble is that every year good people die at the hands of criminals, not because they weren't well-armed, but because they weren't ready to defend themselves. It is a matter of being alert, of having a survival mind-set.

A survival mind-set is nothing more than a powerful will to stay alive in circumstances where it ain't all that easy to do so. It has little, if anything, to do with the "killer instinct" or other such melodramatic terminology. All of us are born with it, to a greater or lesser degree, but like any other instinct, it has to be cultivated.

Odd as it sounds, it all starts with a dose of good self-esteem, the simple recognition that you were placed in this universe for a reason and that no one, short of your Creator, has a right to terminate your existence. It also calls for a fierce dedication to prevail over anyone or anything that would do injury to you or your loved ones, no matter what. It requires also that you relegate criminals to their proper station. The life of a decent citizen is always to be held in higher esteem than that of a predatory felon.

A proper mind-set will also help you in dealing with fear. It has been written that fear and anger are different sides to the same emotion, and there is a lot of truth to that. Truly understanding the nature and depth of these emotions, both in yourself and others, can be the key to unlocking much of your combat potential.

In years past, recruits in police academies were subjected to a cherished rite of passage knows as "boxing week." The nervous rookies would pull on boxing gloves, repair to the police gym, and pummel one another for several hours a day. Few of them emerged as viable contenders for the heavyweight title, but that was never really the purpose of the drill. Each of them did, however, learn about anger—how it hindered, how it helped, and how to use it sensibly to replace and control fear.

We could all take a lesson from that. Nothing will galvanize your skills and abilities more effectively than a controlled, righteous, intelligently applied anger. It is the catalyst that gets all your systems in harmony and helps to sustain your determination to survive. You have every right to get angry at anyone who endangers you or other innocent people.

Alertness and a survival mind-set will allow you to react swiftly to danger. Reaction time refers to how quickly you can initiate a physical response once you perceive an imminent threat. The stages of reaction time involve 1) perception of the threat, 2) evaluation of the threat, 3) forming a plan to deal with it, and 4) initiating your response.

If any one of these four components misfires anywhere along the line, a "mental stall" occurs. This is generally a product of being caught in a state of mental unreadiness. It often explains why people don't fight or flee but simply freeze in their tracks. Another example of a mental stall would be the "buck fever" that can affect a deer hunter who is suddenly confronted with a trophy buck at close range. Avoiding a mental stall requires alertness and mental preparation, plus an iron-willed determination to do whatever it takes.

Right along with the prerequisites of alertness and mind-set comes the ability to shoot well under stress. As we mentioned earlier, the mechanical functions of shooting accurately must be accomplished with very little mental involvement. Like a lot of other things in life, it's largely a matter of accumulated experience. That means practice with the same weapon and hopefully under conditions that thoughtfully approximate real-life circumstances.

Your weapon should be simple to operate and have a balance of size, power, and controllability. It also must be reliable in the extreme. A 35-man infantry platoon that has two jammed rifles still has an overwhelming 94 percent of its available firepower remaining. If you're alone in a stairwell when your handgun malfunctions under fire, you're in deep trouble. Your weapon has to cycle and go bang every time. Keep that in mind when you are selecting your firearm and ammunition.

The type of practice that you engage in should initially be geared toward establishing and improving your marksmanship skills. In time, you'll need to learn to shoot properly from various tactical positions and from behind cover. Any shooting exercise, formal or informal, that promotes either of these goals is certainly worthwhile. Any exercise that promotes both of them simultaneously is even better.

The main thing is to get out and shoot on a regular basis. The more you shoot, the more attuned you become to your weapon. The more attuned you become, the less you have to think about maintaining a proper grip or about how to clear a sudden weapon stoppage. The operation of your firearm must truly become second nature to you. The last thing you need in a gunfight is a weapon that feels like a clarinet that you never quite got the hang of.

The final category of variables is easily the most difficult to comprehend and control. Unless armed criminals would happen to invade your home, you'll probably have little preexisting knowledge about the physical setting where the violence occurs. Familiarity with the battlefield has been a sought-after asset throughout history, even in minor skirmishes. Viet Cong guerrillas sometimes ambushed U.S. soldiers along the same trails and river crossings where their fathers had ambushed French troops and their grandfathers had ambushed the Japanese. It can work out to a real advantage.

When getting set up, police robbery stakeout teams frequently plot firing angles and pace off distances in an effort to control downrange shot dispersion. They also check out available cover, concealment, lighting, access routes, and escape routes. It is a matter of controlling everything they can before the fight even starts. As retired NYCPD stake-out specialist Jim Cirillo puts it, "Shooting well is less than 10 percent of surviving a gunfight." The rest of it is mind-set and tactics.

Good tactics are hard to devise because each scenario is different. The problem is finding a tactical concept that is flexible and yet comprehensive enough to allow us to control as many variables as we can. Some experts advocate closing with your adversary and neutralizing him swiftly. The old timers used to say, "Shoot first, shoot fast, shoot straight, and shoot last." When you think of it, there is a lot of merit to that idea. Police SRT units, on the other hand, live by the maxim, "Isolate, contain and negotiate." You can't argue with their successes. Both of these concepts, however, focus on dealing with the problem only after it has reached a certain level or location.

We know that a high-stress situation can seem to be more than just the sum of its parts. We know that it's not static unless we act to make it so. That might just be the key to the problem. If this type of scenario is like a flowing river, then perhaps we should take our cue from the U.S. Army Corps of Engineers. When those guys have to tangle with a river, they don't look on it as a river, they see it as a riverbed. This viewpoint allows them to lock into the *underlying, solid* factors of a very

fluid problem. Control of the riverbed gives them control of the river.

Any tactical concept that we adopt for a gunfight has to do the same thing. For us, controlling the fluid variables of an armed encounter is also a matter of controlling its underlying factors. These factors are distance, cover, and time.

Distance, as it relates to gunfighting, is one of those areas where the military differs noticeably from the civilian world. Ask a career infantry officer about the distance at which he would prefer to engage his enemy and he will generally give you a range of 3 to 5 kilometers. His ideal goal would be to find and fix enemy units and break them apart with heavy weapons before their attack can form up and get under way.

The military, quite sensibly, does its best to minimize nose-to-nose gunfighting on the part of its infantrymen. They know from long experience that plans often go awry and people get hurt when the fighting gets up close and personal. Their rules of engagement are more wide-open, and they routinely use far more dangerous weaponry than is available to civilians, but that doesn't mitigate the fact that things can get out of control real quick when the distances get short.

In the civilian world, shooting incidents overwhelmingly occur at ranges of 3 to 5 yards. It has been that way for as long as accurate records have been kept on handgun fights. In their excellent treatise, *Shooting To Live*, authors W.E. Fairbairn and E.A. Sykes noted that police-action gunfights of the 1930s typically occurred at 4 yards or "considerably less." The latest statistics from the FBI's annual *Law Enforcement Officers Killed and Assaulted* report show little, if any, change in the distances involved.

We're talking about the distances at which cops normally speak with people and the distances at which crime victims are accosted on the street. These are the distances at which even untrained felons can shoot with deadly accuracy. They are also the distances at which citizens and police officers die with needless regularity. Well-respected combat instructors like Thunder Ranch's Clint Smith refer to this close-range death zone as "the hole" in grim recognition of its adverse effect on your prospects for survival. He and other competent instructors coach their students to think ahead and avoid getting caught in the hole by an assailant. Students who are mistakenly caught there are taught to get out with all possible speed and put distance between themselves and the threat. Even an increase of a few feet can dramatically reduce your attacker's chances of hitting you with gunfire.

Sometimes gunfights erupt too quickly and ultrashort ranges cannot be avoided. Such instances are rare, though, if you're alert. Studies of police gunfights have shown that the officers knew, or should have known, that they were walking into danger. The signs are usually there, and your survival demands that you develop an early warning system of your own. A half-second quick draw isn't nearly as useful as a few seconds of advanced warning. Think about it. How far out of the hole could you move with even a 5 second head start? You have to be alert. You have work to control distance—the distance between you and your attacker and between you and the nearest solid cover.

Cover stops bullets. Someone once said that the three most important factors in surviving a gunfight are 1) cover, 2) cover, and 3) cover. It's a little more complicated than that, of course, but only a little. A good position behind solid cover can make you go from being vulnerable to formidable in the space of a heartbeat. The fact that you're armed, angry, and behind good cover is often enough to thwart the plans of even the most ardent felon. His goal is usually an easy mark, not a fair fight of any kind. Being behind cover can make a world of difference in your ability to keep it together under pressure, even if you've already been injured. Recent research done by the San Diego, California, Police Department showed that over 90 percent of its officers who made it to cover after being shot were able to survive the gunfight. Get out of the hole and get behind cover.

Cover awareness is best promoted in hands-on range drills that force the shooter to move to cover before engaging the target. The old Practical Pistol Course (PPC), so long a U.S. police standard, was a good fundamental marksmanship and safety course. From a tactical standpoint, unfortunately, it taught the shooter to stand in the open and put a premium on emptying the handgun as quickly as possible. Not surprisingly, there have been instances of PPC-trained officers in real-life gunfights who have abandoned good cover, stood in the open, and sprayed their weapons dry, just like they had been trained. These officers had been trained to beat the rangemaster's stopwatch instead of a living adversary. Some of them paid for it with their lives.

Get out of the hole and get behind cover. Cover can protect you from your assailant's bullets and maximize your ability to deliver accurate return fire. Most of all, good cover can buy you time.

You can't control time, of course, but you can make it work for you instead of against you. An example of this might be getting on target first and delivering a deadly volume of fire through the smallest window of opportunity. Another example might involve getting behind some solid cover and not shooting at all. It all depends on the variables of the situation. One thing for sure, though—the more time you have, the better you can assess things. Another thing you can be sure of is that if time is working for you, it's working against your adversary. If you're alive, armed, and behind cover, you've put your assailant in a position he can't afford to stay in for very long.

For a predatory felon, time is a commodity that must be budgeted carefully. We noted earlier that criminal assaults are usually based on the principles of stealth, distance, and timing. A criminal has to stick to those principles if he hopes to succeed and avoid apprehension. When a police officer or armed citizen creates distance and takes cover, the felon is forced to make a choice. He can continue the attack on his formerly vulnerable victim, or he can flee the scene. He has to decide quickly. The sirens he hears pounding in the distance only serve to increase his sense of urgency. He knows they're not coming to help him, and the clock is ticking. Conserve your ammo, maintain cover, and let time work for you.

Bullet performance really is a very small part of an enormously large picture. To lose sight of the big picture is to give the advantage, and ultimately your life, to your attacker. *It is crucial that you never give your assailant anything that he can use, build on, or call his own.* You must use your head and work like the very devil to rob him of his advantages before the fight starts. When the fight begins, your goal is to wreck your adversary's plan and give him something new and more pressing to think about, namely, his immediate prospects for survival.

This is not to say that bullet performance is meaningless. Some bullets cycle better than others. Some tend to handle heavy clothing better. Some fragment when they are supposed to. Some drive deep enough to smash heavy bone. We know a lot more about bullet performance, both good and bad, than we did 30 years ago. Failure to capitalize on this wealth of information would be foolish, but we have to keep things in perspective.

Bullet performance will probably always be a variable in the overall scheme of things. You can expect only so much out of a hand-held weapon, but it is one of those variables that we can work to control before trouble starts. The facts contained in the following chapters will help you make informed choices in your selection of bullets and calibers. The authors hope that this knowledge will leave you free to concentrate on controlling the other, more important, variables that you will encounter in an armed confrontation.

Make sure you do some shooting after you read this book. And keep in mind that the name of the game is coming home to your family, alive and well, at the end of the day.

2
Review of Stopping Power Theories

Several theories and testing methodologies have been designed to provide some answers to questions about handgun ammunition performance. The problem with these theories and methodologies is that they have fallen short of what actual shooting incidents in the real world have proven.

Julian Hatcher's Theory of Relative Stopping Power (RSP) based much of its methodology on the deeply flawed Thompson-LaGarde research. Readers can refer to Chapter 3 in our first book, *Handgun Stopping Power*, for a detailed critique of Hatcher's work. Suffice to say here that reality has proven that Hatcher does not answer the critical question of which handgun loads work best.

The Relative Incapacitation Index (RII)/ Computer Man study has been soundly damned by some experts, and while it does fall short of its intended mark, it is vastly superior and brings us closer to the truth than RSP. One critical flaw of this study is the fact that it gives too much credibility to its "Vulnerability Index" in which the extent of wounding at 1.6 inches was found the most favorable while wounding beyond 8.7 inches was totally ignored. Chapter 4 of *Handgun Stopping Power* discusses this and other serious flaws of this study. Sadly, such a well-intentioned study was unable to answer the vital questions asked by handgun carriers.

The Federal Bureau of Investigation Ammunition Tests evolved from the tragic 1986 shootout in Miami, Florida, in which two FBI agents were killed and five wounded. Evan Marshall, one of the members of the original wound ballistic panel that resulted from that incident, found that there was a political and ego-driven agenda that eventually had a negative impact on the search for reliable answers. Subsequently, the FBI set up its own testing methodology, but, like the RII Study, the Bureau had become fixated on an arbitrary penetration distance. It decided that 12 inches of penentration was the minimum needed to produce reliable incapacitation.

An example of the problems with the FBI's methodology was that it resulted in a wounding value of zero for the Cor-Bon 115-grain 9mm +P jacketed hollowpoint. While one may argue the merits of such a round, can anyone really believe it has a *non-wounding* value? Even worse, some .380 loads have been given a negative wounding value, which presumably means that being shot with such loads would have beneficial results! See Chapter 6 of *Handgun Stopping Power* for a detailed analysis of the FBI methodology.

While all three of these studies were well-intended, they have all failed to reflect reality. The problem, of course, is that reality often does not progress in an orderly fashion as mathematical theories love. In the real world there are inconsistancies and contradictions. The results from the street prove, for example, that while the best 9mm loads are light- and medium-weight hollowpoints, the best .357 Magnum is a medium-weight hollowpoint, and the best .45 ACP is a heavy hollowpoint. That's reality, and it rarely reflects the neatness that theories provide.

TABLE 2-1
HATCHER'S RELATIVE STOPPING POWER

CALIBER	LOAD	RSP	ACTUAL
.380 Auto	Fed 95-gr. FMJ	16.2	51.0
9mm	Win 115-gr. FMJ	29.4	63.0
.38 Special (non + P)	Fed 158-gr. RNL	30.8	51.0
.44 Special	Win 246-gr. RNL	60.6	65.0
.45 Auto	Fed 230-gr. FMJ	60.0	63.0
.45 Colt	Win 255-gr. RNL	73.6	69.0

TABLE 2-2
SAMPLE CALCULATION FOR RII*
Speer .45 Auto 200-grain JHP @ 1,227 fps

PENETRATION DEPTH (cm)	VULNERABILITY INDEX (VI)	CAVITY RADIUS r (cm)	$r^2 \times VI$
1	0.0061	4.3	0.113
2	0.0169	5.1	0.440
3	0.0477	5.8	1.604
4	0.0608	6.0	2.189
5	0.0588	6.3	2.333
6	0.0564	6.4	2.309
7	0.0458	6.2	1.761
8	0.0388	6.1	1.444
9	0.0401	5.6	1.257
10	0.0405	5.4	1.181
11	0.0248	5.0	0.621
12	0.0238	4.4	0.460
13	0.0292	4.0	0.467
14	0.0231	3.1	0.222
15	0.0227	2.4	0.131
16	0.0273	2.3	0.144
17	0.0230	2.2	0.111
18	0.0247	1.8	0.080
19	0.0196	1.3	0.033
20	0.0074	1.1	0.009
21	0.0014	0.8	0.001
22	0.0003	0.6	0.000
			16.910

RII equals 16.910 times pi (3.1416)
RII equals 53.1

TABLE 2-3
RELATIVE INCAPACITATION INDEX

CARTRIDGE	BULLET WEIGHT (GRAINS)	BULLET TYPE	MANUFACTURER	RII	ACTUAL
.380 Auto	85	STHP	Winchester	13.4	61.0
.38 Spl. +P	95	S-JHP	Remington	28.9	66.0
.38 Spl. +P	125	S-JHP	Remington	23.2	73.0
.38 Spl. +P+	110	JHP	Q4070, Winchester	17.9	81.0
.38 Spl. +P	158	SWC-HP	Winchester	17.2	78.0
.38 Spl. +P	158	RNL	Federal	8.6	51.0
9mm	115	JHP	Remington	28.2	81.0
9mm	115	STHP	Winchester	27.5	83.0
9mm	115	FMJ	Winchester	10.3	63.0
.45 Auto	185	STHP	Winchester	25.5	82.0
.45 Auto	185	JHP	Remington	18.0	81.0
.45 Auto	230	FMJ	Remington	4.3	65.0
.44 Spl.	246	RNL	Remington	6.3	65.0
.357 Magnum	125	S-JHP	Remington	40.8	96.0
.357 Magnum	110	JHP	Winchester	29.9	85.29
.357 Magnum	158	JSP	Federal	25.6	72.41
.357 Magnum	158	SWC	Remington	17.3	67.60
.41 Magnum	210	JSP	Remington	51.6	81.0
.41 Magnum	210	SWC	Remington	6.2	75.0
.44 Magnum	240	S-JHP	Remington	47.3	88.0
.44 Magnum	240	SWC	Winchester	33.4	82.0

* reprinted from NIJ 101-83

TABLE 2-4
FBI WOUND VALUE VS. ACTUAL RESULTS

	FBI	ACTUAL
.38 Special +P Win 158-gr. SWC-HP	.42	78.0
.38 Special +P Rem 158-gr. SWC-HP	.72	70.0
.357 Magnum Win 145-gr. Silvertip	1.56	85.0
.357 Magnum Win 158-gr. JSP	1.86	74.0
9mm Win 115-gr. Silvertip	.41	83.0
9mm Win 147-gr. JHP OSM	.68	68.54
9mm Fed 147-gr. Hydra-Shok	1.65	74.0
.45 Auto Win 185-gr. Silvertip	1.01	82.0
.45 Auto Fed 230-gr. Hydra-Shok	2.49	94.0
.45 Auto Rem 185-gr. JHP	1.94	81.0

TABLE 2-5

FBI AMMO BEFORE 1986 MIAMI SHOOTOUT

AMMO	EFFECTIVENESS
.38 Special +P 158-grain SWC-HP	78%
9mm 115-grain STHP	83%

FBI AMMO AFTER 1986 MIAMI SHOOTOUT

AMMO	EFFECTIVENESS
.38 Special +P 147-grain JHP Hydra-Shok	69% (est)
9mm 147-grain JHP Hydra-Shok	78%
10mm 180-grain JHP medium velocity	78% (est)
.45 Auto 230-grain JHP Hydra-Shok	94%

"est" is an estimate based on predictive formulas from actual street results found in Chapter 17 in *Handgun Stopping Power*. The .38 Special results are averages of the 2-inch and 4-inch results for Winchester ammo.

3
Neurogenic Shock
by Dennis Tobin, M.D.

The subject of handgun stopping power has been the focus of decades of emotional debate. This emotion was firmly tied to pet theories about how ammunition "should" work. It has also been fueled by professional jealousies and personality conflicts under the guise of science.

The book *Handgun Stopping Power* was an attempt to objectively document the results of 7,627 actual police-action and civilian shootings. The thrust of the book involved no theory at all. A chalk mark was placed next to a load every time it worked well. After 15 years, all the chalk marks were counted up.

The book was criticized by a group of researchers whose theories differ from those actual results. It has been praised by federal and state agencies alike, who have the wisdom to see that empirical data is always better than theoretical data. But the strongest support by far has come from fellow street cops who understand how sensible and logical this approach is.

Some of the critics have misrepresented the book as "recommending lightweight, high-velocity projectiles." Wrong. The book clearly recommended the use of the heaviest hollowpoint in .45 Auto, the heaviest hollowpoint in .38 Special +P, the midweight hollowpoint in .357 Magnum, and the midweight hollowpoint in 9mm. In just one police caliber, the 9mm +P+, the best street performance has come from a lighter bullet, successfully used in real shootings by the Illinois State Police and U.S. Border Patrol. (And even this 115-grain weight is heavier than the 95-grain 9mm bullets used earlier by the ISP.)

Another misrepresentation of *Handgun Stopping Power* by critics dealt with exactly what data was included in the actual results. Some anecdotal data was "discussed" in the section dealing with specialty ammo like the Glaser Safety Slug, but it *was not* a part of the fully documented results. The book makes this clear.

The detractors have been especially critical of what is called unsupported data, defined as original reports which have not been made widely available. The reason for this restriction is once again easy for street cops to relate to. Some officers supplied unfavorable shooting data on their department's official duty ammo. As a result, they were formally disciplined or reprimanded by the department brass. To gather the huge volume of data we now have, confidentiality became critical.

Ironically, some critics have emphasized that theories developed from lab tests done by other wound ballistic researchers are "scientific" as opposed to our ballistic research. The fact is that *Handgun Stopping Power* is the only published ballistic work that follows the scientific method. To wit, reality is observed, theories are developed, theories are compared to reality, then theories are modified to match reality. Most critics have failed to perform this last and most basic scientific step of modifying theories to adequately predict what really happens. We do that, and we have been criticized for it from the very scientists who should demand we do it if they were faithful to their education.

The October 1992 issue of *Police* magazine contained a cognitive but harsh review of *Handgun Stopping Power*. The *Police* magazine staff writers were especially critical of the concept of neurogenic shock. That chapter of the book was written by Dennis Tobin, M.D., P.A., Diplomate of the American Board of Neurology and Psychiatry, and a specialist in Adult Neurology. Here is Dr. Tobin's response to the *Police* review, followed by his thoughts on handgun stopping power:

For those readers of police journals who have no medical background, I am sure it is disturbing to see such striking disagreement among medical professionals and researchers on a topic that should be understandable at a medical level. However, it must be stressed that there is a great deal that is not known about the neurological mechanisms that affect what happens to a body when an individual is shot.

I think it is unfortunate that the physicians who are quoted in this review brush aside neurogenic shock as if it does not exist. I think that simply because they do not understand the

Definite medical research evidence exists to support the concept of neural shock, according to avid shooter and neurologist Dennis Tobin, M.D., P.A.

mechanism or perhaps have not been exposed to it on a personal level, they seem incapable of admitting that at least it does exist. Anyone who is an experienced police officer, who has interviewed many people who have been involved in gunfights, who has watched films of recorded police shootings in the street survival seminars, or who has had access to data from the Illinois State Police usage of the 9mm +P+ or other departments that have used the .357 Magnum, have no doubt that the phenomenon of the one-shot stop exists.

The concept of neural shock is simply a hypothesis and my personal opinion about a possible mechanism on how it could occur. The *Police* staff writers flagrantly misquote the book and me in stating that the information in this chapter was presented as verified fact. Any objective reading of this chapter will clearly show that it is my personal opinion and a medical hypothesis based on experimental data about how this phenomenon can occur. Nowhere in the article do I draw the conclusion that one should, in fact, rely on this mechanism every time in defense of one's life, nor should one necessarily choose ammo based on this hypothesis. It is simply meant to try to explain a phenomenon that is seen in the real world that we do not yet understand very well.

I think it is disturbing that these physicians and scientists so casually brush aside the very significant experimental work done by Dr. A.M. Goransson in the Fifth Symposium on wound ballistics published in the January 1988 issue of *Journal of Trauma* (Vol. 28, No. 1, Supplement). This study very clearly shows immediate suppression of brain wave EEG activity and periods of apnea at the point of gunshot injury, and the authors rightfully, I think, imply that this supports the fact that there is some sort of remote effect of the central nervous system (CNS) by gunshot trauma. It may have something to do with a temporary cavity in the body being somehow sensed at a local level and conveyed to the higher structures, but as we pointed out in *Handgun Stopping Power*, this is speculative.

The various people quoted in the *Police* article can certainly debate about how often this mechanism accounts for one-shot stops, and it is certainly a legitimate area of debate as to whether you should design your ammo around this particular mechanism or not. I do not think, however, that it is legitimate for them to imply that the phenomenon does not exist simply because they do not understand it or do not have personal experience with it. If they are critical of this data, and since it has been published in the literature, I think that as legitimate researchers and scientists there is a duty on their part to try to duplicate the experiments and disprove them. I throw that challenge out to them if they are really serious about advancing the state of scientific knowledge in this area.

The major failing of a number of the theories from our detractors is that they simply do not match reality. Classically, many of the predictions from their lab testing would imply that the Illinois State Police 9mm 115-grain +P+ and Federal 125-grain .357 Magnum rounds should not be as effective as they are, and yet any police officer who has lived on this planet for the last 10 years knows that they are phenomenally successful rounds. This is an indisputable fact.

I think that the failing of these individuals is that their theories simply do not match reality. Their moral and ethical obligation as researchers is to modify their theories to try explain what they see on the street, not try to invent reality or redefine it in their terms to suit their particular theories.

In my opinion, the only valid method of finding out what rounds work on the street is, in fact, long-term collection and analysis of shootings that have occurred on the street, precisely as Mr. Marshall and Mr. Sanow have done. (This was also duplicated by an independent study done by *Police Marksman* and Dick Fairburn. See Chapter 6.)

I urge you to trust your personal experience and the data base provided by many thousands of police officers around the United States in making these critically important decisions rather than accepting blindly a theory put forth by a group of researchers or professionals, no matter how good their credentials may be.

A NEUROLOGIST'S VIEW ON POLICE HANDGUN STOPPING POWER

After many years acting as a reserve police officer, watching films of actual police shootings in street survival seminars, and speaking with officers involved in shootings as both shooter and victim, I have observed the real phenomenon of the "one-shot stop" commonly written of in police ballistics articles. In some cases where the victim is hit with one or two good torso hits and not in the brain, spinal cord, or bony support of the pelvis, he drops almost immediately. The victim later describes suddenly finding himself falling with his legs buckling, or even a momentary lapse of awareness or brief alteration of consciousness. This excludes the cases where the victim subjectively sensed a severe trauma and voluntarily fell or quit the fight to surrender to the officer.

Why do these involuntary stops occur? What happens in the body to account for this? Most importantly, can we choose or design ammo to predictably produce it in a high percentage of cases?

Only a few things explain why people drop instantly. Clearly, vascular shock due to low blood pressure cannot account for this. Even a shot literally exploding the heart with no pressure supplying the brain with blood allows continued brain function for at least 10 to 12 seconds before loss of consciousness. If there is no brain or cord injury, what mechanisms explain the drop?

It can be explained by any of the following:

1. A major support bone in the leg or pelvis is broken, leading to a fall without alteration of brain function.
2. Psychological trauma may cause the person to "freeze up" or fall.
3. Voluntary collapse occurs because the person senses subjectively a severe trauma and decides to terminate the fight, hoping the officer won't shoot him again.
4. Involuntary collapse beyond the person's control can possibly be explained via the mechanism of "neural shock." This is the mechanism we hope our ammo causes.

When the body senses the sudden severe trauma of a bullet entry, perhaps by nerves in the chest or abdomen being stimulated by the temporary cavity effect, impulses are relayed up the spinal cord to the brain stem. These impulses can block certain pathways, resulting in loss of muscle tone in support leg muscles and even a loss of consciousness.

Neural shock is probably the basis of the "sensory overload" phenomenon seen with multiple simultaneous hits from buckshot pellets or submachine gun rounds where felons drop instantly. Neural shock can probably be blocked by drugs such as PCP or heroin or by psychosis. This may explain why drugged felons can occasionally absorb incredible numbers of rounds or even multiple buckshot loads without a stop until they bleed out from vascular shock. Some people have tremendous mental conditioning or high pain thresholds or, in a psychotic state, may be immune to

neural shock, explaining failures of even the most powerful loads.

There is definite medical research evidence supporting the concept of neural shock as a basis for some one-shot stops. The January 1988 issue of the *Journal of Trauma* included a Swedish article on brain wave activity after gunshot wounds. Pigs in moderately deep anesthesia (to eliminate conscious perception of pain as a mechanism) were shot in just hind leg muscles. There was no injury directly to bone, spinal cord, or even organs. The EEG, as an indicator of brain function, showed clear-cut and immediate suppression of brain activity. This drop in brain function varied in length and intensity up to 30 seconds or more in six of nine pigs. The effect on the brain was not decreased blood pressure as a result of shock. Also, six of nine had respiratory arrest for up to 45 seconds. This indicates some remote effect on the brain stem respiratory center in the medulla.

The research doctors postulated that pressure from the "temporary cavity effect" caused electrical interference in nerve fibers. This effect is somehow sensed even at an unconscious level and transmitted to the brain, with immediate suppressive effects on the brain function. They felt this explained "some of the brief behavioral and mental blockage" occasionally seen in nonfatal cases of gun injury.

In my opinion, this mechanism may be the reason why lightweight high-velocity hollow-points with high kinetic energy levels and large temporary cavity volumes seem to correlate best with higher rates of one-shot stops, either involuntary or voluntary.

Some authors aware of this study criticize it by saying that only six of nine pigs showed EEG suppression. This challenge is meaningless. All the experiment proves is that the mechanism of neural shock exists and does not rely on conscious perception of pain. This helps to understand way a felon on PCP still goes down better with certain rounds than others, even if one can't consistently rely on the neural shock mechanism with all drugged subjects. No one knows how many of the animals would have shown the effect if fully awake or under light anesthesia. I suspect all. Rules governing ethical experiments on animals makes these experiments probably impossible in the United States.

Some authors criticize the study because rifle rounds of higher kinetic energy were used and claim we can't apply the results to pistol rounds. This is untrue, as no one knows what level of kinetic energy deposit induces the effect, especially in awake subjects.

These critics seem to miss the critical point. This data is medical evidence proving that neural shock as a mechanism of stopping is real. They can legitimately debate how often it accounts for one-shot stops and if one should design his ammo around this concept. But it's simply a concept that helps explain some of what we see in real shootings.

Neural shock seems to correlate best with increasing levels of kinetic energy such as that produced by light and fast jacketed hollow-point (JHP) ammo. The .357 Magnum 125-grain JHP at 1,400 feet per second (fps) and 9mm 115-grain +P+ JHP at 1,300 fps are two examples. This is as opposed to the momentum-oriented, large-diameter, heavy and slow bullets. Evan Marshall's compilation of actual street results also seems to favor the higher velocity JHPs.

One meaningless criticism of Marshall's data is that there is no separation of voluntary from involuntary stops. It really makes no difference. Assume a certain number of all stops are "voluntary." With round X, 55 percent of people cease hostility, yet with round Y, 85 percent do. Round Y is still statistically the better round regardless of the mechanism. The 30 percent more of the felons probably subjectively felt more severe trauma and decided to quit the fight. I don't believe most stops are voluntary, however, and I predict that when large numbers of drugged felon cases are analyzed as a subset of Marshall's data, it will be found that more went down from +P+ 9mm or .357 125-grain JHPs than .45 ACP loads.

A September 1988 article in *Handguns* by Mr. Goebel analyzed the relationship between one-shot stops and kinetic energy. One-shot effectiveness seemed to increase to but leveled off at about 550 to 600 ft-lbs. of energy. Above this, increased energy levels didn't seem to help much, meaning the .44 Magnum is not really better than the .357 Magnum, and street results agree.

The small group of resistant victims may correlate with subgroups discussed earlier. These are people resistant to neural shock who are constitutionally more resistant to pain or sense of injury, psychotic, or partially anesthetized to the "sense of injury" by drugs.

A major concept of Geobel's article is that although theoretically it's best to get rounds with higher kinetic energy (such as .41 Magnum or 10mm), one must temper this with the ability of the average officer to control excess recoil with rapid multiple accurate hits. This is the severe limitation of .44 Magnum, .41 Magnum, 10mm, and .357 Magnum in duty-length guns. Under stress, very few officers can really shoot these weapons well with a high hit ratio.

Medical research into neural shock suggests that police agencies would be better served with a good 9mm 115-grain +P+ JHP at 1,300 fps. The Illinois State Police load generates 90 percent one-shot stops. Rounds like these rival the 90 to 95 percent stops we see with Federal 125-grain .357 Magnum, but with much better recoil control and better practical accuracy. If you want better than 90 percent reliable one-shot stops, then convince your chief to let you carry a rifle in your car.

4

The Strasbourg Goat Tests

In 1904, the U.S. Army established a "caliber review board" led by ordnance officer Capt. John L. Thompson and medical corps officer Maj. Louis Anatole LaGarde. The Thompson-LaGarde tests on live animals using handgun ammo would influence the next 80 years of small arms decision making.

Eleven different handgun loads were involved in these tests, held primarily at the Chicago stockyards. These calibers included the .30 Luger, 9mm Luger, .38 Long Colt, .38 Auto (before it became the .38 Super Auto), .45 Long Colt, .455 Webley, and .476 Enfield. The testing did not include the .45 Auto cartridge.

During the wound ballistics tests, Thompson and LaGarde shot 16 bulls, cows, and steers with weights ranging from 950 to 1,300 pounds. They also shot 10 cadavers and two horses.

The Thompson-LaGarde tests measured the ability of a bullet to incapacitate the cattle by causing the standing animal to collapse. The shots were placed precisely to hit certain organs and miss others. The tests against cadavers measured the ability of a bullet to break bones and to transfer momentum, since the cadavers were suspended in air.

A wide variety of bullet designs were used, including round-nose lead, flatpoint lead, wadcutter hollowpoint, lead hollowpoint, jacketed softpoint, and full-metal-jacket hardball. No "modern" jacketed hollowpoints were used in this study (the high-velocity hollowpoint was not developed until the mid 1960s). A slightly cup-pointed .455 bullet was also included, as was a very low velocity (700 fps) 220-grain lead hollowpoint in .45 Colt. Although these bullets did expand, they did not prove to be noticeably more effective than nonexpanding styles.

The actual live animal tests were pretty inconclusive, but Thompson and LaGarde somewhat tentatively concluded that heavier, larger caliber, nonexpanding bullets were more effective than faster, smaller caliber, nonexpanding bullets. In their report, they wisely stressed that bullet placement should be paramount.

In his 1914 book, *Gunshot Wounds*, then Col. LaGarde stated, "The tests showed that the .476 caliber lead bullet has the greatest stopping power." This load was the .476 Enfield Mark III that fired a 288-grain round-nose lead bullet at 720 fps. In the final analysis, Thompson and LaGarde concluded, "No pistol smaller than .45 caliber should be considered for military service." From this testing, the .45 Automatic military cartridge with a 230-grain round-nose bullet was eventually developed. (The .45 ACP was originally designed around a 200-grain bullet. However, the U.S. Army wanted an auto-loaded version as close as it could get to the .45 Long Colt, so the bullet weight was increased to 230 grains.)

The Strasbourg Tests included a wide range of frangible and expanding handgun bullet designs. From left: Winchester Silvertip, MagSafe Defender, Federal Nyclad, Glaser Blue, Eldorado Starfire, Winchester Black Talon, and Federal Hydra-Shok.

The Thompson-LaGarde tests were the basis for the "caliber and momentum" theory of stopping power that we still have to this day. This theory was formalized in the 1930s by Gen. Julian Hatcher in his formula for Relative Stopping Power. This formula favors heavy, large caliber bullets with flat bullet profiles.

Between 1928 and 1930, the U.S. Army once again performed ammo tests using live animals. This time the testing was conducted by Col. Frank Chamberlin of the medical corps. These tests were designed to show which rifle calibers would give the most lethality while at the same time accommodating the then-new semiautomatic rifle program that eventually resulted in the M1 Garand. The tests were basically a shootout between the .30-06 Springfield, .276 Pedersen, and a .256-caliber wildcat.

Conducted at the Aberdeen, Maryland, Proving Grounds, these tests began with 200- to 300-pound hogs. Bullet velocities were obtained before and after impact at ranges out to 1,000 yards. The goal was to obtain the foot-pounds of energy lost as the bullets passed through pelvic bone, skull bone, intestines, lungs, and muscles.

After the hog testing was well underway, Chamberlin determined that pig bones did not react at all like human bones when struck with a bullet. Instead of the crisp, splintering fractures that he saw on the battlefield, the hog fractures were "mushy"—the bullet simply perforated the hog bones instead of shattering or splintering them. He traced these unacceptable differences to a pig bone's higher fat content and lower calcium content compared to a human bone.

In 1930, Chamberlin shifted his testing to goats. Goats have the same calcium content in their bones as humans, and their bones react in the same way as human bones when struck by bullets. He continued to use hogs, however, to record bullet effects in heavy tissues. All the hogs and goats were anesthetized.

This testing produced a number of conclusions. First, internal damage is increased when a bullet yaws or tumbles in the target. This damage is done by the large temporary stretch cavity, even for bullets that do not fragment. Second, liquids within the body are put in motion by the hydraulic effects of the stretch cavity. Called "explosive effects," these cause tissue destruction in all directions far beyond the wound path. Third, "secondary missiles" such as bone fragments and teeth set in motion by the bullet also have a destructive effect far beyond the bullet path.

Chamberlin was familiar with all of the various theories of stopping power, how easy it is to get a theory started, and how tough it is to disprove one. Stopping power theories are like noses: everyone has one. Of all the explanations, after all his testing, Chamberlin favored the hydraulic reaction of the body fluids and their effects on the central nervous system. That was 1930. Now, fast forward to 1992 when Chamberlin was proven correct.

Many of us wished that the Thompson-LaGarde tests on cows could be repeated, except this time with expanding bullets, or that the Chamberlin-Aberdeen tests on hogs and goats could be conducted again, this time with handguns and hollowpoints. Actually, it has happened. It is called the Strasbourg Tests.

The Strasbourg Tests involved the seven most popular police and defensive calibers: .380 ACP, .38 Special +P, 9mm Parabellum, .357 Magnum, .40 S&W, 10mm, and .45 ACP. These tests also involved all of the latest bullet designs used in defense and police work: Black Talon, Hydra-Shok, Glaser, MagSafe, XTP, Silvertip, Nyclad, and standard lead and jacketed hollowpoints.

The following report was written by a principal contributor to the Strasbourg Tests:

The lungs are more likely to be hit by gunfire than any other vital organ. For these scenarios, the frangible MagSafe Defender (left) and Glaser Safety Slug (right) were proven to be the best loads by a wide margin.

THE STRASBOURG TESTS

In early 1991, a privately funded research group was formed to study the physiological effects of bullet impact on medium-sized mammals. Electroencephalography and arterial transducers were employed to record an animal's responses prior to, during, and after bullet impact. The primary objective of the study was to isolate the physical mechanism responsible for rapid incapacitation of man-sized targets and to disseminate these findings along with the test results to the military and federal law enforcement agencies. These tests resulted in a time-based rating system of commercially available handgun ammunition. At this time, phase one of the testing has been completed and the results are being correlated. The following is a preliminary report only. A complete report will be issued at a later date.

Methodology

The Strasbourg Tests were initiated on the strength of the premise that briefly amplified systemic pressure of a specific magnitude can cause disorientation and loss of consciousness. It was determined that an accurate means of monitoring this elevated pressure would be to surgically install a custom-designed peak-hold needle transducer into the carotid artery of an animal. While this type of transducer is extremely expensive, it is capable of responding from 0 to peak pressure at the rate of 2,000 times per second. This is fast enough to respond to a bullet violently invading the circulatory system. The signals from such a transducer could be stored into memory using a 486 computer and later transferred into post-processor/amplifier circuitry and, finally, recorded by way of a Vari-Sync strip chart recorder.

With this concept firmly in mind, medical members of the research group discussed the merits of a study in which electroencephalograms (EEGs) were used to analyze lowered states of brain activity in anaesthetized animals as the result of projectiles fired into nonvital areas. Unfortunately, EEGs of anaesthetized animals do not show a clear picture of actual incapacitation. To better approximate the real-life situations normally encountered by law enforcement agents and military personnel, a corporate decision was made to conduct the tests using nonanaesthetized, fully conscious animals.

Test Equipment

Equipment inside the test room consisted of:

1. A large tripod assembly to which a Ransom Rest was bolted. The tripod was securely fastened to the floor. The tripod head afforded X, Y, and Z positioning of the test weapons. This system allowed for accurate bullet placement after adjustments were made for a particular load.
2. Transducer/computer/strip chart recorder.
3. Electroencephalograph/strip chart recorder.
4. Two oscilloscopes.
5. TV camera/CRT (monitored loading room activity).
6. One mic-activated digital timer/buzzer system.
7. One mic-activated stroboscope.
8. Two mic-activated motor-driven 35mm cameras.
9. Two manually activated VHS camcorders.
10. Two manually activated exhaust fans.
11. One manually activated dimmer system.

Subjects

The animals selected for testing were French Alpine goats. These animals were chosen because their weight, lung capacity, and thoracic cage dimensions are very similar to those of man. All of the goats were of male gender. These were large, adult animals ranging in weight from 156 to 164 pounds. To reduce the chance of adversely affecting the test results, the goats were certified to be free of a number of serious diseases such as tuberculosis and pneumonia prior to purchase. The health of the animals was continually monitored throughout the tests by an in-house veterinarian. (The researchers were most concerned about having healthy lungs and normal lung efficiency.)

Procedures

After surgically implanting the transducers, the goats were allowed to recover for several days and then placed in narrow stalls where needle electrodes were inserted into their scalp areas and glued in place. After clipping the electroencephalograph leads to the electrodes, the goats were monitored by way of an oscilloscope in an effort to establish a "stable" baseline recording (many artifacts were recognized and disregarded). Food was supplied to the animals during the monitoring period. If a reasonably consistent baseline recording could not be established regarding a particular subject, the animal was rejected as too high-strung (since a nervous or easily adrenalinized individual might affect the test results adversely).

Each animal producing a stable baseline recording and showing no signs of fever was led to the loading area of the test facility and positioned toward one end of a revolving, stainless steel cubicle chamber, where it was confined inside a "rubber fence" (i.e., rubber cords stretched across the entrance). Once confined, the twin cubicle was turned 180 degrees by way of a large bearing assembly so that the animal was inside the test room itself.

Electroencephalograph and transducer leads were connected to the animal's head and neck area and taped to isolate them from each other. The animal (now facing left) was then allowed to eat heavily salted oats from a stationary, conical-shaped container, the opening of which was of a diameter which forced the goat to remain in one position (this greatly assisted the shooter, as the X-coordinate variables were greatly minimized). At this point, the shooter quickly made any minor weapon-positioning adjustments to align the sights with the target area (a 2-inch circle stamped on the animal's chest).

Within 10 to 20 seconds from the time the animal commenced eating, the lights were dimmed and two camcorders were manually activated. Brain wave patterns were again monitored by way of an oscilloscope while the recorder charted a permanent record of the

Hollowpoints that expanded then fragmented were more effective in lung shots than those that merely expanded. From left: the Cor-Bon .38 Special +P+ 115-grain JHP, Remington .357 Magnum 125-grain S-JHP, and Remington .45 Auto +P 185-grain JHP were the best hollowpoints in their calibers.

preinvasive condition of the animal. If the baseline recording was unstable, disconnects were made. The animal was then tagged (rejected) and returned to a holding area. If the baseline recording was stable at the end of this 60-second acclimation period, the technician monitoring the oscilloscope signaled the shooter by way of an LED.

Once the shooter received the signal, the weapon was fired. The muzzle report was picked up by a series of microphones. The mics sent separate signals to various devices. One signal activated a digital timer. Another activated a stroboscope (flashing at the rate of one flash per second). The signals from two other mics electronically opened the shutters of two 35mm cameras, which recorded the goat's reaction (body movement) in the form of strobe-sequenced time-exposures. During this 60-second "flash" period, two assistants (each manning five stopwatches) timed each collapse that occurred.

At the end of this 60-second period, an alarm built into the digital timer sounded. At this point, the camcorders were switched off manually (by way of two solenoids attached to electronic cable releases) and the room lights were turned on. If the animal was still standing or had its head up, two marksmen armed with .22 caliber semiautomatic rifles intervened, humanely terminating the animal by firing rounds into the juncture of head and neck, just below the ear.

Once brain death was confirmed, the electrode and transducer leads were disconnected and the cubicle turned 180 degrees. Personnel in the loading room then wheeled the goat's body and the backup gelatin block to another room, where an autopsy was performed. At this point, the cubicle chamber was thoroughly cleaned and rinsed. Fresh straw was scattered on the floor, the food container filled and the stall area generally prepared for the next subject.

Autopsy

During the autopsy, medical personnel searched for signs of entrance rib contact, disease, genetic deformities, tumors, pierced or burst vessels, and bullet or bone fragments that pierced the heart or spinal cord (anything which could have incapacitated the animal sooner than a direct shot through the lungs). If any physical conditions were found which may have substantially lowered the incapacitation time, the records reflected this and a retest was scheduled. Additionally, the blood and pulped lung tissue were strained for projectile parts and weighed in relation to those recovered from backup gelatin positioned behind the animal. The wound channels created by the bullet and any bullet fragments were traced. If lung damage was slight, obvious bullet instability was noted. Damage to the individual lung walls was estimated in cubic centimeters.

If the autopsy revealed a valid test, technicians began the painstaking task of "real-time correlation." This process amounted to comparing the strip chart tracings produced by the transducer signals (systemic pressure) with the electroencephalography tracings (brain wave patterns). What the technicians looked for was a match between the spiked areas of the transducer tracings (high systemic pressure) and slowed for flat EEG tracings (diminished consciousness or possible brain death). If a spiked pressure tracing corresponded to a flattened or sluggish EEG tracing (which was usually the case), a positive correlation was recorded. It should be understood that the above-referenced correlation process was very time-consuming because the transducer tracings were so highly compressed (in order to correspond to the 1-second vertical chart spacing of the EEG) that they appeared solid in some areas. This was because lines from as many as 2,000 vertical stylus movements were crowded together over a short linear distance.

The fast-expanding JHPs like the Federal .40 S&W 155-grain JHP (left) and Winchester 9mm +P+ 115-grain JHP (right) were the best performing hollowpoints during the Strasbourg Tests.

Given the same bullet weight and energy, the Federal Hydra-Shok (left) was the best performing JHP design, followed by the Winchester Silvertip (right).

Target Area

The lung area was chosen as the impact zone in these tests due to the high probability of a bullet striking a human target in this area, regardless of its angle of entry. The goats used in these tests were shot from the side (at a distance of 10'+/-3"). The bores of the firearms were leveled and every attempt was made to strike the animal as squarely as possible through both lungs. To minimize contact with the heart, the bullets were directed just behind the shoulder and above the centerline of the lungs. The total bullet travel through hair, skin muscle, rib, lung, lung, rib, muscle, skin, and hair was between 11 1/2 and 12 inches.

Physiology and Bullet Performance

Ribs are covered with fatty skin. They comprise somewhat of a hemispherical surface. They are slippery and curve in two directions. After penetrating a layer of fat, a nicely lubricated round-nosed bullet does not mate well with a curved surface. In many instances, there was evidence that a round-nosed bullet or a bullet with a large radius at the nose "skidded" off course if the rib was not struck squarely (and

The uneven expansion of this .45 Auto 230-grain Black Talon was due to partial contact with rib bones. Bullets that struck ribs were less effective.

The Strasbourg researchers concluded that hollowpoint bullets with a round-nose profile (left) were less effective than those with a flat-nose profile (right).

In the 9mm caliber, the Strasbourg team found the 115-grain +P+ JHPs (far left) produced the most rapid collapse times, followed by (from left) 124-grain JHPs, 115-grain JHPs, and finally the 147-grain JHPs.

sometimes even it if was). This sometimes caused the bullet to turn so that it penetrated the lungs at an angle (exposing more surface area to the tissue). Generally, this caused more lung damage than a similar bullet which slipped through the intercostal space between two ribs and remained stable.

It is important that those reading this preliminary report realize the degree to which bullet performance was affected when a rib was struck. More often than not, ribs were struck. This is not to say that the ribs were always struck squarely. They were not. Regardless of whether a rib was centrally impacted or impacted off-center, the expansion (or fragmenting) characteristics of most of the bullets tested were severely impaired. If the nose cavities were plugged with hair and/or deformed badly during impact with the ribs, they did not expand well (if at all). In these cases, the incapacitation times were almost always longer (regardless of bullet velocity) unless the bullet fragmented or propelled portions of the rib into the lungs.

In almost every instance, expanding bullets performed much better if they missed the ribs and penetrated the intercostal muscles.

The thoracic cage of a goat is generally vertical, whereas in man, the ribs run in a generally horizontal direction. Normally, the fourth, fifth, or sixth rib was contacted to some degree. If a rib was punched, fractured, chipped, or grooved, it was recorded (and indicated by a lower care "r"). Because the bullets were directed above the center of the lung and approximately toward the fifth rib, the intercostal spaces were somewhat narrower and the chance of contacting a rib were relatively great. The larger the bullet diameter, the greater the chance of a rib being struck. If the animal was calm and breathing shallowly, the ribs were closer together. While eating, the animals tended not to breath deeply. The shooter ran a 60 percent chance of at least contacting a rib during these tests.

Technical Observations

In a substantial number of cases, the subject was incapacitated almost instantly. Each time this occurred, between two and five pressure spike tracings of high amplitude and short duration were found which immediately preceded and matched corresponding, diffused, or flattened lines (EEG tracings). Normally, the time-lag between the first pressure spike and the beginning of the slowed or flattened lines was between 30 and 40 milliseconds (although there were several cases where this delay lasted as long as 80 milliseconds). How much of this delay can be attributed to a slow electroencephalograph response (an equipment limitation) is unknown.

What *is* known is that:

1. The taller pressure spike tracings always preceded the slowed or flat line tracing.
2. The initial spikes had to be of a certain height in order for the animal to collapse immediately.
3. A secondary group of shorter pressure spikes of diminishing height and longer duration always occurred after the taller spikes occurred. These are believed to be produced by the wake of the bullet and may be indicative of a raised system pressure caused by a rapid compression of lung material (initiated by temporal cavitation). These subsequent spikes are essentially a continuation of the taller, initial spikes.
4. A third group of low-amplitude pressure spikes of still longer duration occur last and are a continuation of the group two spikes. These spikes diminish in intensity, and it is believed that they are produced by the violent oscillation of the lungs after impact and cavitation.

What each of these spike patterns contributes to lowering incapacitation time is unknown. However, it is the general con-sensus of the research staff that the group one and group two pressure spikes work together and act as a catalyst to bring about incapacitation. It is believed that those cases of near-instant incapacitation may be the result of a pressure-related interruption in normal electrochemical activity.

Extent of Testing

Over the course of Phase One testing, 611 goats were terminated. Of this number, 31 were discounted for various reasons. There were 580 valid tests. The results of the valid tests are found in the tables of this report.

Incapacitation

An animal was deemed "incapacitated" if it collapsed and was unable to rise to a standing position.

Animal Reaction

Animal reaction varied greatly and was nearly always dependent on the caliber and particular ammunition used. Some animals collapsed immediately and could not rise. Others collapsed immediately and managed to rise to a standing position, only to collapse and rise again (this was recorded up to five times with some animals, as collapsing two or three times was not uncommon). Many of the animals faltered shortly after bullet impact and did not collapse until much later. Several animals reacted vigorously by jumping over the rubber fence, resulting in "disconnects," subsequently invalidating the test. Some animals faltered or stumbled repeatedly and then collapsed unexpectedly. Others faltered shortly after bullet impact and collapsed within a relatively short time thereafter (it is believed that this common reaction was due to a system pressure level that was near but below some threshold level required to cause immediate incapacitation).

On three occasions (two validated), the animals stayed on their feet in excess of 60 seconds. The most notable of these subjects showed only slight agitation immediately after bullet impact, shifting its position in the stall area several times, and then becoming relative-

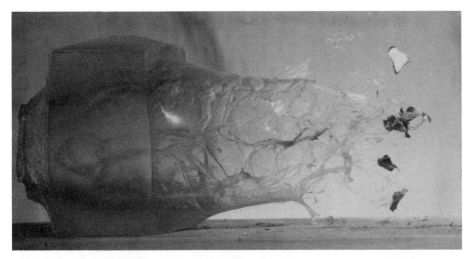

The Quik-Shok 9mm 115-grain +P JHP was the second most effective load in this caliber. It was also one of the few loads tested that produced a collapse in 2 seconds or less.

The Quik-Shok .357 Magnum 125-grain JHP produced the fastest five-shot average collapse time of the Strasbourg Tests. This bullet is now loaded by Triton Cartridge.

ly stationary until approximately 51.3 seconds had elapsed—at which time it made a 2-second attempt at eating! At this point, this rather determined animal began to falter, but remained on his feet until the marksmen intervened. The projectile was a 158-grain RNL bullet fired from a 2-inch barreled .38 Special revolver. Average muzzle velocity for this load was 587 fps. The bullet did not strike a rib.

Conclusions

After lengthy discussions between the surgeons and technical personnel involved in these tests, it was concluded that the most effective ammunition available for an unobstructed lung strike is the high-velocity type which uses prefragmented or fragmenting projectiles or those types that cause immediate expansion on impact. It was found that the more rapid the fragmentation or expansion, the greater the organ damage. Likewise, the more violent the fragmentation or expansion, the higher the system pressure and the more rapid the blood loss. It should be understood that, with few exceptions, most of the ammunition currently available does not fragment (or even expand well) at speeds under 1,200 fps if a rib is struck. The ability of a particular bullet to cause damage was easily assessed by the size of the permanent cavity created in the entrance wall of the first lung.

Recommendations

Based on the results of these tests, this committee strongly opposes the use of 1) all handgun ammunition under .45 caliber which utilizes round-nosed bullets, and 2) any of the so-called "deep-penetrating" ammunition loaded with "expanding" hollowpoint bullets. These bullets consistently penetrated not only the animal but the 6-inch-thick backup gelatin behind the animal. Ammunition employing these two bullet types consistently scored the longest incapacitation times of all the ammunition tested.

Because of the high probability of rib impact, a single handgun bullet cannot be counted on to incapacitate an individual immediately. Multiple rounds should be fired.

The Research Staff

The staff consisted of two retired surgeons, a retired general practioner (M.D.), a former medic, a veterinarian, two diagnostic technicians, a computer programmer, two medical secretaries, an electronics major, and seven additional (classified) personnel.

Time Frame of the Tests

Phase One testing began on April 8, 1991, and ended on September 24, 1992. The tests lasted approximately four months longer than originally anticipated due to an insufficient number of test animals. Initially, the group started testing at the rate of 10 animals per cartridge loading. It was quickly realized that the number of test subjects needed at that rate could not be supplied, even from a draw area consisting of several hundred square miles. Regrettably, the number was reduced to five per loading. Even at this reduced rate, operations came to a standstill from time to time.

Only by a concerted effort on the part of seven members of the groups were we able to locate the number of male animals needed to conclude the tests. It is expected that the group will be faulted for the small number of subjects used in the tests. Under the circumstances, it was the best that could be done. In spite of the numbers, we feel these were the most ambitious tests ever undertaken. It is our hope that the agencies these tests were intended for will find the results useful.

Future Tests

Due to the heavy burden imposed on many of the key members of the research group by an unrelenting test pace over an 18-month period, future tests have not been scheduled. If follow-up tests are conducted, they will be of a limited nature (possibly 70 additional goats). As presently contemplated, the tests will consist of retesting only those loads that scored the lowest incapacitation times. If conducted, these tests should determine a correlation between the consumption of alcohol and incapacitation time.

Due to the sensitive nature of this information, strict anonymity concerning the individuals involved is being maintained. The recipient of this information will be apprised of how to correspond regarding this data by way of various publications.

(End of report)

This data was first openly presented at the 1993 ASLET International Training Conference held in Reno, Nevada, by Ed Sanow, serving as an ASLET staff instructor.

As of mid-1995, only the collapse times are

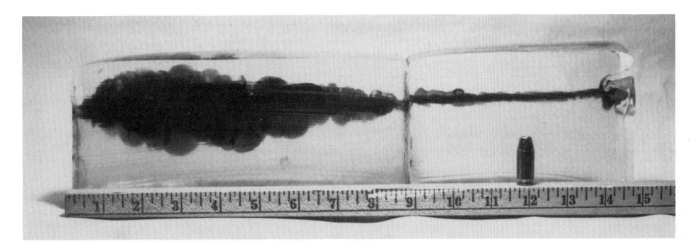

As a rule, late-energy-release loads like the Hornady XTP (.45 ACP 200-grain +P shown here) and the Winchester Black Talon did not perform well during cross-torso lung shots.

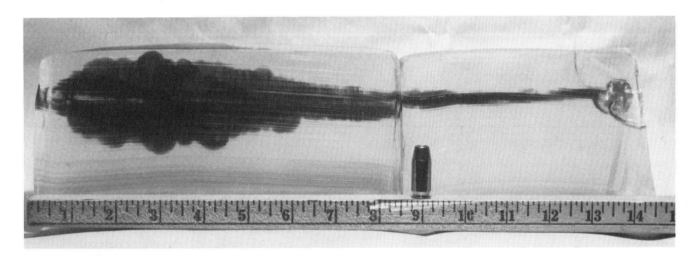

As a rule, the PMC Starfire like the .45 Auto 185-grain SFHP shown here turned in middle-of-the-caliber performance.

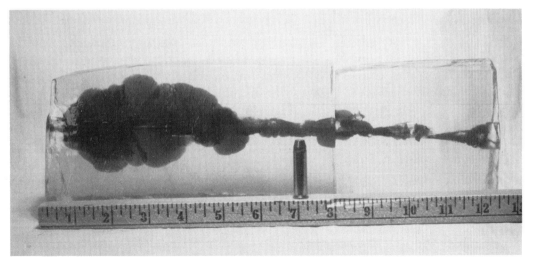

The Cor-Bon .38 Special +P+ 115-grain JHP was based off the original +P+ Treasury Load. This Cor-Bon loaded Sierra JHP was the most effective hollowpoint in .38 caliber during the Strasbourg Tests.

The Federal 9mm 124-grain Nyclad lead hollowpoint produced faster collapse times than many 115-grain and all 147-grain JHPs.

Rapid energy release and controlled penetration hollowpoints like this Federal .45 Auto 185-grain +P Hydra-Shok were proven to have the most stopping power.

As a rule, the Federal Hydra-Shok proved to be the best hollowpoint design during the Strasbourg Tests. This confirms Marshall's high-ranking street results for this design.

available. A correlation between blood pressure spikes, brain wave activity, and instant collapse has not been released. The second study involving blood alcohol levels and incapacitation times has not been scheduled.

The researchers found a link between the "intensity" of the blood pressure spike and the ability to instantly collapse the 160-pound goats with just a lung shot. This is exactly the effect Colonel Chamberlain referred to but could not identify 60 years ago.

The loads that caused a goat to collapse rapidly resulted in a blood pressure spike up to 12 times higher than the blood pressure increase from loads that did not cause a rapid collapse. This spike was of extremely short duration but extremely high amplitude. When this distinctive spike occurred, the EEG immediately dropped or went flat.

This large spike was followed by a series of somewhat shorter spikes in blood pressure caused by the compression of the lungs from the temporary stretch cavity. This series was followed by yet another series of even shorter longer-duration blood pressure spikes. This last set was caused by the oscillation of the lung tissue, just like a block of ordnance gelatin oscillates for some time after a bullet exits.

The first spike was caused by pressure generated ahead of the bullet. The second group was caused by a slower-acting radial pressure generated by the sides of the bullet. This is the temporary stretch cavity. Together, both groups of blood pressure spikes acted in concert to maintain an elevated system pressure. These spikes were far reaching enough to affect the brain, even though the blood-mist-filled lungs were the only organs struck by the bullet.

The research group believes temporary cavitation may be as important in causing incapacitation as the first pressure spike that occurred ahead of the bullet. Since both pressure spikes occurred so close together in time, the researchers feel it is appropriate to treat the first two groups of spikes as a single blood pressure spike.

The final analysis of the Strasbourg Tests is not yet complete. However, the researchers did arrive at a long list of preliminary conclusions. These conclusions are based on both the Average Incapacitation Time (AIT) and on the readings of the brain wave strip charts.

First, prefragmented and frangible bullets work the best in this unobstructed lung shot scenario. This is the shot placement most likely to be achieved in a home defense, police off-duty, civilian concealed carry, police back-up, or carjack defense scenario.

The second finding was that hollowpoints that expand and then fragment incapacitate faster than those that merely expand. The Federal 10mm 155-grain JHP was as effective as the Glaser. The Cor-Bon .38 Special +P 115-grain JHP "Treasury" load was behind the frangible loads but ahead of all the 158-grain lead hollowpoints. The nearly disintegrating Remington .45 ACP +P 185-grain JHP was also slower than the frangibles but faster than all other hollowpoints.

The third conclusion is that hollowpoints that expand immediately are more effective than delayed-expansion or suppressed-expansion JHP bullets. In fact, the Strasbourg researchers specifically stated to avoid deep-penetrating or delayed-expansion bullet designs or bullet weights with those characteristics.

As a rule, the +P or +P+ conventional jacketed hollowpoints worked the best. While many exceptions exist, the Hydra-Shok and Silvertip were next effective. These bullets were designed to be a substitute for extreme velocities and pressures. Next in line, and again exceptions exist, were the Starfire and the standard-pressure jacketed hollowpoints. After these loads, and with fewer exceptions, came the Black Talon. The least effective hollowpoint design in this scenario, without exception, was the suppressed-expansion Hornady XTP.

The Strasbourg researchers found that more rapid rates of bullet expansion caused greater organ damage. They also found that the more violent expansion caused by higher impact velocities also resulted in the highest blood pressure spikes and the most overall blood loss.

The research team also concluded that bullets with little or no expansion had little or no effect. Avoid bullets that do not expand rapidly.

About half the time, the incoming bullet hit a rib. Contrary to the widely held view, this hurts bullet performance. The incapacitation time for bullets that struck a rib was generally slower than the same bullet which penetrated intercostal muscle and missed the rib on entry.

Contrary to current thinking, hollowpoint bullets that hit bone did not expand as well as those that missed bone. In some cases, the hollowpoint cavity plugged up with rib bone or gristle and did not expand. In other cases, the bullet was tipped sideways and either did not expand or expanded unevenly.

The effect the ribs had on expansion was the most obvious on slower bullets that barely expand anyhow. However, not even the blistering .357 Magnum, 9mm +P+, and 10mm hollowpoints could avoid the adverse effects of hitting a rib. This even affected the instantly fragmenting Glaser and MagSafe rounds.

The incapacitation times after hitting a rib were twice as long as when the rib was missed. The shooter has no control whatsoever over this shot placement, nor do the basic bullet designs, from instantly fragmenting to delayed expansion, seem to escape the effects.

The Strasbourg team did conclude, however, that bullet profile played a role in reducing the negative effects of hitting a rib. They recommended against bullets with a round-nose profile or with JHP bullets that are excessively round. Once again, the truncated cone profile for autos and flat-point profile for revolvers were deemed the best.

The Strasbourg Tests had two other findings that some critics will have a hard time accepting. The incapacitation trend within each caliber is a "least squares" match with the actual police shooting results compiled by Evan Marshall. The exact ranking for each load within a caliber varies slightly between Marshall and Strasbourg. However, the trends are the same, both within each caliber and across all calibers.

The Spearman Rank Correlation Coefficient between the Strasbourg Tests and the Marshall study is an impressive .89, even though the exact criteria for bullet effectiveness are radically different. The controlled Strasbourg lab tests are in excellent agreement with the large number of random street results collected by Marshall and vice versa.

The second finding will also upset those with other theories of stopping power. The Strasbourg results are a "least squares" match with the predictive formulas that use both the permanent and the temporary cavities produced in gelatin to predict bullet effectiveness.

These formulas are effective in accurately predicting the stopping power of totally new bullet designs like the Gold Dot and Golden Saber or brand new calibers like the .40 S&W and .357 SIG. The Spearman Rank Correlation Coefficient between the formulas published in *Handgun Stopping Power* and the Strasbourg Tests is a credible .83. This book contains an even more powerful predictive formula (see Chapter 28).

Shot placement will always play a major role in incapacitation. However, the Strasbourg Tests proved again that, given the same shot placement, some bullets work much better than others. We have much more control over bullet selection than we do over bullet placement.

RIB IMMUNITY FACTOR

Analyst Dave Pully reviewed the Strasbourg Tests and offered some comments on the differences in stopping power between when a rib was struck by the bullet and when the ribs were missed. This is his input:

Looking at the Strasbourg Tests data, I was challenged to answer the question, "Can we identify a single factor that correlates to degradation of corpus terminus performance when a rib is struck?"

First, we need a criterion for comparison. This is somewhat arbitrary, but I chose the ratio of incapacitation time of a clean shot to that of a rib shot and called this the Rib Immunity Factor (R.I.F.). A R.I.F. of 1.00 means that the load is impervious to ribs; a R.I.F. of 0.00 indicates that striking a rib renders the load harmless.

Five-hundred and eighty shots were recorded. Normally this is sufficient for finding correlations with good statistical verity. Unfortunately, the testers chose to use a variety of bullet types and calibers rather than to focus on one or two parameters, such as bullet weight and velocity. Thus we have four independent variables introduced into the test—caliber, bullet type, bullet mass, and muzzle velocity. Whether or not a rib was struck introduces a fifth, albeit binary, variable. With five independent variables, 580 samples is simply not enough to statistically isolate the effect of each. However, since the rib variable is binary and every combination of the other four variables occurs with at least one rib and at least one clean hit, we can isolate the effect of the rib variable and hope to identify one or more other variables that correlate to this effect.

I looked at three independent variables—caliber, bullet weight, and muzzle velocity—and two composite parameters—momentum and energy. In each case, I grouped the 580 shots by the parameter in question and within each range compared the clean hits to the rib hits, deriving the R.I.F. as a function of the chosen parameter. It is important to remember that statisical accuracy is compromised by the fact that the other variables are not necessarily distributed uniformly within the groups. For instance, looking at the comparison of bullet weight to R.I.F., it may be that a different portion of the heavy bullets are of a fragmenting type as compared to the light bullets. None-theless, a definite correlation does emerge.

In conclusion, the single factor that determines how adversely rib contact affects the corpus terminus performance of a load is velocity. It is unfortunate that the shotgun approach used in this important experiment has left us with insufficient data samples to extract quantative correlations. We are left with only intuition and genius to fill in the gaps.

TABLE 4-1
R.I.F. VS. MASS

FROM GR	TO GR	CLEAN HIT AIT	RIB HIT AIT	RIB IMMUNITY FACTOR
60	79	3.89	7.56	0.51
80	99	8.27	11.71	0.66
100	119	5.80	11.51	0.50
120	139	6.66	12.00	0.54
140	159	9.40	12.76	0.65
160	179	6.80	8.67	0.78
180	199	6.37	10.11	0.64
200	219	6.47	11.19	0.57
220	239	7.73	12.28	0.61

There does not appear to be any correlation here. Or, to state it more accurately, any correlation that may exist is smaller than the uncertainty in the results.

TABLE 4-2
R.I.F. VS. CALIBER

CALIBER	CLEAN HIT AIT	RIB HIT AIT	RIB IMMUNITY FACTOR
.38 Special	12.73	14.95	0.85
.380 Auto	11.07	13.92	0.79
.40 S&W	6.98	9.51	0.73
10mm	6.04	10.04	0.60
.45 Auto	6.00	10.22	0.59
9mm	5.66	11.66	0.49
.357 Magnum	4.66	10.48	0.44

Taking caliber to represent bullet diameter, we see no correlation—both the highest and the lowest R.I.F. belong to bullets of the same diameter. There is, however, a property in which the .38 Special and the .357 Magnum differ considerably, leading us into the next chart.

TABLE 4-3
R.I.F. VS. VELOCITY

FROM FPS	TO FPS	CLEAN HIT AIT	RIB HIT AIT	RIB IMMUNITY FACTOR
600	799	35.18	30.29	1.08
800	999	8.91	12.45	0.71
1,000	1,199	7.09	11.63	0.61
1,200	1,399	5.25	10.60	0.51
1,400	1,599	3.25	9.56	0.34
1,600	1,799	3.08	6.21	0.50
1,800	1,999	2.20	8.60	0.26

Finally a correlation emerges. Ribs clearly affect fast bullets more so than slow bullets. Does this mean that, all else the same, slow bullets perform better than fast bullets when ribs are hit? No, only that fast bullets are more adversely affected. Again, we haven't enough data points to isolate the other variables here, but it appears that the increase in stopping power gained by speeding up the bullet is reduced but not entirely negated by rib contact.

TABLE 4-4
R.I.F. VS. MOMENTUM

FROM LB. SECS.	TO LB. SEC.	CLEAN HIT AIT	RIB HIT AIT	RIB IMMUNITY FACTOR
0.30	0.40	12.49	15.77	0.77
0.40	0.50	18.53	17.72	0.92
0.50	0.60	7.60	11.99	0.60
0.60	0.70	5.20	10.92	0.48
0.70	0.80	6.67	10.40	0.65
0.80	0.90	5.54	10.46	0.53
0.90	1.00	5.79	10.10	0.59

Momentum is a composite parameter comprised of mass and velocity. We look at momentum here to answer the question, "Is velocity correlated to R.I.F. because it is a component of momentum?" Actually, we already know the answer to be "no" because we found no correlation between mass and R.I.F.

TABLE 4-5
R.I.F. VS. ENERGY

FROM FT-LBS.	TO FT-LBS.	CLEAN HIT AIT	RIB HIT AIT	RIB IMMUNITY FACTOR
100	199	23.14	22.64	0.94
200	299	9.43	12.45	0.75
300	399	7.10	11.69	0.61
400	499	5.28	10.44	0.50
500	599	4.85	9.71	0.51
600	699	5.02	7.77	0.63

Energy is akin to momentum in being a composite of mass and velocity, but it is one in which velocity is given double significance. The weak correlation here is a result of the velocity correlation being "diluted" by the lack of correlation (and consistency) in the mass component.

TABLE 4-6
.380 ACP (3.625-INCH BARREL)

	LOAD	FPS	AIT	FT-LBS.	LB. SEC.
1	MagSafe 60-gr. +P	1,338	7.12	238.57	.3566
2	Glaser 70-gr. (Blue)	1,313	7.94	268.03	.4083
3	Fed 90-gr. Hydra-Shok	1,008	10.94	203.10	.4030
4	Fed 90-gr. JHP	1,007	11.06	202.70	.4026
5	Cor-Bon 90-gr. +P	1,041	11.12	216.62	.4162
6	Win 85-gr. STHP	980	12.88	181.31	.3700
7	CCI 88-gr. JHP Blazer	965	13.40	182.01	.3772
8	Rem 88-gr. JHP	996	13.46	193.89	.3893
9	Hornady 90-gr. XTP-HP	984	15.58	193.55	.3934
10	*Fed 95-gr. FMJ (c)	934	22.80	184.07	.3941

*control round

TABLE 4-7
.38 SPECIAL (2-INCH BARREL)

	LOAD	FPS	AIT	FT-LBS.	LB. SEC.
1	Rem 158-gr. LHP +P	776	15.52	211.32	.5446
2	*Fed 158-gr. RNL (c)	587	46.58	120.92	.4120

*control round

TABLE 4-8
.38 SPECIAL (4-INCH BARREL)

	LOAD	FPS	AIT	FT-LBS.	LB. SEC
1	Glaser 80-gr. +P (Blue)	1,667	4.72	493.76	.5924
2	MagSafe 65-gr. +P+	1,841	4.76	489.30	.5316
3	Cor-Bon 115-gr. JHP +P	1,243	8.98	394.64	.6350
4	Win 158-gr. LHP +P	996	10.76	348.12	.6990
5	Fed 158-gr. LHP +P	982	10.80	338.40	.6892
6	Fed 129-gr. HS +P	951	10.84	259.12	.5449
7	Rem 158-gr. LHP +P	924	10.86	299.61	.6485
8	PMC 125-gr. Starfire +P	946	10.88	248.45	.5253
9	Fed 125-gr. JHP +P	998	10.92	276.52	.5441
10	Win 110-gr. JHP +P+	1,136	11.02	315.29	.5551
11	CCI 125-gr. JHP +P Lawman	947	11.36	248.98	.5258
12	Rem 95-gr. JHP +P	1,138	11.38	273.25	.4802
13	Win 110-gr. JHP +P	999	11.66	243.82	.4881
14	Win 125-gr. JHP +P	938	11.70	244.27	.5208
15	Rem 125-gr. JHP +P	935	11.74	242.71	.5192
16	Hornady 125-gr. XTP-HP	936	14.82	243.23	.5197
17	*Fed 158-gr. RNL (c)	708	33.68	175.90	.4969

*control round

TABLE 4-9
.45 AUTO (5-INCH BARREL)

	LOAD	FPS	AIT	FT-LBS.	LB. SEC.
1	MagSafe 96-gr. +P	1,644	4.68	576.28	.7011
2	Glaser 140-gr (Blue)	1,355	4.72	570.90	.8427
3	Rem 185-gr. JHP +P	1,124	7.98	519.11	.9237
4	Fed 230-gr. Hydra-Shok	847	8.40	366.48	.8654
5	Cor-Bon 185-gr. JHP	1,156	8.56	549.09	.9500
6	Win 185-gr. STHP	1,004	8.82	414.19	.8251
7	PMC 185-gr. Starfire	924	8.88	350.81	.7593
8	CCI 200-gr. JHP Lawman	936	8.92	389.17	.8316
9	Win 230-gr. Black Talon	829	9.14	351.07	.8470
10	Cor-Bon 200-gr. JHP	1,043	9.22	483.23	.9266
11	Fed 185-gr. JHP	1,011	9.24	419.98	.8308
12	Hornady 185-gr. XTP-HP	939	10.66	362.29	.7717
13	*Fed 230-gr. FMJ (c)	839	13.84	359.59	.8572

*control round

TABLE 4-10
.40 S&W (4-INCH BARREL)

	LOAD	FPS	AIT	FT-LBS.	LB. SEC.
1	MagSafe 84-gr.	1,753	4.52	573.32	.6541
2	Glaser 105-gr. (Blue)	1,449	5.34	489.65	.6758
3	Win 155-gr. STHP	1,210	7.86	504.03	.8331
4	Fed 155-gr. JHP	1,142	7.90	448.97	.7863
5	Fed 180-gr. Hydra-Shok	991	8.32	392.62	.7923
6	Rem 155-gr. JHP	1,136	8.40	444.27	.7822
7	Cor-Bon 150-gr. JHP	1,183	8.42	466.25	.7882
8	Cor-Bon 180-gr. JHP	1,044	8.66	435.74	.8348
9	Win 180-gr. Black Talon	989	8.86	391.04	.7908
10	Rem 180-gr. JHP	988	8.90	390.25	.7900
11	CCI 155-gr. JHP Blazer	992	8.92	338.77	.6830
12	Hornady 155-gr. XTP-HP	1,157	10.38	460.84	.7966
13	*Win 155-gr. FMJ-TCM (c)	1,118	13.76	430.29	.7698

*control round

TABLE 4-11
10mm (4.25-INCH BARREL)

	LOAD	FPS	AIT	FT-LBS.	LB. SEC.
1	MagSafe 96-gr.	1,729	4.48	637.41	.7373
2	Fed 155-gr. JHP	1,311	7.56	591.69	.9027
3	Glaser 105-gr. (Blue)	1,624	7.60	615.06	.7575
4	Cor-Bon 150-gr. JHP +P	1,286	7.66	550.97	.8569
5	Win 175-gr. STHP	1,267	7.92	623.95	.9849
6	Cor-Bon 180-gr. JHP +P	1,155	7.94	533.33	.9235
7	Fed 180-gr. Hydra-Shok	995	8.22	395.80	.7956
8	Rem 180-gr. JHP	1,202	8.26	577.61	.9611
9	PMC 180-gr. Starfire	955	8.38	364.62	.7636
10	Fed 180-gr. JHP	1,018	8.46	414.31	.8140
11	Win 200-gr. Black Talon	986	8.76	431.86	.8760
12	Rem 180-gr. JHP	996	8.88	396.59	.7964
13	CCI 180-gr. JHP	1,133	8.96	513.20	.9059
14	Hornady 200-gr. XTP-HP	1,121	10.22	558.21	.9959
15	*Win 155-gr. FMJ-TCM (c)	1,103	13.98	418.83	.7594

*control round

TABLE 4-12
.357 MAGNUM (4-INCH BARREL)

	LOAD	FPS	AIT	FT-LBS.	LB. SEC.
1	Quik-Shok 125-gr. JHP	1,409	4.40	551.17	.7824
2	MagSafe 68-gr.	1,757	4.62	466.24	.5307
3	Glaser 80-gr. (Blue)	1,687	4.82	505.68	.5995
4	Rem 125-gr. JHP	1,458	7.34	590.18	.8096
5	Fed 125-gr. JHP	1,442	7.44	577.29	.8007
6	Cor-Bon 125-gr. JHP	1,419	7.66	559.02	.7879
7	Fed 110-gr. JHP	1,351	7.72	445.92	.6601
8	Win 125-gr. JHP	1,382	7.76	530.25	.7674
9	CCI 125-gr. JHP Lawman	1,367	7.78	518.80	.7590
10	Fed 158-gr. Hydra-Shok	1,213	7.84	516.34	.8513
11	Win 145-gr. STHP	1,285	7.86	531.78	.8277
12	Rem 110-gr. JHP	1,334	7.90	434.77	.6518
13	Rem 125-gr. JHP	1,277	7.94	452.74	.7091
14	Win 110-gr. JHP	1,281	7.98	400.91	.6259
15	CCI 140-gr. JHP Lawman	1,322	8.06	543.43	.8221
16	Fed 158-gr. JHP	1,205	8.28	509.55	.8457
17	Rem 158-gr. JHP	1,220	8.30	522.32	.8563
18	Win 158-gr. JHP	1,246	8.34	544.82	.8745
19	Fed 158-gr. Nyclad HP	1,188	8.42	495.27	.8338
20	CCI 158-gr. JHP Lawman	1,221	8.48	523.17	.8570
21	Hornady 125-gr. XTP-HP	1,314	10.88	479.35	.7296
22	*Rem 158-gr. JSP (c)	1,224	12.80	525.75	.8591

*control round

TABLE 4-13
9mm (4.25-INCH BARREL)

	LOAD	FPS	AIT	FT-LBS.	LB. SEC.
1	MagSafe 68-gr. +P	1,747	4.74	460.95	.5277
2	Quik-Shok 115-gr. +P+	1,301	4.82	432.32	.6646
3	Glaser 80-gr. (Blue)	1,555	7.42	429.64	.5526
4	Fed 115-gr. JHP +P+	1,311	8.90	438.99	.6697
5	Cor-Bon 115-gr. JHP +P	1,333	8.92	453.85	.6809
6	Fed 124-gr. Hydra-Shok +P+	1,267	8.96	442.11	.6979
7	Rem 115-gr. +P+	1,290	8.98	425.04	.6590
8	Win 115-gr. JHP +P+	1,288	8.98	423.73	.6580
9	PMC 115-gr. Starfire	1,181	9.02	356.25	.6033
10	Fed 124-gr. Hydra-Shok	1,126	9.28	349.18	.6202
11	Fed 124-gr. LHP-Nyclad	1,105	9.28	336.28	.6087
12	Fed 115-gr. JHP	1,175	9.30	352.64	.6002
13	Win 115-gr. STHP	1,199	9.36	367.19	.6125
14	Rem 115-gr. JHP	1,166	9.36	347.26	.5956
15	Fed 147-gr. Hydra-Shok	958	9.58	299.64	.6256
16	Hornady 90-gr. XTP-HP	1,286	9.62	330.58	.5141
17	Cor-Bon 124-gr. XTP-HP +P	1,258	9.66	435.85	.6929
18	Win 147-gr. Black Talon	962	9.68	302.15	.6282
19	CCI 115-gr. JHP Lawman	1,149	9.80	337.20	.5870
20	Fed 147-gr. JHP	979	9.84	312.92	.6393
21	Cor-Bon 147-gr. XTP-HP +P	1,093	9.86	390.04	.7137
22	Win 147-gr. JHP	890	9.90	258.61	.5812
23	Hornady 115-gr. XTP-HP	1,134	12.02	328.45	.5793
24	*Win 115-gr. FMJ (c)	1,163	14.40	345.47	.5941

*control round

TABLE 4-14
.380 ACP (3.625-INCH BARREL)

LOAD	VELOCITY FPS	AIT SEC	IT-1 SEC	IT-2 SEC	IT-3 SEC	IT-4 SEC	IT-5 SEC
MagSafe 60-gr. +P	1,338	7.12	9.1 r	7.9 r	8.7 r	5.1	4.8
Glaser 70-gr. (Blue)	1,313	7.94	6.6 r	6.8	10.1 r	8.8 r	7.4
Fed 90-gr. Hydra-Shok	1,008	10.94	10.4 r	9.4	8.2	13.0 r	13.7 r
Fed 90-gr. JHP	1,007	11.06	9.6	12.9 r	11.7 r	10.2	10.9 r
Cor-Bon 90-gr. +P	1,041	11.12	8.8	13.3 r	9.7 r	12.8 r	11.0
Win 85-gr. STHP	980	12.88	11.9 r	12.2 r	13.8 r	16.6 r	9.9
CCI 88-gr. JHP Blazer	965	13.40	8.9	18.0 r	13.5	9.8	16.8 r
Rem 88-gr. JHP	996	13.46	14.5 r	13.7	10.9 r	14.6 r	13.6
Hornady 90-gr. XTP-HP	984	15.58	12.7	17.1 r	15.2	19.6 r	13.3
*Fed 95-gr. FMJ (c)	934	22.80	24.8 r	20.7 r	22.6	21.4	24.5 r

*control round

TABLE 4-15
.380 AUTO (RIB HITS)

	AIT	MFG.	WEIGHT	BULLET TYPE	VELOCITY
1	8.50	Glaser	70	Glaser	1,313
2	8.57	MagSafe	60	MagSafe	1,338
3	11.83	Fed	90	JHP	1,007
4	11.93	Cor-Bon	90	JHP	1,041
5	12.37	Fed	90	Hydra-Shok	1,008
6	13.33	Rem	88	JHP	996
7	13.63	Win	85	STHP	980
8	17.40	CCI	88	JHP Blazer	965
9	18.35	Hornady	90	STP-HP	984
10	23.33	Fed	95	FMJ	934

TABLE 4-16
.380 AUTO (NO RIB HITS)

	AIT	MFG.	WEIGHT	BULLET TYPE	VELOCITY
1	4.95	MagSafe	60	MagSafe	1,338
2	7.10	Glaser	70	Glaser	1,313
3	8.80	Fed	90	Hydra-Shok	1,008
4	9.90	Cor-Bon	90	JHP	1,041
5	9.90	Fed	90	JHP	1,007
6	9.90	Win	85	STHP	980
7	10.73	CCI	88	JHP Blazer	965
8	13.65	Rem	88	JHP	996
9	13.73	Hornady	90	STP-HP	984
10	22.00	Fed	95	FMJ	934

TABLE 4-17
.38 SPECIAL (2-INCH BARREL)

LOAD	VELOCITY FPS	AIT SEC	IT-1 SEC	IT-2 SEC	IT-3 SEC	IT-4 SEC	IT-5 SEC
Rem 158-gr. LHP +P	776	15.52	18.7 r	14.4	18.1 r	12.3	14.1
*Fed 158-gr. RNL (c)	587	46.58	39.8 r	60+	35.3 r	37.8 r	60+
*control round							

TABLE 4-18
.38 SPECIAL (4-INCH BARREL)

LOAD	VELOCITY FPS	AIT SEC	IT-1 SEC	IT-2 SEC	IT-3 SEC	IT-4 SEC	IT-5 SEC
Glaser 80-gr. +P (Blue)	1,667	4.72	9.4 r	6.3 r	1.8	4.4 r	1.7
MagSafe 65-gr. +P+	1,841	4.76	2.4	8.9 r	1.7	2.5	8.3 r
Cor-Bon 115-gr. JHP +P	1,243	8.98	12.2 r	9.8 r	14.1 r	5.4	3.4
Win 158-gr. LHP +P	996	10.76	8.8	9.1	12.9 r	10.0 r	13.0 r
Fed 158-gr. LHP +P	982	10.80	12.5 r	9.6	9.7 r	14.1 r	8.1
Fed 129-gr. Hydra-Shok +P	951	10.84	13.3 r	12.7 r	11.6 r	8.4	8.2
Rem 158-gr. LHP +P	924	10.86	9.5	13.6 r	9.0	11.3 r	10.9 r
PMC 125-gr. Starfire +P	946	10.88	11.4 r	9.1	8.7	13.4 r	11.8 r
Fed 125-gr. JHP +P	998	10.92	9.9	13.7 r	11.8 r	9.9 r	9.3
Win 110-gr. JHP +P+	1,136	11.02	14.4 r	8.8	9.6	9.8	12.5 r
CCI 125-gr. JHP +P Lawman	947	11.36	10.9 r	11.8 r	13.4 r	10.6	10.1
R-P 95-gr. JHP +P	1,138	11.38	10.5	10.7 r	9.8	11.9 r	14.0 r
Win 110-gr. JHP +P	999	11.66	9.4	11.5	13.1 r	12.0 r	12.3 r
Win 125-gr. JHP +P	938	11.70	13.1 r	13.6 r	10.7	9.8	11.3
Rem 125-gr. JHP +P	935	11.74	8.9	10.3	14.6 r	12.6 r	12.3
Hornady 125-gr. XTP-HP	936	14.82	14.8 r	18.9 r	13.7	11.6	15.1 r
*Fed 158-gr. RNL (c)	708	33.68	27.7	36.2 r	24.1 r	41.7 r	38.7 r
*control round							

TABLE 4-19
.38 SPECIAL (RIB HITS)

	AIT	MFG.	WEIGHT	BULLET TYPE	VELOCITY
1	6.70	Glaser	80	Glaser	1,667
2	8.60	MagSafe	65	MagSafe	1,841
3	11.80	Fed	125	JHP	998
4	11.93	Rem	158	LHP	924
5	11.97	Win	158	LHP	996
6	12.03	CCI	125	JHP Lawman	947
7	12.03	Cor-Bon	115	JHP	1,243
8	12.10	Fed	158	LHP	982
9	12.20	Rem	95	JHP	1,138
10	12.20	ECC	125	Starfire	946
11	12.47	Win	110	JHP	999
12	12.53	Fed	129	Hydra-Shok	951
13	13.35	Win	125	JHP	938
14	13.45	Win	110	JHP	1,136
15	13.60	Rem	125	JHP	935
16	16.27	Hornady	125	XTP-HP	936
17	18.40	Rem	158	LHP	776
18	34.83	Fed	158	RNL	708
19	37.63	Fed	158	RNL	587

TABLE 4-20
.38 SPECIAL (NO RIB HITS)

	AIT	MFG.	WEIGHT	BULLET TYPE	VELOCITY
1	1.75	Glaser	80	Glaser	1,667
2	2.20	MagSafe	65	MagSafe	1,841
3	4.40	Cor-Bon	115	JHP	1,243
4	8.30	Fed	129	Hydra-Shok	951
5	8.85	Fed	158	LHP	982
6	8.90	PMC	125	Starfire	946
7	8.95	Win	158	LHP	996
8	9.25	Rem	158	LHP	924
9	9.40	Win	110	JHP	1,136
10	9.60	Fed	125	JHP	998
11	10.15	Rem	95	JHP	1,138
12	10.35	CCI	125	JHP Lawman	947
13	10.45	Win	110	JHP	999
14	10.50	Rem	125	JHP	935
15	10.60	Win	125	JHP	938
16	12.65	Hornady	125	XTP-HP	936
17	13.60	Rem	158	LHP	776
18	31.95	Fed	158	RNL	708
19	60.00	Fed	158	RNL	587

TABLE 4-21
9mm (4.25-INCH BARREL)

LOAD	VELOCITY FPS	AIT SEC	IT-1 SEC	IT-2 SEC	IT-3 SEC	IT-4 SEC	IT-5 SEC
MagSafe 68-gr. +P	1,747	4.74	7.6 r	1.8 r	7.7 r	2.3	4.3
Quik-Shok 115-gr. +P+	1,301	4.82	9.2 r	3.2	2.0 r	3.3	6.4 r
Glaser 80-gr. Blue	1,555	7.42	2.4	11.4 r	9.5 r	10.2 r	3.6
Fed 115-gr. JHP +P+	1,311	8.90	13.3 r	13.0 r	7.9	4.6	5.7
Cor-Bon 115-gr. JHP +P	1,333	8.92	10.9 r	5.7	3.9	11.9 r	12.2 r
Fed 124-gr. Hydra-Shok +P+	1,267	8.96	7.7 r	13.1 r	3.6	7.6 r	12.8 r
Rem 115-gr. +P+	1,290	8.98	4.1	13.8 r	9.2 r	8.4 r	9.4 r
Win 115-gr. JHP +P+	1,288	8.98	11.9 r	3.5	11.5 r	14.6 r	3.4
PMC 115-gr. Starfire	1,181	9.02	5.4	13.8 r	4.1	13.2 r	8.6 r
Fed 124-gr. Hydra-Shok	1,126	9.28	11.7 r	4.4	11.9 r	5.1	13.3 r
Fed 124-gr. LHP-Nyclad	1,105	9.28	14.0 r	9.9 r	6.1	11.2 r	5.2
Fed 115-gr. JHP	1,175	9.30	4.8	8.6 r	13.9 r	5.4	13.8 r
Win 115-gr. STHP	1,199	9.36	4.8	12.6 r	13.4 r	11.8 r	4.2
Rem 115-gr. JHP	1,166	9.36	11.0 r	10.6 r	11.0 r	7.3	6.9
Fed 147-gr. Hydra-Shok	958	9.58	6.7	11.5 r	5.3	12.0 r	12.4 r
Hornady 90-gr. XTP-HP	1,286	9.62	14.2 r	7.1	13.9 r	6.4	6.5
Cor-Bon 124-gr. XTP-HP +P	1,258	9.66	6.9	13.7 r	14.1 r	7.9	5.7
Win 147-gr. Black Talon	962	9.68	12.3 r	12.3 r	6.6	6.4	10.8 r
CCI 115-gr. JHP Lawman	1,149	9.80	8.9	7.1	12.0 r	9.9 r	11.1 r
Fed 147-gr. JHP	979	9.84	12.5 r	11.3 r	13.1 r	6.1	6.2
Cor-Bon 147-gr. XTP-HP +P	1,093	9.86	9.0	9.6 r	10.9 r	7.1	12.7 r
Win 147-gr. JHP	890	9.90	14.1 r	8.9 r	5.2	9.7 r	11.6 r
Hornady 115-gr. XTP-HP	1,134	12.02	15.7 r	13.3 r	9.0	12.9 r	9.2
*Win 115-gr. FMJ (c)	1,163	14.40	9.7	16.6 r	20.1 r	15.6 r	10.0

*control round

TABLE 4-22
9mm (RIB HITS)

AIT	MFG.	WEIGHT	BULLET TYPE	VELOCITY
1	5.70	MagSafe	68	MagSafe	1,747
2	5.87	QuikShok	115	Quik-Shok	1,301
3	10.20	Rem	115	JHP	1,290
4	10.30	Fed	124	Hydra-Shok	1,267
5	10.37	Glaser	80	Glaser	1,555
6	10.87	Rem	115	JHP	1,166
7	11.00	CCI	115	JHP Lawman	1,149
8	11.07	Cor-Bon	147	XTP-HP	1,093
9	11.08	Win	147	JHP	890
10	11.67	Cor-Bon	115	JHP	1,333
11	11.70	Fed	124	LHP-Nyclad	1,105
12	11.80	Win	147	Black Talon	962
13	11.87	PMC	115	Starfire	1,181
14	11.97	Fed	147	Hydra-Shok	958
15	12.10	Fed	115	JHP	1,175
16	12.30	Fed	124	Hydra-Shok	1,126
17	12.30	Fed	147	JHP	979
18	12.60	Win	115	STHP	1,199
19	12.67	Win	115	JHP	1,288
20	13.15	Fed	115	JHP	1,311
21	13.90	Cor-Bon	124	XTP-HP	1,258
22	13.97	Hornady	115	XTP-HP	1,134
23	14.05	Hornady	90	XTP-HP	1,286
24	17.43	Win	115	FMJ	1,163

TABLE 4-23
9mm (NO RIB HITS)

	AIT	MFG.	WEIGHT	BULLET TYPE	VELOCITY
1	3.00	Glaser	80	Glaser	1,555
2	3.25	Quik-Shok	115	Quik-Shok	1,301
3	3.30	MagSafe	68	MagSafe	1,747
4	3.45	Win	115	JHP	1,288
5	3.60	Fed	124	Hydra-Shok	1,267
6	4.10	Rem	115	JHP	1,290
7	4.50	Win	115	STHP	1,199
8	4.75	PMC	115	Starfire	1,181
9	4.75	Fed	124	Hydra-Shok	1,126
10	4.80	Cor-Bon	115	JHP	1,333
11	5.10	Fed	115	JHP	1,175
12	5.20	Win	147	JHP	890
13	5.65	Fed	124	LHP-Nyclad	1,105
14	6.00	Fed	147	Hydra-Shok	958
15	6.07	Fed	115	JHP	1,311
16	6.15	Fed	147	JHP	979
17	6.50	Win	147	Black Talon	962
18	6.67	Hornady	90	XTP-HP	1,286
19	6.83	Cor-Bon	124	XTP-HP	1,258
20	7.10	Rem	115	JHP	1,166
21	8.00	CCI	115	JHP Lawman	1,149
22	8.05	Cor-Bon	147	XTP-HP	1,093
23	9.10	Hornady	115	XTP-HP	1,134
24	9.85	Win	115	FMJ	1,163

TABLE 4-24
.357 MAGNUM (4-INCH BARREL)

LOAD	VELOCITY FPS	AIT SEC	IT-1 SEC	IT-2 SEC	IT-3 SEC	IT-4 SEC	IT-5 SEC
Quik-Shok 125-gr. JHP	1,409	4.40	1.9	1.4	7.9 r	2.2	8.6 r
MagSafe 68-gr.	1,757	4.62	9.9 r	1.7	2.1	1.9 r	7.5 r
Glaser 80-gr. (Blue)	1,687	4.82	3.3	9.1 r	2.9 r	6.7 r	2.1
Rem 125-gr. JHP	1,458	7.34	10.4 r	4.8	9.8 r	8.6 r	3.1
Fed 125-gr. JHP	1,442	7.44	2.9	2.2	11.9 r	11.5 r	8.7 r
Cor-Bon 125-gr. JHP	1,419	7.66	11.8 r	3.3	11.6 r	7.4	4.2
Fed 110-gr. JHP	1,351	7.72	5.7	13.8 r	2.9	5.7	10.5 r
Win 125-gr. JHP	1,382	7.76	14.2 r	6.4	3.6	3.8	10.8 r
CCI 125-gr. JHP Lawman	1,367	7.78	12.6 r	10.8 r	3.9	6.0	5.6
Fed 158-gr. Hydra-Shok	1,213	7.84	8.6 r	3.3	9.3 r	7.3 r	10.7 r
Win 145-gr. STHP	1,285	7.86	3.7	14.1 r	9.5 r	3.4	8.6 r
Rem 110-gr. JHP	1,334	7.90	9.4 r	13.0 r	4.1	8.7 r	4.3
Rem 125-gr. JHP Med. Vel.	1,277	7.94	8.9 r	4.2	13.3 r	9.4 r	3.9
Win 110-gr. JHP	1,281	7.98	4.5	11.2 r	11.8 r	3.8	8.6 r
CCI 140-gr. JHP Lawman	1,322	8.06	10.8 r	4.5	12.0 r	3.2	9.8 r
Fed 158-gr. JHP	1,205	8.28	11.6 r	8.7 r	8.5	9.1 r	3.5
Rem 158-gr. JHP	1,220	8.30	13.9 r	4.3	9.4 r	5.9	8.0
Win 158-gr. JHP	1,246	8.34	4.0	8.9	11.4 r	7.2	10.2
Fed 158-gr. Nyclad HP	1,188	8.42	8.9 r	10.0 r	4.5	9.0 r	9.7 r
CCI 158-gr. JHP Lawman	1,221	8.48	8.7	4.9	10.6 r	9.4 r	8.8
Hornady 125-gr. XTP-HP	1,314	10.88	8.6	6.8	11.4 r	14.0 r	13.6 r
*Rem 158-gr. JSP (c)	1,224	12.80	15.8 r	12.8 r	14.1 r	7.6	13.7 r

*control round

TABLE 4-25
.357 MAGNUM (RIB HITS)

	AIT	MFG.	WEIGHT	BULLET TYPE	VELOCITY
1	6.23	Glaser	80	Glaser	1,687
2	6.43	MagSafe	68	MagSafe	1,757
3	8.25	Quik-Shok	125	Quik-Shok	1,409
4	8.98	Fed	158	Hydra-Shok	1,213
5	9.40	Fed	158	Nyclad	1,188
6	9.60	Rem	125	JHP	1,458
7	9.80	Fed	158	JHP	1,205
8	10.00	CCI	158	JHP Lawman	1,221
9	10.37	Rem	110	JHP	1,334
10	10.53	Rem	125	JHP	1,277
11	10.53	Win	110	JHP	1,281
12	10.70	Fed	125	JHP	1,442
13	10.73	Win	145	STHP	1,285
14	10.87	CCI	140	JHP Lawman	1,322
15	11.40	Win	158	JHP	1,246
16	11.65	Rem	158	JHP	1,220
17	11.70	CCI	125	JHP Lawman	1,367
18	11.70	Cor-Bon	125	JHP	1,419
19	12.15	Fed	110	JHP	1,351
20	12.50	Win	125	JHP	1,382
21	13.00	Hornady	125	XTP-HP	1,314
22	14.10	Rem	158	JSP	1,224

TABLE 4-26
.357 MAGNUM (NO RIB HITS)

AIT		MFG.	WEIGHT	BULLET TYPE	VELOCITY
1	1.83	Quik-Shok	125	Quik-Shok	1,409
2	1.90	MagSafe	68	MagSafe	1,757
3	2.55	Fed	125	JHP	1,442
4	2.70	Glaser	80	Glaser	1,687
5	3.30	Fed	158	Hydra-Shok	1,213
6	3.55	Win	145	STHP	1,285
7	3.85	CCI	140	JHP Lawman	1,322
8	3.95	Rem	125	JHP	1,458
9	4.05	Rem	125	JHP	1,277
10	4.15	Win	110	JHP	1,281
11	4.20	Rem	110	JHP	1,334
12	4.50	Fed	158	Nyclad	1,188
13	4.60	Win	125	JHP	1,382
14	4.77	Fed	110	JHP	1,351
15	4.97	Cor-Bon	125	JHP	1,419
16	5.17	CCI	125	JHP Lawman	1,367
17	6.00	Fed	158	JHP	1,205
18	6.07	Rem	158	JHP	1,220
19	7.47	CCI	158	JHP Lawman	1,221
20	7.58	Win	158	JHP	1,246
21	7.60	Rem	158	JSP	1,224
22	7.70	Hornady	125	XTP-HP	1,314

TABLE 4-27
.40 S&W (4-INCH BARREL)

LOAD	VELOCITY FPS	AIT SEC	IT-1 SEC	IT-2 SEC	IT-3 SEC	IT-4 SEC	IT-5 SEC
MagSafe 84-gr.	1,753	4.52	2.4	7.7 r	3.3 r	4.0 r	5.2 r
Glaser 105-gr. (Blue)	1,449	5.34	8.9 r	3.9 r	4.2	7.5 r	2.2
Win 155-gr. STHP	1,210	7.86	9.7	9.9 r	8.6 r	6.3 r	4.8
Fed 155-gr. JHP	1,142	7.90	10.1 r	8.6 r	8.9	4.5	7.4 r
Fed 180-gr. Hydra-Shok	991	8.32	7.7	4.6	9.6 r	9.2 r	10.5 r
Rem 155-gr. JHP	1,136	8.40	4.8	8.8 r	10.3 r	8.2	9.9 r
Cor-Bon 150-gr. JHP	1,183	8.42	11.1 r	7.8 r	9.1	9.5 r	4.6
Cor-Bon 180-gr. JHP	1,044	8.66	9.6 r	5.6	10.2 r	9.0 r	8.9
Win 180-gr. Black Talon	989	8.86	9.4	8.7 r	7.8 r	8.4	10.0 r
Rem 180-gr. JHP	988	8.90	8.5 r	8.4	6.6 r	10.1 r	10.9 r
CCI 155-gr. JHP Blazer	992	8.92	7.2	11.0 r	10.3 r	6.5	9.6 r
Hornady 155-gr. XTP-HP	1,157	10.38	11.2 r	10.9 r	13.1 r	8.5	8.2
*Win 155-gr. FMJ-TCM (c)	1,118	13.76	13.9	16.3 r	10.9	16.6 r	11.1

*control round

TABLE 4-28
.40 S&W (RIB HITS)

	AIT	MFG.	WEIGHT	BULLET TYPE	VELOCITY
1	5.05	MagSafe	84	MagSafe	1,753
2	6.77	Glaser	105	Glaser	1,449
3	8.27	Win	155	STHP	1,210
4	8.70	Fed	155	JHP	1,142
5	8.83	Win	180	Black Talon	989
6	9.03	Rem	180	JHP	988
7	9.47	Cor-Bon	150	JHP	1,183
8	9.60	Cor-Bon	180	JHP	1,044
9	9.67	Rem	155	JHP	1,136
10	9.77	Fed	180	Hydra-Shok	991
11	10.30	CCI	155	JHP Blazer	992
12	11.73	Hornady	155	XTP-HP	1,157
13	16.45	Win	155	FMJ-TCM	1,118

TABLE 4-29
.40 S&W (NO RIB HITS)

	AIT	MFG.	WEIGHT	BULLET TYPE	VELOCITY
1	2.40	MagSafe	84	MagSafe	1,753
2	3.20	Glaser	105	Glaser	1,449
3	6.15	Fed	180	Hydra-Shok	991
4	6.50	Rem	155	JHP	1,136
5	6.70	Fed	155	JHP	1,142
6	6.85	CCI	155	JHP Blazer	992
7	6.85	Cor-Bon	150	JHP	1,183
8	7.25	Cor-Bon	180	JHP	1,044
9	7.25	Win	155	STHP	1,210
10	8.35	Hornady	155	XTP-HP	1,157
11	8.40	Rem	180	JHP	988
12	8.90	Win	180	Black Talon	989
13	11.97	Win	155	FMJ-TCM	1,118

TABLE 4-30
10mm (4.25-INCH BARREL)

LOAD	VELOCITY FPS	AIT SEC	IT-1 SEC	IT-2 SEC	IT-3 SEC	IT-4 SEC	IT-5 SEC
MagSafe 96-gr.	1,729	4.48	3.8	4.9 r	5.3 r	1.8	6.6 r
Fed 155-gr. JHP	1,311	7.56	8.8 r	9.9 r	11.0 r	3.4	4.7
Glaser 105-gr. (Blue)	1,624	7.60	10.5 r	6.8 r	9.8 r	4.8	6.1
Cor-Bon 150-gr. JHP +P	1,286	7.66	4.1	8.9 r	8.6 r	6.5 r	10.2 r
Win 175-gr. STHP	1,267	7.92	7.7 r	4.4	9.2	8.4 r	9.9 r
Cor-Bon 180-gr. JHP +P	1,155	7.94	2.9	3.3	10.6 r	9.8 r	13.1 r
Fed 180-gr. Hydra-Shok	995	8.22	5.3	10.7 r	4.3	11.6 r	9.2
Rem 180-gr. JHP	1,202	8.26	8.7 r	7.3	10.2 r	8.5	6.6 r
PMC 180-gr. Starfire	955	8.38	6.1	9.4 r	10.4 r	11.1 r	4.9
Fed 180-gr. JHP	1,018	8.46	10.4 r	8.8 r	7.8 r	3.2	12.1 r
Win 200-gr. Black Talon	986	8.76	11.6 r	5.6	8.0	6.1	12.5 r
Rem 180-gr. JHP	996	8.88	5.5	10.8 r	7.6 r	11.9 r	8.6
CCI 180-gr. JHP	1,133	8.96	10.6 r	9.7 r	8.4 r	6.0	10.1
Hornady 200-gr. XTP-HP	1,121	10.22	8.7	7.5	13.5 r	9.7 r	11.7 r
*Win 155-gr. FMJ-TCM (c)	1,103	13.98	17.4 r	13.3 r	11.6	16.0 r	11.6 r

* control road

TABLE 4-31
10mm (RIB HITS)

	AIT	MFG.	WEIGHT	BULLET TYPE	VELOCITY
1	5.60	MagSafe	96	MagSafe	1,729
2	8.50	Rem	180	JHP	1,202
3	8.55	Cor-Bon	150	JHP	1,286
4	8.67	Win	175	STHP	1,267
5	9.03	Glaser	105	Glaser	1,624
6	9.57	CCI	180	JHP	1,133
7	9.78	Fed	180	JHP	1,018
8	9.90	Fed	155	JHP	1,311
9	10.10	Rem	180	JHP	996
10	10.30	PMC	180	Starfire	955
11	11.15	Fed	180	Hydra-Shok	995
12	11.17	Cor-Bon	180	JHP	1,155
13	11.63	Hornady	200	XTP-HP	1,121
14	12.05	Win	200	Black Talon	986
15	14.58	Win	155	FMJ-TCM	1,103

TABLE 4-32
10mm (NO RIB HITS)

	AIT	MFG.	WEIGHT	BULLET TYPE	VELOCITY
1	2.80	MagSafe	96	MagSafe	1,729
2	3.10	Cor-Bon	180	JHP	1,155
3	3.20	Fed	180	JHP	1,018
4	4.05	Fed	155	JHP	1,311
5	4.10	Cor-Bon	150	JHP	1,286
6	5.45	Glaser	105	Glaser	1,624
7	5.50	PMC	180	Starfire	955
8	6.27	Fed	180	Hydra-Shok	995
9	6.57	Win	200	Black Talon	986
10	6.80	Win	175	STHP	1,267
11	7.05	Rem	180	JHP	996
12	7.90	Rem	180	JHP	1,202
13	8.05	CCI	180	JHP	1,133
14	8.10	Hornady	200	XTP-HP	1,121
15	11.60	Win	155	FMJ-TCM	1,103

TABLE 4-33
.45 AUTO (5-INCH BARREL)

LOAD	VELOCITY FPS	AIT SEC.	IT-1 SEC.	IT-2 SEC.	IT-3 SEC.	IT-4 SEC.	IT-5 SEC.
MagSafe 96-gr. +P	1,644	4.68	4.4	4.2	4.8 r	6.8 r	3.2 r
Glaser 140-gr. (Blue)	1,355	4.72	2.1	3.5	6.6 r	8.3 r	3.1 r
Rem 185-gr. JHP +P	1,124	7.98	9.6 r	10.8 r	3.9	4.6	11.0 r
Fed 230-gr. Hydra-Shok	847	8.40	5.5	7.5 r	11.7 r	12.9 r	4.4
Cor-Bon 185-gr. JHP	1,156	8.56	6.6 r	11.4 r	8.0 r	13.2 r	3.6
Win 185-gr. STHP	1,004	8.82	12.9 r	9.6 r	6.1	4.1	11.4 r
PMC 185-gr. Starfire	924	8.88	6.2	5.4	10.9 r	12.1 r	9.8 r
CCI 200-gr. JHP Lawman	936	8.92	8.9 r	12.6 r	4.9	9.3 r	8.9 r
Win 230-gr. Black Talon	829	9.14	7.6	10.7 r	9.8 r	11.8 r	5.8
Cor-Bon 200-gr. JHP	1,043	9.22	10.4 r	11.6 r	11.5 r	4.9	7.7
Fed 185-gr. JHP	1,011	9.24	7.3	12.0 r	12.4 r	8.6 r	5.9
Hornady 185-gr. XTP-HP	939	10.66	6.8 r	11.2	9.9 r	12.3 r	13.1 r
*Fed 230-gr. FMJ (c)	839	13.84	14.1 r	17.3 r	12.9	10.2	14.7 r

*control round

TABLE 4-34
.45 AUTO (RIB HITS)

	AIT	MFG.	WEIGHT	BULLET TYPE	VELOCITY
1	4.93	MagSafe	96	MagSafe	1,644
2	6.00	Glaser	140	Glaser	1,355
3	9.80	Cor-Bon	185	JHP	1,156
4	9.93	CCI	200	JHP Lawman	936
5	10.47	Rem	185	JHP	1,124
6	10.53	Hornady	185	XTP-JHP	939
7	10.70	Fed	230	Hydra-Shok	847
8	10.77	Win	230	Black Talon	829
9	10.93	PMC	185	Starfire	924
10	11.00	Fed	185	JHP	1,011
11	11.17	Cor-Bon	200	JHP	1,043
12	11.30	Win	185	STHP	1,004
13	15.37	Fed	230	FMJ	839

TABLE 4-35
.45 AUTO (NO RIB HITS)

	AIT	MFG.	WEIGHT	BULLET TYPE	VELOCITY
1	2.80	Glaser	140	Glaser	1,355
2	3.60	Cor-Bon	185	JHP	1,156
3	4.25	Rem	185	JHP	1,124
4	4.30	MagSafe	96	MagSafe	1,644
5	4.90	CCI	200	JHP Lawman	936
6	4.95	Fed	230	Hydra-Shok	847
7	5.10	Win	185	STHP	1,004
8	5.80	PMC	185	Starfire	924
9	6.30	Cor-Bon	200	JHP	1,043
10	6.60	Fed	185	JHP	1,011
11	6.70	Win	230	Black Talon	829
12	11.20	Hornady	185	XTP-HP	939
13	11.55	Fed	230	FMJ	839

5

Navy/Crane
9mm Ammo Tests

In 1991, the Naval Weapons Support Center at Crane, Indiana (NWSCC), conducted performance tests on 10 types of commercially available 9mm ammo. The purpose was to determine the best hollowpoint for use by the Naval Investigative Service (NIS) in its 9mm XM11 compact pistols. The tests included chamber pressure, velocity, accuracy, expansion, penetration, muzzle flash, and functioning reliability and involved the Beretta 92SM, Smith & Wesson 6906, Sigarms P225, Glock 19, and Heckler & Koch P7M8 auto pistols.

Critically, the performance tests were weighted in terms of significance. Functional reliability was given 50 percent of the weighting. Penetration distances in both bare gelatin and gelatin after glass were given a 25 percent weighting. Expansion in gelatin and 50-yard group sizes were each rated at 10 percent of the overall score. Retained bullet weight in gelatin was given a 5 percent score weighting. The diameter and intensity of the muzzle flash was for information only.

Excerpts from the unclassified report prepared by Scott K. Karcher, mechanical engineer, Ammunition Branch, NWSCC, are as follows:

In September 1982, the Deputy Under Secretary of Defense for Research and Engineering deleted the reference to the concealable handgun from the 9mm handgun Joint Service Operational Requirement (JSOR). Removal of the concealable handgun from the original JSOR allowed the Army to proceed with a standard handgun procurement while the concealable handgun requirements were being completed and a separate JSOR was being initiated. Further action was delayed until after the selection of the M9 Beretta as the standard military 9mm pistol.

In the spring of 1986, the issue of a JSOR for a concealable handgun was again raised because the M9 Beretta was too large and heavy for use as a concealed weapon. The concealable handgun was termed the Personal Defense Weapon (PDW), and in May 1988 the

Compact Pistol, Joint Service Operational Requirement (JSOR), for a Personal Defense Weapon (PDW), Standard Service Sidearm Pistol, 9mm Semiautomatic was completed. The PDW has been designated the XM11.

The XM11 is intended to be a compact concealable weapon that is carried in a holster beneath civilian clothing in order to reduce the probability of appearing armed to the public. The XM11 will replace the Smith & Wesson Model 10 .38 caliber revolver and will be issued to those individuals in the U.S. Army Criminal Investigation Command, Military Police Corps, and other selected DOD security and military intelligence agencies, including the Naval Investigative Service (NIS), who currently use the S&W Model 10 as well as the Ruger .357 Magnum NIS revolver, S&W Model 19 .357 Magnum, S&W Model 36 .38 Special, and S&W Model 39 9mm semiautomatic pistol.

In February 1990, Naval Weapons Support Center Crane (NWSCC), at the request of the NIS, generated a program plan for the evaluation of commercially available 9mm jacketed hollowpoint cartridges in order to determine the optimum round for their use in the XM11 pistol.

Based on a market survey and with concurrence from the NIS, NWSCC selected commercially available 9mm JHP cartridges to be tested. Those are:

Federal 115-gr. JHP
Federal 115-gr. JHP +P+
Federal 124-gr. Hydra-Shok
Federal 124-gr. Hydra-Shok +P+
Federal 124-gr. Nyclad
Winchester 115-gr. JHP +P+
Winchester 115-gr. STHP
   (Silvertip hollowpoint)
Winchester 147-gr. JHP
CCI 115-gr. JHP
Hornady 147-gr. JHP
Federal 147-gr. Hydra-Shok

For testing purposes, 12,000 rounds of each type of cartridge listed above were procured. M882 ball cartridges were used as comparison rounds in some tests.

Weapon types used for this evaluation were the same weapon types used by the U.S. Army for the XM11 9mm compact pistol Technical Feasibility Test conducted at Aberdeen Proving Ground (APG), Maryland, from May 1990 to January 1991. Those weapon types are:

Beretta 92FS
Smith & Wesson 6904
Sig Sauer P225
Glock 19
Heckler & Koch P7M8

The performance tests which were conducted on the test cartridges and the associated scoring values were determined by NWSCC and NIS representatives. The scoring values stress the relative importance to the users of each test result. Performance tests and their scoring values were:

Function	50%	(MRBF* 45%, Shooter survey 5%)
Penetration	25%	(Gelatin 20%, Glass/gelatin 5%)
Expansion	10%	(Gelatin 8%, Glass/gelatin 2%)
Mass Retention	5%	(Gelatin 4%, Glass/gelatin 1%)
Accuracy	10%	(Test barrels 5%, Weapons 5%)
Muzzle Flash	0%	(For information only)
	100%	

* Mean Rounds Between Failures

The chamber pressure produced by each cartridge type was measured at three different temperature ranges using a piezoelectric conformal transducer. The temperature ranges were 70 plus or minus 5 degrees F, 125 plus or minus 5 degrees F, and -40 plus or minus 5 degrees F. Cartridges were fired from a 4.0-inch test barrel which conformed to ANSI/SAAMI standards mounted in a universal receiver. Twenty cartridges of each type were fired with the powder positioned at the primer end of the cartridge after conditioning for two hours at each temperature range. In addition, 20 rounds of each type were fired with the powder positioned at the bullet end of the cartridge after conditioning for two hours at 70 plus or minus 5 degrees F to determine sensitivity to powder positioning.

Concurrent with the chamber pressure test, velocity of all test cartridges at 15 feet from the muzzle of the test barrel was recorded.

TABLE 5-1
CHAMBER PRESSURE AND VELOCITY

CARTRIDGE	TEMPERATURE	AVERAGE CHAMBER PRESSURE (PSI)	AVERAGE VELOCITY (FPS)
Fed 115 JHP	70 degrees F (p)	29,441	1,180
	70 degrees F (b)	26,383	1,129
	125 degrees F	29,687	1,180
	-40 degrees F	28,929	1,130
Fed 115 JHP +P+	70 degrees F (p)	35,479	1,324
	70 degrees F (b)	35,586	1,331
	125 degrees F	32.667	1,294
	-40 degrees F	46,823	1,398
Fed 124 Hyd-Shk	70 degrees F (p)	28,662	1,132
	70 degrees F (b)	26,963	1,130
	125 degrees F	27,995	1,120
	-40 degrees F	35,869	1,176
Fed 124 Hyd-Shk +P+	70 degrees F (p)	31,905	1,229
	70 degrees F (b)	31,781	1,224
	125 degrees F	27,983	1,174
	-40 degrees F	41,138	1,284
Fed 124 Nyclad	70 degrees F (p)	29,301	1,133
	70 degrees F (b)	27,280	1,120
	125 degrees F	29,899	1,158
	-40 degrees F	28,361	1,095
Win 115 JHP +P+	70 degrees F (p)	36,384	1,302
	70 degrees F (b)	35,341	1,300
	125 degrees F	31,717	1,234
	-40 degrees F	39,520	1,317
Win 115 STHP	70 degrees F (p)	26,091	1,140
	70 degrees F (b)	25,805	1,142
	125 degrees F	23,613	1,068
	-40 degrees F	29,806	1,178

NAVY/CRANE 9MM AMMO TESTS

CARTRIDGE	TEMPERATURE	AVERAGE CHAMBER PRESSURE (PSI)	AVERAGE VELOCITY (FPS)
Win 147 JHP	70 degrees F (p)	33,495	989
	70 degrees F (b)	32,682	989
	125 degrees F	26,595	910
	-40 degrees F	35,277	1,007
CCI 115 JHP	70 degrees F (p)	28,524	1,169
	70 degrees F (b)	25,833	1,141
	125 degrees F	27,786	1,165
	-40 degrees F	31,644	1,176
Horn 147 JHP	70 degrees F (p)	34,444	960
	70 degrees F (b)	33,566	958
	125 degrees F	31,336	941
	-40 degrees F	50,999	1,045
M882 124 Ball	70 degrees F (p)	36,372	1,200
	70 degrees F (b)	33.409	1,189
	125 degrees F	36,830	1,209
	-40 degrees F	42,960	1,224
Fed 147 JHP	70 degrees F (p)	29,589	962
	70 degrees F (b)	29,557	969
	125 degrees F	32,437	1,008
	-40 degrees F	34,461	971

(p) Powder at primer end of cartridge
(b) Powder at bullet end of cartridge

NOTE: ANSI/SAAMI recommended maximum average chamber pressure (transducer method) at 70 degrees F is 37,400 psi.

A minimum of 10 valid rounds of each type of ammunition were tested for expansion and penetration in ballistic gelatin. Five valid rounds minimum of each type were fired from a Smith & Wesson 6906, which has a barrel length of 3.5 inches. This is the shortest barrel of the five weapon types used and therefore produces the lowest bullet velocity. Five valid rounds minimum of each type were also fired from a Beretta 92SM pistol, which has a barrel length of 4.3 inches. This is the longest barrel of the five weapon types used and therefore produces the highest bullet velocity.

The gelatin blocks were made from standard ordnance gelatin, Pharmagel Type A, manufactured by Kind and Knox. The gelatin powder was mixed with water to form a 20 percent by weight mixture, which the Wound Ballistic Lab at the Letterman Army Institute of Research has determined is the best simulant of muscle tissue. Empty M2A1 ammunition cans were used as molds, forming blocks approximately 5 x 7 x 11 inches.

The gelatin blocks were placed 15 feet from the muzzle of the test weapon on a wooden stand. A sandbag was placed on top of each block to keep it secure. For cartridges that exhibited penetration in excess of 11 inches, two blocks were placed end to end to provide sufficient gelatin to stop the bullet. Penetration into the block was measured after each shot and the bullet was recovered to measure expanded diameter and final weight.

The desired expansion/penetration charac-teristics of JHP cartridges for maximum lethality are penetration of 7 to 12 inches, high percentage expansion, and high percentage mass retention. Penetration in excess of 12 inches is not desirable due to possible injury to innocent bystanders. Penetration of less than 7 inches may not reach vital organs and thus fail to incapacitate the target. The cartridge types which displayed the best

TABLE 5-2
GELATIN EXPANSION/PENETRATION

CARTRIDGE	WEAPON	AVG. PEN. (IN)	AVG. EXPANSION		AVERAGE MASS RETENTION		AVG. VEL. (FPS)
			DIA. (IN)	% EXP.	WT. (GR)	% RET	
Fed 115 JHP	Ber.	6.8	.604	70%	114.9	100%	1,079
	S&W	9.8	.553	56%	114.7	100%	1,052
Fed 115 JHP +P+	Ber	9.0	.507	43%	78.5	68%	1,263
	S&W	8.7	.596	68%	104.9	91%	1,245
Fed 124 Hyd-Shk	Ber	8.4	.620	74%	111.9	90%	1,067
	S&W	7.8	.620	74%	123.2	99%	1,051
Fed 124 Hyd-Shk +P+	Ber	8.3	.507	43%	72.7	59%	1,151
	S&W	7.6	.648	82%	117.4	95%	1,166
Fed 124 Nyclad	Ber.	7.2	.632	78%	123.7	100%	1,059
	S&W	11.0	.481	35%	123.5	100%	1,004
Win 115 JHP +P+	Ber.	6.1	.758	113%	110.3	96%	1,262
	S&W	6.9	.660	86%	113.1	98%	1,244
Win 115 STHP	Ber.	7.5	.636	79%	114.5	100%	1,112
	S&W	8.1	.579	63%	115.2	100%	1,096
Win 147 JHP	Ber.	11.6	.549	54%	147.6	100%	938
	S&W	11.3	.504	42%	147.4	100%	937
CCI 115 JHP	Ber.	10.7	.543	53%	115.3	100%	1,101
	S&W	12.0	.467	31%	115.1	100%	1,080
Fed 147 JHP	Ber.	9.2	.554	56%	147.9	100%	891
	S&W	11.8	.497	40%	147.8	100%	901

combination of these characteristics from the two test weapons were the Winchester 147 JHP, Federal 147 JHP, Federal 124 Hydra-Shok, and Winchester 115 STHP cartridges types.

The four cartridge types which exhibited the best expansion/penetration performance in the gelatin test were tested for effectiveness against automobile glass. Those four types were the Winchester 147 JHP, Winchester 115 STHP, Federal 147 JHP, and the Federal 124 Hydra-Shok. Blocks of 20-percent ballistic gelatin were placed 18 inches behind a single layer of laminated automobile glass, 7/32 inch thick and 16 inches square. Five rounds minimum of each ammunition type were fired from one each Beretta 92FS and one each Sig Sauer P225 with the glass perpendicular to the line of fire, and five rounds minimum of each type were fired from one each of the two test weapons with the glass at an angle of 45 degrees to the line of fire. The 45 degree glass was positioned so that a ricocheted bullet would travel upward.

All four ammunition types which were tested exhibited similar performance characteristics. All rounds easily penetrated the glass at both angles, leaving approximately 1 inch diameter holes in the glass. The different velocities created by the two weapon types appeared to have little effect on the performance of the cartridges. When tested against glass placed at 90 degrees to the line of fire, the bullets retained most of their mass and expanded to at least double the original

TABLE 5-3
GLASS/GELATIN EXPANSION AND PENETRATION

CARTRIDGE	WEAPON	GLASS ANGLE	AVG. PEN. (IN)	AVERAGE EXPANSION DIA. (IN)	% RET.
Fed 147 JHP	Beretta	90 degrees	5.0	.672	100%
		45 degrees	7.3	.500	77%
	Sig Sauer	90 degrees	3.9	.731	89%
		45 degrees	5.8	.554	75%
Fed 124 Hyd-Shk	Beretta	90 degrees	4.9	.683	87%
		45 degrees	7.9	.488	72%
	Sig Sauer	90 degrees	6.1	.488	56%
		45 degrees	6.4	.487	72%
Win 147 JHP	Beretta	90 degrees	3.9	.702	94%
		45 degrees	5.9	.530	67%
	Sig Sauer	90 degrees	5.3	.708	95%
		45 degrees	6.1	.504	72%
Win 115 STHP	Beretta	90 degrees	3.6	.784	100%
		45 degrees	8.1	.470	75%
	Sig Sauer	90 degrees	4.1	.719	100%
		45 degrees	6.0	.475	70%

diameter. Due to this large frontal area, however, penetration in the gelatin blocks was limited to 4 to 6 inches.

With the glass placed at a 45 degree angle to the line of fire, the jackets of nearly all of the bullets appeared to be stripped off upon impact with the glass. The lead core would then penetrate the gelatin 6 to 8 inches while the jacket would penetrate 0 to 2 inches, usually at a point about 2 inches to the lower left of the lead impact point. The lead core retained approximately 75 percent of the bullet's original mass, but expansion was limited to only 30 percent to 50 percent without the jacket. The Winchester 147 JHP bullet was deflected approximately 2 to 3 inches upward upon passage through the 45 degree glass. The other three cartridge types remained on or close to their original line of flight after penetrating the glass.

Fifty rounds of each type of ammunition were tested for accuracy at 50 yards from a test barrel. Twenty-five rounds of each type were fired in five-shot groups from two each test barrels which were 4 inches in length and conformed to ANSI/SAAMI standards. The test barrels were mounted in a universal receiver and were cleaned before each new type of ammunition was fired.

One hundred cartridges of each type were tested for accuracy at 50 yards from the test pistols. Twenty rounds of each type were fired in five-shot groups from one each of the five types of pistols used in this evaluation. The weapons were mounted in a Ransom Rest. Four five-shot groups were then fired through each of the five pistols. Weapon barrels were dry swabbed between ammunition types.

It should be noted that in both the test barrel accuracy test and the weapon accuracy test, four of the five most accurate cartridge types were loaded with 115-grain bullets. This indicates that the heavier bullets do not stabilize as well as the lighter bullets from the short barrels of these compact pistol. The high velocity of the +P+ cartridges did not appear to give those rounds a significant accuracy advantage, as only one of the three +P+ loads (the Federal 115 JHP +P+) finished in the top five of each test.

Function testing was performed using both laboratory techniques as well as the NIS Training Sequence. NIS agents performed the Training Sequence testing and assisted with the laboratory testing conducted at 70 degrees F.

Laboratory testing was conducted at three

TABLE 5-4
TEST BARREL ACCURACY

CARTRIDGE	AVERAGE EXTREME SPREAD
Fed 115 JHP	2.23"
Fed 115 JHP +P+	2.79"
Fed 124 Hydra-Shok	4.05"
Fed 124 Hydra-Shok +P+	4.15"
Fed 124 Nyclad	4.85"
Win 115 JHP +P+	4.08"
Win 115 STHP	2.34"
Win 147 JHP	3.47"
CCI 115 JHP	3.11"
Fed 147 JHP	1.92"
M882 124 Ball	4.96"

TABLE 5-5
WEAPON ACCURACY

CARTRIDGE	SIG SAUER E.S.	BERETTA E.S.	S&W E.S.	GLOCK E.S.	H&K E.S	OVERALL AVERAGE" E.S.
Fed 115 JHP	4.25	5.83	8.33	5.83	7.98	6.44
Fed 115 +P+	4.10	7.15	7.55	5.38	6.18	6.07
Fed 124 Hydra-Shok	6.23	6.03	6.28	6.58	7.15	6.45
Fed 124 Hydra-Shok +P	4.48	9.53	6.00	7.48	8.83	7.26
Fed 124 NYCLD	5.28	11.65	8.98	9.48	10.13	9.10
Win 115 JHP+P+	6.13	8.23	5.75	9.58	9.20	7.78
Win 115 STHP	5.55	6.85	5.38	8.38	7.95	6.82
Win 147 JHP	6.60	10.25	6.85	11.60	12.58	9.58
CCI 115 JHP	3.25	5.15	5.30	4.53	4.05	4.46
Fed 147 JHP	9.43	4.98	8.83	5.58	8.00	7.36
M882 124 Ball	8.85	13.45	7.95	6.38	11.60	9.65

temperature ranges (-40 degrees F, 70 degrees F, and 125 degrees F) using all five types of test weapons. Extended cycles were also fired using the Beretta and Sig Sauer pistols to determine ammunition performance in dirty weapons.

Weapons were field stripped and thoroughly cleaned between ammunition types and temperature ranges. All shooters fired the weapons using a two-handed grip, arms fully extended, and with no artificial support for the arms or hands. The first round of each magazine was fired in the double-action mode, except for in the Glock and H&K, which have no double-action mode.

Two NIS agents conducted function testing of each ammunition type using the NIS Training Sequence. Each shooter performed the sequence three times with each ammunition type, once each with a Sig Sauer P225, a Beretta 92FS, and a Smith & Wesson 6904 pistol.

The total number and type of stoppages attributable to the ammunition which occurred during the two function tests are shown in Table 5-6. Also shown is the Mean Rounds Between Failures (MRBF), which is the number of stoppages attributable to the ammunition per number of rounds fired. Malfunctions were attributed to the ammu-

nition unless it could be concluded with confidence that the failure was caused by a weapon or magazine problem.

(Most of the stoppages were the stovepipe of a live round, failure to feed the cartridge, or failure to pick up the cartridge from the magazine. Occurring much less frequently were the stovepipe of an empty case, failure to eject the spent case, failure of the slide to lock back after the last round, and failure to chamber the cartridge.)

The Federal 124 Hydra-Shok was the most reliable cartridge by a slight margin over the Federal 147 JHP, with the Federal 115 JHP and Federal 124 Nyclad virtually tied for third. It should be noted that the three +P+ cartridges had the three lowest MRBF of the 10 types tested. Most of these stoppages were failures to feed, probably due to the increased slide velocity caused by the high chamber pressure these cartridges produce.

During the 70 degree F laboratory function test and the NIS Training Sequence test, the two NIS shooters were asked to give their opinions of the various ammunition types that they had fired. After firing each ammunition type, shooters ranked the ammunition on a scale of 0 (unacceptable) to 10 (outstanding) in

TABLE 5-6
FUNCTION AND CASUALTY TEST

CARTRIDGE	MALFUNCTIONS	# RNDS FIRED	MRBF
Fed 115 JHP	5	9,312	1,862
Fed 115 JHP +P+	22	9,288	422
Fed 124 Hydra-Shok	2	9,168	4,584
Fed 124 Hydra-Shok +P+	17	9,168	539
Fed 124 Nyclad	5	9,168	1,834
Win 115 JHP +P+	31	9,168	296
Win 115 STHP	8	9,168	1,146
Win 147 JHP	16	9,048	566
CCI 115 JHP	15	9,048	603
Fed 147 JHP	3	9,306	3,102

the following categories: functioning reliability, accuracy (bullet drop related to sights), controllability (perceived recoil), powder fouling, muzzle flash, training sequence performance, and overall performance.

The shooters felt that the Federal 147 JHP and the Federal 124 Hydra-Shok cartridges were significantly superior in the above categories to the other eight candidates. The most common comments from the shooters were complaints about the excessive residual powder from the Winchester ammunition and concerns regarding the ability of female agents to maintain control of the +P+ loads during rapid firing.

Ten rounds of each ammunition type were tested for muzzle flash. This test was conducted for information only and was not factored into the overall ranking of the cartridges. Five rounds of each type were fired from a Smith & Wesson 6906, which has the shortest barrel of the five weapon types (3.5 inches), and five rounds of each type were fired from a Beretta 92SM, which has the longest barrel of the five weapon types (4.3 inches).

The test weapon was mounted in a Ransom Rest in a blacked-out range. The muzzle of the test weapon was placed through a hole in a grid surface marked with a white grid of 1-inch squares. The grid surface was also marked with an 8-inch diameter white circle centered on the muzzle hole. A 35mm camera was placed 68 inches downrange and 10 inches off the flight path. The shutter of the camera was opened, one cartridge was fired, and then the shutter was closed and the film advanced. This procedure was repeated for the remaining samples.

Upon developing the film, the image of the flash appeared superimposed on the grid background. The image of the flash was then compared relative to the grid scale.

For each performance test conducted, cartridge types were ranked in order of performance from one to ten, with one being the best. The function scoring consisted of two separate rankings. To determine the first ranking for the function test, worth 45 percent, the cartridge with the highest Mean Rounds Between Failures (MRBF) was ranked first, the second highest second, and so on. The second function ranking, worth 5 percent, was based on the results of the NIS shooter survey. The cartridge type with the highest average score was ranked first, the second highest second, and so on.

Accuracy consisted of two separate rankings, each worth 5 percent. The first accuracy ranking was based on the average of the 10 mean radii of the shot groups fired from test barrels. The second accuracy ranking was based on the average of the 20 mean radii fired from the test pistols (four groups from each of five pistols). In both cases, the cartridge with the smallest average mean radii (tightest group) was ranked first, the second smallest second, and so on.

Expansion and mass retention each consisted of two separate rankings. Expansion in ballistic gelatin was worth 8 percent, mass retention in ballistic gelatin was worth 4 percent, expansion in ballistic gelatin behind automobile glass was worth 2 percent, and mass retention in ballistic gelatin behind automobile glass was worth 1 percent. The cartridge type which had the greatest average expansion was ranked first in the gelatin expansion test, followed by the cartridge type with the second greatest average expansion, and so on. The cartridge type which had the greatest average percent mass retained was ranked first for gelatin mass retention, the second highest percent second, and so on. Cartridge types with equal average percent mass retained were ranked equally.

For the glass/gelatin test, the cartridge types which penetrated the glass at 0 degrees *and* 45 degrees obliquity were ranked highest, with the highest average expansion and highest percent mass retained ranked first, second highest second, and so on. Those cartridge types which only penetrated the glass at 0 degrees obliquity were ranked after those types that penetrated at 0 degrees and 45 degrees, according to the same criteria. Those cartridge types which did not penetrate the glass at either angle were ranked equally below those types which did penetrate the glass. The cartridge types which did not participate in this test were ranked equally below the four types which were tested.

Penetration consisted of two separate rankings. Penetration in ballistic gelatin was worth 20 percent and penetration in ballistic gelatin behind automobile glass was worth 5 percent. The cartridge type which produced the greatest average penetration which was less than or equal to 12 inches and greater than or equal to 7 inches was ranked first in the gelatin penetration test, followed by the

second greatest penetration in this range, and so on. Penetration which exceeded 12 inches is considered overpenetration and penetration less than 7 inches is considered under-penetration. Those cartridge types that pene-trated in excess of 12 inches were ranked higher than those that penetrated less than 7 inches, beginning with the cartridge type that produced the least penetration in excess of 12 inches. Any cartridge types which displayed a tendency to overpenetrate, even if their average penetration was less than 12 inches, were ranked below those which consistently penetrated 7 to 12 inches.

For the glass/gelatin penetration test, the cartridge types which penetrated the glass at 0 degrees *and* 45 degrees obliquity were ranked highest. Those cartridge types which only penetrated the glass at 0 degrees obliquity were ranked after those types that penetrated at 0 degrees and 45 degrees. Those cartridge types which did not penetrate the glass at either angle were ranked equally below those types that did penetrate the glass. The cartridge types which did not participate in this test were ranked equally below the four types which were tested.

To calculate the overall score for each cartridge, a numerical value was substituted for the rank value in accordance with Table 5-7. This numerical value was then multiplied by the scoring percentage for that test to get the score for that test. The scores for each of the individual tests were then added up to get the overall score for each cartridge type.

Based on the results of these tests, two cartridge types are considered acceptable for NIS use in the MX11 pistol. The Federal 124 Hydra-Shok and the Federal 147 JHP cartridge types both exhibited an excellent combination of functioning reliability and terminal performance. The Federal 124 Hydra-Shok was the most reliable round tested and displayed outstanding expansion while retaining over 90 percent of its mass and penetrating an average of 8.1 inches. Although lower than several other rounds tested, this penetration depth is within the

TABLE 5-7
INDIVIDUAL TEST RANKINGS

CARTRIDGE	A	B	C	D	E	F	G	H	I	J
Fed 115 JHP	3T	5	4T	1T	-	-	-	2	3	10
Fed 115 JHP +P+	9	4	7	9	-	-	-	4	2	8
Fed 124 Hyd-Shk	1	6	2	8	1	4	4	9	4	2
Fed 124 Hyd-Shk +P+8		7	4T	10	-	-	-	8	6	6
Fed 124 Nyclad	3T	3	6	1T	-	-	-	10	10	4
Win 115 JHP +P+	10	10	1	7	-	-	-	7	8	9
Win 115 STHP	5	8	3	1T	3	3	3	3	5	7
Win 147 JHP	7	1	8T	1T	4	2	1	6	9	5
CCI 115 JHP	6	9	10	1T	-	-	-	5	1	3
Fed 147 JHP	2	2	8T	1T	2	1	2	1	7	1

TABLE 5-8
FINAL RANKINGS OF CARTRIDGES

CARTRIDGE	SCORE
Federal 147 JHP	84.3
Federal 124 Hydra-Shok	79.5
Federal 115 JHP	67.4
Federal 124 Nyclad	65.3
Winchester 115 STHP	59.2
Winchester 147 JHP	56.8
CCI 115 JHP	44.1
Federal 115 JHP +P+	37.3
Federal 124 Hydra-Shok +P+	34.8
Winchester 115 JHP +P+	21.4

desired range of 7 to 12 inches. An area in which this round received a low ranking was test barrel accuracy. Its average mean radius of 1.48 inches at 50 yards, however, is certainly acceptable.

The Federal 147 JHP cartridge also proved to be an extremely reliable round. Although lacking the expansion of the Hydra-Shok cartridge (74 percent average expansion for the Hydra-Shok, 48 percent average expansion for the 147 JHP), this round retained 100 percent of its mass and penetrated an average of 10.5 inches in ballistic gelatin, more than 2 inches

deeper than the Hydra-Shok. Its only low ranking other than expansion was in weapon accuracy, where it produced an average mean radius of 2.52 inches at 50 yards, which is also quite acceptable.

No other cartridge types which were evaluated are recommended for NIS use. Although the third and fourth place rounds were not far behind the first two in overall score, each exhibited deficiencies in terminal performance. The Federal 115 JHP and the Federal 125 Nyclad both tended to under-penetrate from the Beretta, while from the

Smith & Wesson several rounds overpenetrated and expanded very little. The lethality of these rounds is questioned because of this inconsistent performance, and they are therefore not recommended for law enforcement use.

It is interesting to note that the three lowest-ranked cartridges were the three +P+ loads. This was due in a large part to the large number of stoppages which occurred during function testing of these rounds and their tendency to fragment when tested for expansion and penetration in ballistic gelatin.

It is recommended that the NIS initiate procurement of the Federal 147 JHP cartridge. In addition to its outstanding performance in this evaluation, this cartridge is recommended because a Navy specification for this round is already in place and it has been granted a limited release by the Weapons Systems Explosives Safety Review Board (WSESRB). This will permit a timely procurement and release in order to have ammunition in place when the XM11 pistols are delivered.

(End of Report)

The test methodology for weapon functioning developed by the NWSCC researchers represents a clear misunderstanding of the police shooting scenario. Do not be misled by the military funding or site of the naval study. This ammo study was clearly stated to be for NIS agents. These are civilian investigators who will face *exactly* the same kind of shooting scenarios as *any* plainclothes police detective.

An average of 9,184 rounds were fired during the function and casualty test. Of this number, 8,900 were fired under lab conditions and 288 were fired using Police Pistol Combat (PPC) stances.

An excellent argument can be made that PPC stances, grips, and shooting positions have nothing to do with the reality of the police shooting environment. Therefore, cycle reliability testing conducted under those idealistic range conditions is equally meaningless.

Some police firearms instructors watch millions of rounds of ammo go downrange during training and then use this observation to claim their ammo causes reliable functioning. They just don't get it.

We will leave that two-sided argument to the "martialists" versus "gamesmen" since the NWSCC committed an even clearer and more blatant error. As it turned out, the PPC portion of the cycle tests would have actually been more street relevant than the way it tested the bulk of the ammo.

Weapon functioning is a three-component system made up of the gun, the ammo, and the shooter. If any one part of this reliability triangle doesn't do its part, a stoppage will occur. Let's focus on the shooter as a firing platform.

When shooters report to the range, they are fresh and alert. They know they will be shooting. It is never a surprise. Their grip is nearly always correct and firm. Range conditions are ideal. Range officers are spaced every four shooters to instantly correct any errors. The shooter is thus an ideal platform. The guns are as clean as they'll ever be. The ammo can be marginal and still cycle well because the shooter and the pistol are doing their part.

In the main part of the NWSCC test, the shooter was essentially removed from the system, for 97 percent of the firing for the cycle reliability tests were done as follows: all shooters fired the weapons using a two-handed grip with arms fully extended. This is the most rigid, idealistic platform possible, not to mention the fact that the weapons were being fired by NIS agents of substantial enough stature and weapons-orientation.

Now, how about factoring in the fatigue of being 9 hours into a 10-hour shift with a caffeine-induced headache. One last paper to serve or one last traffic summons will call the day complete. From nowhere, the officer is called to draw and fire. Most cops are much more familiar with where the radio and the cuffs are on their gun belt than exactly where the pistol grip is.

Will the draw be range-perfect or will the cop grip slightly low? Will he fully extend both arms or fire before he gets that far? Will he snap-fire one handed before he "locks" his wrist? Will he fire a little limp-wristed unless he uses both hands? Even then? Will he be struggling with his opponent as he fires? Will the use of a flashlight in his other hand compromise his grip? Will he get so far behind cover that to fire, the slide really does rub the "barricade"?

The NWSCC study included subjective ratings from two NIS agents concerning functioning reliability and perceived recoil. The most common comments included concern regarding the ability of female agents to maintain control of the +P+ loads during rapid firing. Ignore for a moment the sexist implication that only women will have trouble or that smaller stature men will not. The facts are that +P+ ammo produces enough slide velocity to operate a recoil-operated pistol under adverse conditions. Standard-pressure ammo is less tolerant of the shooter platform not being perfect. Subsonic ammo is even less tolerant than that. This +P+ ammo is actually more reliable than lower pressure loads under actual police scenarios, not less reliable as the NWSCC study concluded.

The NWSCC researchers had the answer right in front of them but could not recognize it. They said, "Most of these stoppages were failures to feed, probably due to the increased slide velocity caused by the high chamber pressures these cartridges produce."

Had the researchers developed a more street-realistic cycle test, they would have instead said, "Most of these stoppages from the subsonic loads were failures to extract or eject, probably due to the decreased slide velocity caused by the low bullet velocities these cartridges produce."

The facts are that both too much and too little slide velocity cause stoppages. However, the reality of the gunfighting scenario is that everything the shooter does wrong reduces the slide velocity: a low grip, unlocked wrist, limp wrist, flexed or unlocked arms, thumbs or barricades rubbing the slide, shooting one handed, shooting weak handed, dirt and debris in the auto pistol, ammo at the bottom

end of the power band. Each and every one of these factors reduces slide velocity and gets one step closer to a stoppage.

Only clean guns, with locked wrists and arms, a solid stance, and a shooter of above average stature under lab conditions could possibly cause a stoppage from too much slide velocity. That is exactly what happened at Crane. And that is why it happened. On the street, the exact opposite happens. (See Chapter 15.)

The largest police experiment in the world has proven that the way to reduce shooter-induced stoppages is to use +P+ pressure ammo. We respectfully refer to the New York City Police Department and the most diverse mix of uniformed law enforcement officers anywhere. The one load that reliably cycles the NYCPD auto pistols is the 124-grain at +P+ pressures. (For a while, the NYCPD backed off to 115-grain loads to reduce overpenetration risks until a 124-grain +P+ hollowpoint could be approved.)

Let's see. Who gets involved in more gunfights, the NYCPD or NIS? Which agency has more diversity among its members? And which agency is made up of less weapons-oriented officers?

The NWSCC was clearly wrong in testing cycle reliability the way it did. Remember now that cycle reliability made up a full 50 percent of the overall score.

We did some number crunching to see how the final ranking would be affected by correcting the cycle tests. This assumes that we accept, without any challenges, the minimum penetration requirements of 7 inches of 20-percent gelatin. Since the U.S. Secret Service set 5.9 inches of 20-percent gelatin as the minimum, we are not willing to give the NWSCC a pass without a challenge. However, for the sake of just this cycle issue, let's assume we ignore all tests except the cycle tests.

Slide velocity is a function of both muzzle energy and muzzle momentum. The loads that produce the most of each of these will be the most cycle-reliable in actual police scenarios.

The loads that produce the least energy and the least momentum will be the least likely to cycle reliably.

When we run the numbers to correct for the errors in the cycle testing and in the subjective opinions, the best overall load is now the Federal 115-grain JHP +P+ followed by the Winchester 115-grain Silvertip and then the Federal 124-grain Hydra-Shok +P+. And, again, that is giving the other challenges a pass. The top three loads under the incorrect cycle testing methodology fall to seventh, fifth, and eighth, respectively.

The assumptions that went into the development of the NWSCC cycle test greatly affected the outcome. With more police-oriented, street-realistic assumptions, the NWSCC would have joined the Illinois State Police, U.S. Secret Service, U.S. Marshals Service, U.S. Border Patrol, Royal Canadian Mounted Police, and the New York City PD in specifying a +P+ load for its 9mm pistols.

TABLE 5-9
NAVY/CRANE 9mm AMMO RANKINGS
(CORRECTED FOR POLICE-SCENARIO CYCLE TEST METHODS)

LOAD	SCORE
Federal 115-grain JHP +P+ (9BPLE)	76.8
Winchester 115-grain Silvertip	64.8
Federal 124-grain Hydra-Shok +P+	63.8
Winchester 147-grain JHP (OSM)	61.2
Federal 124-grain Hydra-Shok	60.0
Winchester 115-grain JHP +P+ (Q4174)	55.9
Federal 147-grain JHP (9MS-2)	53.8
Federal 115-grain JHP (9BP)	40.9
CCI-Speer 115-grain JHP	37.6
Federal 124-grain Nyclad hollowpoint	30.8

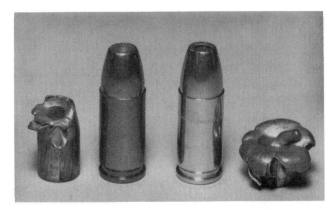

The U.S. Navy test protocol favored the Federal 147-grain JHP 9MS-2 (left), followed closely by the Federal 124-grain Hydra-Shok (right) for its NIS agents.

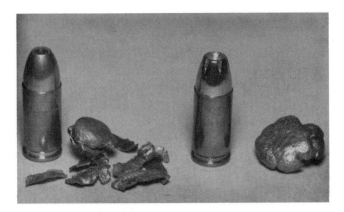

When the navy test protocol is corrected to more realistically test for cycle reliability, the winners are the Federal 115-grain +P+ JHP 9BPLE (left), followed by the Winchester 115-grain Silvertip (right).

6
Police Marksman/ Fairburn Tests

In 1989, the publisher of the police trade magazine *Police Marksman*, Charles Leslie Dees, and prolific police writer Dick Fairburn joined forces to assess the performance of police ammo under actual police gunfight conditions. Four years later, in the March/ April 1993 issue of *Police Marksman*, they published their results.

Fairburn and Dees took a novel approach to the incredibly difficult job of gathering actual police-action or officer-involved shooting results. Dees published a one-page questionnaire in numerous issues of the magazine for police officers to fill out. Fairburn statistically analyzed the mailed-in results.

The survey depended on the honesty and objectivity of eyewitnesses to the shootings, whether they were the involved officer or a backup unit at the scene. It began with the statement: "Which ammunition has more stopping power? The purpose of the PMA/Fairburn Study is to gather factual data on the stopping power of various ammunition. This is a five-year study. We will only accept reports from police, military police, and trained security officers. Please submit the report in a departmental envelope with some detachable evidence that you are a law enforcement officer (business card). This evidence will be removed as soon as it is received. It is for verification only. Report on an incident that was personally witnessed. Please be as accurate as possible. Only accurate facts derived from these forms can yield the scientifically valid results we are seeking."

Fairburn acknowledged that the data that came from the study were subjective opinions submitted by the observers. He also stated that more is involved when bullets hit a human than mere physiological damage. He quite accurately cautioned that while the phenomenon of stopping power exists, it may never be able to be gauged simply because the number of variables is almost infinite.

Yet Fairburn, like Marshall, took the most logical, simple, and straightforward approach to quantifying stopping power. Rather than develop a theory or test method, Fairburn set out to simply record reality. What happens in the lab in gelatin or water is only the prediction; what happens on the street under actual gunfight conditions and a wide variety of engagement distances and barriers/clothing is reality. The results from enough direct observations are always better than the predictions from even the most complex and interrelated testing.

The readers of *Police Marksman* submitted 241 shooting events involving 876 shots fired. The range of calibers involved ran from the .22 Long Rifle to the .44 Magnum in handguns and included eight incidents with centerfire rifle cartridges and 17 events with the 12-gauge shotgun.

Evan Marshall restricted his data base to single shots and torso shot placements. Head and extremity shots and multiple shots were excluded. Fairburn, however, took a different but equally relevant approach. His totals included all shot placements, including head shots, and all multiple shots.

The other methodology difference is that Marshall required 10 shootings of each make, caliber, and weight before he reported it as a result. Fairburn required five shootings by caliber and weight but in general lumped all the makes together. In other words, all makes of .38 Special 158-grain SWC-HP went into the result of that load. This assumes that all these different makes perform the same, and in reality, this assumption is correct.

Fairburn focused on the four major police calibers: .38 Special +P, 9mm, .357 Magnum, and .45 ACP. The .40 S&W and 10mm were not included in his summary. The results from these four police duty calibers were based on 187 shooting reports and 700 shots fired. The study has profound merit and deserves its place in history along with all other serious attempts to measure stopping power.

The first of Fairburn's conclusions was a success ratio by caliber. He found that statistically, the 9mm, .357 Magnum, and .45 Auto calibers have a similar degree of overall effectiveness when all loads within one caliber are compared to all loads within other calibers. Compared to these three calibers, the .38 Special +P caliber produces a statistically lower level of success, and as an overall caliber the .38 Special is less effective than the other three when all shootings with all loads within that caliber are analyzed.

The comparison of Fairburn's overall success by caliber to Marshall's weighted one-shot stops by caliber is as follows. Keep in mind that the percentages represent differences in data-gathering techniques:

FAIRBURN (187 REPORTS)

.45 Auto	54.5%
.357 Magnum	53.8%
9mm Luger	49.0%
.38 Special	39.0%

MARSHALL (7,020 REPORTS)

.357 Magnum	90.8%
9mm Luger	79.7%
.45 Auto	75.7%
.38 Special	65.6%

The trends between these two studies are the same. Fairburn's data ranks the .45 Auto, .357 Magnum, and 9mm in one distinct group and the .38 Special in another. Marshall's results put the .357 Magnum in one group, the 9mm and .45 Auto in another, and the .38 Special in a third.

Fairburn went on to list the success ratio from various loads within each caliber. As a rule, his ranking from best to worst within each caliber exactly matches Marshall's results. This makes sense. When both men set out to find the truth, and both actually find it, you would expect that the two truths would agree!

In the .38 Special, and of the loads surveyed, the 158-grain SWC-JHP was far and away the best police load in the caliber. No controversy whatsoever surrounds this conclusion. Originating with the St. Louis, Missouri, Police Department circa 1972, this load gained street fame with the Chicago Police, Metro-Dade (Miami) Police, and the

FBI. It will forever be remembered as the bullet that ended the 1986 FBI shootout in Miami.

In the 9mm caliber, Fairburn found the 115-grain JHPs to have a statistically significant greater success ratio than the 147-grain JHPs. This is what noted gun writer Massad Ayoob wrote in the July 1993 issue of *Guns* magazine when he reviewed Fairburn's study:

"At the same time, the 147-grain 9mm subsonic (that [Dr. Martin] Fackler and his followers can be said to have popularized) performed less well than the Silvertip it was intended to replace, let alone the more effective supersonic 115-grain 9mm JHPs, and this contradicts the doctrine of those who favor this deep-penetrating bullet."

The 147-grain subsonic JHP is the least effective expanding bullet in the 9mm caliber, according to Fairburn (who is from the heavy bullet, deep penetration school). According to Marshall, all of the 115- and 124-grain +P JHPs and all of the 115- and 124-grain standard-pressure JHPs/LHPs are more effective than even the best 147-grain JHP.

In the .357 Magnum caliber, Fairburn found the most successful load to be the 125-

	FAIRBURN		MARSHALL	
.38 SPECIAL	TOTAL SHOOTINGS	SUCCESS RATIO	TOTAL SHOOTINGS	ONE-SHOT STOPS
158-gr. SWC-HP (all makes)	9	77.7%	654	75.8%
125-gr. JHP (all makes)	15	46.6%	459	71.2%
110-gr. JHP (all makes)	5	40.0%	111	69.4%
158-gr. JHP (all makes)	6	33.3%	n/a	n/a
158-gr. SWC (all makes)	5	20.0%	370	52.7%

	FAIRBURN		MARSHALL	
9mm LUGER	TOTAL SHOOTINGS	SUCCESS RATIO	TOTAL SHOOTINGS	ONE-SHOT STOPS
115-gr. JHP (non-STHP)	12	58.3%	510	81.0%
115-gr. Silvertip	17	52.9%	304	82.9%
147-gr. JHP (all makes)	11	50.0%	588	76.5%
115/124-gr. FMJ (all makes)	4	25.0%	256	62.9%

	FAIRBURN		MARSHALL	
.357 MAGNUM	TOTAL SHOOTINGS	SUCCESS RATIO	TOTAL SHOOTINGS	ONE-SHOT STOPS
125-gr. JHP (all makes)	13	76.9%	985	94.5%
145-gr. Silvertip	8	75.0%	84	84.5%
158-gr. JHP (all makes)	10	50.0%	188	79.3%

grain JHP. Again, this should surprise absolutely no one who has seriously studied wound ballistics. And again, Fairburn and Marshall had exactly the same relative ranking within the caliber.

In .45 Auto, and of the loads with survey results, the Federal 230-grain Hydra-Shok was the clear winner. Fairburn's results did, however, show a clear difference from Marshall's results when it came to the effectiveness of the 185-grain Silvertip.

Based on nine shootings, Fairburn showed the Silvertip to be a poor choice for duty use. In 73 shootings, Marshall, however, showed it to perform far above 230-grain FMJ hardball and to be about average for the caliber. Whatever else is made of this ranking, this stark difference in street results shows that Fairburn is no minion of Marshall.

All of Fairburn's data has been based on all shots fired and all shot placements. In a separate display, and for comparison to the one-shot stop methodology, he excluded the shooting reports with multiple bullet hits and with head and extremity shot placements.

While not an outright antagonist or bitter detractor of Evan Marshall, Dick Fairburn is certainly a philosophical opponent and thoughtful critic of Marshall's research and conclusions. Fairburn simply set out to find the truth about bullet effectiveness himself.

Fairburn did not trust Marshall's results because Marshall does not generally release the sources of his raw data. This prevents independent corroboration of the results and requires that the rest of us rely on the integrity of Evan Marshall. Some are not willing to do that.

By his own admission, Fairburn was solidly aligned with the heavy bullet, deep penetration school of thought. He did exactly what Marshall urges all his critics to do: gather your own street results and then let's talk. While Fairburn's data gathering and analyzing methodology was very different than Marshall's, the overall results from the street, the relative rankings within each caliber, are the same.

Do not think that Fairburn based his smaller sample size of records on Marshall's work. Fairburn specifically wrote that to make his findings more objective, he had purposely not read the book *Handgun Stopping Power*.

	FAIRBURN		MARSHALL	
.45 AUTO	TOTAL SHOOTINGS	SUCCESS RATIO	TOTAL SHOOTINGS	ONE-SHOT STOPS
230-gr. Hydra-Shok	5	60.0%	71	94.5%
230-gr. FMJ (all makes)	11	45.4%	469	63.3%
185-gr. Silvertip	9	33.3%	73	82.2%

	FAIRBURN		MARSHALL
CALIBER	MULTIPLE SHOTS AND ALL SHOT PLACEMENTS	ONE-SHOT AND TORSO PLACEMENT	ONE-SHOT AND TORSO PLACEMENT
.38 Special	39.0%	48.0%	65.6%
9mm Luger	49.0%	55.5%	79.7%
.357 Magnum	53.8%	71.4%	90.8%
.45 Auto	54.5%	66.6%	75.7%

Massad Ayoob reviewed Fairburn's ammo effectiveness study in the July 1993 issue of *Guns* magazine. In the polarized area of wound ballistics, Ayoob is one of the few police writers to remain totally neutral and uncommitted to either faction. Ayoob wrote, "What PMA and Dick Fairburn have given us is useful, important and valid."

He also wrote, "It is well known among professionals that the debate between the followers of Marshall and Sanow and those of Dr. Martin Fackler may be the most acrimonious exchange in the history of firearms journalism. The fact is that Fairburn's work largely validates that of Marshall and Sanow, even though that was certainly not his intent."

Many of us have a choice of what caliber or load within a caliber to carry on duty or for defense. Since this chapter is devoted to Fairburn's research, it is only fair that we print what Fairburn concluded in a memo written the month his study was published.

"Given the choice, I will use a major caliber sidearm with a heavy weight projectile that gives 12 to 15 inches of penetration and the most expansion possible."

Fairburn's study went beyond wound ballistics. The survey also requested information on number of shots fired, distance to the target, and the hit ratio all by caliber.

Since the 1970s, we have been taught that the average police gunfight involves 2.5 rounds of ammo. Fairburn updated this number and broke it out by caliber. These results have a profound impact on firearms instruction, especially with regards to fire-control discipline and liability from causing a downrange hazard.

CALIBER	SHOTS PER INCIDENT
.357 Magnum	2.3 rounds
.45 Auto	2.7 rounds
.38 Special	3.6 rounds
9mm Luger	5.5 rounds

The overall shots per incident average from these four police calibers is 3.5 rounds. The fact that officers who carry 9mm pistols shoot a lot more rounds per gunfight is not a surprise to most police trainers. The hit ratio numbers are interesting when they are broken down by caliber.

CALIBER	HIT RATIO
9mm Luger	47.3%
.38 Special	57.3%
.45 Auto	61.5%
.357 Magnum	78.2%

These ratios raise a number of additional questions and challenge a number of old myths. First, felt recoil appears to have nothing to do with hit probability. The .357 Magnum had a far greater hit ratio than the .38 Special, and the .45 Auto had a significantly higher hit ratio than the 9mm. Obviously, comments in the gun press against the ability to be effective in a gunfight with the heavy-recoiling .357 Magnum are wrong. In fact, taken on face value, Fairburn's results would instead argue that everyone should be using a .357 Magnum revolver. After all, the purpose of shooting is hitting.

However, the .357 Magnum revolver is obviously "out" and one of the auto pistol calibers is obviously "in." With that in mind, consider Fairburn's comments on the 9mm.

"The hits/shots ratio of 47.3% for the 9mm is the lowest shown. When the two aspects are combined (shots per incident and hit ratio), it can be said with certainty that the high-capacity, semiauto pistols need some careful attention paid to the aspects of marksmanship and fire control during training."

Dick Fairburn is now a full-time police trainer and consultant specializing in weapons, tactics, and officer survival issues. He can be reached though the Police Marksman Association. Subscriptions to *Police Marksman* magazine can be obtained by writing:

Police Marksman Association
6000 E. Shirley Lane
Montgomery, AL 36117

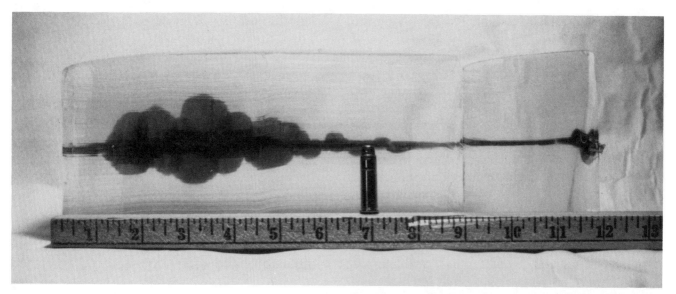

Of the survey responses, Fairburn found the 158-grain SWC-HP to be the most effective hollowpoint in the .38 Special +P caliber.

Fairburn documented the Federal 9mm 115-grain JHP 9BP (shown here) to be more effective than the 147-grain subsonic JHP and clearly superior to all hardball ammo.

Fairburn that concluded the 125-grain JHP (shown here) was the top .357 Magnum load, followed closely by the 145-grain Silvertip.

Fairburn agrees with Marshall that the .45 Auto 230-grain Hydra-Shok is the best load in the caliber and is clearly more effective than 230-grain hardball.

The police officers responding to Fairburn's survey indicated that the .38 Special +P 158-grain SWC-HP had a 78 percent success ratio. This agrees with Marshall's stats.

7

Royal Canadian Mounted Police Ammo Tests

In September 1994, the Canadian Police Research Center compared the performance of various 9mm Luger and .40 S&W loads to their .38 Special +P 158-grain SWC-HP in ballistic gelatin. This study was performed by Dean B. Dahlstron and Kramer D. Powley, Firearms Section, Forensic Laboratory, Royal Canadian Mounted Police (RCMP), Regina, Saskatchewan, Canada.

The text of the RCMP report shows the Canadian researchers were heavily influenced by the FBI and the deep penetration, crush-cavity-only thinking of the late 1980s. However, they do not place the seven-to-one emphasis on defeating barriers as the Bureau does. Nor did the RCMP researchers develop a misleading, crush-only formula to predict wound effectiveness as the Bureau did. The RCMP did, however, add a unique twist to the gelatin test. As Col. Frank Chamberlin did in the 1930s, the RCMP researchers added pig ribs to the gelatin. They conducted three separate tests: bare gelatin, gelatin covered with clothing, and gelatin with the embedded

rib. These tests were fired at 3 meters and again in their entirety at 50 meters.

The testers used the Federal .38 Special +P 158-grain SWC-HP fired from a S&W Model 10 with a 5-inch barrel as a control. This was a special "fast" version loaded by Federal specifically for the RCMP. It has a 5-inch muzzle velocity of 1,000 fps minimum. They used the performance of this proven load as a baseline to evaluate eight 9mm and nine .40 S&W loads. These two auto pistol calibers were fired from 4-inch S&W pistols, and all of the tests were repeated with the 9mm loads fired from an HK MP5 submachine gun with a 9-inch barrel.

The RCMP researchers focused on just four test results: total penetration, recovered diameter, weight retention, and the percent of retained weight.

Like the FBI, loads were disqualified for penetrating less than 12 inches of 10-percent gelatin. (Rigid adherence to the 12-inch minimum is being rethought by the same folks that came up with the arbitrary distance. See

Chapter 27.) Unlike the Bureau, however, the RCMP wisely disqualified loads for penetrating more than 18 inches of 10-percent gelatin. The RCMP also disqualified loads that produced less expansion than its .38 Special +P 158-grain SWC-HP.

The RCMP researchers did *not* select any one best load in either 9mm or .40 S&W. Instead, they left the final decision up to the various agencies using the data and selecting the ammo.

Although we disagree with some of the statements in the text—especially discounting the affects of temporary cavities, minimum penetration requirements, and bullet fragmentation—we applaud the RCMP for its test methodology. The testers are also to be commended for their ability to at least partially break away from the "deeper-is-better," barrier-intensive thinking of the late 1980s.

Without further comment, the text from the Technical Report TR-01-95 by Dahlstrom and Prowley, reproduced with the permission of the Royal Canadian Mounted Police, now follows in its entirety.

EXECUTIVE SUMMARY

Currently the trend in police issue sidearms is the adoption of a high capacity pistol in calibre 9mm Parabellum or .40 Smith & Wesson. The purpose of this paper is to compare terminal ballistic performance of commercially manufactured 9mm Parabellum and .40 Smith & Wesson ammunition with the current Royal Canadian Mounted Police issue .38 Special 158 semiwadcutter hollowpoint (SWCHP) cartridge.

Ammunition supplied by various commercial manufacturers was chronographed and fired into 10-percent ordnance gelatin blocks under three conditions at distances of 3 meters and 25 or 50 meters depending upon the barrel length of the firearm utilized as dictated by RCMP training standards. At each distance, five rounds of each type of ammunition was fired into bare gelatin, gelatin covered with clothing, and gelatin with pigs' ribs embedded 1 to 2 inches under the entrance surface.

The ability of a projectile discharged from a handgun to incapacitate a human should be a subject of crucial importance to law enforcement agencies since the handgun is usually the law enforcement agent's primary weapon of defense. Based on previous research, it is generally accepted that at handgun velocities, temporary cavitation produced by a projectile is a minimal wounding agent, particularly in the case of torso shots. In such cases, the expansion of the bullet must be relied upon to physiologically incapacitate an individual. There must be sufficient blood loss to effectively disrupt the central nervous system, since psychological incapacitation is unpredictable. To achieve this desired result, a projectile should reach vital organs within the body and damage as much tissue as possible.

In 1982, Dr. M. Fackler of the Wound Ballistics Laboratory of the Letterman Army Institute of Research developed a scientific approach to the study of wound profiles based on an understanding of the effects of projectiles on body soft tissues. The procedure for the RCMP study was developed on the basis of Dr. Fackler's research, with some additional modifications that more closely simulate actual field conditions.

The terminal performance of calibres 9mm Parabellum and .40 Smith & Wesson ammunition were measured with respect to penetration depth, expansion, weight retention, and percent weight retention. Results were recorded and compared to similar tests conducted for caliber .38 Special, 158-grain semiwadcutter hollowpoint ammunition. An easily interpreted tabular form of the resulting data was developed to assist law enforcement agencies in the selection of a suitable calibre and ammunition type for police use.

From the limited ammunition types tested, there are both calibre 9mm Parabellum and .40 Smith & Wesson ammunition which are comparable or exceed the terminal performance of the RCMP issue calibre .38 Special 158-grain SWCHP ammunition. The significance of the performance difference is an issue which may only be determined by those agencies involved in the selection of a suitable firearm ammunition combination for law enforcement use. This selection process must be based upon individual force protocol and may rely upon factors outside the listed events such as shooting through intermediary targets.

INTRODUCTION

Handguns have historically been the primary source of defense for regular duty law enforcement officers. Because it is the duty sidearm which is generally used in confrontational situations, the firearm ammunition combination must be relied upon to incapacitate a human aggressor.

In handgun projectile wounds, incapacitation is caused by two factors: 1) psychological incapacitation, and 2) physiological incapacitation.

Psychological incapacitation is nonpredictable and thus a model of reaction to being shot cannot be developed. "Psychological incapacitation is completely independent of any inherent characteristics of a specific bullet and is totally unrelated to the potential for any given bullet to cause physiological incapacitation."

Physiological incapacitation has been well documented and is the result of the mechanical effects of the projectile producing physical damage to the human body.

As a handgun bullet enters the human body, it must first crush and destroy tissue. The space once occupied by this tissue is called the permanent cavity.

Temporary cavity is "the lateral transient dispersion of tissue from the wound track," and at handgun projectile velocities, the tissue generally does not stretch beyond its elastic limits and there is no significant contribution to the wound mechanism.

Certain organs within the body, including the brain, spleen, liver, and bones, are more susceptible to damage from the temporary cavity due to their inelasticity; however, damage to these is limited. Overall, it is generally recognized that at handgun velocities, temporary cavity is not a reliable wounding mechanism.

The only reliable method of stopping a human with a handgun bullet is to "decrease functioning capability of the central nervous system." This may be done in one of two ways: Type I is direct disruption of the central nervous system by bullet penetration. Type II is by lack of oxygen to the brain caused by bleeding. The only wounds which result in immediate incapacitation are those which damage the essential brain matter such as the brain stem or cervical spinal cord.

Because the central nervous system occupies such limited space within the human body, it is not feasible to expect or train for direct CNS shots, particularly in confrontation situations.

In nondirect central nervous system bullet injuries, the size and location of the wound are important. Wolberg states, "The rate of incapacitation is directly proportional to the rate of blood flow and the organs or structures hit."

Bullets must be able to penetrate deeply enough in order to disrupt major organs and blood vessels within the human torso to cause hemorrhaging which results in incapacitation. However, an individual who has been shot in the heart or major blood vessels may not be affected for many seconds or minutes. Therefore, the expectation that a bullet striking a vital organ aside from the brain will cause immediate incapacitation is a dangerous misconception.

The exact quantity of blood loss a person can tolerate before collapsing is difficult to determine because it is dependent upon age, health, activity, presence of drugs or alcohol, and psychological state. McKenny, however, states 2,000 mL is the point at which "serious incapacitation" takes place. Newgard states that for blood loss greater than 25 percent of total volume, compensation will not adequately keep the brain and heart supplied with sufficient oxygen, and progression of this condition will lead to irreversible shock and death.

Vital anatomical structures are located deep within the body protected by various layers of tissue. The average thickness of an adult human torso is 9.4 inches. The major blood vessels in the torso are located approximately 6 inches from the ventral skin surface. From oblique and transverse angles, the heart and major blood vessels of the torso can be over 7.9 inches deep. Bullets must be able to penetrate 12 inches of soft tissue the "minimum depth necessary to ensure disruption of the major organs and blood vessels in the torso from any angle and despite intermediate obstacles." Bullets that penetrate beyond 18 inches are wasting tissue disruption potential which could be used to make a larger hole in the ideal 12- to 15-inch range of penetration required for handgun bullets.

Of the bullets which attain desired penetration depth, those of larger diameter are the most effective, crushing more tissue. Shape and configuration of the bullet can also be an important factor. Cutting is a variation of the crush factor and is far more efficient in disrupting tissue than is stretching. Expanded bullets which are sharp edged are more likely to cut tissue along the wound track compared to blunt edges, which tend to stretch tissue aside during their passage.

If handgun bullets fragment, wound severity is generally not increased since the bullet fragments are usually found within 1 cm of the main permanent cavity formed by the bullet path.

The wound profile method for measuring the damage caused by penetrating projectiles was developed at the Wound Ballistics Laboratory of the Letterman Army Institute of Research in 1982. Its purpose was to clarify the interaction of penetrating projectiles with body soft tissues and establish a quantitative predictive model for human wounds. This method was based upon shooting projectiles into 10-percent ordnance gelatin at 4 degrees C and recording the projectiles' penetration depth, its yaw pattern, and its deformation (including fragmentation and the size and location of the temporary cavity it produced). The wound ballistic profile method has been validated by Dr. Davis' colleagues at the Miami-Dade Medical Examiners office, who conducted ballistic testing of swine tissue and

gelatin and compared findings to that of gunshot victims at autopsy. Wolberg, testing 147-grain subsonic Win 9mm, stated "this gelatin can be a useful predictor of this bullet's penetration and expansion characteristics in shots in the human torso."

Although 10-percent gelatin has many proponents, and Dr. M. Fackler's wound profile is currently used by many researchers and police agencies, there are also critics.

Dr. Ragsdale, in a letter to the editor of the *Journal of American Medical Association*, states "Gelatin is in fact a very misleading tissue simulant, since a body comprises a complex array of layers with different densities around organs, supported by bone and enveloped by elastic skin."

Ragsdale states a 20-percent gelatin concentration reproduces bullet retardation of animal tissue the size and shape of temporary cavities in pig muscle and incurs a permanent cavity similar to tissue wounds.

Ragsdale further states, "The simple expedient of injecting epoxy glue into permanent cavities in gelatin blocks details the structural complexity of radial fissures. They are actually an overlapping series of lobulated leaf-like projections that spiral (due to bullet spin) from the central track of penetration. This fissure complexity is a major cause for the imprecise correlation of fissure calculations and actual temporary cavity."

"The wound profile method of Fackler is basically the creation of a comparative series of sketches of the permanent cavities created in 10-percent gelatin with superimposed outlines of the temporary cavity, as inferred by mathematical calculations. In view of the demonstrated lack of correlation between fissure calculations and actual temporary cavities, the Wound Profile diagrams cannot be taken as accurately showing likely cavitational effects in gelatin, let alone tissue."

Various researchers have modified Dr. Fackler's wound profile method by inserting bones or organs into 10-percent gelatin blocks. Dr. Lane and Ted Hallabough, Firearms Training Unit FBI, have conducted tests inserting swine femur into 10-percent ballistic gelatin blocks, advising swine bone is similar to human bone.

Lewis, Clark, and O'Connell stated, "The placement of organs in gelatin is of great value in studying the effects of missile trauma on various organs and tissues and produces a model which more closely simulates the human body than does gelatin alone.

"The symmetrical damage revealed in homogeneous translucent gelatin can be expected to be substantially modified if the incoming missile is destabilized by an intermediate target or strikes bone early in its penetration. Also, the complex structure of the human body has layers of variable density (skin, fat, muscle, fascia), and irregularly shaped viscera and visci variously filled with air and fluid. This complexity means there will be an almost infinite array of possible wound channel configuration, unlike those in homogeneous tissue simulant.

"Gelatin/bone target probably has more relevance to human wounding than a plain gelatin block, since the latter cannot be compared to the complex regional density differences within the body."

Fackler states, "Since most shots in the human body traverse various tissues, we would expect the wound profiles to vary somewhat, depending on the tissue traversed. However, the only radical departure has been found to occur when the projectile strikes bone: this predictably deforms the bullet more than soft tissue, reducing its overall penetration depth, and sometimes altering the angle of the projectiles course. Shots traversing only soft tissue in humans have shown damage patterns of remarkably close approximation to the wound profiles."

Kinetic energy and tissue trauma has been a subject debated in the modern concept of terminal wound ballistics. Duncan MacPherson, in a paper presented at the Wound Ballistic seminar at the FBI Academy in 1/19-22/93, stated there is a lack of correlation between kinetic energy and damage in some physical processes. The reason for this is that physical damage is the result of stress (force per unit area), not energy. Higher kinetic energy usually increases the induced stress, but this stress only creates damage if it produces strains above the elastic limit. Most body tissues have a relatively high elastic strain limit, well above the level produced by handgun bullet temporary cavities. Since much of the kinetic energy of a bullet is associated with producing the temporary cavity volume, there is a lack of correlation between handgun bullet kinetic energy and wound trauma.

Ragsdale states, "The severity of a wound is directly related to the amount of kinetic energy lost by the bullet in the body, because the kinetic energy of a missile is dissipated in bullet deformation and tissue damage. Nine millimetre pistol wounds of the abdomen create hemorrhagic lesions on the intestinal walls that may look innocent but may develop into dangerous intestinal perforations if they are left untreated. For a given aim point, the bullet producing the largest temporary cavity at the proper depth, defined by the location of vital organs, should have the greater likelihood of producing incapacitation."

In the spring of 1994, it was determined that the Royal Canadian Mounted Police would adopt a new duty sidearm and ammunition combination, based upon the expected need for a higher capacity firearm.

Because the Federal .38 Special SWC HP ammunition fired from the S&W Model 10 in both 5- and 2-inch barrels had performed as required in police involved shootings by the RCMP, it was decided that the adoption of a new firearm ammunition combination would have to be as reliable.

The Royal Canadian Mounted Police armourers did an exhaustive series of tests of submitted commercially manufactured semiauto pistols in calibres 9mm and .40 S&W. At the completion of testing, short list of firearms were submitted to the Firearms Section of Forensic Laboratory Regina for ammunition testing.

Previous research in the field of ammunition testing and terminal wound ballistic studies suggested that the wound profile method for measuring damage caused by penetrating projectiles should be followed with very few exceptions. Perhaps the most notable exception to this profile was the addition of pigs' ribs into the gelatin as one of the test procedures. The reason it was felt this was necessary was based upon RCMP protocol. Members of the RCMP who encounter situations where the use of "deadly force" is warranted are trained to shoot for the "critical centre of mass." In order for the bullet to penetrate to the desired vital organs, it is apparent from previously examined shootings within the Firearms Section, Forensic Laboratory Regina, that the projectile must pass through not only soft tissue but a combination of rib, muscle, and cartilage.

The addition of the pigs' ribs used in testing, although similar in diameter to human ribs measured at autopsies and with connective tissue still present, was not meant to simulate human bone necessarily but to add a medium of different density that the bullet would likely strike in order to achieve desired outcome. The ribs were introduced during this test to determine and accentuate any undesirable attributes that a specific ammunition type may display during impact with a structure of different density, i.e. fragmentation, core jacket, separation, nonexpansion.

Based upon previous research and discrepancies in measuring temporary cavities, it was decided that no form of measurement for the temporary cavity would be included in this research.

Three tests were conducted with each firearm ammunition combination at two distances.

Distances of 3 m and 50 m were chosen based upon RCMP firearms training protocol. Three metres is the distance at which RCMP recruits must instinctively be able to hit critical centre of mass of their intended target, and 50 m is the maximum distance at which trainees are still expected and required to hit the centre of mass. The media used for the three test events were:

Test 1: bare 10-percent ballistic gelatin.

Test 2: 10-percent ballistic gelatin covered with a layer of cotton undershirt material, one layer of shirt material, and a heavy RCMP stormcoat. Conditions which one would expect to encounter outdoors during a typical Canadian winter.

Test 3: 10-percent ballistic gelatin with marrow containing pigs' ribs and connective tissue embedded 1 to 2 inches behind the entrance side of the gelatin block.

The 10-percent gelatin blocks were produced in molds 21"x19x"16" with each mold weighing approximately 130 lbs. to more closely simulate an adult human and to ensure that movement of the block was not a factor during testing.

Five rounds of each ammunition type firearm combination was fired into the gelatin block for each test type. In each case, the orientation of the projectile at rest, penetration, remaining bullet length, expansion, and retained bullet weight were recorded.

Twenty shots were fired into each block, avoiding intersection of fissures.

The gelatin was reheated only a maximum of two times and not heated to above the maximum of 40 degrees C, so a possible change in gelatin properties would not be an introduced factor to the test procedures. Gelatin which contained pigs' ribs was not reused for any further testing.

METHODS AND MATERIALS

Two potential service pistols were submitted for testing by the Royal Canadian Mounted Police Armourer's Shop:

A Smith & Wesson Model 5943, calibre 9mm Parabellum with a 4-inch barrel, Serial No. VAC1271, and a Smith & Wesson Model 4046, calibre .40 Smith & Wesson with a 4-inch barrel, Serial No. VAA3369.

A Beretta 92 Centurion and compact variation of the forementioned Smith &

Wesson pistols were also submitted, but chronographed variations upon test firing were no greater than lot to lot variations, so they were not used in testing.

Two Royal Canadian Mounted Police service sidearms were also used in testing: 1) a Smith & Wesson, Model 10-5 revolver, calibre .38 Special with a 5-inch barrel, Serial No. 3D01411, and 2) a Smith & Wesson, Model 10-5, calibre .38 Special with a 2-inch barrel, Serial No. 2D87607. Also a Force issue, Heckler & Koch (H&K) Model MP5, calibre 9mm Parabellum with a 9-inch barrel, Serial No. C315857, was tested.

All of the test pistols had approximately 10,000 rounds fired through them as received. The service revolvers had approximately 1,500 rounds fired through them prior to testing.

Ammunition was submitted for testing by five commercial manufacturers in calibres 9mm Parabellum and .40 Smith & Wesson and consisted of the following:

9mm PARABELLUM

115-grain Federal Jacketed Hollowpoint
115-grain Winchester Silvertip
124-grain PMC Starfire
147-grain Federal Hydra-Shok
147-grain Winchester Black Talon
147-grain Winchester Full Metal Jacket
147-grain Remington Golden Saber
147-grain Speer Gold Dot

.40 SMITH & WESSON

155-grain Winchester Silvertip
155-grain Federal Hydra-Shok
155-grain Speer Gold Dot
165-grain Federal Hydra-Shok
180-grain Winchester Ranger SXT
180-grain Winchester Full Metal Jacket
180-grain Winchester Subsonic
180-grain PMC Starfire
180-grain Speer Gold Dot

In calibre .38 Special, the RCMP's adopted service round 158-grain Federal semiwadcutter hollowpoint ammunition was used for all tests.

Kind and Knox 250A ordnance gelatin Lot 30 was used as the tissue simulant for all tests. Dr. M. Fackler's recipe for manufacturing 10-percent ordnance gelatin as outlined by S. Post and E. Thompson was followed. The gelatin powder was mixed with cold water (7-10 degrees C) in the ratio of 1,000 g to 9,000 mL.

The mixture was gently agitated and allowed to hydrate for two hours at room temperature.

The ordnance gelatin was heated in an Escan Model 104P60 60-gallon steam kettle and the solution was not allowed to exceed 40 degrees C. Once the particulate matter had dissolved, the mixture was poured into plastic molds, measuring 21"x19"x16", which had previously been sprayed with vegetable oil to act as a release agent. The approximate weight of each completed mold was 130 pounds.

Propionic acid was initially used in solution to prevent bacterial growth; however, because the molds were used within a five-day period, the addition of acid was eliminated and no bacterial growth was recorded as was initially reported by Lucien Haag.

Once the solution was poured into the molds, any foam on the surface was skimmed off and the molds were placed in a walk-in cooler and stored at 5 degrees C.

Initially, the molds were not covered to prevent a build up of condensation, but were subsequently covered after an initial cooldown period.

When racks of pigs' ribs were embedded into the gelatin molds, the gelatin was first allowed to slightly cool. The racks were cut to fit dimensions of the mold and the ribs and connective tissue were slightly dried by patting to remove moisture and grease prior to insertion. The racks were then placed into the molds and suspended in place approximately 1 to 2 inches from the entrance surface with wire.

All gelatin blocks were allowed to set a minimum of 60 hours before any tests were conducted.

Prior to any gelatin blocks being tested, they were calibrated by shooting into them with calibre .177 copper-coated BBs from a

Crossman Model 766 Pneumatic rifle, Serial No. 380004954, and measuring both the velocity and penetration of the BBs. Five pumps of the air rifle generated a velocity approximately the desired 590 feet per second, at an instrumental distance of 10 feet. All blocks were calibrated to achieve 8.5 plus or minus 1.5 cm of penetration at a velocity of 590 feet per second. BBs were fired initially into four corners of the blocks, two prior to testing and two after; however after successive tests with very minute differences, only two corners were calibrated prior to testing.

Temperatures of the gelatin blocks were recorded prior to test shots and then again after to ensure no variation existed during test procedures. Once it was determined that only very slight (less than 1 degree C) variation existed, temperatures were taken only prior to testing, measuring both in the centre of the block and at one corner.

All tested ammunition was fired from the test firearms and chronographed through a Model 4040 Chronograph manufactured by the Electronic Counters Division of MV Ordnance Industries at an instrumental distance of 20 feet.

All tests were conducted in a 125-meter single-lane indoor range at a temperature of between 60-68 degrees F. Shooting was from a sandbag rest for all test events.

Three tests were conducted at two distances for each firearm ammunition combination. With each test event there was no overlap of fissures allowed within the gelatin block, or that specific result was retested.

Test Event I was firing into bare gelatin at a distance of 3 m. Five rounds of each firearm ammunition combination was fired for this test and a total of 20 rounds was fired into each block.

Test Event II was a block of gelatin covered with a layer of 65/35 polyester/cotton mix T-shirt material whose weight was 145 grams/meter^2. This in turn was covered with a shirt produced with a 50/50 cotton/polyester mix and a weight of 200 grams/meter^2. An RCMP issue storm coat covered the other two materials. The storm coat was comprised of three layers: a nylon cotton mix shell with a weight of 170 grams/meter^2, a polyester insulation with a weight of 300 grams/meter^2, and a nylon lining with a weight of 84 grams/meter^2. Again, five rounds of each firearm ammunition combination was fired at the covered block, ensuring no random impact with buttons, zippers, etc.

The third test was comprised of a gelatin block with pigs' ribs and connective tissue embedded 1 to 2 inches from the entrance surface. Five rounds of each firearm ammunition combination was recorded in this test as in the previous test.

At the completion of all firearm ammunition combinations for the three test events, distances were then varied to 50 meters, or 25 meters for the Smith & Wesson Model 10-5 with a 2-inch barrel following RCMP training protocol.

Upon completion of test events into each block (20 rounds), gelatin was removed in layers from the top surface using a fixed blade knife so the bullet paths could be more easily observed. Bullet penetration depths were measured from the exterior of the entrance surface to the furthest point of the bullet or, in some situations, to where the bullet path ended, the bullet having rebounded slightly within the gelatin.

Permanent cavity diameter was measured using a Mitutoyo Digimatic Caliper. This measurement, although recorded, was not presented for this particular research.

The bullet's orientation at rest was recorded as well as fragmentation or core jacket separation.

Bullet penetration through the pigs' ribs was measured using a rod of known length to project into the bullet path. To determine what the bullet came into contact with when shooting through ribs, a finger was inserted into the block of gelatin to differentiate between muscle or bone fragmentation. Measurements of the rib diameter was recorded for each test containing the racks of pigs' ribs.

When the bullets were removed from the gelatin, maximum and minimum expansions were recorded along with the remaining bullet length. Any protruding jacket fragments were included in these measurements. Black Talon bullets were measured from the tip of each protruding point for maximum expansion values.

Remaining length measurements of Hydra-Shok bullets were taken from the tip of the post to the base of the bullet or any portion of the jacket protruding beyond the base.

All recovered bullets were weighed after removing as much foreign material as possible. Those bullets which still weighed more than the reported weight were recorded as 100 percent weight retention. When bullets fragmented, the largest remaining fragment was measured and weighed.

RESULTS AND DISCUSSION

Although terminal performance of the RCMP issue calibre .38 Special 158-grain SWCHP has been satisfactory, there are commercially manufactured ammunitions in calibres 9mm Parabellum and .40 S&W which exceed these performances in test medium. The heavier calibre 9mm Parabellum 147-grain hollowpoint ammunitions manufactured by Winchester in their Black Talon round, Remington Golden Saber, and Federal Hydra-Shok ammunition compared favourably to the calibre .38 Special round in most test events when comparing penetration depth, degree of expansion, weight retention, and percent retained weight of the fired bullet. Slight differences in bullet expansion may not be significant due to the experimental limitations and sample size. The significance of differences in percent weight retention must be analyzed with respect to remaining bullet weight and degree of secondary projectiles as a result of bullet fragmentation. The full-metal-jacketed Winchester 147-grain ammunition failed to expand after excessive penetration.

CCI 147-grain Gold Dot ammunition, although providing adequate penetration, had inadequate expansion when compared to the calibre .38 Special RCMP adopted round.

The lighter 115-grain and 124-grain bullets in calibre 9mm Parabellum were all unacceptable performers, failing to penetrate 10-percent ordnance gelatin to the desired 12-inch depth, and for both the 115-grain bullets in particular, there was excessive fragmentation. In addition, the 124-grain PMC Starfire bullet, when discharged from the H&K Model MP5 submachine gun, failed to cycle the action due to the brass flowing into the fluted chamber, preventing the cartridge case from being extracted or ejected from the weapon.

The majority of calibre .40 Smith & Wesson ammunition types compared favourably to the current RCMP issue calibre .38 Special round in all test events at both distances.

One exception to this acceptable performance was the Winchester 180-grain full-metal-jacketed truncated cone bullet, which consistently had excessive penetration and inadequate expansion in all test events.

The Winchester Black Talon, or Ranger SXT bullet as it is now marketed, not only met all the terminal ballistic requirements in both calibres 9mm Parabellum and .40 Smith & Wesson, but it was the only bullet recovered which had extremely sharp deformed surfaces which may assist in the cutting of tissue along the wound track.

During the course of testing, many observations of ammunition/firearm performance were made and, although they do not pertain directly to the data recorded for this research, they may be significant to law enforcement agencies in the selection of a suitable duty sidearm ammunition combination.

The 158-grain SWCHP bullet when fired from the S&W calibre .38 Special with a 2-inch barrel, overpenetrates 10-percent ordnance gelatin and gelatin covered with layers of clothing; however, when ribs were embedded into the gelatin medium, both adequate penetration and expansion result. Although accuracy was not one of the test events in measuring ammunitions' terminal performance, it is obvious that a bullet must strike an intended target to achieve the desired result. For those test events at 50 m, shooting the gelatin blocks from a sandbag rest using calibre 9mm Parabellum, 124-grain PMC Starfire ammunition was a challenge and a 200 round supply of ammunition was depleted prior to finishing the test events.

The H&K MP5 submachine gun was introduced as a test firearm because it is an RCMP issue firearm, and the adoption of any calibre 9mm Parabellum round would be used in this weapon as well as any handgun which may be chosen. From the tabular results, it is apparent that any performance problems associated with ammunition type were accentuated when fired from this submachine gun.

CONCLUSION

From the limited ammunition types tested, there are both calibre 9mm Parabellum and .40 Smith & Wesson ammunition which are comparable or exceed the terminal performance of the RCMP issue calibre .38 Special 158-grain SWCHP ammunition. The significance of the performance difference is an issue which may only be determined by those agencies involved in the selection of a suitable firearm ammunition combination for law enforcement use. This selection process must be based upon individual force protocol and may rely upon factors outside the listed events such as shooting through intermediary targets.

TABLE 7-1
BARE GELATIN

CAL.	LOAD	PEN.	EXP.	RET. WT.	% RET.
.38 Special	158-gr. SWC-HP	12.0250	0.6290	156.0380	98.76
9mm	115-gr. Win ST	9.2500	0.6597	113.4820	98.68
9mm	115-gr. Fed JHP	9.9250	0.6170	107.5240	93.50
9mm	124-gr. PMC SF	11.0000	0.6355	123.8520	99.47
9mm	147-gr. Fed HS	12.2250	0.6292	145.2380	98.80
9mm	147-gr. Rem GS	13.8500	0.6152	146.9980	99.84
9mm	147-gr. Win BT	13.7250	0.6258	144.8400	98.53
9mm	147-gr. CCI GD	15.5000	0.5171	146.2200	99.44
9mm	147-gr. Win FMJ	29.1000	0.3522	146.6400	99.76
.40 S&W	155-gr. Fed HS	12.7750	0.6145	156.2980	99.48
.40 S&W	155-gr. Win ST	11.7750	0.6824	156.7220	99.75
.40 S&W	155-gr. CCI GD	13.1750	0.7189	155.6600	100.00
.40 S&W	165-gr. Fed HS	13.4750	0.6261	159.9400	96.93
.40 S&W	180-gr. Win Ranger SXT	13.2500	0.7079	179.1600	99.42
.40 S&W	180-gr. Win Subsonic	14.6250	0.6565	177.9880	98.62
.40 S&W	180-gr. Win FMJ	28.5750	0.3959	180.5000	100.00
.40 S&W	180-gr. PMC SF	11.9250	0.7101	180.9500	99.94
.40 S&W	180-gr. CCI GD	13.4500	0.6914	182.6540	100.00

TABLE 7-2
CLOTH AND GELATIN

CAL.	LOAD	PEN.	EXP.	RET. WT.	% RET.
.38 Special	158-gr. SWC-HP	12.9000	0.5638	156.3440	98.95
9mm	115-gr. Win ST	11.6000	0.5717	115.2720	99.80
9mm	115-gr. Fed JHP	11.2000	0.5901	114.8420	99.74
9mm	124-gr. PMC SF	13.2000	0.5646	124.3460	99.91
9mm	147-gr. Fed HS	13.5750	0.5804	147.1840	99.92
9mm	147-gr. Rem GS	15.1000	0.6109	146.0140	99.33
9mm	147-gr. Win BT	15.3250	0.6160	147.1840	99.57
9mm	147-gr. CCI GD	16.7750	0.4795	147.4600	99.97
9mm	147-gr. Win FMJ	27.8250	0.3512	146.4600	99.63
.40 S&W	155-gr. Fed HS	14.7000	0.6031	156.6240	100.00
.40 S&W	155-gr. Win ST	13.7750	0.6427	155.7660	99.99
.40 S&W	155-gr. CCI GD	13.0250	0.6645	155.2000	99.99
.40 S&W	165-gr. Fed HS	14.4750	0.6000	164.3000	99.58
.40 S&W	180-gr. Win Ranger SXT	14.2500	0.7499	180.0120	99.87
.40 S&W	180-gr. Win Subsonic	14.4250	0.6296	181.1980	100.00
.40 S&W	180-gr. Win FMJ	28.3250	0.3975	180.4000	99.96
.40 S&W	180-gr. PMC SF	13.3250	0.6510	180.5180	100.00
.40 S&W	180-gr. CCI GD	13.5500	0.6208	180.0260	99.92

TABLE 7-3
GELATIN AND RIB

CAL.	LOAD	PEN.	EXP.	RET. WT.	% RET.
.38 Special	158-gr. SWC-HP	14.6500	0.6111	156.5600	99.09
9mm	115-gr. Win ST	9.5750	0.6553	111.0800	96.52
9mm	115-gr. Fed JHP	12.7250	0.5073	82.4000	71.65
9mm	124-gr. PMC SF	11.9000	0.6252	123.4400	99.55
9mm	147-gr. Fed HS	13.9750	0.6443	147.3800	99.76
9mm	147-gr. Rem GS	15.2250	0.6064	146.0600	99.20
9mm	147-gr. Win BT	14.1500	0.6251	146.4000	99.20
9mm	147-gr. CCI GD	15.8250	0.4906	146.7800	99.81
9mm	147-gr. Win FMJ	23.0750	0.3536	146.4800	99.65
.40 S&W	155-gr. Fed HS	12.9250	0.6592	147.6800	95.21
.40 S&W	155-gr. Win ST	11.0250	0.7139	155.2000	99.85
.40 S&W	155-gr. CCI GD	12.7750	0.6994	155.6400	100.00
.40 S&W	165-gr. Fed HS	13.3000	0.6151	162.4600	98.46
.40 S&W	180-gr. Win Ranger SXT	12.0750	0.7089	179.1600	99.53
.40 S&W	180-gr. Win Subsonic	13.7000	0.6345	165.9800	92.21
.40 S&W	180-gr. Win FMJ	29.4500	0.3968	180.8800	100.00
.40 S&W	180-gr. PMC SF	11.2000	0.7192	177.8400	98.43
.40 S&W	180-gr. CCI GD	13.3500	0.6555	179.9200	99.92

The Royal Canadian Mounted Police established its .38 Special +P 158-grain SWC-HP at 1,000 fps as a benchmark. It disqualified 9mm and .40 S&W hollowpoints that penetrated under 12 inches or over 18 inches or those with smaller recovered diameters than this .38 Special +P duty load.

8

Secret Service Ammo Tests

In the late 1980s, the FBI gained national attention with its ammunition tests conducted in the wake of the tragic 1986 shootout in Miami in which two FBI agents were killed and five wounded. Since then, the Bureau has maintained a high profile in ammo development and testing. Copies of its test results are mailed upon request to any police agency, and periodic updates on ammo appear in *The FBI Bulletin*, which is mailed free of charge to every police department in the country.

The FBI methodology had been so heavily self-promoted that it totally overshadowed other views on stopping power. To this day, many cops and civilians alike are surprised to find out that most other federal police agencies *do not* agree with the Bureau's opinion on wound ballistics.

These other agencies, including the U.S. Marshal's Service and INS/Border Patrol, perform their own testing but on a much more limited basis and with a much lower profile. Frankly, these agencies do not need to perform exhaustive gelatin testing. They already have a

good idea of what does and does not work simply because they shoot a lot of people. Again, large enough numbers of shooting results are always, and will always be, vastly superior to even the most complex and rigorous gelatin testing.

The FBI is famous for its eight-media gelatin test methodology and for the resulting development and adoption of the 9mm 147-grain subsonic hollowpoint (see Chapter 16). However, it has recently de-emphasized its complex, assumption-based gelatin tests. It has also stopped publishing the "wound efficiency" number for each load, which we have proven is misleading at best and statistically invalid at worst (see *Handgun Stopping Power*, Chapter 6). The FBI has also, but with very low profile, stated that its barrier-oriented gelatin tests are applicable to Bureau shooting scenarios and are not necessarily to those of uniformed state and local police officers and private civilians.

To be sure, there is as much disagreement among federal agencies on the best loads for

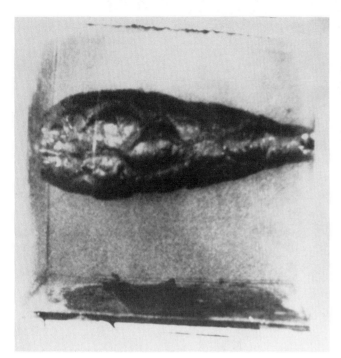

ABOVE: The Winchester 9mm 115-grain +P+ JHP used by the Illinois State Police was the outright winner of the 1987 Secret Service ammo effectiveness study.

LEFT: The Secret Service used high-speed photography to record energy transfer into blocks of 20-percent gelatin. According to the Secret Service, the greater the energy transfer, the more rapid the incapacitation. (Photo credit: Winchester)

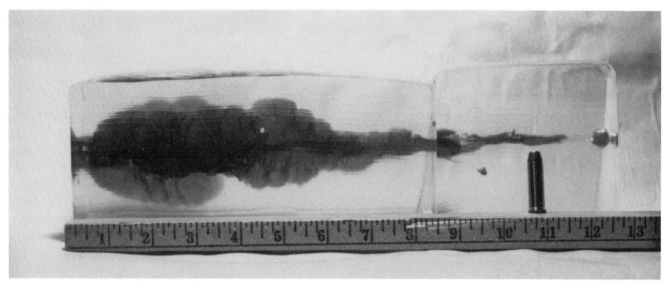

The .38 Special +P+ 110-grain JHP "Treasury Load" was selected by the Secret Service after its 1972 ammo evaluation.

police work as there is in the popular gun press. The FBI favors 147-grain subsonic hollowpoints in 9mm. Many other federal agencies favor the 115- and 124-grain +P+ hollowpoints in 9mm. In .40 S&W, the Bureau methodology leads it to the 180-grain subsonic hollowpoint or the 165-grain medium-velocity hollowpoint. Other federal agencies were, in fact, the force behind development of the 155-grain hollowpoint.

In this spirit, we now shed some light on the FBI's rival in federal circles, the U.S. Secret Service. Just as its name states, the Secret Service is "secret" about things. It does not intend to be a part of a Bureau-style, high-profile ammo debate to influence state and local agencies. However, that does not mean that it doesn't exist, that it has done no testing, or that it agrees with the more publicized results from other federal agencies.

To respect its long-standing quest for secrecy, we will only discuss the Secret Service's 1972 .38 Special testing and its 1987 first look at 9mm ammo effectiveness. Ammo investigations since then will be kept confidential. However, the point remains: at the highest levels of the most prestigious federal police agencies, a profound disagreement about ammunition exists.

In its purest, most rhetoric-free form, the disagreement is based on the shooting scenario each agency is preparing to face. The FBI is committed to giving its agents ammo that will never, ever allow another "Miami" to occur. The fact that nearly all police tacticians consider Miami to be a once-a-century encounter is beside the point.

Other federal agencies are committed to giving their agents ammo that will work the best in all the other gunfight scenarios—the kind of gunfights where other people are around, so excessive penetration must be avoided. They select the kind of ammo that has worked well in the past under a wide variety of shooting scenarios, not just in one specific event.

As a side note, the Secret Service used, and continues to use, a 20-percent gelatin ratio fired at room temperature instead of a 10-percent gelatin ratio fired at refrigerator temperature. As the personal communication at the end of this chapter explains, this gelatin mixture came from the U.S. Army. To this day, the U.S. Army and Navy still use this denser 20-percent ratio. Like the army, the Secret Service data base of results based on 20-percent is simply too big to now adopt the 10-percent ratio currently used by ammo manufacturers and most police agencies.

The following are direct excerpts from the 1972 Secret Service report entitled "Ammunition Effectiveness Study."

AMMUNITION EFFECTIVENESS STUDY

The experimental procedures and the results of a study to evaluate the relative terminal effectiveness of selected .38 Special, 9mm, and .357 Magnum handgun ammunition are reported below. This study was conducted at the Biophysics Division, Biomedical Laboratory, Edgewood Arsenal, Maryland, at the request of Frankford Arsenal, Philadelphia, Pennsylvania.

The handguns in use were a Smith & Wesson Model 15 (.38 Special) with a 4-inch barrel, a Smith & Wesson Model 19 (.357 Magnum) with a 2.5-inch barrel, and a Smith & Wesson Model 39 (9mm) with a 4-inch barrel.

Striking velocities refer to the bullet velocity just prior to impact with the gelatin block and were measured over a 1 meter baseline fitted with silver grid screens. This break circuit baseline was coupled to 1.0 Mc electronic counter chronographs. Set-up distances were maintained constant throughout the exercise so that the striking velocities listed were always recorded (30.2 ft.) from the muzzle of each weapon.

Remaining velocities refer to the bullet velocity just after perforation of the 15-inch gelatin block and were determined from high-speed movie films. These movies, taken at approximately 27,000 frames per second, also recorded the passage of bullet through the block.

Striking energies, the kinetic energy of the bullet just prior to impact with the gelatin block, were determined from the above mentioned movie film. They were computed using the equation $E = .5MVV$, where E is the kinetic energy, M is the listed bullet weight, and V is the listed striking velocity. This velocity was recorded 9.2 yards from the muzzle and 0.8 yards prior to impact with the gelatin block. All energies were initially determined in joules to three decimal places. Conversion of all energy values to the closest ft-lb. was accomplished using the relationship of 1 joule=0.73756 ft-lb.

The energy deposit by the bullets between 1 and 5.9 inches of the gelatin block was determined from analysis of the high-speed film.

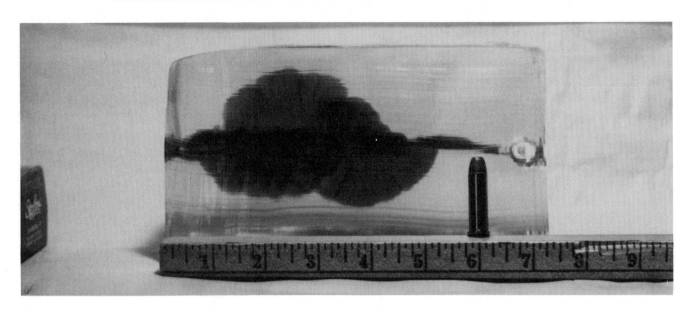

The Remington .38 Special +P 95-grain S-JHP had the highest efficiency in the first 5.9 inches of 20-percent gelatin of any caliber or bullet tested by the Secret Service in 1972.

The Winchester 9mm 115-grain Silvertip did well in Secret Service tests. At 83 percent one-shot stops, this is still a better police duty load than any 9mm subsonic hollowpoint.

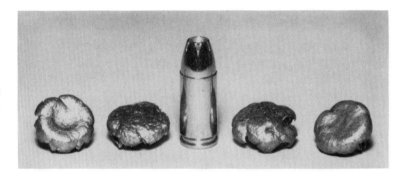

The 1- to 5.9-inch penetration is significant since generally against human targets the more vital organs in the path of penetration should be reached within that distance span.

Remaining energies, the kinetic energy of the bullet just after perforation of the 15-inch gelatin block, were also determined from the movie film. As with the striking energies, the remaining energies were computed using the equation $E=.5MVV$, with V being the remaining velocity as determined from the film.

The bullet efficiency value listed is the ratio of the energy deposited in 5.9 inches of gelatin to the striking energy expressed as a percentage.

All bullet weights listed are a mean value for a sample of three selected randomly from each type of ammunition.

Generally, gelatin penetration distances listed are distances at which the bullet came to rest in the gelatin. Those entries containing the plus (+) symbol are cases where no "backup" block was present or where the bullet exited from the side of the backup block and total penetration values could not be obtained. In other words, those penetration entries with the (+) symbol had remaining velocity after perforating the first 15-inches of gelatin block and therefore had the potential for additional gelatin penetration. The gelatin blocks used were 20 percent by weight Pharmagel "A" and 80 percent by weight water.

The table summarizes the mean energy deposit in 5.9 inches of 20-percent gelatin and serves as an indicator of the relative wounding

The Secret Service ammo tests ranked the 9mm 115-grain JHP at both standard and +P+ velocities (Black Hills shown here) over the 140-grain JHP Type B.

effectiveness of the bullets tested. *Since wounding is directly related to energy deposit in the target, the greater the energy deposit, the greater the anticipated tissue damage and the more rapid the incapacitation of a chosen target.* [Emphasis added.]

The table includes remaining velocity after a nominal 15 inches of soft target penetration and serves as an indicator of the penetrating potential of the bullets tested. The 15-inch block length has no specific significance in itself but has been maintained as a standard at this laboratory over a period of years to maintain compatibility of results obtained. For purposes of this study, however, a bullet which perforates the gelatin block and has remaining velocity, and thus remaining energy, potentially poses a threat to an unintentional secondary target.

A rough quantitative evaluation of this secondary target hazard from the bullets tested may be obtained through consideration of the 58 ft-lb. criterion. This criterion states that any projectile striking the body with an energy of 58 ft-lbs. or more would produce a serious wound, and anything striking with less energy would be relatively harmless.

It should be pointed out that bullets which did not perforate the 15-inch block still may pose a potential threat to an unintentional secondary target. However, it can be assumed that as the depth of bullet penetration in gelatin decreases, the probability of perforating and hitting an unintentional secondary target will also decrease.

The table also summarizes bullet efficiency. While somewhat academic in nature, this table does show that the hollowpoint round is the most efficient of the types tested. Additionally, it may be seen that the fully metal jacketed round is generally the least efficient and the jacketed softpoint round has an efficiency somewhere between these two extremes.

The table also summarizes the bullet efficiency. Although academic to a wound ballistician, it is important to a weapons designer. From the bullet's efficiency, the weapon's designer may obtain an idea of the effects that striking velocity, bullet deformation, jacket and core material, bullet mass, and other design parameters may have on resultant energy deposition.

One final generalized point of interest regarding the prime objectives of a weapon-ammunition system bears mentioning in this brief report. Examination of the energy data, whether it is presented as energy deposit in 5.9 inches of gelatin, the efficiency of the round, or the "stopping power" rating of the bullets and regardless of the weapon from which it was fired, consistently showed the hollowpoint round to be the most effective. While achieving this effectiveness against the intended target, the hollowpoint bullet permits reduced hazard potential to an unintentional secondary target as evidenced by the penetration or remaining velocity data.

It can be seen that the jacketed hollowpoint bullets, generally, are more efficient, have shorter gelatin penetrations, and have a higher kinetic energy deposition within the gelatin targets.

As listed in the results, the Winchester-Western .38 Special 158-grain semiwadcutter bullet has a very decreased energy deposition within the 5.9 inches of the gelatin target as compared to that of the "standard," the Super Vel JHP 110-grain bullet. The result of this is a decrease in the relative "stopping power" of the semiwadcutter.

In the gelatin target, the semiwadcutter bullet did not deform, as did the other bullets. The total penetration distance of the semiwadcutter bullet was longer. This bullet has a great penetrating capability in tissue. This may result in an increased potential hazard to unintentional secondary targets as compared to the penetrating capability of the other .38 Special JHP bullets.

(End of Report)

TABLE 8-1
9mm AMMUNITION EFFECTIVENESS STUDY
JAMES J. ROWLEY TRAINING CENTER
UNITED STATES SECRET SERVICE, MARCH 1987

MAKE	WT. GR.	TYPE	MUZZLE VEL.	CHAMBER PRESSURE	STRIKING ENERGY	ENERGY DEPOSITED	% EFFIC-IENCY
Win-Olin	115	JHP Q4174 +P+	1,302	38,090	430.1	353.5	.8229
Rem. Arms	115	JHP R9MM1	1,164	29,960	364.4	288.3	.7909
Win-Olin	115	Silvertip	1,190	31,070	363.5	285.0	.7838
Glaser SS	80	Blue, flat-point	1,554	39,230	452.1	354.1	.7829
Fed. Cart.	115	JHP 9BP	1,121	28,810	337.7	256.0	.7577
Dynamit Nobel	87	Action Safety	1,236	32,500	364.1	270.4	.7428
Soc. Francaise DeM.	47	THV (brass)	1,913	29,360	359.2	239.0	.6657
Win-Olin	140	JHP Q4192 Type B	928	24,440	278.6	183.3	.6575
Fed. Cart.	95	JSP 9CP	1,209	26,730	324.1	205.8	.6351
Reference Lot	115	FMJ hardball	1,201	36,450	406.8	117.3	.2890

*This is the energy deposited in the first 5.9 inches in 20-percent gelatin.

TABLE 8-2
1972 SECRET SERVICE AMMO EVALUATION

CAL.	LOAD GRAIN	STRIKE VEL. FPS	STRIKE ENERGY FT-LBS.	ENERGY* DE-POSIT	EFFIC-ICENCY	REMAIN VEL.** FPS	REMAIN ENERGY FT-LBS.**	TOTAL PEN. INCH	EXIT 15" 20% GEL-ATIN
.357 Mag	Rem 158 JSP	1,285	574	237	41.2	524	96	15+	8 of 8
.357 Mag	Super Vel 110 JSP	1,366	460	271	58.9	151	6	15+	7 of 8
.357 Mag	Super Vel 110 JHP	1,369	460	344	74.9	none	none	8.5	none
.38 Spl	Win 158 RNL	754	200	62	31.2	14	none	13.4	1 of 6
.38 Spl	Rem 130 FMJ	796	184	63	34.4	none	none	13.4	none
.38 Spl +P	Super Vel 110 JSP	1,200	353	167	47.3	317	25	15+	6 of 6
.38 Spl +P	Super Vel 110 JHP	1,200	353	271	76.8	none	none	8.4	none
.38 Spl +P	Speer 140 JHP	876	239	142	59.8	none	none	12.8	none
.38 Spl +P	Speer 125 JHP	983	268	190	70.7	none	none	9.8	none
.38 Spl +P	Speer 110 JHP	1,036	262	208	79.4	none	none	7.7	none
.38 Spl +P	Win 110 JHP	981	234	189	80.7	none	none	5.4	none
.38 Spl +P	Norma 110 JHP	1,076	283	217	76.3	none	none	9.2	none
.38 Spl +P	Rem 95 S-JHP	1,030	223	191	85.2	none	none	5.7	none
.38 Spl	Win 158 SWC	726	185	68	36.6	n/a	n/a	16.0	2 of 4
.38 Spl+P+	Win 110 JHP	1,045	267	219	82.0	n/a	n/a	5.7	none
9mm	Win 115 FMJ	1,223	381	104	27.2	378	36	18.5	6 of 6
9mm	Frankfort 125 JSP	1,085	333	127	38.2	494	68	23.0	6 of 6
9mm	Rem 115 FMJ	1,189	360	117	32.4	329	27	18.1+	6 of 6
9mm	Super Vel 90 JHP	1,414	397	319	80.4	none	none	6.3	none

*Energy deposit in 5.9 inches of 20-percent ordnance gelatin.
**Velocity and energy remaining after 5.9 inches of gelatin.

9

10mm and 10mm Medium Velocity Ammo

The 10mm cartridge was covered briefly in Chapter 18 of the book *Handgun Stopping Power*. Since then, poor shooter acceptance has demoted it to being considered as just another stepping-stone on the way to the .40 S&W. Early on, the FBI, Virginia State Police, and Kentucky State Police adopted the 10mm for police duty. These were the exceptions.

The 10mm ultimately proved itself to be either too powerful, with too much recoil and too much penetration in its full-power loadings, or too much like the .45 Auto 185-grain JHP in its medium-velocity 180-grain JHP loadings. The Virginia State Police has since adopted the 9mm. This leaves the Kentucky State Police as the only major agency using the full-power version of the 10mm and the FBI as the only major agency using the medium-velocity load, which was originally developed by them.

The 10mm cartridge has certainly had its share of ups and downs in its short life. It was the talk of all shooters when it was introduced in the Dornaus & Dixon Bren Ten. Although praised by big-bore and high-velocity types

alike, Bren Ten magazine availability and slide cracking problems eventually cast a shadow on both gun and ammo. The powerful 10mm ammo made by FFV Norma AB was too hot and the resulting recoil too high. With no guns to shoot it, the 10mm cartridge faded into near obscurity.

Colt solved the handgun availability problem in 1987 with the release of its single-action Delta Elite. The Government Model-based auto pistol was tough enough for the original 10mm Norma ammo. With plenty of guns and an increasing variety of ammo, the 10mm cartridge grew in popularity.

THE 10mm TODAY

The 10mm is available today in a number of full-power loads. This includes the light 135-grain JHPs, the medium 150- to 155-grain JHPs, the heavy 170- to 180-grain JHPs, and exotic loads like the MagSafe and Glaser. Unlike the original Norma hollowpoints weighing 165 and 170 grains, the American-made hollowpoints all expand to large recovered diameters or in some cases expand and then fragment. A hollowpoint that fragments in gelatin will at least expand in different kinds of soft tissue.

A couple of 10mm and 10mm Medium Velocity loads stand out from the rest. Of the heavyweight 170- to 180-grain full-power 10mm hollowpoints, the Winchester 175-grain Silvertip appears to be the best load. The downside of the Silvertip is that it also produces the most recoil of any load in the 10mm caliber. This is quite odd since the Silvertip in the other heavy-recoiling calibers like .41 Magnum and .44 Magnum are all moderately loaded. Regardless, the Silvertip in 10mm has a velocity of 1,266 fps. The JHP bullet uses nickel-plated copper jackets with the excellent "crease-fold" jacket serration design.

The Silvertip penetrates between 12.5 and 13.5 inches of 10-percent gelatin. Most importantly, it expands to and retains a full .81 caliber mushroom. Silvertip bullets as a group do an excellent job of keeping their full expanded diameter. As a result, the 10mm Silvertip produces the largest permanent crush cavity of any load in the caliber. This means the bullet actually comes in contact with more tissue over the entire penetration distance. The Silvertip also produces the largest temporary stretch cavity of any heavy 10mm hollowpoint.

Of the medium-weight 150- to 155-grain hollowpoints, the load to beat is the Federal 155-grain JHP (which came in second in the caliber during the Strasbourg Tests). This 1,311 fps JHP violently expands on impact and then fragments. The result is a moderate crush cavity and an extreme stretch cavity. The round also expands reliably after all kinds of secondary barriers, especially wallboard and heavy clothes. This 592 ft-lb. bullet transfers all of its energy in the first 12 to 12.5 inches of penetration to produce ideal wounding.

Other medium-weight 10mm loads that rival the Federal 155-grain JHP are the Cor-Bon 150-grain Sierra JHP and Remington 155-grain JHP. In fact, nearly all the 10mm full-power 150- to 155-grain loads work extremely well, almost regardless of bullet design. Like the .357 Magnum 125-grain JHP, the 10mm 150- to 155-grain JHP has enough velocity to overwhelm minor JHP design differences.

All of the full-power 150- to 155-grain 10mm JHPs from major and regional loaders penetrate between 12 and 14.5 inches, expand violently, and fragment back to recovered diameters of .61 to .67 inch. The overall wound ballistics are too close to call for all of these loads. At velocities between 1,300 and 1,350 fps, these lightweight JHPs produce less recoil than the heavy hollowpoints and

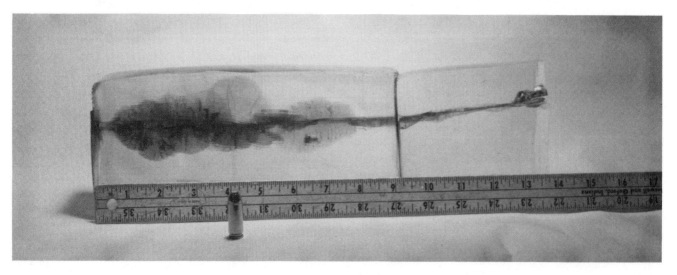

The Federal 10mm Medium Velocity 180-grain Hydra-Shok penetrates 13.8 inches of gelatin. This load equals the .45 Auto 185-grain JHP.

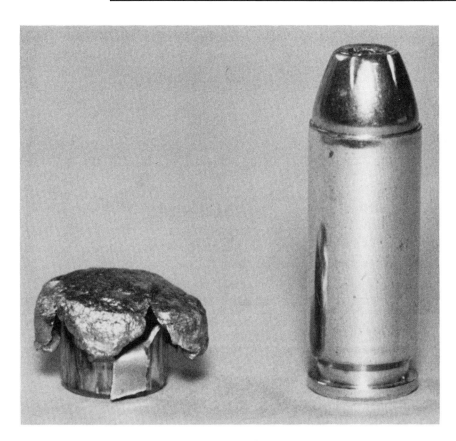

ABOVE: The Federal 10mm Medium Velocity 180-grain Hydra-Shok is estimated to be 87 percent effective. This bullet expanded to .67 caliber.

LEFT: The Winchester 10mm Medium Velocity 180-grain Subsonic JHP has the best street record of these mid-range loads at 82 percent.

also produce .41 Magnum-like temporary stretch cavities.

Even more impressive is what the 150-grain Sierra JHP does in that 12 inches of penetration. The round expands and fragments to become one of the very few 10mm bullets to produce secondary missiles.

Most 10mm JHP bullets expand, and most shed the lead around the hollowpoint opening. These are recovered as bits and pieces of lead lying in the main bullet path in the wake of the bullet. These pieces produce no secondary wounding independent from the main bullet at all. In fact, they reduce wounding because when they shear off, the bullet diameter is reduced.

Secondary missiles are pieces of bullets or bone that leave the main bullet path to engage tissue missed by the bullet core. This greatly increases the potential for stopping power. The Sierra 150-grain JHP, loaded especially by Cor-Bon but also by many companies, expands and spins off six to seven deadly secondary missiles, and the slug still has a recovered

diameter of .68 inch. The results are shredded blocks of gelatin and .41 Magnum-like stretch cavities measuring a whopping 4 inches in diameter. The Cor-Bon version of the 150-grain Sierra JHP has the best street record in this caliber of the reported loads.

The most exciting category of full-power 10mm ammo is the lightweight 135-grain Nosler and Sierra bullets loaded by Cor-Bon and Triton Cartridge. With velocities around 1,400 fps and muzzle energies at 587 ft-lbs., these loads are quickly proving to be the most effective in the caliber. In fact, they may have peaked in terms of wound ballistics against a human target. With this much energy, and the energy all transferred by 11.9 inches of penetration, it may be the maximum amount of wounding possible from a handgun. Other handgun calibers like the .44 Magnum have more muzzle energy, but they are not available in bullet weights light enough to transfer all of the energy inside a human torso.

But it is not energy at the muzzle that matters; it is energy transferred in the first 11 to 12 inches. In this regard, the 10mm full-power 135-grain JHPs appear to be the best possible auto pistol load against a human target. They are estimated at 95 percent (plus) effective, just like the revolver-fired .357 Magnum 125-grain JHP. Improvements in one-shot stops beyond a 90 percent rating are unlikely and beyond a 95 percent rating are almost impossible given the variables of shooting scenarios.

Of all the 10mm ammo, the MagSafe 96-grain Defender distinguishes itself in a number of critical areas. The first is muzzle velocity. MagSafe claims its ammo has a 5-inch velocity of 1,780 fps. Our Custom Chronograph with accurate printed screens clocked it at a screaming 1,854 fps. When fired from the 6.5-inch Grizzly, the MagSafe recorded a near double-sonic velocity of 1,992 fps. The Strasbourg researchers achieved 1,729 fps.

Even at these astonishing handgun velocities, the felt recoil due to the light bullet weight was quite low. The .45 Auto with 230-grain hardball kicks a lot more than this 10mm MagSafe load. The shot-to-shot response time with the MagSafe is excellent.

Most important, however, is the phenomenal wound ballistics produced by this improvement over the Glaser 105-grain Blue Safety Slug at 1,550 fps. The MagSafe Defender won the Strasbourg Tests outright.

Like the Glaser, the MagSafe bullet is made up of a copper jacket filled with birdshot. In the case of the MagSafe 10mm, it is 13 pieces of hardened and nickel-plated number 2 birdshot. (That is number 2, not number 12.) The shot is held in place in a bed of epoxy resin. The Glaser is a copper jacket filled with number 12 birdshot that has been compressed and fused into a solid core. Both loads fragment on impact to saturate surrounding tissue with birdshot, making it look like a contact shotgun wound.

The MagSafe produces between 9 and 16 inches of pellet penetration, which is considerably deeper than other prefragmented designs. The combination of incredible impact velocity and saturating fragmentation produce the largest temporary stretch cavity in the cal-iber. With 13 separate secondary missiles, all of which penetrate deeply, the MagSafe is the king of the hill in 10mm wound ballistics.

10mm vs. .45 ACP

The full-power 10mm was developed before the +P version of the .45 Auto. Many wonder how these two big-bore cartridges compare since both boast high energies and both are fired from large-frame auto pistols. Here is how the typical full-power 10mm 180-grain JHP compares to the typical +P pressure .45 Auto 185-grain JHP.

Both the .45 Auto +P and full-power 10mm produce an equally stiff recoil. This is especially noticeable in pistols with shorter barrel lengths. Both cartridges are equally reliable in weapon functioning. The .45 is significantly more accurate than the 10mm. Both calibers overpenetrate in hardball form. Both produce adequate and controlled penetration in hollowpoint loadings. The 10mm 180-grain JHP produces the larger permanent crush cavity. The .45 Auto +P 185-grain JHP produces the larger stretch cavity. In the 180- to 185-grain bullet weight, the .45 Auto +P and the full-power 10mm are, for all practical purposes, equal. The medium-velocity 180-grain 10mm came down to rival the standard-pressure .45 Auto hollow-points. The +P version of the 185-grain .45 Auto has come up to rival the full-power 10mm hollowpoints.

In spite of the superior wound ballistics of the 10mm over the 9mm and .45 Auto, stout recoil kept the cartridge from becoming a total success. For literally decades, the great gun writers of the past like Bill Jordan, Skeeter Skelton, and Elmer Keith dreamed of the ideal auto pistol cartridge. This would be a .40 to .41 caliber bullet, weighing 180 to 200 grains, and driven between 950 and 1,050 fps. All previous attempts, including the .40 Guns & Ammo, .41 Action Express, and full-power 10mm, fell short of that lofty title for one reason or another.

The police-only Winchester 10mm Medium Velocity 200-grain Ranger SXT (Black Talon) expands to .68 caliber and carries an 87 percent one-shot stop estimate.

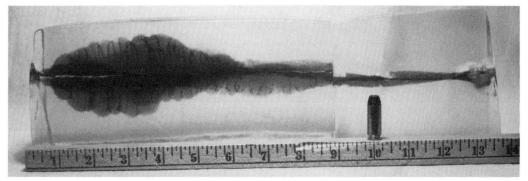

The Winchester 10mm Medium Velocity Ranger SXT shows controlled penetration and a wound profile well-suited to cross-torso shots.

THE FBI AND THE 10mm

In late 1988, the FBI was in the middle of its unique testing looking for a replacement for the horribly ineffective 9mm 147-grain JHP. Reports started surfacing that the Bureau was interested in a "modified" 10mm. At the time, the industry was buzzing with conflicting reports, even among ammo company insiders. First, the talk was of a new 9.8mm auto, then a 10mm auto that fired a shortened 10mm cartridge.

Finally, the story became clear. The FBI had specified a 10mm reduced-velocity load. Federal Cartridge made a special run of Sierra 180-grain JHP bullets in Federal-Norma brass. It loaded them to the 1,035 fps level specified by the FBI. (This was from a 6-inch test barrel.) The Bureau published restricted copies of side-by-side ammo evaluations in December 1988, January 1989, and March 1989.

The powerful 10mm cartridge as it was originally released had changed. It was no longer only available as a wrist-snapping rival to the .41 Magnum. The Federal "FBI load" produced *exactly* the same felt recoil as a .45 Auto with 185-grain JHP ammo. The shooting industry

came to realize that the key to success with the 10mm, in civilian and police circles alike, was reduced loads—not wimpy mid-range loads but not stout .41 Magnum loads either. The FBI effort to develop a medium-velocity 10mm load as an all-around police duty round kept the cartridge from experiencing the same fate as the .41 Magnum. (In fact, the 10mm and .41 Magnum are quite similar. Both are .40 to .41 caliber bullets with weights in the 170- to 210-grain range and velocities from 1,200 to 1,300 fps.)

THE 10mm MEDIUM VELOCITY

The 10mm Medium Velocity was born, and the 10mm auto pistol became popular for the third time. State, county, and city police agencies delayed adoption of either a 9mm or .45 Auto pending the final outcome of the FBI tests. The FBI had solved one of the two major drawbacks to the full-power 10mm, and that was excessive recoil. The solution to excessive auto pistol bulk would come later. At the time, the 10mm Medium Velocity appeared to be the ultimate combat ammo.

After the multimedia testing was complete,

RIGHT: This PMC 10mm Medium Velocity 180-grain Starfire expanded to .70 caliber in gelatin. This load should produce 84 percent one-shot stops.

BELOW: This PMC 10mm Medium Velocity 180-grain Starfire shows a long and tolerant stretch cavity and extremely controlled penetration depth.

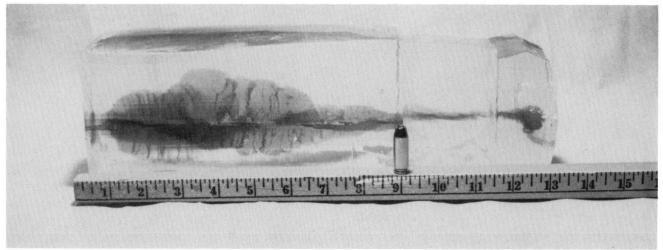

the FBI standardized on a 180-grain JHP at 950 fps from a 5-inch auto pistol. Federal was the first out with two 180-grain loads. One was an FBI-spec jacketed hollowpoint. The other was a 950 fps Hydra-Shok. The Federal JHP expands to .68 caliber and penetrates between 14 and 15 inches of gelatin. The Hydra-Shok expands to .68 caliber and penetrates between 12 and 13.5 inches of gelatin.

Remington and Winchester quickly developed their versions of the 950 fps hollowpoint. Both loads expanded in the .62- to .66-inch range and penetrated 15 to 15.5 inches of gelatin. Hornady studied the FBI tests and results and then designed a hollowpoint bullet specifically to excel in those tests. The resulting 180-grain XTP-HP bullet at 950 fps produced .60 caliber expansion and up to 18 inches of penetration.

Since all 10mm Medium Velocity hollowpoint bullets weigh 180 grains and have the same 950 fps average velocity, all loads produce the same muzzle energy. The average was 364 ft-lbs. of energy. As a comparison, a .45 Auto 185-grain JHP at 940 fps produces 363 ft-lbs. Make no mistake: these medium-velocity 10mm hollowpoint loads *are* .45 Auto hollowpoints in every regard.

With the same bullet weight and roughly the same velocity, these 10mm loads also produce the exact same impulse or momentum, otherwise known as kick or recoil. And this recoil exactly matches the .45 Auto 185-grain JHP. The full-power 10mm loads, in comparison, kicks 20 percent more than the .45 Auto 230-grain FMJ and the .357 Magnum 125-grain JHP.

You can change the felt recoil by changing either the ergonomics or the weight of the

The Cor-Bon 10mm full-power 150-grain Sierra JHP has achieved an actual one-shot stop record of 90 percent.

The Winchester 10mm full-power 175-grain Silvertip expands to .81 caliber and has the best calculated wound ballistics in the caliber.

firearm. For example, a heavier Model 1006 with a 5-inch barrel will feel more controllable than a lighter Model 1066 with a 4.25-inch barrel. Likewise, a Colt will feel slightly different in recoil from a S&W or a Glock of the same barrel length. But when these 10mm loads are all fired from the same gun, it is impossible to tell one from the other in terms of recoil control or shot-to-shot recovery time.

Any time a handgun produces more felt recoil than the .45 Auto or .357 Magnum, a real recoil problem exists. At best, the scenarios in which that gun would be effective are greatly restricted. It is quite significant that the FBI chose to exactly match the felt recoil of the .45 Auto with its Federal load.

Since all the 10mm Medium Velocity loads are so similar in terms of exterior ballistics, it should come as no surprise that they are also similar in terms of wound ballistics. These loads are all 81 to 82 percent effective with one torso shot based on actual shootings.

From a technical viewpoint, the Hydra-Shok should be the best load. This was the top-ranked 10mm Medium Velocity round during the Strasbourg Tests, followed in order by the PMC/Eldorado 180-grain Starfire, Federal 180-grain JHP, Winchester 200-grain Black Talon, and Remington 180-grain JHP. The Hydra-Shok should also perform better against heavily clothed perps. However in reality, these loads all perform the same. In fact, the Winchester-Ranger JHP holds a slight edge.

As a rule, all of the medium-velocity 10mm hollowpoints produce the same stopping power as the average .45 Auto hollowpoint. Again, they have the same felt recoil. The 10mm Medium Velocity, however, has a slightly greater ability to penetrate tactical obstacles.

We compared the Federal .45 Auto 185-grain JHP at 940 fps to the Federal 10mm Medium Velocity 180-grain JHP at 948 fps (the JHP used by the FBI, not the Hydra-Shok) using five of the FBI eight-media test methodologies. In the tests, the .45 Auto averaged a permanent crush cavity of 4.8 cubic inches. In exactly the same tests, the 10mm averaged a slightly smaller cavitation at 4.5 cubic inches. The .45 produced penetration in the FBI ideal range twice, excessive penetration twice, and underpenetration once. The 10mm produced ideal penetration once, excessive penetration three times, and underpenetration once. The .45 Auto averaged 17 inches versus 20 inches for the 10mm.

Overall, the .45 Auto still clearly appears to be a better law enforcement load than the reduced-velocity 10mm. And the full-power 10mm produces entirely too much recoil for general issue police use.

CONCLUSION

The .45 Auto equals the permanent cavitation performance of the 10mm and produces greater temporary cavitation. It is in general far more accurate than the 10mm. The .45 also generally produces adequate but more controlled penetration than the often excessive 10mm. The 10mm is an interesting police load, but the .45 Auto remains a better choice.

The 10mm started off with 165- and 170-grain Norma hollowpoints that were too hot for the guns. These early hollowpoints rarely expanded beyond .55 caliber and as a result produced excessive penetration and small crush and stretch cavities. The next step was a small variety of American-made 150- to 180-grain full-power JHPs that indeed expanded as designed but still produced too much recoil for most shooters. But the saving step was the medium-velocity version of the 180-grain JHP that produced acceptable ballistics and a controllable recoil. Finally, the 10mm has come full circle—the latest loads are the 135- and 155-grain full-power JHPs that provide explosive performance.

The 10mm and 10mm Medium Velocity were two important steps in bringing us what most consider the ultimate combat auto pistol cartridge, the .40 S&W. The .40 S&W, in turn, has made obsolete both 10mm versions. The .40 S&W is available in 180-grain loads that absolutely duplicate the 10mm Medium Velocity rounds. The .40 S&W is also available in 135- and 155-grain JHPs that rival these same bullets from the full-power 10mm.

TABLE 9-1
.45 AUTO vs. 10mm MV vs. .40 S&W

Caliber	.45 Auto	10mm MV	.40 S&W
Weight & Style	185-gr. JHP	180-gr. JHP	180-gr. JHP
Make	Federal	Federal	Winchester
Muzzle Velocity	940 fps	948 fps	956 fps
Muzzle Energy	363 ft-lbs.	359 ft-lbs.	365 ft-lbs.
Recoil Impulse	.77 lb-sec.	.76 lb-sec.	.76 lb-sec.
Ordnance Gelatin Only			
Expansion	.68 cal	.68 cal	.64 cal
Penetration	13.5 in	15.0 in	14.6 in
Crush Cavity	4.9 in3	5.4 in3	4.7 in3
Stretch Diameter	2.45 in	3.10 in	3.2 in
Stretch Cavity	18.3 in3	25.2 in3	31.1 in3
Heavily Clothed Gelatin			
Expansion	.45 cal	.41 cal	.40 cal
Penetration	23.5 in	26.5 in	22.0 in
Gelatin After Sheet Steel			
Expansion	.61 cal	.54 cal	.40 cal
Penetration	16.0 in	21.0 in	18.0 in
Gelatin After Plywood			
Expansion	.45 cal	.41 cal	.40 cal
Penetration	25.0 in	26.5 in	22.0 in
Gelatin After Plate Glass			
Expansion	.80 cal	.68 cal	.78 cal
Penetration	6.8 in	10.0 in	8.5 in
Average Expansion	.60 cal	.54 cal	.52 cal
Average Penetration	17.0 in	19.8 in	17.0 in
Average Crush Cavity	4.8 in3	4.5 in3	3.6 in3
Actual Stopping Power	87%	81%	81%

10

10mm and 10mm Medium Velocity Street Results

Co-author Evan Marshall was one of the panel members of the original FBI Wound Ballistics Panel that was convened after the infamous Miami shootout in 1986. The focus of that panel was whether the FBI should adopt the 9mm or .45 ACP to replace the then issue .357 Magnum. Eventually, of course, the Bureau developed and selected the 10mm.

While the 10mm is an excellent handgun hunting cartridge, it is outperformed by the .40 S&W in law enforcement/defensive applications. The .40 S&W can be carried in 9mm-sized handguns, while the 10mm must be utilized in weapons massive enough to reliably handle the full-power 10mm offering. In addition, the length of the round makes a high-capacity magazine a massive, unwieldy option.

Reliability problems with the 10mm handgun selected by the FBI quickly cooled interest in law enforcement/defensive circles. The round is actually quite accurate and produces excellent stopping power with the right load. The actual shooting results are listed in Table 10-1.

TABLE 10-1
10mm AND 10mm MV ACTUAL RESULTS

	TOTAL SHOOTINGS	ONE-SHOT STOPS	PERCENTAGE
1. Cor-Bon 150-gr. JHP	10	9	90
2. Win 180-gr. JHP	44	36	82
3. Fed 180-gr. JHP	27	22	81
4. Rem 180-gr. JHP	31	25	81

• • • • •

The SWAT team member prepared for the raid by checking his submachine gun and S&W 10mm pistol one last time. It was supposed to be a straightforward, uncomplicated drug raid. Unfortunately, the team was unaware of the fact that an escaped murderer was in the process of purchasing drugs when they made entry.

The killer's response was instantaneous as he shot the entry man in the face. Our hero, the number two man, experienced a stoppage when he fired a burst from his submachine. Dropping the weapon, he drew his pistol and fired three shots. The killer fell to the floor, dead.

He had taken two Cor-Bon 150-grain jacketed hollowpoints in the chest. The entrance wounds were exactly 1 inch apart. The bullets had an average recovered diameter of .73 inch, and the recovered weight was 120 grains.

• • • • •

The state trooper carried his 10mm both on and off-duty. Other troopers complained about its size, but this particular cop considered the weapon's bulk reassuring.

Living in a rural area, he and his wife made a weekly trip to a nearby large city for groceries and other purchases. On this day they parked in the lot of a large urban shopping center. As they were walking to the market, they were approached by two young men who asked them for money. Denying their request, the trooper and his wife started to walk away when the young men announced a holdup. Pushing his wife down behind a parked car, the trooper drew his 10mm and opened fire. One holdup man made good his escape, but the other took a couple of steps before collapsing.

Responding officers found a dead holdup man and a visibly shaken state trooper. Rolling the man over in an attempt to render first aid, he had recognized the young man as the son of one of the secretaries at state police headquarters.

The recovered Cor-Bon hollowpoint had a diameter of .77 inch and weighed 136 grains.

• • • • •

The liquor store he owned was right on the edge of encroaching urban blight. He had watched the changes with increasing concern and had decided to purchase a pistol because of the deteriorating conditions.

He watched the FBI's ammunition selection process with great interest. When the announcement was made concerning the 10mm, he went to a nearby gun shop and placed an order for a 10mm handgun to keep on the premises. A few months later the gun arrived, which he purchased and took to work. A couple of years later, he purchased a box of Cor-Bon 150-grain jacketed hollowpoints for it. He test fired the gun and then placed it on a shelf near the cash register.

It was almost 2 A.M. when the man entered. The bottle of expensive liquor he selected contrasted starkly with his dress and demeanor. The store owner's concern increased when the asked for 10 cartons of cigarettes. As the owner placed all of this on the counter, the man produced a butcher knife and demanded all the cash in the register.

The store owner grabbed his 10mm and opened fire. The first seven rounds missed, but the eighth took effect and the man collapsed in the doorway. It had traversed the chest cavity, stopping under the skin on the far side. Its recovered diameter was .79 inch, while its recovered weight was 119 grains.

• • • • •

He was a cop who belonged to a department that offered officers the option of carrying one of a number of different handguns. He had selected a Glock 10mm pistol and Cor-Bon's 150-grain jacketed hollowpoint.

Assigned to narcotics, he carried the high-capacity 10mm because backup was often either far away or nonexistent. He was working a potential buy with a group of dope dealers who were supposed to provide him with 5 kilos of cocaine. Unfortunately, it was to be a rip-off, not a sale.

As the officer approached the meet location, he looked for his backup and was gratified when he didn't see it. Unfortunately, he did not see them because of their concealment skills but because they had gone to the wrong location.

As he exchanged the money for what he thought was cocaine, he waited for the backup to appear and make the arrest. He couldn't understand what had gone wrong. He had used the agreed-upon signal and nothing had happened.

He began to look around as concern started to turn to panic. His sellers asked him what was wrong. Then they began to look around and, smelling a trap, started to produce weapons. The undercover officer produced his weapon and identified himself as a cop. The drug dealers response was to open fire. Ducking behind his undercover vehicle, he returned fire. During a brief lull in the gunfight, he removed a portable radio from the trunk of his car and called for help.

His opponents had started to outflank him when he heard the welcome sound of sirens. All of the dealers but one turned and started to run away. The remaining dealer advanced on him with an SKS rifle. The officer fired three rounds at him before experiencing lockback. He was in the process of reloading when the dope dealer leaned over the vehicle and shot him in his left shoulder. Collapsing from the wound, he fell on his side. As he lay there, he heard his attacker coming around the car. He struggled to pick up his pistol, then emptied it in the direction of his attacker and collapsed.

He woke up in the hospital without his left arm. It been amputated due to irreparable damage. He attacker had taken one round in the throat and was DOA. The bullet had a recovered diameter of .74 inch and a recovered weight of 131 grains.

• • • • •

The junior high teacher had returned to his old neighborhood to teach. The quiet tree-lined neighborhood had changed, and narcotics trafficking and gang warfare had become depressingly commonplace.

After he was mugged twice, he went to a local gun shop, purchased a Colt 10mm pistol, and loaded it with Cor-Bon 150-grain jacketed hollowpoints. The gun was placed in the shoulder bag in which he carried his school supplies.

He was a popular teacher with the parents and staff alike because he kept a watchful eye on the young men who often loitered across the street. They would respond with obscenities and gang symbols, but he had no idea they were planning to murder him because he often called the police and let them know who was selling drugs.

It was a pleasant afternoon, and he had just completed grading papers in the teacher's lounge. Walking across the street, he ignored the taunts of the street dealers. As he got mid block, he stopped at a neighborhood store to buy a bottle of apple juice. He went to drop the lid into a nearby trash barrel when a car pulled to the curb. Looking up, he saw the man in the backseat raise a shotgun.

As he turned to run back inside the store, he was shot in the legs. Fortunately, the weapon was loaded with birdshot, not buckshot or slugs. Falling inside the doorway, the teacher scrambled to pull the pistol from his bag. He finally felt it in the bottom and pulled it out just as his attacker exited the vehicle.

The thug fired again, this time missing his target. Desperate now, the teacher opened fire with his 10mm pistol. The first round struck the shotgun, knocking it out of his hands. One of the subsequent rounds struck the dope dealer just below the heart, mortally wounding him.

The bullet had a recovered diameter of .65 inch and a recovered weight of 129 grains.

11

.40 Smith & Wesson Ammo

Decades of searching for the ultimate combat auto pistol cartridge are probably over—the .40 Smith & Wesson is the ideal cartridge for personal defense and law enforcement. After nearly a century of debate on the merits of the 9mm and .45 Auto, the real answer lies midway between them. The .40 S&W is the perfect compromise.

Some of what makes the .40 S&W so good is the fact that it was designed from scratch as a police caliber and not a military caliber. The .40 S&W was also originally designed to use hollowpoints and not full-metal-jacket loads.

The 9mm cartridge fires a .355-caliber bullet weighing typically 115 to 147 grains at velocities of 1,150 to 950 fps respectively. Higher pressure +P and +P+ loadings push the velocity of a 115-grain bullet just over 1,300 fps.

The .45 Auto cartridge fires a .451-caliber bullet weighing typically 185 to 230 grains at velocities of 1,000 to 850 fps respectively. Higher +P loadings push the velocity of a 185-grain bullet to 1,150 fps.

The .40 S&W cartridge fires a .400-caliber bullet weighing typically 135 to 180 grains at velocities of 1,300 to 950 fps respectively. The .40 S&W firearms are exactly the same size and weight as 9mm auto pistols. Both hold 10 rounds of ammo in their magazines.

The 9mm has the right weapon size, enough velocity for good bullet expansion, and a recoil controllable by all shooters. The standard-pressure 9mm bullet packs up to 365 ft-lbs. of energy. The "energy theory" of stopping power rallied around the 9mm. The .45 Auto has the big initial bullet diameter and enough weight for adequate penetration. Most .45 Auto pistols hold fewer bullets, but the average .45 Auto bullet is 85 percent effective, while the average 9mm is 73 percent effective. With 350 fps of energy but 44 percent more momentum than the 9mm, the .45 Auto is favored by fans of the "momentum theory" of stopping power.

DEVELOPMENT OF THE .40 S&W

The FBI has been looking for the "ideal" police cartridge and bullet ever since the April

The Cor-Bon .40 S&W 135-grain Nosler JHP produces 96 percent one-shot stops. This equals the .357 Magnum 125-grain JHP.

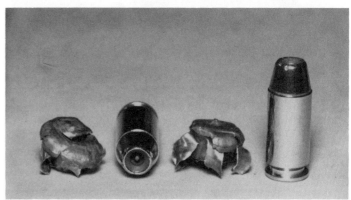

The Federal .40 S&W 155-grain JHP expands to .65 caliber and penetrates 12 inches. This has a 94 percent one-shot stop rating.

The Federal .40 S&W 155-grain Hydra-Shok achieves 93 percent one-shot stops. It expands to .68 caliber.

11, 1986, shootout in Miami. The Bureau quickly dropped the 9mm Winchester 115-grain Silvertip and adopted the low-velocity 9mm Winchester 147-grain Olin Super Match JHP. Many civilian shooters and police agencies misunderstood this move. Many still do not understand it.

This 9mm JHP was not the "ideal" bullet. It was specifically labeled by the FBI as an "interim" load, nothing more. The 147-grain load gives up a lot of wound ballistics to get greater penetration. This was exactly what the FBI wanted until it could sort everything out. Actual police-involved shootings show that the 147-grain JHP is less effective than all other 9mm hollowpoints. But it does penetrate deeply.

Working with Federal Cartridge, the FBI specified a lower-recoil version of the hot 10mm cartridge. It called for a 180-grain Sierra "power jacket" serrated JHP at 950 fps. The full-power 10mm kicked too much for fast follow-up shooting. Over 40 percent of police-action shootings involve multiple offenders, and certainly the duo of Michael Platt and William

Mattix drove this point home. The FBI wanted a load that recoiled no more than a .45 Auto, and the mid-range 10mm met that requirement.

The FBI designed a series of tests using 10-percent ordnance gelatin that included penetration and bullet expansion both in bare gelatin and in gelatin after first penetrating common tactical obstacles (heavy winter clothing, car body sheet steel, building materials, and vehicle glass). The 10mm 180-grain JHP at mid-range velocities swept these tests and was approved. Smith & Wesson was awarded the contract for the FBI 10mm auto pistols. The result was a 10mm weapon based on a .45 Auto big-bore frame. (The .45 ACP S&W Model 4506 and the 10mm S&W Model 1076 are virtually identical.)

Somewhere along this development, Smith & Wesson committed to the FBI to "optimize" its Model 1076. This meant a smaller-framed auto pistol and a smaller 10mm cartridge case.

Smith & Wesson was in a perfect position to design a smaller .40-caliber, mid-range 10mm cartridge. Some years past the company had designed a prototype .40-caliber load based on the 9mm case length and 9mm rebated rim design, calling it the .40 S&W. The round was never released, not even as a wildcat.

At any rate, the official version behind the .40 S&W is that Smith & Wesson approached Winchester-Olin and offered to downsize the Model 1076/1066 if Winchester-Olin would design a cartridge for the gun. Jerry Bersett, who was then with Winchester-Olin, and Steve Melvin, then with Smith & Wesson, met in June 1989 at the SAAMI meeting to discuss an "optimized" 10mm. By the January 1990 SHOT Show, they jointly announced a 10mm-based cartridge and a 9mm-based auto pistol.

Smith & Wesson and Winchester were concerned enough about the rebated rim design to change it on the new .40 S&W to the more conventional rimless design like the .45 Auto and 10mm. (In a so-called rimless design, the extraction rim is the same diameter as the case; a rebated rim case has the rim smaller than the case.) The rest was simple. Winchester dumped in enough ball powder to hit

950 fps from the 10mm "short" case and loaded a 180-grain Silvertip-serration JHP.

Smith & Wesson, for its part, modified a 9mm frame Model 5900-series auto pistol to accept the new .40 S&W. The result was the compact Model 4006. After nearly a half dozen attempts, the shooting world had a .40/10mm-sized bullet fired from a compact 9mm-sized auto pistol.

By mid-1990, the influential California Highway Patrol adopted both the S&W gun and the Winchester ammo. (Officially this is Smith & Wesson's cartridge. It is the first one to be headstamped S&W since the obsolete .35 S&W was introduced in 1913.) Dozens of other agencies followed. As of mid-1995, the .40 S&W is in use by the U.S. Border Patrol, U.S. Marshal's Service, U.S. Customs Service, U.S. Forestry Service, and the state police or highway patrol in California, South Carolina, Missouri, Arkansas, Ohio, Nevada, Rhode Island, Nebraska, Alaska, Iowa, Mississippi, North Carolina, Pennsylvania, and Minnesota along with countless sheriff's departments, county police, city police, and town marshals.

All of the earlier .40 caliber/10mm cartridge combinations had nagging problems ranging from lack of shooter interest to excessive recoil to design-related feeding problems to excessive weapon size. The .40 S&W is the end result of a long search for a .40-caliber bullet weighing from 180 to 200 grains and driven between 950 and 1,050 fps. The great gun writers of the past like Bill Jordan, Elmer Keith, and Skeeter Skelton all worked to get such an ideal handgun load.

The FBI, working with Federal Cartridge, almost made the perfect .40-caliber cartridge. Its downloaded 10mm "reduced velocity" 180-grain JHP at 950 fps met all the requirements except one—weapon size. When Smith & Wesson got the FBI pistol contract for the Model 1076, it agreed to "optimize" the gun. It didn't take a .45-caliber-framed gun to handle the 10mm FBI load; a 9mm-framed gun would do just fine.

Downloading the 10mm full power to meet the FBI medium velocity specs meant less

The Cor-Bon .40 S&W 150-grain Sierra JHP is in the "top five" for this caliber with 92 percent stops.

powder and more airspace in the case. Smith & Wesson and Winchester basically removed that airspace by shortening the 10mm case length. The shorter case worked with the 9mm-sized guns and the result was the S&W Model 4006 with both slide- and frame-mounted decocking levers.

The .40 S&W case is not actually a shortened 10mm case. The 10mm cartridge has much thicker case walls and a large pistol primer. However, the .40 S&W can technically be fired from the 10mm auto pistols, although this is not recommended. The .40 S&W cartridge will headspace on the extractor instead of the case mouth. The bullet will jump a .142 inch freebore just like a .38 Special fired from a .357 Magnum. If the cartridge is not held by the extractor, the chances for a ruptured primer are great.

Of all the attempts at a .40 auto pistol cartridge, the .40 S&W is already the most successful. It was designed to have the exact same ballistics as the 10mm Medium Velocity FBI load except from a smaller gun. It does that so successfully that everyone wanted in on the action right away.

The ammo companies originally watched the full-power 10mm with caution. It splashed with the Bren Ten, then fizzled. The 10mm flashed again with the Delta Elite, then sputtered. No one wanted to be a part of another

9mm Magnum, .357 Maximum, or 9mm Rimmed project. However, none of this industry caution was evident with the .40 S&W. Winchester and Smith & Wesson scooped everyone with a cartridge that finally answered the age-old demand. Everyone else scrambled to get in on a cartridge that was obviously right for the times.

Winchester set the pace with its 180-grain JHP with Silvertip-style jacket serrations. The prototype ammo produced 990 fps muzzle velocities, but this required an extremely dense load of ball powder. Winchester has since backed off to 950 fps nominal.

Hornady was the quickest to respond to Winchester with a 180-grain XTP hollowpoint at 950 fps. It quickly followed up with a 155-grain XTP at a sizzling 1,180 fps. The Hornady XTP is different from many jacketed hollowpoints because the company specifically designed it to penetrate deeper with better weight retention and more controlled expansion.

Aiming to avoid overexpansion and fragmentation, Hornady created the XTP bullet using a wax/grease media and water as a test media, but the company plans to use ordnance gelatin in its design and testing in the future. The HP-XTP is easily recognized by very shallow hollowpoint cavities and very narrow hollowpoint cavity openings.

The Winchester .40 S&W 155-grain Silvertip was the first "lightweight" bullet in this caliber. This 1,205 fps JHP is ranked at 91 percent.

The Federal .40 S&W 180-grain Hydra-Shok is the best of the 180-grain JHPs at 89 percent effective.

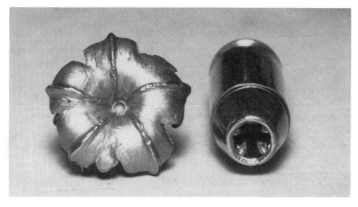

LEFT: This PMC .40 S&W 180-grain Starfire expands to .75 caliber due to the unique, fluted hollowpoint cavity.

BELOW: The PMC .40 S&W 155-grain Starfire shows a progressive energy release and controlled yet adequate penetration.

MagSafe Ammo was the next out. The MagSafe projectile is based on the Glaser Safety Slug. It uses number 2 birdshot embedded in epoxy as the bullet core. Glaser Blue uses number 12 birdshot and Glaser Silver uses compressed number 6 birdshot. All these frangible loads fragment on impact to scatter birdshot inside the target like a contact shotgun wound. The MagSafe load penetrates deeper with its copper- and nickel-plated magnum-hard shot. The first MagSafe load was the 84-grain Defender with a screaming 1,800 fps muzzle velocity. This projectile uses the jacket from the 150-grain Sierra JHP with a wide hollowpoint opening.

Pete Pi from Cor-Bon next introduced a .40 S&W load. We have come to expect maximum velocities from Cor-Bon ammo. Sure enough, the company's 150-grain Sierra JHP averaged 1,200 fps.

Black Hills is a source for both new and reloaded ammo. It typically uses Hornady HP-XTP bullets and Winchester primed cases. The 950 fps velocities for its .40 S&W ammo are typical for 180-grain bullets in accordance with FBI specs. Black Hills also loads a 180-grain copper-plated FMJ bullet at 950 fps and a 155-grain HP-XTP at 1,150 fps.

Federal Cartridge had been at full capacity supplying the FBI with 10mm Reduced Velocity JHP ammo and supplying civilian shooters with 10mm Reduced Velocity Hydra-Shoks. It made a small run of .40 S&W ammo for the California Highway Patrol to test but got right back to the 10mm. Just before the 1991 SHOT Show, Federal released two 180-grain .40 S&W loads at 950 fps. One was a conventional JHP based on the aggressive Sierra design. The other was the Hydra-Shok.

The Hydra-Shok, of course, is the superior load; the street results have proven this. The post in the center of the hollowpoint cavity forces the bullet to expand to larger diameters at lower impact velocities. Compared to the regular JHP, the Hydra-Shok design is most effective through heavy clothing. But since some refuse to face the facts from the street or because they misunderstand the basics of fluid physics, Federal made an ordinary JHP for the .40 S&W.

THE "SECOND WAVE" OF .40 S&W AMMO

At the beginning of the .40 S&W project, the goal was to equal the 10mm Medium Velocity specified by the FBI. For the first .40 S&W loads, the emphasis at most companies was on making 180-grain hollowpoints to match the original Winchester .40 S&W load. With the 950 fps heavy hollowpoints in production, the focus then turned to finding the "perfect" load for the .40 S&W.

Companies that made 180-grain JHPs quickly turned to lighter bullets. Those that felt the 180-grain weight was right stepped up the velocity. Exotic fragmenting and duplex loads appeared. And importantly, a great deal of training and practice ammo is now available in three bullet weights. The "second wave" of .40 S&W ammo arrived.

Most of the sizzle in the .40 S&W caliber comes from the 150- and 155-grain hollowpoints. The first of the hand-held missiles in this class is the Pro Load 150-grain Sierra JHP pushed to 1,190 fps. That 470 ft-lbs. of energy should calm the nerves of officers transitioning from the .357 Magnum to the .40 S&W. The .40 S&W Pro Load far exceeds the punch of the .357 Magnum 110-grain JHP at 1,295 fps.

Cor-Bon has also released a special-order-only load that uses the 155-grain HP-XTP for deeper penetration. Black Hills also loads the 155-grain HP-XTP for both civilian and police shooters. The Black Hills emphasis has always been economy and accuracy.

After a long wait, the 155-grain Winchester Silvertip finally became available. This 1,205 fps controllable lightweight packs a full 500 ft-lbs. of energy. The Silvertip style "crease-fold" jacket serrations are proven in providing reliable expansion. This load produces ideal penetration in ordnance gelatin at exactly 13.5 inches.

CCI-Speer developed the totally metal-jacketed (TMJ) copper plating process as an economical way to get jacketed bullets for its

Blazer aluminum cases. A surprise benefit of this TMJ technology is great jacketed hollowpoints. The jacket on the plated hollowpoint (PHP) holds to the lead with a chemical bond greater than the lead has to itself. As a result, its PHP expands as violently as the best hollowpoints, but it does not fragment. Unless fragments leave the main bullet path (and they rarely do), the bullet with the largest recovered diameter usually produces the most stopping power. The CCI 155-grain PHP is one of the very few lightweight hollowpoints to both expand violently and hold that diameter—the best of both worlds.

The 155-grain JHP from Remington is significant in that it was designed to work at lower velocities. While other lightweight loads push closer to 1,200 fps, this load is 60 to 80 fps slower on purpose. The recoil is a closer match to the standard 180-grain loads.

.40 S&W PRACTICE AMMO

For any caliber to gain widespread acceptance, ammo for practice, training, target shooting, qualifying, and plinking is absolutely required. In fact, the number one reason why police agencies that looked at the .40 S&W in the early 1990s did not adopt it was lack of low-cost training ammo. All that has changed. The small companies were the first out with practice ammo, and now the big boys have made it available.

Winchester has two loads for this purpose. The first is a 180-grain FMJ flatpoint loaded, of course, to 950 fps. This is a "Q" load, otherwise known as USA White Box ammo. The second is a 155-grain FMJ Match flatpoint loaded to 1,125 fps. This round impacts the target to the same point of aim as the 155-grain Silvertip at 25 yards.

The economical Federal .40 S&W load, marketed as American Eagle ammo, uses a 180-grain truncated cone lead bullet at 950 fps. This swaged bullet is made from 6 percent antimony, making it the hardest noncast lead bullet available.

CCI-Speer, of course, has approached low-cost training ammunition from another angle with its aluminum-cased Blazer ammo. With specially heat-treated aluminum and a new Teflon lubricant on the cases, Blazer ammo is as reliable as brass-cased ammo. The Teflon makes extraction easier and eliminates aluminum fouling that used to take place in the chambers. In fact, due to continuous improvement projects at CCI, some of the Blazer ammo is more reliable in full-auto submachine guns than some ball loads.

The practice loads from Federal and CCI-Speer are extremely significant for handgunners who shoot steel reaction targets. Shooters must use lead or plated lead bullets against steel. Jacketed hollowpoints and especially full-metal-jacket bullets do not vaporize when they hit the steel like lead and plated bullets. As a result, the jacket and big chunks of lead bounce back at the shooter.

Injuries from as far back as 15 yards are common when firing FMJ ammo against steel. All this is solved by firing lead and copper-plated bullets. One study conducted by CCI-Speer found the bounce back from its copper-plated PHP to be less than 1 yard. The all-lead American Eagle load is the same. Do not shoot jacketed bullets against steel.

FRAGMENTING AND DUPLEX .40 S&W AMMO

The .40 S&W now includes fragmenting and duplex loads. Glaser is the oldest and most established of all the specialty ammo companies. Police officers have fired Glaser for 35 years now, and civilian shooters have had them for 20. The Glaser is proven. The company's Blue ammo uses loose-packed number 12 birdshot housed in a copper jacket and sealed with a blue plastic ball. The Silver uses a compressed load of number 6 birdshot. The 105-grain Blue and Silver both loads have velocities of 1,450 fps.

At the relentless urging of Ed Sanow and based on the success of the .45 Auto SWAT, Joe Zambone of MagSafe has developed a .40 S&W SWAT round. All the SWAT loads in the MagSafe lineup are designed for minimum

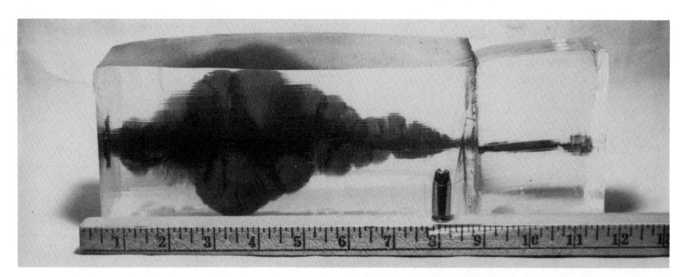

ABOVE: The Remington .40 S&W 165-grain full-power Golden Saber is tied for second in the .40 S&W caliber at 94 percent one-shot stops.

The Remington .40 S&W 165-grain Golden Saber uses aperture-style spiral-cut jacket serrations. This is Cpl. Ed Sanow's duty load by choice.

The Winchester .40 S&W 180-grain police-only Ranger SXT (Black Talon) produces 80 percent one-shot stops. This late-energy-release bullet expands to .72 caliber.

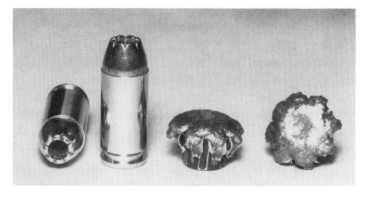

The defanged Winchester .40 S&W 180-grain Supreme SXT expands to .68 caliber. The deep sump-type cavity is tolerant of heavy clothes and debris.

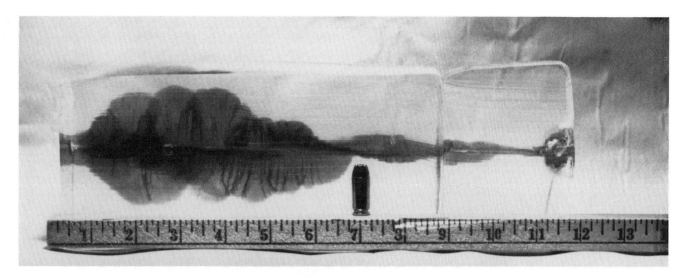

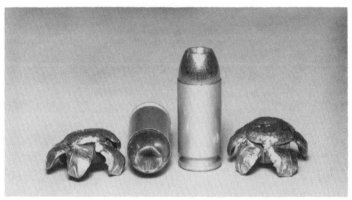

ABOVE: The Winchester .40 S&W 180-grain Supreme SXT penetrates a very controlled 12 inches of calibrated gelatin to earn an 86 percent rating.

The CCI-Speer .40 S&W 155-grain Gold Dot expands to .70 caliber. This copper-plated hollowpoint should produce 89 percent one-shot stops.

penetration in building materials, which makes them perfect for home defense.

In .45 Auto and .40 S&W, the SWAT load uses a heavy Remington jacket filled with nothing more than tough marine epoxy. The .40 S&W slug weighs a mere 46 grains and crosses the chronograph screens at 2,100 fps. It has the least recoil of any .40 S&W load, hits as hard as most hollowpoints, and is by far one of the safest.

LATER .40 S&W DEVELOPMENT

Far from being "Slow & Weak," the .40 S&W is able to produce as much if not more stopping power than the very best 9mm, 9mm +P+, .45 Auto, and .45 Auto +P loads. The best .40 S&W ammo produces exactly the same wound ballistics as the best .357 Magnums. The 125-grain JHP in .357 Magnum has the best actual street record of any load in any caliber, with one-shot stops 96 percent of the time. The best from the other auto pistols are 89 to 91 percent for the 9mm +P+ and 91 to 94 percent for the .45 Auto and .45 Auto +P. The .40 S&W checks in with conventional JHP ammo at 93 to 96 percent. The detailed wound ballistics results are listed in Table 12-1.

The first generation of .40 S&W loads were all 180-grain JHPs driven to 950 fps. These equalled the FBI-spec 10mm Medium Velocity ammo and rivaled the average .45 Auto hollowpoint. The second wave of .40 S&W ammo was the crop of 150- to 155-grain JHPs loaded at 1,150 to 1,200 fps. These have proven to be among the most effective of all auto pistol loads.

The third era of .40 S&W ammo was the absolutely sizzling 135-grain JHPs. This ammo came from two sources—Cor-Bon and Triton—loading two makes of bullet: Nosler and Sierra.

These are the loads that have a 96 percent stopping power record. They are tied with the .357 Magnum 125-grain JHP as the most effective handgun loads in police and defensive shooting scenarios, period.

Cor-Bon, as usual, was the first out with its 135-grain JHP at 1,300 fps. The pre-1995 Cor-Bon loads used Nosler bullets; ammo loaded in 1995 and later used 135-grain bullets made exclusively for Cor-Bon by Sierra. Triton Cartridge has remained with the original Nosler bullet.

These 135-grain bullets, packing 526 ft-lbs. of energy, penetrate between 10 and 11 inches of gelatin. One school of thought claims that this is not enough penetration. Wrong. The street results from two dozen police-action and civilian shootings prove that it is enough.

These loads expand violently and fragment to produce a smallish crush cavity but a massive stretch cavity. One school of thought claims that stopping power is only determined by the crush cavity and the size of the stretch cavity is meaningless. Wrong again. The .357 Magnum 125-grain JHP performs exactly the same way in gelatin as the .40 S&W 135-grain JHP. These two loads prove that a large stretch cavity, which is a sign of rapid energy transfer, is one of the best measures of stopping power.

The fourth generation of .40 S&W loads are based on the 165-grain bullet weight. Use *extreme* caution when selecting this weight of .40 S&W ammo. Some are full-power loads while others are medium-velocity. For example, the Cor-Bon- and Triton-loaded 165-grain Sierra JHP and Remington 165-grain Golden Saber are *full-power* loads. The Federal 165-grain Hydra-Shok and CCI-Speer 165-grain Gold Dot are *medium-velocity* loads. The medium-velocity loads are *not* clearly labeled as such. There is an enormous difference in stopping power between these two pressure levels.

The only ways to tell a full-power from a medium-velocity load are to check the ammo makers catalog or chronograph them yourself. The full-power 165-grain ammo has a muzzle velocity around 1,125 fps, the medium velocity 165-grain ammo around 950 fps.

The Cor-Bon and Triton ammo use Nosler hollowpoints. With 13.8 to 14.7 inches of penetration and fragmenting bullet expansion, these 1,125 fps JHPs are a very good choice for law enforcement or similar defensive scenarios calling for deeper but controlled penetration. This ammo expands reliably even after heavy clothes and has the ideal penetration depth for cross torso shots.

The Federal .40 S&W 165-grain load uses a Hydra-Shok hollowpoint. Again, this is a *medium-velocity* load pushing just 950 fps. It was developed in cooperation with the FBI, which wanted a lower chamber pressure version. The advantage of this load is reduced recoil, less muzzle rise, and faster follow-up shots.

The bullet performance from the medium-velocity Hydra-Shok, however, is only marginal due to its lower mid-range velocities. While producing acceptable penetration, the permanent and temporary cavitation from this load calculate to just an 82 percent effectiveness. That is just above the .38 Special and 9mm subsonic range. This .40 S&W Medium Velocity round makes some sense when fired from the very lightest guns such as the Glock 23 and Glock 27 in the hands of the most recoil-shy. But except for 180-grain FMJ ball, in terms of wound ballistics these medium-velocity hollowpoints are the worst performers in the caliber. They also raise serious concerns about ammo-induced cycle stoppages.

One of the most dynamic of all .40 S&W loads—and the ammo currently in Ed Sanow's Glock 22 used on sheriff's patrol—is the Remington 165-grain Golden Saber. For 1994, the Saber's high-performance jacket (HPJ) has been redesigned with the most aggressive jacket serrations ever made. The spiral-cut serrations lower the threshold of expansion by 125 fps to just 700 fps.

The Golden Saber was designed specifically to perform in the FBI multiple-barrier tests. However, this brass-jacketed hollowpoint also produces a credible temporary stretch cavity. It expands to .68 caliber in gelatin *after* heavy clothes or *after* wallboard and still produces a controlled 14 inches of penetration. The

Remington 165-grain full-power Golden Saber has achieved an impressive 94 percent one-shot stops based on a number of police-action shootings.

CONCLUSION

What is the future for the .40 S&W now that dozens of loads in the caliber are available? Ammo industry insiders are convinced that the .40 S&W is the police and defensive cartridge for the 1990s and beyond. It produces both a big-bore crush cavity and a high-velocity stretch cavity. The .45 Auto will always have a small, hardened core of followers—that has not changed since 1905. The 9mm will see only slight growth in popularity, if any. (The 1995 gun legislation that bans the production of auto pistols with magazine capacities larger than 10 rounds has probably done more to hurt the 9mm and help the .40 S&W and .45 Auto than any other recent event.) The .40 S&W will be the cartridge of choice for civilians looking for their first auto pistol and for police agencies transitioning from revolver to auto.

So the police and defensive calibers of the future will probably shake out to be the .40 S&W and, to a lesser degree, the .357 SIG. The 9mm and .45 Auto are destined to play a lesser role. The .357 SIG appeals to those unhappy with the 9mm but who are still energy-oriented. The .40 S&W, however, appeals to both sides of the stopping power argument. It has energy like the 9mm +P+ but an initial caliber close to the .45 Auto. As Chapter 28 makes clear, the keys to stopping power involve both energy and initial caliber. For this reason, the .40 S&W is the caliber of the future.

TABLE 11-1
CALIFORNIA HIGHWAY PATROL AMMO COMPARISON TEST
MAY 1990

CALIBER	MANUFACTURER	BULLET WEIGHT GRAIN		AVERAGE VELOCITY FPS	MUZZLE ENERGY FT-LBS.	EXPANSION INCH	PEN. 10% GEL. (IN)
9mm	Win	115	STHP	1,090	303	.625	11.5
10mm (full)	Win	175	STHP	1,170	531	.702	15.25
10mm (MV)	Fed	180	JHP	879	308	.701	16.5+
.45 ACP	Win	185	STHP	953	373	.767	13.5
.38 Spl. +P	Win	110	JHP	1,044	246	.670	10
.357 Mag.	Rem	125	JHP	1,450	582	.576 (f)	12.25
.40 S&W	Win	180	JHP	930	345	.776	15.5

TABLE 11-2
.40 S&W AMMO

MAKE	VELOCITY FPS	ENERGY FT-LBS.	EXPAN. INCH	PEN. INCH	CRUSH CAVITY CU. IN.	STRETCH CAVITY CU. IN.	ONE SHOT STOP %
MagSafe 84-gr. Defender	1,800	604	frag	13.0	2.0	61.8	91
MagSafe 46-gr. SWAT	2,100	450	frag	6.0	1.4	44.2	89
Glaser 105-gr. Blue Safety	1,450	490	frag	7.8	7.0	33.3	90
Cor-Bon 135-gr. Sierra JHP	1,325	526	.59 f	10.4	2.8	59.0	91
Triton 135-gr. Nosler JHP	1,300	507	.56 f	9.8	2.4	69.1	91
Federal 155-gr. Hydra-Shok	1,175	475	.68	13.3	4.8	47.9	93
CCI 155-gr. Gold Dot	1,186	484	.70	12.3	4.7	20.2	89
Cor-Bon 150-gr. Sierra JHP	1,200	480	.55 f	14.0	3.3	48.2	92
Cor-Bon 155-gr. Hornady XTP	1,175	475	.68	14.0	5.1	44.6	88
Federal 155-gr. JHP	1,140	448	.65 f	12.0	4.0	56.9	94
Winchester 155-gr. Silvertip	1,205	500	.70	13.5	5.2	46.8	91
Remington 155-gr. JHP	1,140	448	.61	16.5	4.8	41.2	86
Pro-Load 150-gr. JHP	1,190	472	.53 f	14.5	3.2	48.4	88
Master 150-gr. Sierra JHP	1,100	403	.73	14.5	6.1	47.6	85
Hornady 155-gr. XTP-HP	1,180	480	.68	14.0	5.1	44.6	88
PMC 155-gr. Starfire	1,160	463	.75	10.8	4.8	37.7	89
Georgia Arms 155-gr PHP	1,200	496	.80	12.0	6.0	52.3	90
Winchester 155-gr. FMJ-Match	1,125	435	.40	22.0	2.3	12.8	79
Remington 165-gr. Golden Saber	1,150	485	.68	12.0	4.4	41.1	94
Cor-Bon 165-gr. Nosler JHP	1,125	464	.66	13.8	4.7	50.5	88
Triton 165-gr. Nosler JHP	1,125	464	.55 f	14.7	3.5	34.5	88
Federal 165-gr. Hydra-Shok MV	950	331	.61	13.8	4.0	18.3	82
CCI 165-gr. Gold Dot MV	970	345	.66	14.5	5.0	20.4	82
Master 170-gr. SWC	925	323	.40	22.0	2.8	14.5	73

TABLE 11-2 (CONTINUED)
.40 S&W AMMO

MAKE	VELOCITY FPS	ENERGY FT-LBS.	EXPAN. INCH	PEN. INCH	CRUSH CAVITY CU. IN.	STRETCH CAVITY CU. IN.	ONE SHOT STOP %
Federal 180-gr. Hydra-Shok	950	361	.75	15.0	6.6	39.2	89
CCI 180-gr. Gold Dot	950	361	.68	11.6	4.2	18.3	85
Winchester 180-gr. Black Talon	990	392	.72	13.0	5.3	29.1	80
Winchester 180-gr. Supr SXT	990	392	.68	12.0	4.4	34.4	86
Winchester 180-gr. JHP	1,010	408	.64	14.6	4.7	31.1	81
Cor-Bon 180-gr. JHP	1,050	441	.75	15.0	6.6	39.2	86
Pro-Load 180-gr. JHP +P	1,070	458	.64	17.0	5.5	32.6	86
Remington 180 gr. JHP	950	361	.61	18.0	5.3	32.2	80
Pro-Load 180-gr. JHP	950	361	.60	16.5	4.7	29.1	82
Federal 180-gr. JHP	950	361	.64	17.0	5.5	32.6	82
Hornady 180-gr. XTP-HP	950	361	.64	16.4	5.3	26.2	85
PMC 180-gr. Starfire	985	388	.75	12.0	5.3	42.4	83
Remington 180-gr. Golden Saber	1,015	412	.83	12.9	7.0	27.9	87
Georgia Arms 180-gr. PHP	1,050	441	.72	15.5	6.3	25.6	86
American 180-gr. ADE-HP	990	391	.67	15.5	5.5	31.6	84
CCI 180-gr. TMJ	950	361	.40	25.0	3.1	14.6	70
Winchester 180-gr. FMJ	950	361	.40	25.0	3.1	14.6	71
Federal 180-gr. SWC	950	361	.40	22.0	2.8	14.5	75

12

.40 Smith & Wesson Street Results

As discussed in Chapter 11, the .40 S&W has become highly popular in law enforcement circles because it fills a gap between the 9mm and .45 ACP. It allows those people who are happier with a larger bullet to carry a caliber that gives them a greater magazine capacity than is generally available with the .45 ACP.

Initial reports on the .40 S&W look promising, but we must understand that we will need to see a substantially larger number of shootings before we can be as confident in this caliber as we are with the results for the 9mm and .45 ACP. Realistically, the .40 S&W fills a perceived need. Whether or not it will prove to be dramatically better than the 9mm or .45 ACP remains to be seen. The results of actual shootings are listed in Table 12-1.

TABLE 12-1
.40 S&W ACTUAL RESULTS

LOAD	TOTAL	STOPS	PERCEN.
1. Cor-Bon 135-gr. JHP	24	23	96
2. Fed 155-gr. JHP	34	32	94
3. Rem 165-gr. GS	16	15	94
4. Cor-Bon 150-gr. JHP	38	34	93
5. Fed 155-gr. HS	14	13	93
6. Win 155-gr. ST	22	20	91
7. Fed 180-gr. HS	38	34	89
8. Cor-Bon 180-gr. JHP	22	19	86
9. Black Hills 180-gr. JHP	46	39	85
10. Win 180-gr. JHP	21	17	81
11. Win 180-gr. BT	35	28	80
12. Win 180-gr. FNJ	17	12	71

• • • • •

He had just been issued his Beretta Model 96 double-action-only semiautomatic pistol. His department left ammunition selection up to the individual officer as long as it was loaded by an approved manufacturer. He had selected the Cor-Bon 135-grain JHP based on articles he had read. He found it relatively easy to qualify with and carried it as his duty load.

Because he was assigned to foot patrol in a high crime area of his city, he was supposed to work with a partner. This day, however, his partner was giving a deposition in a civil case.

The officer had written a few parking tickets, broke up a couple of fights, and advised several citizens. He was making his way to his favorite eating place around lunchtime when he heard shots fired in a nearby alley. As he approached the mouth of it, he saw a man stagger out and collapse. Drawing his pistol, he approached the man and saw that he had been shot several times.

After calling for back up and medical assistance, the officer proceeded down the alley. Approximately halfway down he saw a man crouched behind a Dumpster. The man ignored the officers repeated orders to stand and put his hands up. The officer moved so that the Dumpster was between him and the citizen and again ordered him to stand up. This time the man started to rise and turn in a rapid manner. He got about three-quarters of the way around before the officer saw the rifle.

Fearing for his life, the officer fired four times. The man sat, dropped the rifle, and clutched his chest. The officer approached, kicked the rifle away, holstered his weapon, and handcuffed the suspect.

The suspect expired on his way to the hospital, suffering from a single gunshot wound to the upper chest. The slug had a recovered diameter of .79 inch and a recovered weight of 119 grains.

• • • • •

The convenience store owner carried a Glock Model 23 in a Greg Kramer IWB holster. His local gun shop had recommended Cor-Bon ammunition, so he purchased three boxes of 135-grain jacketed hollowpoints.

He had stopped by his store at 7 A.M. to pick up the overnight receipts and deposit them at a local bank. As he walked across the parking lot, he noticed two men in a dark van. As he approached them to get to his vehicle, a squad car pulled into the lot. He waved at the officers, got in his car, and drove off.

While standing at the 24-hour deposit slot, he heard another car pull up. He turned to see the same van that had been in his store's lot. He immediately stepped around a nearby corner of the bank and, dropping the deposit bag on the ground, he drew his pistol and crouched against the wall.

He was in this position when a young male subject turned the corner holding a short-barreled shotgun. Without hesitating, the store owner shoved his gun against the man's stomach and pulled the trigger. The man screamed, turned, and took four steps before falling on his face.

The gunman was conveyed to a local hospital, where he underwent emergency surgery. The slug was removed from the large intestine and had a recovered diameter of .71 inch and a recovered weight of 121 grains.

• • • • •

A veteran of the Vietnam War, he had been confined to a wheelchair since 1968. As a psychologist, he donated several hours a week counseling other veterans. He understood their anger and frustration, although he often was not as sympathetic as other psychologists who had not experienced the war.

Because he was a realist, he carried a compact Smith & Wesson .40-caliber auto loaded with Cor-Bon 135-grain jacketed hollowpoints. He had found that people often equated his condition with a willingness to be a victim for either insults or crime.

He had spent the evening at a veteran's center talking to several members. He wheeled himself to his car and was in the process of getting out of his chair when he heard taunts relating to his condition. Looking up, he saw several young men standing nearby. They came closer and began to alternate ridicule with demands for money. He told them to go find somebody who was impressed by such behavior. The response to this was for two of the young men to produce knives while another waved a piece of pipe in a threatening manner.

As they got closer, one of them jerked his chair away. When he asked them to return it they just laughed. When one of the group started to pull the vet from the car, he shot him. Another advanced on him with a knife, so he shot him too. The others turned and fled. He crawled into his car and, using the cellular phone, called for help. Responding officers found one thug alive and one dead.

The first man had a slug removed from his stomach that had a recovered diameter of .73 inch and a recovered weight of 114 grains. The second thug's slug was removed from his heart at the morgue. It had a recovered diameter of .79 inch and a recovered weight of 109 grains.

• • • • •

As a typical high school student, he enjoyed normal teenage pursuits like dating and waterskiing. In addition, he enjoined going shooting with his cop father. Of all the guns, he most enjoyed shooting his dad's service weapon, a Glock Model 22 .40 S&W. He was a responsible gun handler, and his father kept the weapon loaded on a high shelf in the living room.

It was Saturday morning, and the young man was engaged in the normal weekend routine of mowing the lawn and tending to the yard. He had finished the lawn and was turning his attention to weeding the flower bed when he heard a noise from inside the house. He ignored it at first, but then puzzled by it, he walked inside.

He stepped in the door and, hearing nothing, turned to go back out when he heard his mother's voice. He didn't understand what she was saying, but the tone was one of

desperation. Moving to the living room, he retrieved his dad's Glock. He advanced down the hallway, stood next to his parent's bedroom, and listened. Then he understood. She was begging not to be hurt.

Pushing the door open, he was shocked to see his mother naked and face down on the bed. A man he had never seen before was standing over her with his pants down around his ankles. Not hesitating, the young man shot him in the back. Pulling the rapist off his mother, he covered her with a blanket and called the police.

The rapist was conveyed to the hospital, where it was determined that the bullet had lodged in his spine, permanently paralyzing him. The recovered round had a diameter of .64 inch and weighed 87 grains.

• • • • •

The bank security guard was given the money to purchase a handgun but was allowed to select the weapon himself. He chose a Ruger P91 .40-caliber pistol. The director of security at the bank made it clear that he expected his security force to respond only under the most extreme of circumstances.

It was three days before Christmas and the bank was full of customers. Fifteen minutes before closing time, a fight broke out in the lobby. As the guard started to move toward the disturbance, one of the men involved produced a handgun and shot the other man.

Drawing his Ruger, he ordered the man to drop his weapon. Instead of complying, the shooter turned and fired three times at the guard. Two of those rounds struck him in the head, causing minor wounds. He brought his pistol up and fired four rounds, striking his attacker in the left chest. The man fell to the floor, and the guard sat in a chair and called for help.

Both men were brought to the hospital, where they were operated on. The felon had a Cor-Bon .40 S&W 135-grain jacketed hollow-point removed from his lung, where it had a recovered diameter of .59 inch and a recovered weight of 119 grains.

13

.357 SIG Ammo

The new .357 SIG cartridge is a joint effort between Federal Cartridge and Sigarms. Sigarms imports all SIG-Sauer auto pistols from Germany. It also assembles some SIG-Sauers domestically and produces many of the slides used on the pistols.

SIG-Sauer itself is a 1975 joint venture between the Swiss company Schweizerische Industrie Gesellschaft (SIG) and the German arms maker J.P. Sauer & Sohn (Sauer). This merger allowed SIG to get around strict Swiss laws against exporting arms. Pistols would be made in Germany, and now the United States, instead of Switzerland. As a side note, this same Sauer factory, located on the Baltic Sea, made torpedoes for German U-boats during World War II.

Federal Cartridge has been a partner in a number of new cartridges over the past 10 years. Some will remember the 9mm Federal Rimmed, which gave genuine 9mm ballistics to .38 Special revolvers. The use of a fully rimmed 9mm case was a solution to complex revolver extractor mechanisms while avoiding the need

for half-moon or full-moon clips. Charter Arms was among the first to chamber a revolver for the 9mm Federal Rimmed, but the cartridge did not become a commercial success.

The next joint venture was between Federal and the FBI. They downloaded the excessively recoiling 10mm to a level equalling the .45 Auto. The result was the incredibly influential 10mm Medium Velocity, which was adopted by the FBI.

The most recent collaboration has been with Smith & Wesson on its .356 TSW, yet another attempt to hot-rod the 9mm caliber. TSW means either Tactical Smith & Wesson or Team Smith & Wesson, depending on whom you talk to. Since the first pistols chambered for the .356 TSW were made only by Smith & Wesson's Performance Center and specifically for IPSC competition, Team Smith & Wesson is probably the correct term.

Handgunners have been trying to bump up the power of the 9mm for nearly as long as it has been a cartridge. In 1929, the .38 Super, aka the .38 Super Auto, was developed. This high-pressure version of the original .38 Auto (circa 1900) uses a 9x22.9mm case. The biggest differences between the .38 Super and .356 TSW are the Super's longer overall case length and semirimmed case design.

The .356 TSW is based on the European 9x21mm. This caliber was designed for use in countries that forbid their citizens to own handguns chambered in military calibers like the 9x19mm Luger. The 9x21mm caliber was a successful competition cartridge but not a popular defensive caliber.

The .356 TSW case is identical to the 9mm in all regards except case length. It has a tapered-wall 9x21.5mm cartridge case in comparison to the 9mm's tapered 9x19mm case. They have the same overall cartridge length to allow them both to be fired from 9mm pistols. This means the .356 TSW bullets must be deep seated, which in turn means both cases have identical powder capacities.

The .356 TSW is a high-pressure, high-velocity cartridge. The higher velocities of the .356 TSW are simply the result of high pressures, not more powder capacity. The whole purpose of the caliber is to push a .355-caliber bullet fast enough to achieve a "major" power factor designation in IPSC competition. (IPSC competition is divided into major and minor classes. During competition, center hits are scored equally. However, marginal hits earn more points for a major caliber shooter than for the same shot placement from a minor caliber.) Thus the .356 TSW was developed as a competition cartridge first and a defensive cartridge second.

These two IPSC bullet classes are based on their "power factor," which is really a simplified calculation for felt recoil or momentum. Momentum, or impulse, increases one to one with both bullet velocity and bullet weight. To calculate power factor, multiply the bullet weight in grains times the muzzle velocity in fps and divide by 1,000. To qualify for major, a load must have a power factor of 175 or above. This works out to an impulse of .778 lb-sec.

Recoil from the .356 TSW is beyond brisk. The Federal .356 TSW pushes a 147-grain FMJ bullet at 1,220 fps. That is fast enough to make it feel like the .45 Auto 230-grain bullet driven to 780 fps. For those handgunners who want their competition gun to double as a defensive piece, Federal now makes a 135-grain Hydra-Shok driven to 1,250 fps in .356 TSW. Additionally, Cor-Bon loads a 124-grain Gold Dot to 1,450 fps. Triton Cartridge produces both a 115-grain Sierra JHP and a 124-grain Hornady XTP for the .356 TSW caliber.

BIRTH OF THE .357 SIG

The .357 SIG is the first handgun or rifle cartridge to ever bear the name SIG. The Swiss have made a number of rifle cartridges, including the .41 Swiss Rimfire, but these all had the headstamp "Swiss" rather than "SIG." For its part, Sauer had a number of rifle cartridges with its headstamp before the company teamed up with SIG. These include the 6.5x48mm R Sauer, 8x58mm R Sauer, and 9.3x72mm R Sauer.

SIG is one of the oldest companies in Europe, having produced firearms well back into the black powder era. The Swiss have actually had a strong input into small arms development. One of the most historic was the full-metal jacket (FMJ) bullet pioneered by a Major Rubin. An officer and engineer in the Swiss Army, Rubin perfected a deep draw process for the copper cup used in a FMJ bullet. In the late 1800s, the world's armies found that smokeless powder could drive bullets faster than the lead bullets could be stabilized. Specifically, a lead bullet could only be driven so fast without stripping out in the rifling, which caused long-range accuracy problems. The French were the first to solve this problem by developing a solid bronze bullet. The Swiss were the second to solve it by developing a copper-jacketed lead core bullet. The rest is small arms history.

Sigarms approached Federal Cartridge on the .357 SIG project in June 1993, though the cartridge concept dates back to February of that year. Alan Newcomb, marketing director at Sigarms and formerly with Federal

ABOVE: The .357 SIG (left) is the result of a joint effort between Federal Cartridge and Sigarms to develop an auto pistol caliber that equals the .357 Magnum. It does.

ABOVE RIGHT: The .357 SIG (left) uses a bottleneck case to get maximum velocities from the 9mm bullet. Other attempts to hot rod the 9mm include the .356 TS&W (center) and the .38 Super Auto (right).

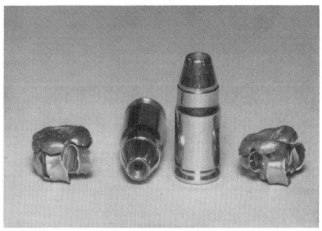

RIGHT: Both Federal and Sigarms wanted the .357 SIG 125-grain JHP to remain intact after impact. A softer but thicker jacket and a harder core resulted in a .59 caliber full mushroom..

Cartridge, had always been a bottleneck pistol cartridge enthusiast. Sigarms decided to use the case capacity of a bottleneck cartridge to get as close as possible to the ballistics of the legendary .357 Magnum when it was fired from a 2 1/2- or 4-inch revolver.

The official Sigarms goal for the .357 SIG was for it to achieve over 1,300 fps in muzzle velocity and over 500 ft-lbs. in muzzle energy. The hottest of the 9mm +P+ ammo gets over 1,300 fps but only generates 450 ft-lbs. The hottest of the .45 ACP +P ammo produces over 500 ft-lbs. of energy but has velocities well under 1,200 fps. The only other cartridge to exactly achieve the Sigarms goal for the .357 SIG is the .40 S&W, but only when loaded with 135-grain JHPs from Cor-Bon and Triton.

Sigarms also spent a good deal of time deciding on the name of the cartridge. The name .357 SIG was selected to emphasize the similarity of its cartridge to the .357 Magnum, even though the .357 SIG bullet measures .355 caliber.

The demand for such a cartridge originated in the auto pistol transition craze of the mid-1980s. At that time, most cops were armed with the potent .357 Magnum. For the record, with a weighted average one-shot stop ranking of 95 percent, based on 985 officer-involved or police-action shootings, the .357 Magnum 125-grain JHP has the best actual stopping power record of any handgun load. So by going to auto pistols, these cops gained a few more shots between reloads but gave up a lot in terms of stopping power. At the time, the top-ranked 9mm was the Winchester 115-grain Silvertip with an 83 percent effectiveness. In spite of the Silvertip's good street record, many cops instead were issued the Winchester 147-grain JHP with a 74 percent rating.

The 9mm clearly is ballistically inferior to the .357 Magnum. The highly effective 9mm +P+, pioneered by Federal Cartridge and the Illinois State Police, was available at the time, but police departments and pistol manufacturers alike were cautious of the load. It was only available to police departments that signed a liability waiver. Pistol makers were concerned about accelerated weapon wear.

Many felt that the 9mm +P+ was an attempt to make the 9mm something it was not. Unhappy with the ballistics of the 9mm, some cops turned to the .45 Auto. However, the best big-bore load for most of the 1980s was the CCI-Speer 200-grain JHP with an 88 percent one-shot stop record. That was better than the 9mm loads but not up to the success of the .357 Magnum.

The 10mm Medium Velocity and .40 S&W were tried next. The 10mm Medium Velocity in its best version was an 82 percent load. In its original 180-grain offering, the .40 S&W was also just 81 percent effective. Other .40

S&W loads were developed, like the 135- and 155-grain JHPs, and these loads *do* equal the street record of the .357 Magnum, but the lower performing 180-grain JHPs remain in wider use due to the erroneous subsonic, deep penetrator myth of stopping power.

With the release of the .357 SIG auto pistol, Sigarms and Federal have taken the handgunning world full circle back to the ballistics of the revolver-fired .357 Magnum. For the record, the .357 SIG fires a .355-inch bullet just like the .380 Auto, 9mm, and .38 Super. The .357 Magnum and .38 Special both fire a .357-inch jacketed bullet and a .358-inch lead bullet. Sigarms tried all of the available bullet weights in both .355 and .357 caliber before deciding upon the classic 125-grain bullet weight in .355.

The .357 Magnum level of velocity was targeted next. The goal was to gain as much velocity as possible while maintaining moderate levels of recoil. Federal did not want another stiff-kicking .356 TSW.

Federal and Sigarms pushed the .357 SIG chamber pressures past the .357 Magnum

The Federal .357 SIG 125-grain JHP penetrates 13.7 inches of gelatin and produces a street-tolerant stretch cavity. This works out to 88 percent one-shot stops.

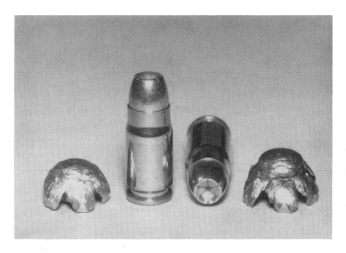

The CCI-Speer .357 SIG 125-grain Gold Dot has been adopted by the Delaware State Police, which wanted better performance against windshields than what the 9mm subsonic offered.

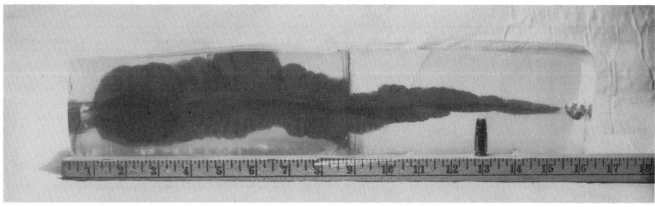

The CCI-Speer .357 SIG load uses the same basic 125-grain Gold Dot bullet as its .357 Magnum load. The result is a .68 caliber recovered bullet and this very long stretch cavity.

mark before they settled on a nominal velocity of 1,350 fps from a 3.8-inch Sigarms P229. This rivals the velocity and energy from a 2 1/2-inch .357 Magnum. The 2 1/2-inch .357 Magnum produced about 50 fps less than a 4-inch .357 Magnum. Compared to the 179 power factor for the .356 TSW, the .357 SIG works out to a power factor of 169.

A major difference exists in the way barrel lengths are measured between revolvers and auto pistols. The auto pistol barrel length is measured from the muzzle to the breech face, which houses the extractor. The P229 has a 3.8-inch barrel, which *includes* the .858-inch cartridge case. The revolver barrel length is measured from the muzzle to the entrance of the forcing cone at the front of the cylinder.

The S&W Model 19 has a 2.5-inch barrel, which *excludes* the 1.288-inch cartridge case. Except for a .008-inch cylinder to barrel gap, which bleeds off a little chamber pressure, in auto pistol terms, the 2.5-inch magnum revolver also as a 3.8-inch barrel.

THE .357 SIG BOTTLENECK DESIGN

The bottleneck pistol cartridge has a well-established precedent in the .30 Luger and .30 Mauser. As a historical perspective, the 9mm is a .30 Luger necked *up* to .355 caliber. Other bottleneck handgun cartridges include .22 Remington Jet, .256 Winchester Magnum, .32-20, .357 Bain & Davis, .38-40, .44-40, .38/.45, 9mm Action Express, and .357 Auto Mag.

Bottleneck pistol cartridges themselves are not new, but a commercially successful bottleneck pistol might be.

The .357 SIG is one of the most powerful bottleneck auto pistol cartridges ever designed. It has the highest chamber pressure of any popular police or defensive cartridge, with a maximum average pressure of 40,000 psi. This compares to 38,500 psi for the 9mm +P and 35,000 psi for the .357 Magnum, .40 S&W, .38 Super, and standard-pressure 9mm. The 9mm +P+ designation is not recognized by SAAMI. (The chamber pressure for the 9mm NATO cartridge is measured using a different test method, although the estimated chamber pressure under the SAAMI protocol is 42,000 to 43,000 psi.) The .45 Auto, .38 Special, .44 Special, and .45 Colt are very low-pressure rounds.

Sigarms and Federal put a lot of research and development into three specific areas: making the bottleneck cartridge case itself, selecting the right powder burn rates and charges, and keeping the high-velocity JHP bullet from flying apart on impact.

The .357 SIG case is not simply a .40 S&W case necked down to .355 caliber, nor is it based on a .40 S&W case that has been lengthened slightly to make up for the length reduction from the bottleneck operation. Instead, the .357 SIG uses a special case with a case wall designed for bottleneck cartridge manufacturing. In addition to having a slightly longer case blank than the .40 S&W before the bottleneck operation, the lower wall of the .357 SIG is stronger as well.

The .40 S&W has an overall cartridge length of .850 inch. The .357 SIG is slightly longer at .860 inch. Again, while the case head diameter, extractor groove, and primer pocket are identical between the .357 SIG and .40 S&W, the overall length, headspacing, and interior wall profile are *different*. Therefore, it is much more meaningful and correct to think of the .357 SIG as a bottlenecked, large-case-capacity 9mm than merely a necked down .40 S&W.

Quite unlike nearly all bottleneck cartridges, the .357 SIG headspaces off the case mouth and not the shoulder. According to Sigarms, the headspace is easier to control if it is based on overall length rather than midway up the shoulder. This is a problem for those who hand-form .357 SIG cases from .40 S&W cases, as these shorter cases will headspace on the shoulder rather than the case mouth. Consequently, accuracy will suffer and the case mouth rim in the chamber will be eroded more easily.

The bottleneck cartridge has different flame front characteristics than a tapered auto pistol case or a straight wall revolver case. As a result, the powder selection and load development were a bit trickier according to Federal. This was especially true since the .357 SIG cartridge operates at high pressures. It simply required a lot of up-front development.

With that work out of the way, loading and reloading the .357 SIG is almost the same as any other pistol cartridge. Like reloading all bottleneck cases, care must be taken not to collapse the shoulder. A lubricant is required. The overall length must be monitored closely and the cases trimmed to length if the .860-inch overall length is exceeded.

The bottleneck pistol cartridge has a number of technical advantages over the conventional tapered auto pistol case. The most significant is feed reliability. Simply put, with the .357 SIG it is easy to reliably feed a small .355-caliber bullet into a big .40-caliber hole. This is easier than both putting a .355-caliber bullet in a .355-caliber hole like the 9mm and feeding a .40-caliber bullet into a .40-caliber hole as the .40 S&W pistols do.

The second advantage of the bottleneck case is the enhanced ratio of the case capacity to the bore diameter. This allows more room for propellant and, as a result, improves the ability to get the velocity up.

(Because of its feed reliability and increased case capacity, all of the great semiauto and fully automatic military rifle cartridges have been of the bottleneck design. This includes everything from the .223 Remington to the .50 Browning.)

The use of bottleneck cartridges to boost

velocities is as old as smokeless gunpowder and as new as the wildcat 9x25mm Dillon. Around 1987, Eric Harvey and Randy Shelly of Dillon Precision necked down 10mm Auto brass to 9mm. The goal was to get as much slow-burning powder in the case as possible in yet another attempt to get a 9mm bullet travelling fast enough to qualify for the IPSC major category. The short-necked and steep-shouldered 9x25mm Dillon holds twice the powder of a .38 Super Auto case and pushes a 115-grain JHP to the incredible velocity of 1,650 fps.

The .357 SIG is somewhat similar to the little-known 9mm Action Express. The 9mm AE is based on a .41 Action Express case, which was necked down to 9mm. The Action Express case uses a rebated rim, while nearly all auto pistol cases except the .38 Super and .25 Auto use a technically more cycle-reliable rimless design. The .357 SIG actually has more design similarities to the 9x25mm Dillon than the 9mm Action Express.

It is only fair to also discuss the disadvantages of the bottleneck cartridge. As far as the shooter sees it, there are no disadvantages. For the ammo maker, the bottleneck case is a little harder to manufacture than a straight-wall revolver or tapered-wall auto pistol case. The initial propellant selection and the internal ballistics are trickier too. However, once these have been established, they do not remain on-going disadvantages.

THE .357 SIG BULLET

With the chamber pressures, muzzle velocity, and bullet weight finalized, it was up to Federal to develop the projectiles. The company selected a conventional jacketed hollowpoint and a full-metal-jacket flatpoint. For its part, Federal insisted that the 125-grain JHP used in the .357 SIG remain intact upon impact. This is quite unlike its dominating 125-grain JHP in .357 Magnum, which expands violently and then fragments to around 60 percent retained weight. But Sigarms agreed with this position, and both

companies decided that the bullet should have a high weight retention for best performance. Whether or not this is a correct approach is less significant than the fact that both companies insisted the bullet stay together when pushed hard.

The Federal version of the .357 SIG 125-grain JHP uses a thicker jacket with a special anneal to make it softer and less brittle. The bullet also uses a harder, higher antimony core compared to the 125-grain JHP used by Federal in its .357 Magnum load. The .357 SIG bullet expands to .59 inch in bare gelatin and does indeed have a 100 percent retained weight. This produces about the same estimated stopping power but a much smaller stretch cavity than the Cor-Bon .357 SIG 115-grain JHP. This Sierra JHP loaded by Cor-Bon has a recovered diameter similar to the Federal version. However, the Cor-Bon round shows fragmentation in gelatin like the revolver-fired .357 Magnum 125-grain JHPs always did.

The CCI-Speer 125-grain Gold Dot bullet and the CCI-Speer 124-grain Gold Dot bullet are very different in appearance. The 125-grain bullet, when measuring .357 inch, is used in its .357 Magnum ammo. It has a very shallow, cup-point type of hollowpoint cavity. But looks are deceiving. This load expands very well in gelatin, and the shallow cavity simply has no space for wood and clothing debris to plug up. As a result, it also expands very well after passing through these common barrier materials. With a copper-plated jacket that cannot separate from the bullet core, the Gold Dot is the very best bullet to use against auto glass and thermopane windows.

CCI-Speer uses this same basic .357 Magnum Gold Dot bullet in its .357 SIG load. This makes sense. Both cartridges are in the same 1,350 fps muzzle velocity bracket. The .357 SIG Gold Dot, however, has a .355-inch bullet diameter.

CCI-Speer also developed a 124-grain, .355-inch diameter Gold Dot for its 9mm and 9mm +P cartridges. This Gold Dot has a much deeper hollowpoint cavity. It was designed to expand reliably at the 9mm velocities of 1,150

Cor-Bon uses the same 115-grain Sierra JHP in its .357 SIG ammo as it does in its top-rated 9mm +P ammo. Fragmentation in gelatin is a good thing.

The Cor-Bon .357 SIG 115-grain Sierra JHP at 1,450 fps produces 12.5 inches of penetration and the largest stretch cavity of any hollowpoint in this caliber.

to 1,250 fps. The 124-grain Gold Dot has a lower threshold of expansion than its 125-grain counterpart. Cor-Bon selected this faster expanding bullet for one of its .357 SIG loads.

When both of these 124- and 125-grain Gold Dot bullets are loaded to the same velocities and energies, they achieve the exact same one-shot stop rating. Both penetrate 16.5 inches of calibrated 10-percent gelatin. Both produce roughly the same size stretch cavity. The .357 Magnum-based 125-grain version expanded to .68 caliber from the .357 SIG and exhibited only a slight amount of bullet breakup. The 9mm-

based 124-grain version expanded and then fragmented back to a recovered diameter of .60 caliber. Actually, both bullets had a 100-percent weight retention. The broken-up 124-grain bullet was literally held together by the copper-plated jacket. This is something a conventional copper jacket would never do.

Both the 124- and 125-grain Gold Dot bullets work very well when fired from the .357 SIG. Of the two, however, the 124-grain version seems more likely to fully expand under a wider range of defensive scenarios. It wanted to fragment, but the jacket wouldn't let

Cor-Bon selected the 124-grain Gold Dot bullet for one of its .357 SIG loads. This is the same bullet used by CCI-Speer in its 9mm +P ammo.

The MagSafe .357 SIG 64-grain Defender fragments on impact and saturates 11 inches of the target with number 3 birdshot. This will produce a 92 percent one-shot stop.

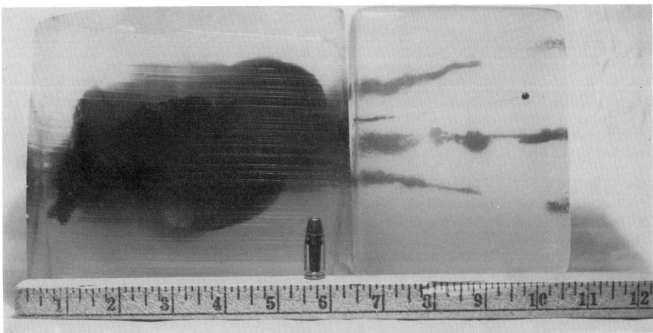

it. It is this willingness to fragment that gives this particular bullet expansion reliability in a variety of street scenarios.

(Cor-Bon has always favored bullets that expand violently and even fragment after expansion. Bullets that expand and fragment in gelatin will at least expand in combinations of soft and hard living tissue. A hollowpoint that may fragment in gelatin will be effective under the widest variety of shooting scenarios. This bullet selection philosophy explains why Cor-Bon ammo leads the actual stopping power results in .380 Auto, .38 Special, 9mm, .40 S&W, and 10mm.)

MagSafe uses the same 64-grain frangible bullet for both its 9mm Stealth +P and .357 SIG Defender loads. This projectile uses nine pieces of number 3 birdshot. MagSafe started off driving its .357 SIG load to 2,230 fps, but it has recently backed the pressure down to 2,150 fps. We fired both versions, and no difference in wound ballistics exists.

The MagSafe 64-grain Defender fragments on impact. The nine large pellets penetrate between 10.5 and 12 inches of gelatin. This formed the largest stretch cavity of the eight .357 SIG loads tested. The Defender also produced the highest stopping power prediction at 92 percent one-shot stops.

Hornady uses 124- and 147-grain XTP hollowpoints for the .357 SIG in its Hornady Custom line of ammo. It also sells these XTP bullets as reloading components to large loading outfits and individual handloaders alike. These are the same XTP bullets used in its 9mm ammo.

Hornady was the first to design a line of bullets specifically to pass the FBI's eight-barrier test protocol. The company's approach was to actually suppress hollowpoint expansion and totally eliminate fragmentation. As a result of designing a late-energy release load, the actual and estimated stopping power from most XTP bullets has been lower than many other premium or even standard hollowpoints. Hornady has tweaked the XTP for a little more expansion and a little less penetration, but as a rule, these are still the least expanding hollowpoints available.

The .357 SIG solves that completely. This powerful new caliber pushes both the 124- and 147-grain well beyond their minimum expansion velocities. The .357 SIG 124-grain XTP expands reliably and has a controlled penetration of 14.5 inches. The wound ballistics calculate to a very impressive 87 percent one-shot stop. This is comparable to the best from Federal, CCI-Speer, and Cor-Bon. The .357 SIG 147-grain XTP is close behind with an 84 percent rating. Instead of penetrating in excess of 18 inches of gelatin as the 9mms do, the .357 SIG version stops in 16.2 inches. That is a noted improvement.

The .357 SIG is the best caliber to use if 147-grain bullets are required. The concept is simple. Whatever the hollowpoint design, the bullets must be driven fast enough to expand. The 9mm velocities do not reliably achieve expansion for the 147-grain XTP, but the .357 SIG velocities do.

As we go to press, Remington is rumored to be developing a .357 SIG Golden Saber weighing from 125 grains to as heavy as 147 grains. The .357 SIG does have the velocity potential to make the 147-grain JHPs perform. It is also reasonable to expect the smaller ammo companies like Black Hills and Master

Cartridge/Georgia Arms to offer some sort of .357 SIG loading as soon as cartridge cases become more readily available.

.357 SIG RECOIL

Given pistols of the same weight, action, and ergonomics, the felt recoil of the .357 SIG 125-grain JHP is less than either the .40 S&W 155- or 180-grain loads but more than the 9mm 115- and 124-grain +P+ and 147-grain loads.

It is not valid to compare the calculated impulse of the .357 SIG to the revolver-fired .357 Magnum. However, in subjective terms of perceived recoil, the .357 SIG from a P229 is far more controllable than either a 2 1/2- or 4-inch medium-frame .357 Magnum. Actually, there is no comparison. The .357 SIG is significantly easier to get follow-up hits with than the .357 Magnum. Only when the .357 Magnum was fired from the 4-inch S&W 686 and Ruger GP-100 were the shot-to-shot times even close when all the shots had to stay inside the B-27 8-ring from 10 yards.

Many .357 Magnum handgunners use one of the two 125-grain medium-velocity JHPs in their snubbies to improve the revolver's controllability. The 125-grain Remington .357 Magnum Medium Velocity JHP and 125-grain Golden Saber produce 83 percent one-shot stops. All of the .357 SIG hollowpoints are better stoppers than these medium-velocity .357 Magnum loads.

.357 SIG STREET PERFORMANCE

The actual and estimated street results show the .357 SIG to be more effective than the 9mm and comparable to the 9mm +P+ and more effective than most 180-grain .40 S&W loads. However, the .357 SIG does not produce higher one-shot stops than the 135-, 165- (full power), and 155-grain .40 S&W loads.

Some shootists have bluntly asked why they need a .357 SIG when they can simply go to lighter weight, higher energy bullets in the .40 S&W. The answer—and the whole logic behind the .357 SIG caliber—is that not everyone has a choice to switch to the higher velocity .40 S&W loads or would not do so even if they had the choice. The 180-grain JHP is considered by many to be *the* .40 S&W load. It was the original load, and it is the one preferred by deeper-is-better subsonic advocates. Bullets lighter than 180 grains are simply not politically correct in the .40 S&W, and it is a fact that politics plays a much greater role in bullet selection than does wound ballistics. Therefore, many law enforcement agencies have improved upon the stopping power of the politically correct 9mm 147-grain JHP by switching pistols, holsters, and spare magazines to fire the equally politically correct .40 S&W 180-grain JHP.

Many cops have found that the expense of changing entire calibers is easier to sell to some police brass than simply changing the bullet weight away from 147 grains. Any of the 115- and 124-grain 9mm bullets would give a similar stopping power increase as the change to the .40 S&W 180-grain JHP. In fact, the 9mm +P+ versions of these weights generally outperform all the .40 S&W 180-grain JHPs.

The new .357 SIG cartridge avoids the politics of a bullet weight change. It also avoids the apprehension surrounding the use of +P or +P+ ammo. (Sigarms is among the pistol makers that are reluctant to endorse the use of 9mm +P+ ammo.) The .357 SIG falls neatly into the wrong but popular mind-set that it is the caliber that determines stopping power instead of proper bullet selection within the caliber.

Put another way, the .357 SIG in its original loading of 125 grains is a better stopper than the .40 S&W in its traditional loading of 180 grains. It is *not* a better stopper than the .40 S&W loads that broke tradition like the 155-grain Silvertip, 155-grain Hydra-Shok, 135-grain Cor-Bon, and 165-grain Golden Saber.

CONCLUSION

As an overall conclusion, with the correct bullet selection, the .357 SIG does indeed produce .357 Magnum ballistics from a compact, high-capacity auto pistol. However, a few 9mm +P+ loads, some .38 Super loads, and many .40 S&W loads already rivaled the mighty .357 Magnum.

Perhaps the greatest significance of the .357 SIG caliber is its role in greatly improving upon the wound ballistics, tactical penetration, and cycle reliability of the politically correct 9mm 147-grain JHP and offering a better alternative to many .40 S&W 180-grain JHPs.

The first two major (100-man) police departments to adopt the .357 SIG as their duty caliber were the LaPorte County, Indiana, Sheriff's Department, followed by the Porter County, Indiana, Sheriff's Police. LaPorte County firearms instructors wanted something better than the 9mm 147-grain subsonic JHP they were carrying. They didn't even consider the .40 S&W. Specifically, LCSD officers wanted the stopping power and the 50-yard accuracy of the .357 Magnum they used to carry. The department now issues the Federal .357 SIG 125-grain JHP. Porter County kept the .357 Magnum revolver as its duty weapon until an auto pistol cartridge with .357 Magnum ballistics was developed.

Recently, the Delaware State Police became the first state police or highway patrol to adopt the potent .357 SIG. The DSP had been using the 9mm auto pistol with the 147-grain subsonic JHP, but its troopers wanted a load with better cycle reliability than the 9mm subsonic, while DSP SWAT team members wanted something that was able to defeat car windshields. Energy is the ability to do work, like defeating car bodies and glass, and the .357 SIG has 80 percent more energy than the 147-grain subsonic. Consequently, the DSP has selected the CCI-Speer .357 SIG 125-grain Gold Dot as its duty load. It joins a growing list of police departments, including San Francisco, California, Police and the Marion County, Indiana, Sheriff, that have abandoned the feeble 147-grain subsonic.

As this book is being finalized in late 1995, the only firearms manufacturer to offer the .357 SIG is Sigarms in its excellent P229. However, the industry is buzzing with talk of .357 SIG retrofit barrels for Glocks, Smith & Wessons, and Berettas. Bar-Sto Precision and Bill Jarvis Gunsmithing are two such sources. Sigarms also indicated that it will offer .357 SIG barrels for P229s chambered in .40 S&W in 1996. As more police agencies recognize the merits of the .357 SIG and admit to the failure of the 9mm subsonic, the pressure will be on Glock, Smith & Wesson, Ruger, Beretta, Heckler & Koch, and others to chamber auto pistols for this potent newcomer. The .357 SIG is here to stay.

TABLE 13-1
.357 SIG EXTERIOR BALLISTICS

CALIBER	MAKE	WEIGHT & STYLE	VELOCITY FPS	ENERGY FT-LBS.
.357 SIG	MagSafe	64-gr. Defender	2,230	707
.357 SIG	Cor-Bon	115-gr. Sierra JHP	1,450	537
.357 SIG	Federal	125-gr. JHP	1,352	507
.357 SIG	Hornady	124-gr. XTP	1,350	502
.357 SIG	CCI-Speer	125-gr. Gold Dot	1,398	543
.357 SIG	Cor-Bon	124-gr. Bonded HP	1,400	540
.357 SIG	Hornady	147-gr. XTP	1,190	460
.357 SIG	Federal	125-gr. FMJ	1,352	507

TABLE 13-2
.357 SIG WOUND BALLISTICS

CALIBER	MAKE	WEIGHT & STYLE	PENE-TRATION INCHES	EXPAN-SION INCHES	CRUSH CAVITY CU. IN.	STRETCH CAVITY CU. IN.	ONE-SHOT STOP %
.357 SIG	MagSafe	64-gr. Defender	11.3	frag	frag	69.5	92 est.
.357 SIG	Cor-Bon	115-gr. Sierra JHP	12.5	.58 (f)	3.3	58.6	89 est.
.357 SIG	Federal	125-gr. JHP	13.7	.59	3.7	43.4	88 est.
.357 SIG	Hornady	124-gr. XTP	14.5	.55 (f)	3.4	42.5	87 est.
.357 SIG	CCI-Speer	125-gr. Gold Dot	16.5	.68	6.0	51.7	86 est.
.357 SIG	Cor-Bon	124-gr. Bonded HP	16.5	.60	4.7	48.1	86 est.
.357 SIG	Hornady	147-gr. XTP	16.2	.58	4.3	33.7	84 est
.357 SIG	Federal	125-gr. FMJ	32.0	.36	1.8	12.8	59 est.

14
Pocket Pistol Calibers and Street Results

We have included results of shootings in .22 LR and .25 ACP due to incessant requests from readers. Neither author recommends that either caliber be selected for defensive purposes. While some loads in these calibers work significantly better than others, they are not reliable stoppers and should be avoided.

The .22 LR and .22 ACP are often chosen because of cost, size, and recoil concerns. While these are legitimate concerns, they should not take precedent over stopping power. A surprisingly high percentage of these "mouse guns" are kept in bedside drawers or elsewhere in the home, so concerns about concealment are not valid. Additionally, .380

and .38 Special produce modestly more recoil but with significant stopping-power increases and are available in the same basic price range.

.22 LONG RIFLE

The .22 Long Rifle is a surprisingly popular caliber for self-defense. Unfortunately, it is a dismal performer, and neither of the authors can recommend it for such purposes. Case studies will not be provided for either this caliber or the .25 ACP because the authors do not want to encourage their use. It would be too easy for some readers to rationalize that, because it worked in certain instances, it will work for them. The latest results are listed in Table 14-1.

TABLE 14-1
.22 LONG RIFLE ACTUAL RESULTS

LOAD	TOTAL	STOPS	PERCENTAGE
1. CCI Stinger	395	134	34
2. Fed HP	612	184	30
3. Win HP	567	164	29
4. Rem HP	879	237	27
5. Win RNL	1,469	308	21

.25 ACP

Like the .22 Long Rifle, this caliber is a dismal stopper and should be avoided at all costs by those interested in protecting life and limb. There are a variety of "expanding bullet" offerings in this caliber, but they apparently offer little if any performance advantage over the full-metal-jacket versions. They are best avoided given the poor quality of most pistols chambered in this caliber. The results are listed in Table 14-2.

.32 ACP

The authors original intent was to neither recommend the .32 ACP nor include case studies for it, but a surprisingly high number of shootings involving this caliber were reported where the Winchester Silvertip hollowpoint worked rather well. While neither author would rely on this caliber for primary self-defense usage, Evan Marshall has a Seecamp .32 Auto that he routinely puts in a Kramer pocket holster as a backup to his Karl Sokol customized Browning Hi-Power. The latest results are shown in Table 14-3.

• • • • •

A West Virginia coal miner, he lived for those days when he could grab his fishing gear and head for his favorite spot. After he had been bitten by a poisonous snake years before, he had taken to carrying a Walther PP .32 ACP that he had liberated during the Korean War. The only ammunition available at a local gun shop had been Silvertip hollowpoints, so he purchased a box, loaded his pistol, and carried it for several years without incident.

He got up at 5 A.M. and drove to a local 24-hour gas station to get some pop and snacks for the day's fishing. As he pulled up, he noticed that the young female clerk who worked the midnight to 8 A.M. shift was not behind the counter.

He entered the store, quickly gathered up his purchases, and walked to the counter. After standing there for a couple of minutes, he began to wonder where she might be when he heard a noise from the stockroom. He started to walk that way prepared to kid her about goofing off when he heard a scream.

Ignoring his purchases, he quickly exited

TABLE 14-2
.25 ACP ACTUAL RESULTS

LOAD	TOTAL	STOPS	PERCENTAGE
1. Win Expand Point	119	30	25
2. Win FMJ	2,406	553	23
3. Fed FMJ	1,864	410	22
4. Rem FMJ	1,977	435	22

TABLE 14-3
.32 ACP ACTUAL RESULTS

LOAD	TOTAL	STOPS	PERCENTAGE
1. W-W ST	83	52	63
2. W-W FMJ	123	62	50

the store, picked up one of the pay phones outside, and dialed 911. He gave the information to the police and was prepared to stand by for their arrival when he heard an even louder scream. Running to his truck, he removed his pistol and verified that it was loaded. He entered the store, hurried to the stockroom, and slowly pushed the door open. He was horrified to see the young clerk naked on the floor. She was being held down by one young male while another raped her.

His horror quickly turned to anger and, bringing the gun to eye level, he shot both perpetrators. As the rapist rolled onto his back, he noticed that the other hand held a knife, so he shot him four more times. Hearing the sirens of approaching police units, he threw his pistol into a corner and walked out to notify the responding officers that the paramedics were needed.

The rapist expired on the way to the hospital, while his partner survived a single gun shot wound that had collapsed his lung. The average recovered weight of the six slugs was 51 grains, with an average recovered diameter of .375 inch.

• • • • •

He was a graduate student at one of this

The CCI .22 Long Rifle Stinger starts out as lead wire. A massive hollowpoint cavity and a small hollow base are swaged next. Finally, the cavity walls are formed into the bullet profile.

Neither the .22 Long Rifle 37-grain LHP (left) nor the 40-grain RNL (right) expands when fired from handguns.

The CCI .22 Long Rifle 32-grain Stinger does not expand when fired from handguns. It does, however, produce the most one-shot stops in the caliber at 34 percent.

The Remington .25 Auto 50-grain FMJ has the worst wound ballistics of any recorded cartridge. This load produces just 22 percent one-shot stops.

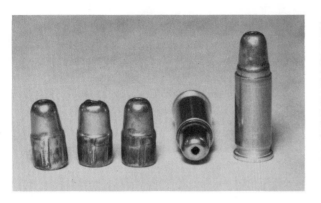

The CCI .25 Auto 45-grain PHP does not expand in gelatin or tissue. It produces just 25 percent one-shot stops.

The Winchester .25 Auto 45-grain Expanding Point expands slightly in gelatin. The steel number 4 birdshot assists feeding but not expansion.

countries most prestigious universities who had grown up in the inner city, the son of an African-American store owner. Unlike his liberal and politically correct colleagues, he had no illusions about the innate cruelty of some people, seeing two of his brothers murdered while involved in the narcotics trade.

Before leaving for school, his uncle had requested that he stop by because he had a gift for him. This particular uncle was a big city homicide lieutenant, and the gift was a Seecamp .32 Auto in an ankle holster. His uncle's only advice was to try not to outsmart himself and to always wear the gun. The student found that the gun's small size and light weight made it easy to carry. He also found its presence reassuring when walking back to his dorm after late-night study sessions in the graduate library.

Four years of graduate school went by without incident until two weeks before he was to receive his Ph.D. in Economics. He had successfully completed his dissertation and had received his first bound copy of it. Hurrying across campus to show it to a friend, he was too absorbed to notice his surroundings. When he realized he was not alone, he looked to see two young white males dressed in the garb of a local street gang.

"Well," one remarked, "Look what we have here. Another educated nigger." The other gang member made a similar remark.

The graduate student looked around and realized that his options were extremely limited. He tried to talk his way out of it, but gave that up when both of his assailants produced homemade clubs. Remembering the Seecamp, he went to one knee and produced it quickly. He ordered them to go away, but they just laughed and made comments that there was probably a correlation between the size of his male organ and his pistol. One took a step forward, and the student did what any reasonable person would do—he pointed the pistol at the attacker's center of mass and pulled the trigger. The round struck the gang member 2 inches above the heart, piercing a major blood vessel. The young man took three steps before collapsing. His partner turned and escaped.

After extensive surgery, the thug recovered to stand trail for felonious assault and was convicted and given probation. The student missed his graduation, as he was sentenced to six months in prison for possession of an unregistered handgun! The recovered slug weighed 48 grains and had a diameter of .36 caliber.

• • • • •

The pharmacist was not a happy man. He was a recent graduate from pharmacy school and the newest member of the staff at a chain drugstore. When the store decided to offer 24-hour prescription service, he was assigned the midnight shift. His wife was two months pregnant in a new town several thousand miles from family. She was distinctly uncomfortable with her circumstances and made her concerns known on a daily basis.

Having left the military shortly after participating in the invasion of Panama, he had seen more than his share of action. Based on those experiences and an increasing drug problem in his new community, he decided that a little personal security was in order. He left a loaded S&W .357 Magnum revolver on the bed stand next to his wife to make her feel safer, while he carried a Colt .32 Auto that his dad had packed from Normandy to Germany during World War II. He felt reasonably comfortable with the Silvertip hollowpoints it was loaded with. Its flat shape concealed well under his pharmacist's smock.

It was almost 3 A.M. when the woman entered with a prescription for a controlled substance. It had all the appearances of being altered, so he called 911. Attempting to stall the woman until police arrived, he offered several excuses as to why it was taking so long to prepare. The woman suddenly shouted an obscenity and started to climb over the counter. When he attempted to shove her back, she shot him in the chest with a previously unnoticed .22 revolver. Pulling up his smock, he produced the Colt and fired five rounds. She collapsed next to the cash register just as the pharmacist suddenly felt short of breath and slumped to the floor. Paramedics conveyed both to a local hospital, where the woman expired in emergency surgery from a gunshot wound to the heart while the pharmacist survived after a lengthy recovery. He was still in the hospital when his wife delivered a healthy 7 lb. 8 oz. girl.

Today the pharmacist works at the same location, but his smock conceals a Second Chance vest and a Glock Model 23 in a Mitchell Rosen holster. The recovered slug weighed 49 grains and had a diameter of .334 inch.

• • • • •

The big city cop had been assigned to the Felony Response Team for years. Having a talent for going in harm's way on a regular basis, members of this unit carried bigger handguns than the issue .38 Special. Additionally, virtually every member carried at least two handguns and one shotgun.

The subject of this incident relied on a S&W Model 57 .41 Magnum with a 6-inch barrel as his duty piece. His backup gun was a Walther PPK in .32 ACP that he had purchased from an inner city store owner who wanted something bigger. The cop, of course, thought that its small size and flat profile made it an excellent second gun. He had carried it for almost 11 years loaded with full-metal-jacketed ammunition before the Silvertip arrived upon the scene.

It had been one of those days that cops assigned to such units hated. Absolutely nothing was going, and even a significant amount of money spread among informants had not produced anything worthwhile. He and the rest of his four-man crew had decided to stop for lunch at the usual place. In spite of their plainclothes attire, it was obvious that they were cops. As they sat down at the lunch counter, they placed their hand-held radios nearby and divided their attention between the menu and the constant stream of communication.

They had no sooner placed their lunch order when the radio erupted with the call all cops dread: "Two officers shot!" Realizing the location was almost directly behind the restaurant, two crew members ran to the car to grab shotguns while the other two ran through the kitchen and out the back door.

As the first two officers arrived at the location, they found two uniformed officers lying face down on the floor with their hands cuffed behind their backs. Both had been executed by gunshots to the back of the head. Informing responding officers that both officers were DAS (dead at scene), they grabbed a citizen and demanded to know what had happened. The citizen responded that he

The Winchester .22 Long Rifle 37-grain LHP tumbles on impact and is recovered base forward. This is a 29 percent load.

had seen two men run out of the room where the officers were found and had escaped down into the basement.

After instructing their partners to cover the basement windows from outside, both officers entered the basement with guns drawn. They had no sooner started to make their way through the basement when one officer was grabbed by the two cop killers. They placed their guns to his head and instructed the second officer to drop his .41 Magnum. Hesitating a second, the hostage officer told him, "Go ahead, Pete, drop the gun." His partner had remembered the tactics they had rehearsed so many times. By calling him by his middle name, which he never used, his partner had let him know that compliance was the last thing on his mind.

Simultaneous with dropping his .41 Magnum, his partner went limp and fell to the floor. Before the bad guys could respond, both officers pulled their weapons. The officer who moments before had been a hostage opened fire with a .357 Magnum while the second officer produced his .32 Auto and fired twice. One cop killer took a .357 125-grain jacketed hollowpoint

just above the right ear, killing him. The other took a Silvertip through the heart. He quickly slumped to the floor, where he expired prior to the arrival of the paramedics.

The Silvertip slug weighed 48 grains when recovered at the morgue and had a diameter of .407 caliber.

• • • • •

His newsstand had occupied the same corner in the big city for 40 years. It had provided him with a steady, if modest, income. He had a number of regular customers who remembered him on his birthday and holidays. Fortunately, this urban center was one with a moderate climate, so he avoided the harsh winters of his northern counterparts.

Having been robbed and beaten severely a year earlier, he had "obtained" a Colt .32 Auto. Gun laws in his town made it almost impossible for him to legally own a pistol, so he had bought it off a local pimp for $200. It came loaded with Winchester Silvertips. He stuck it in the back of his cash box and forgot about it.

It was a lovely spring day, and he had just removed his sweater when he was confronted by a young man obviously strung out of drugs. The junkie quickly produced a butcher knife and demanded money. The stand owner had decided to comply, when the robber grabbed a framed picture of his mother and smashed it on the ground.

Angered by this senseless display of violence, the man reached in the cash box and produced the pistol. He pointed it at the robber and pulled the trigger without result. As his assailant came around the side of the stand and entered the doorway, he was able to chamber a round and shove the gun against the left side of the robber and pull the trigger again. This time the weapon discharged. The Silvertip slug entered just under the nipple and traversed the chest cavity, exiting out the right side. The robber stabbed the newsstand owner once in the neck before collapsing. Both were rushed to a local hospital, where they eventually recovered from their wounds. The slug was never recovered.

.380 ACP

The .380 is another of those marginal calibers that individuals should carry with considerable caution. While the better loads offer significant advantages over the traditional full-metal-jacket rounds, they do not turn the .380 into a major caliber. Carriers of .380 pistols need to understand this and not fall into the trap of thinking that the mere display of a handgun will cause hostilities to cease.

The best load in this caliber is the Cor-Bon 90-grain jacketed hollowpoint. The results are listed in Table 14-4.

• • • • •

The traveling salesman's route included both urban and rural customers. His company vehicle was a van marked with the name of the major electronics firm he represented. It had been broken into twice, but his employer declined his suggestion to repaint it and remove all clues as to its contents.

Concerned about the national increase in carjackings, he had purchased an AMT .380 Auto and loaded it with Cor-Bon 90-grain jacketed hollowpoints. He carried it in a briefcase that he placed between the bucket seats in his van.

It was a stormy Friday night and he was on the way home along a stretch of rural road when he saw a car pulled over with its hood up. A woman stood next to it and began to wave anxiously when he approached. He pulled over and started to exit his van when something told him to grab the pistol and place it in his overcoat pocket. That action was to save his life.

TABLE 14-4
.380 ACP ACTUAL RESULTS

LOAD	TOTAL	STOPS	PERCENTAGE
1. Cor-Bon JHP	20	14	70
2. Fed JHP	109	75	69
3. Fed HS	58	40	69
4. Win ST	82	50	61
5. Rem JHP	51	29	57
6. CCI JHP	57	33	58
7. Hornady JHP	26	14	54
8. Fed FMJ	131	67	51

The .22 Magnum rimfires do expand in gelatin. The Winchester 40-grain JHP (left) expanded to .32 inch, while the CCI 30-grain Maxi-Mag+V (right) reached .34 inch.

The Winchester .22 Magnum 40-grain JHP produces adequate penetration and achieves a 42 percent one-shot stop rating.

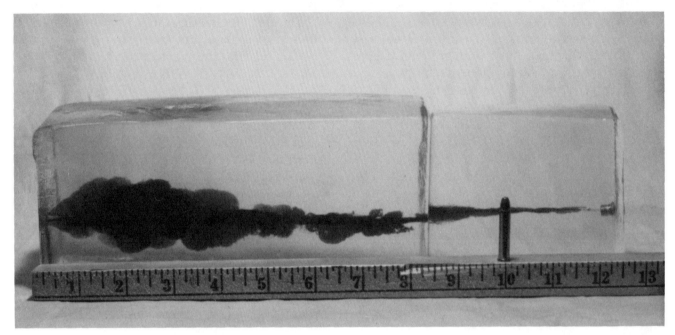

The woman asked him to look under the hood to see if he could tell what was wrong. As he did so, he was suddenly struck across the head. He laid unconscious for a short period before he heard a woman and man talking. The man said, "Get his wallet and car keys and we'll kill him and drag the body into the trees."

He was able to remove his pistol without being noticed. After brushing the blood out of his eyes, he shot both his assailants. He then dragged himself to his van and made it behind the steering wheel, where he passed out. When he awoke, the sun was starting to rise. Looking in the rearview mirror, he noticed the man and woman lying near the front of their

car. He grabbed his cellular phone and called the state police. Responding officers found both robbers dead. The man had been shot once in the eye, while the woman had been shot in the left breast. The recovered slugs had an average weight of 72 grains and a recovered diameter of .47 caliber.

The salesman suffered permanent brain damage and today works at company headquarters as a supervisor.

• • • • •

An undercover agent recently assigned to narcotics enforcement, he had taken a quick

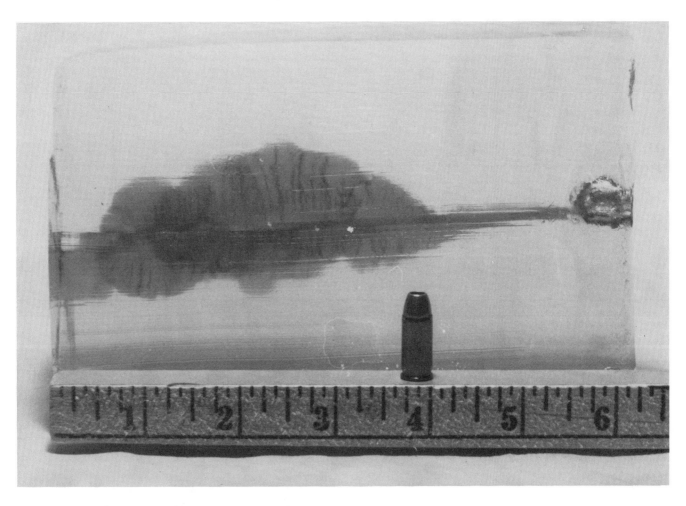

The Winchester .32 Auto 60-grain Silvertip only penetrates 6.5 inches of gelatin but produces 63 percent one-shot stops.

The Winchester .32 Auto 60-grain Silvertip uses a pure aluminum, nonserrated jacket. It expands to .57 caliber.

look at what the other guys and gals were carrying and bought a Walther PPK in .380. Small, light, and compact, he thought it ideal for his duties. He was tragically wrong.

It was his first case, and he accompanied several veteran agents to a briefing prior to a raid. As they walked to their vehicles, he was reminded to stay in the background and observe. They drove to the scene and the rookie agent quickly put on his body armor and took up a position behind a tree at the rear of the drug house.

After he heard entry being made, he drew his .380 Auto and brought it to eye level.

ABOVE: The Hornady 90-grain XTP is one of the few .380 Auto bullets to penetrate 12 inches. It has a 54 percent rating.

RIGHT: The Winchester 85-grain Silvertip is one of the only .380 Auto bullets to expand beyond .60 caliber. It produces 61 percent one-shot stops.

The Federal .380 Auto 90-grain Hydra-Shok expands to .58 caliber and gives 69 percent one-shot stops.

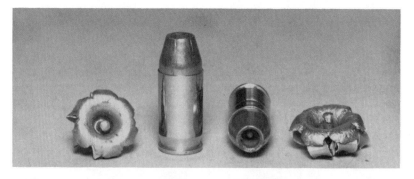

The .25 Auto Glaser 36-grain Safety Slug (left) and the MagSafe 29-grain Defender (right) are the top loads for this caliber with 33 and 41 percent one-shot stops, respectively.

LEFT: The .32 Auto MagSafe 50-grain Defender expands to .56 caliber and releases nine pellets that form separate crush cavities.

BELOW: The Federal .380 Auto 90-grain Hydra-Shok achieves an optimum balance between expansion and penetration.

Moments later he heard gunfire and saw three men armed with long guns exit the rear of the premises. Leaving his position of cover, he identified himself and ordered the men to drop their weapons. Their only response was to open fire at him. He returned fire, wounding one of the assailants. The other two quickly surrendered. Turning his back on the downed suspect, he had almost reached the other two when he was fatally shot from behind. Responding agents shot the agent's murderer. The .380 slug recovered from the drug dealer's left lung weighed 72 grains and had a diameter of .401 inch.

• • • • •

The grandfatherly older man with full head of white hair was known by all his neighbors as the kindest man in the area. Quick to help with any task, he had earned the love and respect of all.

He had never mentioned to his neighbors that he had spent 25 years as a big city cop, most of it as a SWAT team leader. He felt it wasn't really anybody's business, and besides, who wanted to listen to boring cop stories from an old fart. He would much sooner talk about his grandchildren or his fruit trees.

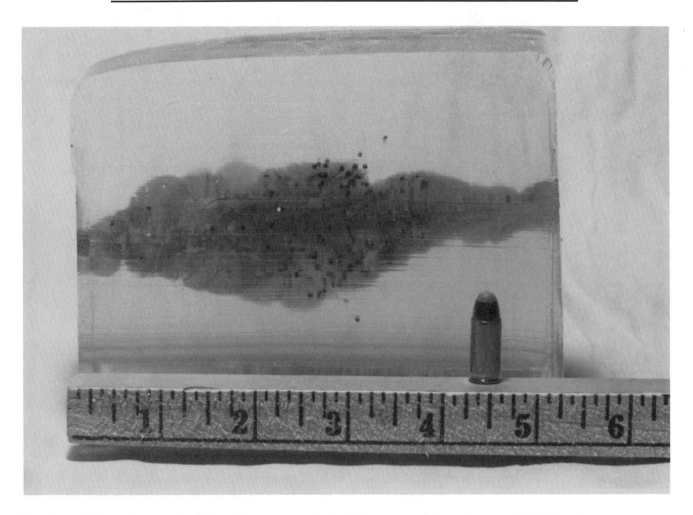

The Glaser .32 Auto 50-grain Blue Safety Slug saturates the first 5 inches of gelatin with number 12 birdshot.

He had not, however, lost the eye for detail that had kept him alive during his police career. In addition, he felt it was prudent to carry a little extra insurance—a Walther PPK .380 Auto in a Milt Sparks Summer Special holster. His expanding waistline concealed the small pistol nicely, and it felt comforting there.

Walking through the neighborhood on a mild fall evening, he noticed with satisfaction how well Mrs. Johnson's new fruit trees were doing. He had encouraged her to plant them and then helped to water, prune, and tend them. She had been hesitant at first but had gradually begun to share his enthusiasm.

He decided to stop by and commend her for her efforts when he heard breaking glass at the rear of her house. Walking to the rear, he observed the hips and legs of a large male crawling through her rear window. He walked back across the street, knocked on the Simmons' front door, and asked Mr. Simmons to call the police and inform them that there was a breaking and entering in progress at the Johnson house.

He had decided to stand by for responding officers when he heard Mrs. Johnson call for help. He told Mr. Simmons to inform responding officers that there was a retired officer at the scene. Then he produced his .380 Auto and ran across the street. Finding the Johnson's door locked, he put his size 14 foot to it and forced it open. He checked the downstairs and found nothing, then started upstairs when he heard another scream.

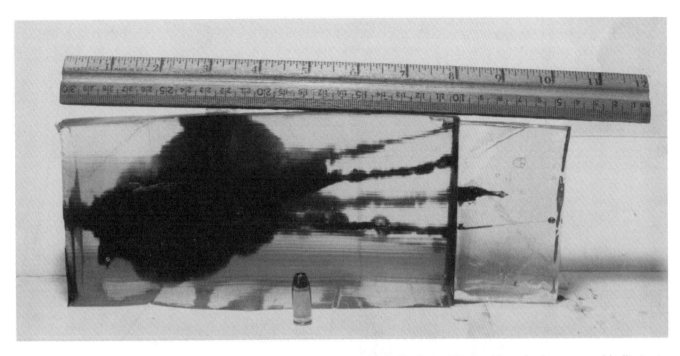

The MagSafe .380 Auto 52-grain MAX +P+ penetrates a full 11 inches of gelatin. This load has the best wound ballistics in the caliber, with an 81 percent rating.

Moving quickly down the hallway, he found Mrs. Johnson laying on the bed with a male in his twenties on top of her with his pants down around his ankles. He ordered the rapist to freeze, but instead the young man turned with a small pistol and opened fire. Struck in the head, the retired cop slumped against the wall, but he quickly regained his composure, sighted the gun, and fired three times. The rapist collapsed on top of his victim.

Responding officers found Mrs. Johnson slumped in one corner crying while the retired officer held a corner of the bedspread against a minor wound on the left side of his head. The rapist lay across the bed, obviously dead. One of the officer's rounds had struck him under the right arm pit. The slug has traversed his chest, piercing both lungs and the heart. It was recovered under the skin on the far side with a weight of 79 grains and diameter of .438 inch.

• • • • •

The 19-year-old college student worked in her father's inner city grocery store after school and on weekends. The great granddaughter of a slave, her family was proud of the fact that she was the first member of her family to attend college.

While the neighborhood's crime rate had increased dramatically, her father had a well-deserved reputation for fairness and charity. Based on his standing in the community, she had unwisely concluded that there was no risk attached to her employment.

It was almost closing time when two young men entered the store. They went to the cooler and removed several bottles of beer. Questioning their age, she asked for identification as her father had instructed her. The men responded with a long string of profanities and threw the money on the counter. She again politely requested identification and once again the men responded with obscene language.

She picked up the phone and attempted to dial 911 when one of the men leapt over the counter. He pushed her to the floor and was in the process of emptying the cash register when she reached up under the counter and grabbed the Colt .380 Auto that was hanging there.

The .380 Auto MagSafe 60-grain Defender (left) and Glaser 70-grain Blue Safety Slug (right) fragment on impact. These are 71 to 75 percent loads.

The .380 Auto Remington 88-grain JHP has been redesigned with a thinner and serrated jacket and new cavity dimensions. This round-nose JHP now expands.

Pointing it at the man, she ordered him to drop the money and leave. His response was to kick her in the side and start to climb back over the counter. She pointed the pistol in his direction and emptied it rapidly. The man collapsed on the counter while his companion grabbed the beer and escaped.

The man was dead at the scene with a Cor-Bon .380 hollowpoint lodged in his spine. The recovered weight was 69 grains and the recovered diameter was .58 inch.

• • • • •

As an entertainer at a local night club, he realized that while he was capable of drawing good audiences locally, he had neither the talent or drive to succeed at the national level. It provided him with a good income, however,

and allowed him to pursue his first love—photography. Every spare dollar went into photographic equipment of the finest quality.

Over the last year or so he had taken to monitoring the police scanner after the club closed at 2 A.M. By responding to calls of a serious nature, he was hoping to produce the same sort of gritty realistic photos that had been the speciality of a New York photographer of an earlier era. After once arriving at a gang-related shooting before the cops, he had decided a little self-protection might be in order. He went to a local gun shop, where he purchased a Walther PP in .380 ACP. He liked its compact size and moderate recoil.

It was shortly after 3 A.M. on a hot July Saturday night when the scanner announced a shooting at an inner city bar. While responding to the location of the shooting, he heard the police dispatcher announce that officers were on the scene and were being fired on.

Pulling up to a nearby intersection, he exited his vehicle and quickly selected a 600mm lens for his Nikon. He steadied the camera against the corner of the building and began to take a series of photos that tragically depicted the critical wounding of a police officer. He saw the officer go down and watched in horror as his attacker approached the downed cop with his weapon pointed at his head. Reacting instinctively, the photographer drew the .380, brought it to eye level, and fired five shots. He was gratified to see the felon collapse. He ran to the officer's assistance and attempted to control the bleeding until additional officers and paramedics responded to the scene.

The officer and his attacker were both hurried to the nearest hospital, where they both survived lengthy emergency surgery. The bad guy had taken the Cor-Bon 90-grain jacketed hollowpoint in the base of the neck. It came to rest just short of the spine and had a recovered weight of 67 grains and a recovered diameter of .394 inch.

15
Updated Street Results

The readers of this book need to understand that what is contained in this chapter is not some complex theory about what bullets *might* do in actual shootings. Rather, what follows is the product of close to 20 years of collecting the results from actual shootings. As with the proceeding book by the authors, *Handgun Stopping Power: The Definitive Study*, it is the result of thousands of hours studying this fascinating subject. Shooting reports and autopsy results were analyzed carefully. Officers and citizens who had been involved in shootings were interviewed and occasionally interrogated. Evan Marshall's experience with the homicide section of the Detroit Police Department on two separate occasions during a 20-year career was invaluable in evaluating the information obtained.

Handgun Stopping Power created a lot of controversy when the results from actual shootings that it chronicled didn't agree with long-held and deeply cherished theories about handgun wound ballistics. Shortly after the book was published, there were claims of fraud and "made up" statistics, but these charges have not stood the test of time. Both authors have heard from agency after agency and officer after officer who have followed our recommendations with satisfying results. Conversely, we have had a number of calls from individuals and agencies who relied on other "expert" opinions and selected loads that looked great in gelatin but proved to be dismal failures in the most realistic laboratory of all—the street.

CRITERIA

In order to accurately evaluate the data contained in this book, it is critical that readers understand the criteria used. There has been some carping about this criteria, but since the authors are the ones who did the work and collected the data, we will be the one's to develop the criteria to be used.

1. Only torso hits were used. We thought it unrealistic to include shootings where the victim was hit in a nonvital area and then use that incident to criticize the rounds "ineffectiveness."
2. Multiple hits were also discarded. Again,

Bullets recovered from people rarely resemble those recovered from gelatin.

we did not think it was a fair indicator of a round's performance if we included shootings where, for example, an individual took six hollowpoints in the upper thoracic cavity and then collapsed. How could we include these with incidents where a single round was effective? If we had counted multiple hits, this study could have been effectively attacked on the grounds that multiple hits are not a reliable indicator of any round's effectiveness.

3. We have defined a stop as follows: if the victim was assaulting someone when shot and collapsed without being able to fire another shot or strike another blow. If he was fleeing, he collapsed within 10 feet.

4. In order to include a shooting in this study, we insisted on either having or at least being able to review some of the following: police-action shooting reports; evidence technician reports; statements by the victim; homicide reports; autopsy reports; officer, civilian, and medical examiner

interviews; press videotapes of actual shootings; and photos. Whenever possible, we also talked to the emergency room physicians.

5. Recovered bullets were either personally examined or photographed by us, or we were provided with photographs of the bullets. Interestingly enough, there were a number of stops where hollowpoints did not expand, reinforcing the fact that bullet placement is the key.

6. A minimum of 10 shootings were required before a load could be included in this study. Fortunately, we have been able to accumulate much more than that, and the actual number of shootings (at the time of publication) is included.

ACTUAL STREET RESULTS

The rest of this chapter covers actual street results for common calibers and loads issued to or carried by police officers and civilians concerned about personal defense. The dialogue and narrative were taken directly from these sources or in some cases paraphrased from numerous accounts.

.38 SPECIAL

Long the traditional police caliber in the United States, this round has been replaced by the 9mm among law enforcement types. The customary police service load, the 158-grain round-nose lead, was appropriately named "The Police Widow Maker." It is impossible to determine how many people have died because they relied on this round, but it is unacceptably high.

Fortunately, technology has done wonders with this caliber, and several excellent loads are available that make the .38 Special a reasonable choice for self-defense. The Winchester 158-grain lead hollowpoint is the best stopper out of 2-inch barrels, but the Cor-Bon 115-grain +P+ jacketed hollowpoint is the top performer out of longer barrels.

The results are listed in Table 15-1.

TABLE 15-1
.38 SPECIAL, 2 INCH, ACTUAL RESULTS

LOAD	TOTAL SHOOTINGS	ONE-SHOT STOPS	PERCENTAGE
1. Win 158-gr. LHP +P	106	71	67
2. Fed 158-gr. LHP +P	111	73	66
3. Rem 125-gr. JHP +P	91	59	65
4. Rem 158-gr. LHP +P	81	53	65
5. Fed 125-gr. JHP +P	103	67	65
6. CCI 125-gr. JHP +P	53	34	64
7. Win 125-gr. JHP +P	63	39	62
8. Fed 125-gr. Nyclad +P	29	18	62
9. Rem 95-gr. JHP +P	118	71	60
10. Win 110-gr. ST	91	47	52
11. Fed 158-gr. SWC	167	82	49
12. Fed 158-gr. RNL	319	157	49

• • • • •

The big city cop's department restricted its officers to the .38 Special revolver. Fortunately, they had switched from the 158-grain round nose lead to the Winchester 158-grain lead hollowpoint. Assigned to the detective bureau, he carried the issue S&W Model 64 stainless steel revolver with 2-inch barrel.

It was a typical summer day with blistering heat and excessive humidity. He had only been at work for a couple of hours when his wife called and informed him that their large air conditioning unit had quit working and while she had been trying for two hours to reach the person who did their heating and cooling work, all she had gotten was a busy signal. Knowing that the proprietor often took the phone off the hook so he could get his work done, the cop promised to drop by the store and ask him to drop by and look at their unit.

As the detective pulled up in front of the shop, he noticed the unusual clutter that obscured a view inside the premises. He had advised Harvey to clear it up so passing patrol units could see the interior of the building, but the store owner had ignored his advice.

Opening the door, he saw a man he did not recognize behind the counter. "Where's Harvey?" he asked the man. "Oh, he doesn't work here anymore," the man responded. Knowing this wasn't correct, the detective just nodded and walked outside. Crossing the street and getting out of sight of the shop, he produced his cellular phone and called the direct line to police dispatch. He informed the dispatcher of what might be a crime in progress, described himself, and explained where he would be located.

A few minutes later an unmarked car containing three uniformed officers pulled up. Members of the SWAT team, they were streetwise and heavily armed. They donned their body armor as the detective explained the situation to them. Instructing him to cover the rear, they indicated they would make an entry through the front door.

Getting in position behind a pickup truck at the rear of the premises, he drew his revolver and badge. Moments later, he heard shots and a lot of shouting. The rear door flew open and the man he had seen inside earlier ran out accompanied by a young woman. He ordered them to freeze, but their response was to open fire with handguns. He returned fire,

This Federal .38 Special LHP +P stopped a gunfight.

and the woman quickly collapsed while the man continued to flee. He was reloading his revolver when the SWAT guys burst through the back door.

They pursued the man around the corner, and several shots were fired. Running to the corner, he saw the three officers standing over the downed felon. Both suspects were dead, as was the owner of the heating and cooling shop. The woman had taken a Winchester 158-grain lead hollowpoint through the heart. It was recovered from her spine with a diameter of .58 inch and a weight of 123 grains.

• • • • •

As a security guard for a central business district jewelry store, he had argued long and hard for permission to be armed. It had taken two rather vicious armed robberies to convince the owner of the necessity of having armed security on the premises. The store owner, concerned about liability, insisted that

the security personnel be restricted to concealed .38 Special revolvers. Fortunately, he had no objections to the security officers wearing concealable body armor. Dressed in blazers and slacks, they presented an image consistent with the upscale clientele the establishment attracted.

It had been a busy afternoon, with several well-dressed customers browsing and occasionally making an expensive purchase. It was just before closing time when the three men entered. While their attire matched that of previous visitors, their demeanor did not. They appeared nervous, and two paced back and forth while the third examined a number of expensive rings.

The guard and his partner started to approach the three men when they suddenly produced handguns and announced a holdup. The first security guard quickly raised his hands in the universal sign of surrender, while the second knelt behind a display case and drew his Smith & Wesson Bodyguard from an ankle holster. Just as he was ordering the thugs to surrender, he was shot several times. As he lay helpless on the floor, one of the men executed him with a shot to the back of the head.

The first security guard, realizing the error of his ways, quickly drew his Taurus .38 snub and opened fire. One subject was struck in the eye and killed instantly. The other two opened fire, striking the guard three times in the chest. Fortunately, his body armor stopped all the rounds, although the pain was intense. He clicked the revolver on several empty chambers before he realized the need to reload. After completing the task with an HKS loader carried in his blazer pocket, he staggered outside to see the remaining two felons climbing into a waiting vehicle. Steadying himself against the wall, he fired five rounds from his snub.

Responding officers found three dead holdup men. The slugs averaged a recovered diameter of .49 inch and an average weight of 131 grains. The security guard was exonerated in the shooting but dismissed by his employer for his "rash behavior."

•••••

The recent graduate from the police academy carried the issue S&W Model 64 .38 Special revolver with 4-inch heavy barrel until he could afford to buy a smaller revolver for off-duty. He was soon the proud purchaser of a stainless five-shot revolver, which he promptly loaded with the department issue Winchester 158-grain lead hollowpoints.

He was attending school at night, working toward an associate degree in criminal justice. He had finished classes for the evening and was walking to his car when he heard a scream from the back of the parking lot. Hurrying to the source of the disturbance, he quickly analyzed the situation and produced his revolver and identification. Unfortunately, what he thought was a rape was a financial dispute between a prostitute and a customer.

The woman's protest ended quickly when she realized this stupid cop was going to arrest her customer before she was paid. She produced a knife and started to threaten the officer. Confused, he didn't know who to point his gun at. Sensing his uncertainty, the prostitute slashed him across the throat. The young officer emptied his weapon in her direction before dying. She was able to take a few steps before collapsing. Responding officers found both the cop and the whore dead.

The diameter of the slug recovered from her left lung was .421 inch, with a recovered weight of 139 grains.

•••••

It had been a busy day for the delivery driver. He had delivered a truck full of paint, only to have to return and pick up the shipment because it was the wrong type. More disasters followed that one until all he could think about was his easy chair at home and a cool drink.

He was standing behind the counter of his workplace when the young man entered. As the clerk assisted the man, the driver noticed that the customer didn't seem to be paying attention. He also noticed that the man had a rather large bulge under his jacket. Fearing a holdup, he quickly removed the .38 snub kept next to the cash register and held it behind his leg.

His fears were soon realized as the man produced a large revolver and announced his intentions. Pointing the store gun at the holdup man, the driver ordered him to drop his weapon. The felon's response was to shoot the clerk and turn to fire on the delivery man. He got off two rounds before the driver's first round caught him in the upper chest. The holdup man started to bring his gun back up to eye level when a second round struck him in the heart, killing him. The average diameter of the recovered slugs was .51 inch, while the recovered weight was 138 grains.

•••••

Working the graveyard shift at a gas station just off the interstate gave the college student time to study between customers. He was deeply engrossed in a biology text when a new Cadillac pulled in. The driver left a credit card while he filled the tank, but the machine notified the clerk that it was a stolen card.

He called the state police post two miles down the road to notify them of his situation. The dispatcher replied that a unit would be there promptly. The clerk waited nervously until the state trooper pulled into the station and exited his vehicle. As the trooper approached the driver of the Cadillac, the officer was suddenly shot three times.

The clerk watched in horror as the man stood over the trooper but seemed to be having some sort of problem with his weapon. Remembering the Colt .38 snub on the shelf beneath the cash drawer, the clerk grabbed it and exited his secure office. By now the felon had dropped his own pistol and was trying to extract the officer's handgun. The clerk ordered him to stop, then ran closer to the scene and repeated his order. The shooter failed to comply, and as the clerk got close

The Rem .38 Special 158-grain LHP produces excellent expansion in the real world.

diameter of the recovered slug was .54 inch, and its recovered weight was 136 grains.

• • • • •

.38 SPECIAL—4 INCH

Cor-Bon is a relatively new company that produces a superior line of defensive handgun and rifle ammunition. Peter Pi is a genuine wizard when it comes to load designs. The Cor-Bon .38 Special 115-grain JHP +P+ has proven to be the best of the .38 Special loads in a 4-inch or longer barrel. The results of .38 Special loads out of 4-inch or longer barrels are listed in Table 15-2.

• • • • •

enough he shoved the revolver against the bad guy's chest and pulled the trigger once. The man looked up at him, cursed, and collapsed on top of the trooper.

The clerk ran to the police vehicle and placed a call for help. Responding officers applied emergency first aid, and a helicopter conveyed the trooper to a nearby trauma center. He survived surgery while his attacker was pronounced dead at the scene. The

One of his duties as a police officer with a smaller, suburban department was firearms instructor. He had worked hard to convince his chief that they needed a better round than the traditional 158-grain round-nose lead that they had been using in their heavy barrel Smith & Wesson Model 10s. After a careful

TABLE 15-2
.38 SPECIAL, 4 INCH, ACTUAL RESULTS

LOAD	TOTAL SHOOTINGS	ONE-SHOT STOPS	PERCENTAGE
1. Cor-Bon 115-gr. JHP+P+	29	24	83
2. Win 110-gr. JHP +P+	31	25	81
3. Win 158-gr. LHP +P	302	235	78
4. Fed 158-gr. LHP +P	209	161	77
5. Rem 125-gr. JHP +P	106	77	73
6. Fed 125-gr. JHP +P	214	156	73
7. Rem 158-gr. LHP +P	143	100	70
8. CCI 125-gr. JHP +P	74	52	70
9. Win 110-gr. JHP ST	111	77	69
10. Rem 95-gr. JHP +P	119	78	66
11. Win 125-gr. JHP ST	65	42	65
12. Fed 158-gr. SWC	278	144	52
13. Fed 158-gr. RNL	456	231	51

evaluation, he had selected Cor-Bon's 115-grain +P+ jacketed hollowpoint. Averaging over 1,300 feet per second from their service revolvers, he felt confident that the department was getting dramatically increased performance levels without the stigma sometimes attached to the .357 Magnum.

He was assigned to the midnight shift and had taken careful notes at on-duty roll call. Information had been provided about a holdup team that was robbing 24-hour convenience stores in the northeast corner of the state where their community was located.

The first few hours had been busy with a wide variety of calls for police service. He had decided to stop for coffee at a local restaurant when the dispatcher gave another unit a run to a convenience store on a suspicious vehicle. He decided to drive by the location to provide some backup if necessary.

He was halfway there when a person who identified himself as a citizen came on the police radio and indicated that an officer was being held at gunpoint inside the premises. The officer pulled to the side of the building and exited the vehicle. As he approached the door, he observed his brother officer being held by two young males. Both had stainless steel semiautomatic pistols pointed at his head. The officer took cover and notified dispatch of a hostage situation. The dispatcher responded that the sheriff's SWAT team had an ETA of 60 minutes.

The officer attempted to enter into negotiations with the two individuals when they shot the hostage officer in the head and threw him out the front door. The officer engaged them in a gunfight with his .38. He was in the process of reloading when a second officer joined him as the two felons attempted to make good their escape. Both cops opened fire, fatally wounding them.

The first felon had a single Cor-Bon 115 grain +P+ jacketed hollowpoint removed from his liver. It had a recovered diameter of .69 inch and a recovered weight of 73 grains. The second had a slug removed from the left ventricle of his heart. It had a recovered

diameter of .72 inch and a recovered weight of 91 grains.

• • • • •

He had been an armored car driver for 35 years and had seen it all, from a time when they carried Thompson submachine guns and tear gas guns to today, when their armament consisted of .38 Special revolvers and one 12-gauge pump shotgun kept in the truck. It seemed ironic to him that even though the amount of money they carried on a daily basis had increased dramatically, the firepower they carried had diminished.

It was a routine he knew well. It included several stops at major department stores, followed by a delivery to their money storage depot. One unofficial stop was a local bagel bakery for hot onion bagels and coffee. It had been one they made daily for years. This routine had made them sloppy and complacent.

As they pulled into the mall parking lot for their coffee break, they failed to notice a panel truck parked across from the bagel shop. The four men inside were armed with Ruger Mini-14 rifles and soft body armor. Contrary to regulations, the driver left the vehicle to get the food. As he opened the door, he was met by a ski-masked man with a rifle.

The driver quickly surrendered his revolver and was handcuffed and shoved back into the cab of the vehicle. The holdup man jumped in and started to drive off when the guard in the back of the truck attempted to exit the vehicle. One of the holdup men opened fire on him, and the guard quickly closed the door and locked it.

The armored car was driven several miles out of town before it was stopped. The holdup men dragged the driver out and threatened to kill him if the guard in the truck did not surrender. The guard inside, however, had no intention of joining his partner in handcuffs. His hope was that someone in the mall had called to report shots fired and that responding officers would locate them in time.

He looked at the shotgun but quickly realized that buckshot would not be a wise choice for this situation. Drawing his revolver, he evaluated the situation and waited for an opportunity to take action. The sound was faint at first, but he soon recognized the sound of police sirens. The holdup men again threatened the life of the driver, but it was obvious they heard the sirens too.

They pushed the driver to the ground and began to run to their vehicle when the guard opened fire through a gun port. One of the men turned with his rifle to return fire when he stumbled and collapsed.

Responding officers arrested the remaining felons and called for the paramedics, but the wounded gunman expired before their arrival. The Cor-Bon 115-grain +P+ had entered between two ribs and traversed the chest cavity, penetrating both lungs and the heart. The recovered diameter of the slug was .61 inch and its recovered weight was 74 grains.

• • • • •

Although she was a big city cop, she was restricted by regulation to the .38 Special and 158-grain semiwadcutter ammunition. A rather dramatic ammunition failure in an adjoining precinct had caused her to rethink the issue ammunition, so she purchased a box of Cor-Bon 115-grain +P+ ammunition to carry in both her duty and off-duty weapons.

She was assigned to foot patrol in a relatively low crime area of her rather active precinct. Her main responsibility was the enforcement of parking regulations in this primarily commercial area. She had made careful observations as to whether or not vehicles were exceeding the time constraints allowed by law and noticed that one delivery truck had done so.

She went inside the premises that the truck was parked in front of to inquire as to the location of its driver. She was referred to the back of the building, where five men were drinking coffee and engaged in casual conversation. Identifying the driver, she advised him that the vehicle had to be moved. The driver's response was brief and obscene.

This CCI 125-grain JHP +P .38 Special produced excellent expansion in a bad guy.

Rather than engage in an argument, she simply returned to the curb and called for a tow truck. While waiting for the truck, she proceeded to write a ticket for the appropriate violation.

The truck had just started to hook up to the delivery vehicle when its driver came running out of the premises. Swearing in a loud voice, he grabbed the officer and threw her against the building. He then struck her across the face with a piece of iron pipe. Collapsing with a broken nose, she pulled her revolver and ordered the man to drop the pipe. He only response was to come closer. Fearing that she would be injured further, she fired two shots from her service weapon.

The man took two steps before collapsing on the sidewalk. An autopsy determined that one of the rounds had struck him in the left nipple. It had pierced the lung and came to rest in the spine. Its recovered weight was 62 grains and its recovered diameter was .51 inch.

• • • • •

A private citizen who lived in a quiet

suburban neighborhood, he seemed the most reasonable of people. His typical middle class neighbors would have been troubled, however, to know that he routinely went about his business armed. His weapon of choice was a S&W Model 19 .357 Magnum with a 4-inch barrel and night sights. He had tried various magnum loads but had decided that a high-performance .38 Special was decidedly more controllable. After reviewing the popular literature, he had selected Cor-Bon's 115-grain jacketed hollowpoint +P+ offering. He carried the weapon in a Greg Kramer horse-hide holster.

His concern for his personal safety was due to his involvement in a rather notorious money laundering case in a neighboring state. He had discovered that the bank where he worked had been doing favors for a major drug dealer. He shared that knowledge with both the police and a jury. In the process, his life had been threatened repeatedly.

He had declined the recommendation that he change his name and relocate at federal expense. Instead, he simply moved 500 miles from his old residence and assumed a similar position with a bank in his new hometown. He had been able to obtain a concealed weapons permit due to the philosophy of the local sheriff, which was that unless there was a compelling reason not to grant a permit, it would be issued when requested.

Everything had been uneventful until the day he won a large cash prize for sinking a hole in one at a charity golf event. Someone familiar with his testimony and sympathetic with the drug dealer's plight took note and passed the information along. Several weeks later, two individuals were sent to deal with him.

Although the man had declined the offer from a federal agency to be relocated, he had engaged in several conversations in which he had elicited useful information. One agent had told him that if he thought he was being followed, he should make three right turns. If the vehicle was still behind him after that, he could safely assume it was not a coincidence.

His mind was preoccupied in the morning, but as he left for lunch, he noticed a vehicle with two young men and realized that he had either seen the same vehicle or one like it when he had left home for work. Making three right turns, he saw that the vehicle was still there.

He began to formulate a plan. He remembered a nearby self-service car wash. He pulled his vehicle in line, felt the automatic belt catch the car frame, and quickly exited the vehicle, getting wet in the process. Drawing his pistol, he circled around and approached the men from the rear as they waited outside the car wash exit. He noticed that one of them was holding a large gym bag that was partially unzipped.

He ordered the men to freeze, but the one with the bag ignored his order and reached into the bag. As his hand started to leave the bag, the citizen could see that the object inside was a sawed-off shotgun. Realizing his life was in extreme jeopardy, he fired twice at the shotgun-wielding thug. The man dropped the shotgun and fell face forward, dead. His partner quickly surrendered and was placed under arrest by responding officers.

The recovered slug had a diameter of .68 inch and a recovered weight of 75 grains. Our banker relocated once more and now owns a small specialty shop in one of this countries most famous ski resorts.

• • • • •

He had been given his service revolver upon his completion of 25 years as a police officer. He enjoyed the quiet routine on the dead end dirt road where he lived outside a major urban center. His days consisted of walks with his dog, fishing, and working in his fruit orchard. Ignoring his wife's kidding, he routinely stuck the 4-inch-barreled S&W Model 10 in his waistband. Telling himself he needed it for animal protection, he mused on whether the animals that concerned him had four legs or two.

It was a hot August day as he headed

toward the end of his road, where he would cross a large field to reach the fishing hole he favored. As he reached the fence, he heard voices from the field. Thinking nothing of it, he spread the strands of barbed wire and crawled through. As he got closer to the voices, he heard them raised and then he heard a scream. He pulled his revolver and moved behind a tree, where he was finally able to understand the conversation. A woman was begging a man not to rape her.

He stepped out and ordered the man to freeze. The rapist, however, stood up and turned toward the retired cop with a large knife in his hand. Not hesitating, the retired cop shot him in the chest. The rapist started to turn and fell on his face. He took the woman back to his house and waited for the police to arrive.

Responding officers found the man dead. The bullet had a recovered diameter of .55 inch and a recovered weight of 61 grains.

• • • • •

9mm

The 9mm has been a popular police and civilian self-defense caliber for several years now. The .40 S&W has started to erode its position, but it remains extremely popular among those who rely on a handgun for defensive purposes. The most effective load in this caliber is the Cor-Bon 115-grain jacketed hollowpoint +P. The results of actual shootings are shown in Table 15-3.

• • • • •

He had been extremely skeptical of his department's decision to replace Federal's excellent 9BP offering with a popular 147-grain jacketed hollowpoint. Subsequent events had confirmed his suspicions when, in case after case, felons had absorbed multiple 147-grain rounds without any noticeable effect.

TABLE 15-3
9mm ACTUAL RESULTS

LOAD	TOTAL SHOOTINGS	ONE-SHOT STOPS	PERCENTAGE
1. Cor-Bon 115-gr. JHP +P	32	29	91
2. Fed 115-gr. JHP +P+	109	98	90
3. Win 115-gr. JHP +P+	98	88	90
4. Rem 115-gr. JHP +P+	57	51	89
5. Fed 124-gr. HS +P+	63	54	86
6. Fed 124-gr. Nyclad HP	239	200	84
7. Win 115-gr. ST	304	252	83
8. Fed 115-gr. JHP	208	170	82
9. Fed 124-gr. HS	106	86	81
10. Rem 115-gr. JHP	167	136	81
11. CCI 115-gr. JHP	135	107	79
12. Cor-Bon 147-gr. JHP +P	10	8	80
13. Fed 147-gr. HS	278	218	78
14. Fed 147-gr. (9MS)	27	21	77
15. Win 147-gr. BT	26	20	74
16. Win 147-gr. JHP	232	172	74
17. Win 115-gr. FMJ	256	161	63

More concerned with survival than compliance, he bought several boxes of Cor-Bon 115-grain JHP +P ammunition. It fed reliably through his Beretta and averaged 1,350 feet per second from his pistol.

He was assigned to a court security detail responsible for transporting a number of gang members to and from court for their murder conspiracy trial. He and his crew had fallen into the dull sort of routine that can have tragic results. It was the last day before a long holiday weekend, and the deputies were busy discussing their plans. No one paid any attention to the woman who walked up to the transport van with a road map until she showed them the .357 Magnum revolver she had concealed there. The two deputies close to her surrendered their Beretta pistols to her, but the officer in charge stepped back in front of the grill, drew his pistol, and quickly evaluated the situation.

Realizing that any attempt to call for help would most certainly be overheard by the woman, he went prone on the ground. From this position, he could see her feet and ankles. Taking careful aim, he shot the woman in the left instep. She promptly fell to the ground, and he fired again, fatally wounding her.

X-rays taken at the morgue showed that the round that struck the instep had totally fragmented and that the bone it had hit was shattered. The second round was recovered from the woman's left lung with a diameter of .73 inch and a weight of 97 grains.

• • • • •

The store owner had stayed in the core city of a major urban center despite several attempted robberies. One of his son's had been shot and permanently crippled as a result. He still worked at the family store but only had limited mobility aided by crutches.

In response to these circumstances, the father had bought S&W Model 3913 compact pistols for both his son and himself. They loaded their pistols with Cor-Bon 115-grain jacketed hollowpoints and carried them in Milt Sparks Summer Special holsters.

It was a hot Saturday night when the three young men entered and asked for an expensive brand of wine. The father went to the storage room to obtain the wine when he heard his son shout out a warning. The father turned to see two of the three young men running toward him with baseball bats. He pulled his pistol and ordered the men to stop. One complied, but the other raised the bat above his head and charged. The father fired five shots in the attack's direction. He took a few steps, staggered, and collapsed at the father's feet.

At the autopsy, a single jacketed hollowpoint was recovered from the victim's heart. It had a diameter of .81 inch and a weight of 104 grains.

• • • • •

The officer had finished a tough tour of duty in an inner city precinct. On his way home, he decided to stop and get pizza for dinner. He parked in front of the restaurant, grabbed the fanny pack off the front seat, and strapped it on. Inside was a compact cocked-and-locked 9mm auto loaded with Cor-Bon's 115-grain JHP +P ammo.

As he stood in line trying to make up his mind, he suddenly realized all conversation had stopped. Looking around, he realized something was terribly wrong. He glanced to his right and saw a man standing next to the pay phone with something in his right hand. Looking closer, he realized that the man had a gun. He then noticed another unfamiliar person standing next to the cash register. The realization finally made it through his fatigued brain that this was a holdup.

After evaluating the situation, he decided not to take any action. He stood there trying to appear just like another customer when he saw one of the holdup men grab a clerk and strike her in the face with a gun. He immediately stepped behind a support beam and removed his pistol and badge from its place of concealment. Reappearing, he quickly shot the thug holding the clerk and then turned to deal with the second holdup man. Unable to find him, he stepped further away from the pillar and was shot in the side. He fell to one knee, turned, and emptied his weapon without effect.

The first holdup man was conveyed to a local hospital where he survived emergency surgery. The officer was also taken there and treated and released. He had taken a .22 Short that had glanced off a rib and rode around under the skin before stopping on the far side.

The 9mm bullet was removed from the thug's large intestine, where it had a recovered diameter of .59 inch and a recovered weight of 104 grains.

• • • • •

He was a rookie cop who had graduated from the academy run by the state training council. Hired by a smaller, rural department, he looked forward to his new job with the same enthusiasm as big city recruits. He was given considerable latitude in the choice of duty weapons, so he purchased a Ruger P89 9mm pistol and loaded it with Cor-Bon 115-grain 9mm jacketed hollowpoints.

He was assigned to work with a veteran officer for the first 90 days in the hope that he would be appropriately orientated to his new career. He had been careful and attentive to the advice given by his training officer.

It was his first night of midnights, and he looked forward to the opportunity to patrol the part of the interstate that ran through his community. He had yet to make a drug arrest, and he was hoping that access to this segment of freeway would give him that opportunity.

They had stopped a couple of out of state vehicles without the hoped-for result when a Cadillac occupied by two males went by them at a high rate of speed. Giving chase, the training officer instructed the rookie to get a check on the license plate. A couple of minutes later the dispatcher responded that the plate was registered to a rental car that had not been returned.

They called for a backup and then proceeded to pull the vehicle over without waiting for its arrival. As the Cadillac pulled up on the shoulder of the freeway, the passenger exited quickly and started to walk off into the woods nearby. The rookie illuminated this individual with his high-intensity flashlight and ordered him to halt. The passenger continued to walk away until the officer ran up and grabbed him. The subject turned suddenly, shoved a small auto pistol against the officer's chest, and pulled the trigger. The round was stopped by the officer's bulletproof vest, but it felt as if he had been punched by Mike Tyson. He was able to remove his pistol from his holster and open fire on his attacker.

The passenger ran toward the treeline and then turned to fire at the officer again. He again returned fire, and this time the gunman collapsed. The officer handcuffed him and hurried to his partner, who was holding the driver at gunpoint. The rookie then called for an ambulance and handcuffed the driver. Responding paramedics found the passenger

The Cor-Bon 115-grain 9mm JHP +P is the top 9mm performer.

dead at the scene. Three pounds of pure cocaine were discovered in the vehicle's trunk.

The pathologist removed the bullet from the left ventricle of the heart, where it had a recovered diameter of .68 inch and a recovered weight of 84 grains.

• • • • •

The veteran cop carried a S&W Centennial chambered in 9mm as a backup to his H&K P7M13 duty weapon. Both handguns were loaded with Cor-Bon 115-grain +P JHP ammo. Based on seniority, he was assigned to the day shift and his normal duties consisted of transporting evidence from outlying precincts to police headquarters. He felt that since he still wore a uniform and rode in a marked vehicle, a second gun was a very good idea.

He had stopped at his last precinct and was approaching the on ramp to the freeway downtown when he saw a woman being chased by a man armed with a baseball bat. He informed the dispatcher of his circumstances and location before exiting the vehicle. He pulled his duty pistol and was running across the on ramp when he was struck from behind by a passing motorist. Losing possession of his pistol, he found himself flat on his back with a broken leg.

He was in the process of removing his portable radio to call for medical assistance when he was struck across the chest with the baseball bat. The man stepped back and started to swing the bat again when the officer pulled his Centennial from his left front pocket and fired three rounds at his attacker. The man turned to run away and was struck by a vehicle driven by a woman who had seen him attack the officer.

Responding paramedics rushed the man and the officer to the hospital, where the perpetrator died in the emergency room. The slug was removed from his liver at the morgue. It had a recovered diameter of .63 inch and weighed 89 grains.

• • • • •

.357 MAGNUM

For decades, the .357 Magnum was the first choice of both police and civilians concerned with selecting a handgun for defensive use. It is currently the best performer of the various handgun calibers, although performance it has

TABLE 15-4
.357 MAGNUM ACTUAL RESULTS

LOAD	TOTAL SHOOTINGS	ONE-SHOT STOPS	PERCENTAGE
1. Fed 125-gr. JHP	523	501	96
2. Rem 125-gr. JHP	204	196	96
3. CCI 125-gr. JHP	153	143	93
4. Fed 110-gr. JHP	204	184	90
5. Rem 110-gr. JHP	53	47	89
6. Win 125-gr. JHP	105	91	87
7. Win 145-gr. ST	84	71	85
8. Rem 125-gr. JHP-MV	23	19	83
9. Rem 158-gr. JHP	38	31	82
10. Fed 158-gr. Nyclad HP	42	34	81
11. Win 158-gr. SWC	98	71	72

not achieved without heavy recoil, muzzle flash, and muzzle blast. For those who prefer the revolver over the semiautomatic pistol, there is no better choice than the .357 Magnum. Actual shooting results are listed in Table 15-4.

• • • • •

The federal agent working a uniform assignment often found himself alone on the midnight shift. His four-wheel drive vehicle contained a 12-gauge pump shotgun and a .308 sniper rifle. His patrol area included a rural section of the southwestern United States.

His original assignment had gradually shifted to a focus on the control of narcotics. It bothered him, since he had joined this particular agency because of his interest in its original function and it had changed dramatically. He worked hard and was one of the better field agents, but he was looking forward to retirement.

He had parked his vehicle and walked about a quarter mile to a crossing point favored by solitary drug runners. He had left the shotgun in the vehicle since it made search and handcuffing difficult. He took a seated position in some high weeds and waited for some action.

It was several hours later when he realized to his embarrassment that he had dozed off. He started to stand up to stretch when he heard someone splashing across the river. He drew his S&W Model 66 from its holster, removed his flashlight from its holder, and illuminated the area.

To his surprise, he saw three men carrying backpacks crossing the river. Two of them were carrying what appeared to be AK-47 rifles. He ordered all of them to freeze, but instead they separated, and the two started to unsling their rifles. His response was fast and decisive. He fired first at the men with rifles, then extinguished his light and moved several feet away. His response was answered with a volley of rifle fire.

Reloading his pistol, he waited for a short time before briefly illuminating the area and then moving again. The flashlight had shown him that there were two perpetrators face down in the water, but one of the men armed with a rifle was not to be seen. Backing away from the scene, he moved quietly toward his vehicle, where he was able to call for help.

Responding agents and medical personnel found two men face down in the river, dead. One had taken a Federal 125-grain jacketed hollowpoint just above the left eye, while the other had taken a single Federal jacketed hollowpoint through the sternum. Its recovered diameter was .75 inch, and its recovered weight was 104 grains.

• • • • •

The college physics professor lived in an apartment near the urban university center he taught at. Originally a rather fashionable area, it had changed radically over the years. As a veteran of the Korean War, he had no delusions about the capability for violence possessed by most humans.

He had purchased a Colt Python .357 Magnum with 2 1/2-inch barrel, which he routinely carried in his shoulder bag. Loaded with Federal 125-grain jacketed hollowpoints, he found it a comforting presence on those late night walks home after conducting a physics laboratory.

The Federal 125-grain .357 Magnum JHP is the top handgun performer.

It was a mild fall evening, and he had stopped to buy some canned food for his cat. On the walk home, he realized that the two young men who had been loitering outside the neighborhood grocery had followed him for several blocks. He shifted his grocery bag slightly, removed the revolver, and stuck it in his waistband. Crossing the street, he looked back as he turned the corner and saw that the two men had closed the gap. He drew the revolver, stood in a nearby doorway, and waited. The two young men turned the corner and ran past his place of concealment. He then stepped out on the sidewalk and asked if he could be of assistance. The thugs' bravado quickly cooled when they saw the snub nose of the .357.

The professor told them to be on their way and turned to walk away when he was shot in the back. Falling on his face, he heard the two men run up. In their haste to get his money and weapon, they had failed to check on his condition. It was a fatal mistake.

As he was rolled onto his back, he opened fire, killing both his attackers. He was brought to a nearby hospital, where surgery helped him recover most of the mobility on his right side. Today he carries a compact 9mm because of its modest recoil.

The slugs were removed from the lung cavity of one thug and the kidney of another. The average recovered diameter of the two slugs was .68 inch, while the average recovered weight was 104 grains.

• • • • •

Whatever else happened, it couldn't get worse. His new Mercedes had been damaged by a hit and run driver, and his daughter had fallen off her bike and broken her arm. He was a criminal defense attorney who carried a Colt Lawman .357 Magnum with 2-inch barrel in a holster inside the waistband as protection against potential clients.

His wife called him on the car phone to remind him to stop at the travel agent to pick up the tickets for their vacation. After a hectic day in court, he pulled up in front of the travel agent's office. Rushing inside, he found himself in what appeared to be an empty office. He walked to the rear of the building and came upon a woman lying on the floor. As he got closer, he observed a large pool of blood underneath her head. He pulled his gun, then picked up the phone and dialed 911. After relaying the appropriate information, he hung up the phone.

He looked out of the office into the parking lot and noticed a man dragging a woman toward a car. Stepping outside, the lawyer ordered the man to let her go. His response was to shove the woman to the ground and shoot her. The attorney then opened fire with his .357 snub. The man turned, ran to the car, and jumped in. He was trying to get the gear shift lever moved when he collapsed.

Responding officers found three people dead—the receptionist inside and the travel agent and her estranged husband outside. The Federal 125-grain slug had struck him on the right side, traversing the chest cavity and stopping under the skin on the far side. Its recovered diameter was .78 inch and its recovered weight was 103 grains.

• • • • •

The woman had inherited the gun from her cop father. He had retired and had given it to her shortly before his death. She didn't view her urban neighborhood with the same concern her father had, but she kept the S&W Model 686 revolver in her nightstand.

Unlike most owners of a handgun for home defense, she was skilled in its use. She had spent countless hours at the range with her dad and had learned to control the Magnum's vigorous recoil.

It had been a long day at the brokerage office where she worked, and it was almost 9 P.M. before she got home. Juggling a bag of groceries and her cleaning, she managed to get inside her apartment without dropping anything. Unfortunately, she neglected to close the door completely.

Hanging her cleaning in her closet, she turned to see a stranger standing in the doorway of her apartment. She asked him what he wanted, but he just grinned and produced an ice pick. She turned and ran toward her bedroom, grabbed the handgun, and ordered the man to leave. His response was to tell her that she had no intention of shooting him. He then proceeded to describe in very graphic detail the various sexual acts he was going to perform on her.

Her response was almost automatic. Placing the red ramp in the center of his chest, she pulled the trigger. His reaction was to drop the ice pick, place both hands over the wound, and die. The slug was recovered from the heart and had a diameter of .81 inch and a weight of 111 grains.

• • • • •

He belonged to a big city police department that issued the S&W Model 10 but allowed officers to carry a wide variety of personally owned handguns. He had purchased a nickel-plated S&W Model 19 and

This CCI .357 Magnum shows typical street expansion for this load.

loaded it with Federal's excellent 125-grain jacketed hollowpoint ammunition. Although department regulations prohibited hollowpoints, he decided to take the heat over a regulation violation.

Assigned to his department's tactical unit, he and his partner were tasked to stake out a cleaners. A team of robbers had been holding up a chain of cleaners and had simply started downtown and worked their way toward the suburbs. The cleaners the cops were in was the next in line. His partner had a 12-gauge shotgun, while he relied on his .357 Magnum.

It was almost time for their shift to end when three men entered the premises, produced handguns, and announced a holdup. The officers called for help and were waiting for it to arrive when one of the holdup men shot the clerk. The officers burst out of their hiding place in a storage room and ordered the gunmen to surrender. One of the three complied while the other two opened fire. Both officers responded with fatal force, and the two resisting holdup men were quickly down and dead.

One had taken nine pellets of 00 buckshot in the face, while the other took a Federal 125-grain jacketed hollowpoint in the throat. It had a recovered diameter of .77 inch and a recovered weight of 104 grains.

• • • • •

.41 MAGNUM

One of our most unappreciated calibers, the .41 Magnum is an excellent cartridge for both self-defense and hunting. Co-author Evan Marshall carried a S&W Model 58 .41 Magnum revolver loaded with the Remington 210-grain lead semiwadcutter as both an on- and off-duty weapon for years.

The results of actual shootings are listed in Table 15-5.

• • • • •

The big city tactical cop preferred the .41

TABLE 15-5
.41 MAGNUM ACTUAL RESULTS

LOAD	TOTAL SHOOTINGS	ONE-SHOT STOPS	PERCENTAGE
1. Win 170-gr. ST	53	47	89
2. Win 210-gr. JHP	34	28	82
3. Rem 210-gr. JSP	31	25	81
4. Rem 210-gr. SWC	57	43	75
5. Win 210-gr. SWC	43	32	74

Magnum over the newfangled semiautomatic pistols. He had found a first-year production S&W Model 57 revolver with a 6-inch barrel. Others liked high-capacity 9mms, but he took great comfort in those big lead bullets.

The unit was moved around the city in response to crime and crowd control problems. On this particular night, they were assigned to one of the city's quieter precincts. He and his partner had stopped several vehicles without a hoped-for felony arrest.

They had driven past the carry-out restaurant twice and noticed that a late model luxury car was illegally parked in a bus stop. The third time around they decided to write a parking ticket. While one officer wrote the ticket, the other entered the license plate in the in-car computer.

The officer was getting ready to exit the squad car and place the ticket under the windshield of the vehicle when his partner grabbed his arm and pointed at the computer terminal. The vehicle in question was wanted in connection with a multiple homicide in a nearby state.

The officers exited their patrol vehicle and entered the premises. To their right, they observed two males leaning against the wall eating from containers. When the officers asked them for identification, both men wanted to know why they were being hassled. The officers asked them again and the reaction was immediate and deadly—both suspects dropped their food and started to produce handguns.

The first officer grabbed the suspect directly in front of him, deflected his gun, and shoved his .41 Magnum in the suspect's face. That suspect dropped his gun, and the officer was in the process of handcuffing him when several shots were fired to his left. Turning his head, he saw his partner on the ground with blood running out of a wound on his neck and the other suspect standing over him with a gun. He retrieved his gun from his waistband, where he had stuck it while handcuffing the first suspect, and fired one shot, striking the suspect in the chest.

The officer and the bad guy were rushed to a nearby hospital, where both eventually recovered. The bullet taken from the felon had a diameter of .83 inch and a weight of 144 grains.

• • • • •

While hunting bear in the northwestern United States, he carried a S&W Model 57 .41 Magnum with an 8 3/8-inch barrel in a shoulder holster as a backup. loaded with Winchester 170-grain JHPs. He and his hunting partner had spent a frustrating day without even seeing a bear. They had returned their rifles and related equipment to their motel room before going out for dinner.

They were returning to their car when they were approached by a shabbily dressed individual who asked for money. The hunter gave him $5, but the man made a sarcastic remark about the bigger bills in his wallet.

Ignoring him, the hunter turned toward his car when he was struck in the back. Thinking that the panhandler had hit him with his fist, he turned around to see the man holding a large knife in his hand. Realizing that he had been stabbed, he pulled the revolver from the shoulder holster and shot him twice.

The recovered bullets averaged .78 inch in diameter and weighed 156 grains.

• • • • •

The man had received a box of items when his son had died in the line of duty as a county deputy. Included in that box was his son's personal weapon, a S&W Model 58 .41 Magnum. His son's killers had not been found, and he worried about that. Shortly after the funeral, he had begun to receive threatening phone calls. The subject was always the same—the caller would identify himself as his son's killer and promise that he would be by to finish the job.

The person making the call was not the killer, just a street-level drug dealer who had been arrested by his son. His harassment was a stupid practice that would lead to his death. After several months, the dealer decided

This Rem .41 Magnum "Police Load" worked well on a felon!

while in a drug-induced state to drive by the father's home and throw a Molotov cocktail into the house.

In response to events, the father had done two things. He had loaded his son's .41 Magnum with Winchester 170-grain JHPs and had started to sleep on the living room sofa while his invalid wife continued to occupy their bedroom upstairs.

He had just finished watching a late night talk show. He turned off the light and lay down on the sofa when he heard a car stop on his dead end street. He took a quick look and saw that the vehicle really didn't fit in with his neighborhood.

Obtaining the revolver, he watched the man walk past his house, turn, and come back, holding something in his right hand. He thought it was a wine bottle at first, but when the man lit the top of it, he knew instantly what it was. He ran to the door, jerked it open, and opened fire. The first three rounds missed, but the fourth struck the drug dealer just beneath the sternum.

The dealer turned and started to run before falling on his side. Responding officers got an admission from him that he had been the one harassing the slain officer's parents. The bullet recovered during surgery had a diameter of .89 inch and a weight of 159 grains.

• • • • •

It had been one of those days that the cab driver always hated. Drunks, nothing but drunks, had climbed in his cab all day. He didn't mind most of them, but there were always those who would speak disparagingly of his Jamaican origins. The fact that he had a Masters degree in art and was working on a Ph.D. wouldn't have impressed them if he had even bothered to mention it.

While he had never been robbed, he had attended the funerals of fellow cab drivers who had. Because of this, he had purchased a S&W Model 657 .41 Magnum with a 3-inch barrel and round butt. He carried it in a leather portfolio that laid next to him on the front seat.

It was almost midnight when he received what he decided would be his final call of the night, as the dispatcher gave him a call that would take him toward home. He saw the man holding onto a light pole. Another drunk, he thought, but he was wrong. The man was a mentally ill individual who had escaped from a nearby mental health facility. He had been placed there for attacking a number of people on the street with a knife. He had passed by several Caucasians to stab every black he could find before responding officers had arrested him.

The cab had driven just a few blocks when the passenger produced a knife and stabbed him several times in the back. The cab driver slumped forward and then felt his attacker pull his head back. Realizing he was about to get his throat cut, he pulled the revolver from its place of concealment and tried to fire the gun between his side and arm. The first Winchester 170-grain round struck his own body, cutting a groove across his side. The second round struck his attacker in the stomach, and subsequent rounds impacted in his chest.

Five rounds were recovered at the morgue. Their average diameter was .67 inch and the average recovered weight was 164 grains.

• • • • •

He was the night watchman at a foundry, and he had been allowed to arm himself after he had been beaten and robbed on duty. He had found a used Ruger Blackhawk .41 Magnum revolver, loaded it with Winchester Silvertips, and carried it in an inexpensive nylon holster.

Several years had past without incident, and his level of awareness had slipped significantly. It was a bitter February night, and he made his outside rounds as quickly as possible. He returned back to the office building and noticed the door was ajar. Assuming he had left it open, he moved inside quickly and closed it.

As he was making his way upstairs, he was struck from behind by an intruder and knocked to the floor. His attacker pulled the Black Hawk from its holster and attempted to shoot the watchman. Fortunately, the assailant was not familiar with the workings of a single-action revolver and was trying to fire it without cocking it first.

The watchman attempted to take the weapon away from his much younger attacker. They fought fiercely, but the watchman lacked the strength to dominate the situation. He looked down and noticed the revolver was pointed at his opponent and that he had the trigger pulled all the way to rear. The watchman pulled the hammer back and let go, causing the weapon to discharge into his attacker's stomach. The young man collapsed and the watchman staggered off to call for help. When he returned to the scene of the altercation, his attacker was gone.

A search by police followed a blood trail to a nearby warehouse, where the body of the

TABLE 15-6
.44 SPECIAL ACTUAL RESULTS

LOAD	TOTAL SHOOTINGS	ONE-SHOT STOPS	PERCENTAGE
1. Win 200-gr. ST	60	45	75
2. Fed 200-gr. LHP	49	36	73
3. Win 246-gr. RNL	71	46	65
4. Rem 240-gr. SWC	17	11	65

intruder was found. The bullet had a recovered diameter of .59 inch and a recovered weight of 157 grains.

• • • • •

.44 SPECIAL

The .44 Special is one of the venerable calibers that never quite seems to go away. It received a resurgence of popularity with the introduction of the Charter Arms Bull Dog compact revolver. Later, Smith & Wesson introduced the Models 24 and 624 N frame revolvers, which found quick popularity among officers and citizens who prefer large-caliber revolvers. Today, the popularity of the .44 Special caliber continues with the Taurus and Rossi big-bore revolvers.

The actual shooting results are listed in Table 15-6.

• • • • •

A college cop, he was allowed the option of carrying revolvers other than the issue .38 Special as long as they were not magnums. He had chosen a 6-inch-barreled Model 624 and loaded it with Winchester's excellent Silvertip hollowpoints.

He was permanently assigned to the midnight shift so that he could attend law school in the evening. His normal routine was to spend an hour or two in the law library before reporting for work. He finished his library assignment and was heading across campus to the public safety building where he had parked his car.

He was almost there when he heard a car screech to halt behind him. He turned to see three drunken young men exiting a beat-up pickup truck. They started to call him a college punk and began to describe in great deal the various injuries they were planning to inflict on him.

The officer turned and attempted to walk away from trouble when one of the drunks hit him across the shoulders with a baseball bat.

He dropped his law books as he fell to the ground. Another one of the drunks grabbed his notebook and started to rip it apart.

The officer punched that individual in the face and was struck again with the baseball bat. Realizing that a blow from the bat could be fatal, he pulled his .44 Special and told the men they were under arrest. They laughed at him, and the man with the bat charged him. The officer brought the revolver to eye level and fired twice. The man dropped the bat and turned to run before sitting down suddenly with blood running out of his mouth.

He recovered after a lengthy stay at the hospital. The bullet had a recovered diameter of .48 inch and a recovered weight of 178 grains.

• • • • •

He had worked as a bus driver for a large city bus line for almost 30 years. He had watched the city change and the people with it. He was totally mystified by young people these days. They were, loud, vulgar, and uneducated in spite of, or perhaps because of, their schooling.

Next to his driver's seat was an old black leather satchel that contained a number of personal items, including his Bible. A few years earlier he had added something else—a stainless steel Charter Arms Bull Dog loaded with Winchester hollowpoints. He had started carrying it because of an incident on another bus when a mentally ill man had shot two people.

He had worked his regular eight-hour shift when the dispatcher asked him to stay and work an additional four hours. He sighed good naturedly and got out of his bus to get a can of Coke from the machine. Climbing back on the bus, he finished the soda and threw the can in a wastebasket at the coach stop.

Four hours later he had finished his extra tour and was pulling into the garage when he heard a woman screaming for help. He grabbed his pistol and exited the bus. He saw a female bus driver he knew struggling with a man. As he ran to her assistance, the assailant opened a folding knife and stabbed her once in the neck.

He got within a few steps of the man when he started to stab her again. The bus driver shoved the gun against the his side and pulled the trigger. The man turned and stabbed the bus driver in the heart before collapsing. Both men were conveyed to a local hospital, where they were DOA. The bullet had a recovered diameter of .67 inch and recovered weight of 163 grains.

• • • • •

The owner of a junkyard was often plagued by night time intruders who would steal property off the junked vehicles. Since he often worked late, he decided to buy a handgun for protection. He told the gun dealer he wanted a big gun to scare people with. The dealer sold him a long-barreled S&W stainless steel .44 Magnum and suggested he load it with Winchester's Silvertip .44 Special hollowpoints.

It was an early Saturday evening, and he was still in his office trying to get his taxes done. He had just returned from the bathroom and was looking out the window when he thought he saw someone in the yard. Removing the pistol from its hiding place, he walked into the yard to investigate a possible intrusion. As he walked toward the back fence, he suddenly saw a young man crouched behind a fender assembly. He pointed the weapon at him and ordered him to stand up.

As the young man became upright, the junkyard owner saw that he was holding a carburetor in his left hand. He ordered the intruder to drop it, but instead he struck the man in the head. He fired three rounds at the intruder as he staggered back. The young man went to his knees and rolled to his side, screaming for help.

Responding officers found the critically wounded intruder bleeding heavily. After being rushed to a local hospital, he underwent lengthy emergency surgery but expired on the operating table. One bullet was recovered from the liver, where it had a diameter of .54 inch and a weight of 177 grains.

• • • • •

A cop who had been affected by the *Dirty Harry* movies, he had bought a S&W Model 29 with 6 1/2-inch barrel. For years he had carried standard .44 Special 246-grain round-nose lead ammunition because of its modest recoil. When Winchester introduced its Silvertip jacketed hollowpoint, he had switched over to that load.

He rode a motorcycle on street traffic enforcement during the 6 A.M. to 2 P.M. shift. It had been raining, so he waited in the city garage for the rain to lighten to the point where motorcycle patrol would be safe.

While he was walking across the street to a coffee shop for a cup of decaf and a donut, he saw some activity out of the corner of his eye. Turning, he saw a man armed with a shotgun running toward him. He struggled to get his long-barreled magnum out of his rain gear and was shot in the side. He was still trying to get his gun out as he was falling to the ground when he saw the man attempting to reload what appeared to be a single-shot break-open shotgun.

Another officer ran out of the coffee shop and fired 15 rounds of 9mm ammunition at the would-be cop killer at a distance of less than 10 feet without hitting him once! The wounded officer finally freed his .44 from his holster and, cocking the gun carefully, fired one round single-action, striking the man in the upper chest. The bad guy turned, took two steps, and fell on his face.

A single bullet was recovered at the morgue. It had a diameter of .69 inch and weighed 171 grains.

• • • • •

A dedicated hiker, he carried a S&W Model 24 in his backpack to protect himself against the two-legged predators that often lived and grew drugs in the woods. The gun was secured in a Bianchi police duty rig on a belt that contained two HKS speedloaders of Silvertip hollowpoints in addition to the six rounds in the gun.

He was four days into a projected 12-day hike when he encountered his first humans. It was a young couple spending their honeymoon in the great outdoors. It was almost dark when they met, and they inquired if he would mind if they camped nearby. He told them they were welcome to do so. Eating a cold dinner that met his vegetarian life-style, he wrote in his journal for awhile, took a few photos of wild flowers, and went to bed.

He awoke suddenly in the middle of the night to the sound of loud voices. At first he thought the newlyweds were having their first argument, but he soon changed his mind as he listened carefully. Pulling his revolver from its holster, he dropped the speedloaders in his pants pocket and walked quietly toward the disturbance.

As he approached the campsite, he saw three men by the campfire. One was the young man he had met earlier. His face was bloody and one eye was swollen shut. He looked for the young wife and suddenly noticed vigorous physical activity inside the tent. He correctly assumed that a sexual assault was in progress.

He decided that discretion was the better part of valor and waited. As a man exited the tent zipping up his pants, he shot him once in the chest and opened fire on the other two as

they turned to run away. Unfortunately, none of the other rounds took effect, and the other men made good their escape. After reloading the pistol, he ran into camp to assist the young couple.

After a strenuous two-day hike, they were finally able to notify the authorities. At autopsy, a single bullet was removed from the rapist's chest. It had a recovered diameter of .53 inch and a recovered weight of 181 grains.

• • • • •

.44 MAGNUM

Not given serious consideration as a defensive round until the string of *Dirty Harry* movies, the .44 Magnum has since seen a fair amount of use for self-defense. It tends not to produce results as promising as "less powerful" rounds because it almost always overpenetrates, and its heavy recoil makes accurate fire difficult.

The actual street results are shown in Table 15-7.

• • • • •

His duty weapon was a nickel-plated S&W Model 29 .44 Magnum with a 4-inch barrel that he loaded with Winchester's 210-grain jacketed hollowpoint offering. Assigned to precinct plainclothes patrol, he and his

TABLE 15-7
.44 MAGNUM ACTUAL RESULTS

LOAD	TOTAL SHOOTINGS	ONE-SHOT STOPS	PERCENTAGE
1. Win 210-gr. JHP	50	45	90
2. Fed 180-gr. JHP	37	33	89
3. Rem 240-gr. JHP	34	30	88
4. Win 240-gr. JHP	43	36	84
5. Win 240-gr. SWC	44	36	82
6. Fed 240-gr. JHP	35	28	80
7. Rem 240-gr. SWC-MV	55	42	76

STREET STOPPERS

This Federal .44 Magnum SWC expanded and ended a felonious assault.

partner focused on high crime areas in their unmarked Plymouth.

They were moving slowly down a main street when they heard shots fired in a nearby alley. Notifying the dispatcher of their situation, they drove quickly to the mouth of the alley and exited their vehicle. As they moved to a large Dumpster, they were fired upon from two different locations. They called for assistance as they returned fire.

As the sirens got closer, they heard movement down the alley. When they illuminated the alley, they saw two males running toward them. Both of them were armed with M1 carbines. Since ordering them to halt failed to bring the desired result, both officers opened fire. The subjects collapsed and were rushed to a nearby hospital.

One had taken a total of eight rounds of .38 Special 158-grain round-nose lead and was treated in emergency and shipped off to the county jail. The second one was shipped to the morgue, where a single Winchester .44 Magnum hollowpoint was removed from under the skin in the center of his back. It had a recovered diameter of .84 inch and a recovered weight of 189 grains.

• • • • •

He drove a fuel delivery truck in the rural area near his home. Several years before he had run off a pack of wild dogs as they menaced a group of school children. Fearful that something similar could happen again, he had bought a Ruger Redhawk .44 Magnum revolver and loaded it with Winchester 210-grain jacketed hollowpoints.

It was a snowy, slippery day that forced him to stop and put on chains to continue his deliveries. He waved at a locally assigned state trooper as he turned off a state road to make a delivery. A half hour later he returned to the state road and saw that the trooper's vehicle was still parked where it had been earlier. Slowing down, he noticed that the vehicle was empty. He also noticed that there were two sets of footprints leading away from the parked vehicle.

He then saw what appeared to be blood drops in the snow. Grabbing the microphone of his CB radio, he switched over to channel 9 and called for help. He explained the situation to a passing trucker, grabbed his big revolver, exited the truck, and started to follow the tracks.

He had walked about a quarter of a mile when he found the trooper face down in the snow, blood running down the back of his head. The driver found him to be unconscious but with a regular, strong pulse. As he took off his heavy winter coat and placed it over the trooper, he noticed that the officer's handgun and radio were missing.

He followed the single set of footprints for about another mile before coming to an abandoned farmhouse. He found a young woman inside asleep. The trooper's radio was laying next to her, and his 9mm pistol was stuck in her waistband.

He ordered the woman to put her hands up. Her eyes flew open and, seeing the man, she quickly reached for the pistol. Fearing for his life, the trucker fired twice. The woman quickly fell back down, dead. The bullet recovered from her spine had a diameter of .67 inch and a weight of 166 grains.

•••••

A handgun hunter, his favorite pistol was a Ruger Super Blackhawk in .44 Magnum. While he had several other handguns in his home, he kept the Super Blackhawk loaded with Winchester 210-grain JHPs in case a self-defense situation should ever arise. His quiet neighborhood was just minutes from a busy interstate, and over the last few months there had been a rash of daytime burglaries.

He had come down with a summer cold and had taken a few days off to recuperate. His car was inside the garage, so there were no obvious signs that anyone was home.

He was napping on the sofa when he heard glass breaking in the family room downstairs. He quietly but quickly made his way to the bedroom, grabbed his Ruger, and sat at the top of the stairs. His feeling was that while the insurance company could reimburse him for most things, he did not intend to allow his guns to be stolen and used against innocents.

He sat there quietly and listened to someone moving around his house, hoping they would gather several items and leave. It soon became obvious, however, that the individual was slowly working his way upstairs. Cocking the big Ruger, he waited patiently for the intruder.

When he heard footsteps on the stairs, he brought the gun to eye level and was surprised to see a man almost his own age round the corner. He ordered the man to halt just as he noticed a pry bar in the intruder's right hand. The intruder struck him across the gun arm and the revolver fell to the floor.

The home owner dove for the gun and was struck across the neck. He was finally able to pick it up as the man continued to strike him upon the upper body. He shoved the muzzle against the intruder's chest and fired once. His attacker slumped on the stairs and then fell to the landing. He was DOA at a local hospital. The bullet had gone through the bad guy and then through a stairwell window and was not recovered.

This .44 Magnum Hydra-Shok ended a criminal's career permanently!

•••••

The veteran street cop carried a nickel-plated S&W Model 29 with a 6 1/2-inch barrel on duty and a customized Model 629 with 3-inch barrel and rounded butt off duty. An avid jogger, he carried this big pistol in a custom oversized fanny pack that also contained a speedloader, a can of pepper spray, and his police credentials.

He was well into his final mile when a group of four youths walked off the curb and stood in his path. Grimacing, he crossed to the other side, but the young men moved again. Deciding that pepper spray would not be that effective against multiple assailants, he stopped 50 feet away and asked them what they wanted. Their response, while obscene, was clear. The officer replied that he wasn't going to give them anything. One of the young men suddenly produced a small semi-automatic pistol and opened fire. One of the rounds ricocheted off the road and struck him in the instep. The officer fell to the ground and, rolling on his side, produced his handgun and opened fire. His first three rounds missed, but the fourth Winchester 210-grain JHP struck the shooter just above the navel.

The shooter turned and took four steps before sitting down and dying. The rest of his gang made good their escape. The officer was permanently disabled. The bullet removed from the shooter had a diameter of .61 inch and a weight of 179 grains.

• • • • •

He had lived alone since his wife had died four years before. His children often invited him to come and live with them, but while he liked to visit, he soon missed his old dog and garden.

His house was an anomaly, consisting of four acres smack dab in the middle of a large urban center. The large house sat at the rear of the property at the end of a long driveway that divided the garden area.

He loved to work among his fruits and vegetables, often losing track of the time and only stopping when it was too dark to see. He would leave the house early in the morning with a large insulated jug of cold water and would fill his stomach with food from the garden.

The best thing about working in the garden was that it allowed him to forget his former career as a big city cop assigned to the decoy

unit. He had been involved in several fatal shootings and had been denounced in the liberal press as "an assassin in blue." The truth, of course, was that each shooting had been investigated intensively and cleared by both the homicide and prosecutor's office. His handgun had played a prominent role in the stories too. It was a nickel-plated S&W Model 29 .44 Magnum with a 4-inch barrel loaded with heavy handloads. It had proven to be extremely effective, although he had switched to Winchester hollowpoints after a supervisor had reminded him of the department's prohibition against hand loads.

As his neighborhood had started to deteriorate, he had removed the .44 from its lock box, loaded it, and stuck it in his waistband each morning before starting work.

It was a hot summer day, and he worked steadily if slowly. He headed to the house to use the bathroom but first walked to the front gate to check the mail. Walking back to the house, he was too engrossed in his bills to notice the two young men climbing over the side fence.

He was sitting on the toilet when he heard one of the steps leading upstairs creak. Reaching down, he picked up the .44, quietly stood up, and pulled up his pants. He heard

TABLE 15-8
.45 ACP ACTUAL RESULTS

LOAD	TOTAL SHOOTINGS	ONE-SHOT STOPS	PERCENTAGE
1. Fed 230-gr. HS	71	67	94
2. Rem 230-gr. GS	14	13	93
3. Cor-Bon 185-gr. JHP	12	11	92
4. Rem 185-gr. JHP +P	44	40	91
5. CCI 200-gr. JHP	111	98	88
6. Fed 185-gr. JHP	75	65	87
7. Win 185-gr. ST	73	60	82
8. Win 230-gr. BT	36	29	81
9. Rem 185-gr. JHP	114	92	81
10. Rem 230-gr. FMJ	122	79	65
11. Win 230-gr. FMJ	179	112	63
12. Fed 230-gr. FMJ	168	106	63

the men then, and he waited. They walked away from him toward one of the bedrooms. He waited until he heard them open the door. Slipping off his shoes, he moved down the hallway. He caught a glimpse of them in the bedroom mirror and realized that one was carrying a gas can.

Because his old frame house would burn rapidly, he moved quickly. Stepping in the doorway, he ordered both to freeze. As the two young men turned, he could tell they were both high on drugs. Their response to his command was to charge. His response was to shoot them both in the chest.

Responding officers found him sitting on the porch eating a peach. The bullets were removed at the morgue and had an average recovered diameter of .67 inch and an average recovered weight of 178 grains.

• • • • •

.45 ACP

This caliber is highly favored by both cops and civilians concerned about survival. While several loads produce excellent results, hardball is not one of them. The problem is that its popularity was based on the results of shooting half-starved Japanese and German soldiers during World War II. When the same round has been employed against U.S. criminals, it has failed with depressing regularity.

The results are listed in Table 15-8.

• • • • •

As a state trooper, he carried Hydra-Shok hollowpoints in his SIG P220 duty pistol. He enjoyed the fresh air and rugged scenery of the mountainous area in the north end of his state to which he was assigned.

It was 2 A.M. when he was woken from a deep sleep by the telephone. It was the local sheriff's department informing him that one of their units was not responding to the radio.

The trooper dressed quickly and got his K-9 partner from the kennel in back of his house. The dog was a lot happier to go to work than he was. Turning on the lights and siren, he made quick work of the 20 miles to the scene. When he arrived, he got the dog out, obtained the scent from the police vehicle, and took off up the hill.

At the top of the hill, the dog circled for a moment before heading back toward the vehicle. As they approached the sheriff's car from a different direction, he saw what appeared to be blood drops in the sand. Squatting down, he saw that the drops led to a ditch. In the ditch was the body of the deputy. He had been shot in the back of the head at close range.

After notifying the other officers of his tragic discovery, he noticed a ripped red t-shirt laying next to the deputy's body. He directed the dog to it, and the K-9 quickly turned away and headed into the darkness. They had jogged about 50 yards when the dog started to bark loudly. The officer started to swing his flashlight when gunfire erupted. Both the trooper and his dog were wounded. As he fell to the ground, he drew his SIG and opened fire. He heard a scream in the darkness. Reloading his pistol, he grabbed his flashlight and illuminated the area. Laying on his back was a man in his twenties who was obviously dead.

The trooper's vest had stopped the 9mm jacketed hollowpoint, but his dog had been wounded severely. The dog eventually recovered but was retired from service.

At the morgue, a Hydra-Shok .45 ACP bullet was recovered from the cop killer's left lung. It had a diameter of .70 caliber and weighed 204 grains.

• • • • •

The SWAT cop was issued a Smith & Wesson .45 ACP double-action pistol. The duty round for both the pistol and unit's 9mm submachine gun was Federal's Hydra-Shok.

The team's primary role was to assist the narcotics unit on raids, and they averaged one a day. Even though these were daily occurrences, they never took the events for granted and prepared carefully.

The raid location was an apartment on the fourth floor of a large building in a high crime area. They decided to make the forced entry at 3 A.M. on a Tuesday morning in an attempt to avoid detection.

To further assist them in their efforts, they borrowed a delivery truck. As they pulled up in front of the building, two five-man teams moved toward the front door, while a third five-man team headed through the back door.

The officer had a stun grenade in one hand and his .45 ACP pistol in the other. He stood aside while two officers forced the door. As it flew open, he inserted the grenade and followed it in. He was moving to the right when he saw movement out of the corner of his eye. As he turned to identify it, he was shot once with a 12-gauge shotgun. Hoping his tactical armor had stopped the shot, he brought his pistol to eye level and fired three rounds.

After seeing his attacker collapse, he continued to sweep the apartment and checked all the rooms before broadcasting the "all clear" signal. He returned to the living room and saw that his attacker was obviously dead. Closer examination determined that it was the 15-year-old mentally retarded daughter of the dope dealer. The bullet retrieved at the morgue had a recovered diameter of .72 inch and a recovered weight of 204 grains.

The Federal 230-grain Hydra-Shok is the top performer in .45 ACP.

• • • • •

The gun shop owner and all of his employees were armed at all times. Individual choices ranged from the .38 snub to .44 Magnum, but the owner relied on a lightweight Colt Commander loaded with 230-grain Hydra-Shok ammunition.

It was the middle of their annual inventory, and they were extremely busy. He was concentrating on the reloading supplies in a far corner of the shop when he heard some one yell "stop." Turning, he saw a man running out of the store with an expensive over-and-under shotgun. The owner ran outside, pulled his .45, and ordered the man to stop. As the thief jumped in a vehicle at the curb, the driver leaned across and opened fire at the owner. He responded by firing five rounds of .45 ACP into the car.

The car sped away from the curb, traveled about a block, and side-swiped four parked cars before stopping. As the gun shop owner approached, the passenger threw the shotgun out and surrendered. The driver was conveyed to a local hospital, where he died in the emergency room. The bullet had a recovered diameter of .71 inch and a recovered weight of 206 grains.

• • • • •

He had completed an exhausting tour of midnight shifts and was almost home when he realized he had promised his wife he would pick up some milk for the kids' breakfast. He pulled up to a convenience store on the corner and got out. Although he had left his police uniform in the locker at work, his duty Glock .45 ACP rode in a Milt Sparks Summer Special. Most of the cops in his agency opted for smaller and lighter sidearms, but he preferred to carry the handgun he was most familiar with.

As he entered, he realized that the place was almost deserted, something most unusual for this time on a weekday morning. Walking toward the milk cooler, he noticed a young man peek out from the stockroom and jump back quickly. As he walked toward the counter, he started to get "that" feeling.

He stood at the far left end of the counter so that his back was against a cooler filled with juice. As he waited, he looked behind the counter and saw money scattered on the floor. He quickly drew his pistol and badge. Holding them by his side, he waited quietly for something to happen. He saw a man step out of the stockroom, and the officer asked for some service. The man ignored him and ran toward the back of the store.

The officer had taken about five steps in pursuit when he was fired upon. Struck in the ankle, he fell to the floor. He looked to his left and saw a man laying face down, obviously dead. Looking to his right, he saw another man attempting to work the action on a pump rifle. Bringing his Glock to eye level, he fired six rounds. The man fell to the ground and was struggling to point the rifle at the officer when the officer fired again, killing him.

The dead man found by the officer was the store manager. Two .45 ACP Hydra-Shok jacketed hollowpoints were recovered from the holdup man's chest. They had an average recovered diameter of .64 inch and an average recovered weight of 207 grains.

• • • • •

The man had been sitting in the bar for hours waiting for his appointment to arrive. He was a federal agent and his informant was supposed to provide him with some critical information on a drug ring. He was on his eighth glass of 7-UP and was convinced that he had been stood up. He finished his glass of soda, paid his bill, and left.

What he didn't realize was that his snitch had set him up. Walking to his car, he thought he saw movement in the shadows. A streetwise agent, he pulled his Swenson modified .45 Commander and held it behind his leg. As he got closer to his vehicle, he saw more movement. Ducking behind a nearby car, he removed a flashlight from his belt. As he

stood up, he illuminated the area and saw two men with pump shotguns. He opened fire and one assailant went down while the other ducked down behind a parked car. The agent quickly took cover, moved laterally, reloaded his pistol, and waited.

He heard steps on the gravel to his right. He rolled out from behind the car, illuminated the area, and shot the gunman twice.

Both attackers were conveyed to the hospital where they survived emergency surgery. A total of five Hydra-Shok bullets were recovered from both men. They had an average recovered diameter of .64 inch and an average recovered weight of 211 grains.

• • • • •

.45 COLT

Originally a black powder offering, the .45 Colt was a popular defensive round prior to the introduction of magnums. It saw a resurgence with the introduction of Smith & Wesson's Model 25-5 .45 Colt revolver and hollowpoint ammunition from Winchester and Federal. The results of actual shootings are listed in Table 15-9.

• • • • •

He was a member of a 350-officer department. His chief allowed the carrying of other calibers than the issue .38 Special as long as they were not magnums. The officer chose a S&W Model 25-5 revolver with 4-inch barrel. Loaded with Federal lead hollowpoints, he carried it in a Safariland security holster.

He spent the first two hours of the day shift at an elementary school serving as a crossing guard. He had completed his detail and was walking to his patrol car when he saw a man and woman arguing in the parking lot. As he got closer, he saw the man grab the woman and shove her against a parked car.

The officer reached for the man as he ordered him to step away from her. The man

TABLE 15-9
.45 COLT ACTUAL RESULTS

LOAD	TOTAL SHOOTINGS	ONE-SHOT STOPS	PERCENTAGE
1. Fed 225-gr. LHP	69	54	78
2. Win 225-gr. JHP	53	39	74
3. Win 255-gr. RNL	59	41	69
4. Rem 255-gr. RNL	19	12	63

spun around and lunged at him, and the officer realized he had been stabbed in the side. Staggering back, he pulled his revolver and fired five rounds. The man collapsed and died en route to the hospital. The woman was his ex-girlfriend who had gotten a court order to keep him away.

Two Federal lead hollowpoints were removed at the morgue. They had an average recovered diameter of .65 inch and an average recovered weight of 211 grains.

• • • • •

He had inherited the gun from his father. It was a long-barreled Colt New Service revolver in .45 Colt caliber. He had loaded it with Federal lead hollowpoints and put it in his nightstand drawer. He didn't give it another thought until one night several months later. He had turned off the TV and lights and was climbing into bed when he heard someone trying his door. He grabbed the big revolver, quietly walked to the living room, and sat down in one corner where he had a clear view of the doorway.

He waited quietly as the intruder again tried to manipulate the lock. Finally, he started to kick the door. The door held for three kicks and then gave way. The intruder stepped inside and the apartment dweller opened fire. The victim turned, took a few steps, and collapsed. The shooter quickly dialed 911, and responding officers found a very dead burglar. The apartment dweller was

sentenced to 90 days in jail for possession of an unregistered handgun.

One Federal lead hollowpoint was removed from the felon's heart at the morgue. It had a diameter of .56 inch and a weight of 197 grains.

• • • • •

As a casino security guard, she was required to buy her own handgun and leather gear. She had purchased a used S&W Model 25-5 revolver from a local cop. He had included three boxes of Federal lead hollowpoints.

It was shortly after 2 A.M. when she took her hourly tour through the rear parking lot. She was on her way back to the casino when she saw movement by a parked limo. Thinking it was a drunk, she illuminated the area and was horrified to see one man stabbing another one repeatedly. She immediately drew her revolver and fired one round. It missed, and as the attacker turned toward her, she fired two more rounds that also missed.

The man was within arm's length when she shoved the revolver against his chest and fired her last three rounds. The man collapsed at her feet. She was pulling the portable radio from her belt when she felt weak. Looking down, she saw blood running down her leg.

She and her attacker were rushed to a local hospital. He was DOA, while she underwent several hours of surgery. She eventually recovered and returned to work. Her attacker

The Rem .45 Colt load offers good performance with modest recoil.

had been a professional hit man whose target was a loan shark customer who had missed several payments.

The recovered bullets had an average diameter of .62 inch and a recovered weight of 203 grains.

• • • • •

He saw the revolver at a gun show and had fallen in love with it. It was a heavily modified S&W Model 25-5 that featured a hard chrome finish, 3-inch barrel, and a round butt with custom grips. He bought it and threw it in the briefcase that accompanied him as he made his rounds as an insurance adjuster.

He had taken a break for lunch and decided to eat it on the shore of a local lake. He wanted to read some claims before making his next appointment so he carried his briefcase with him. He was engrossed in his tuna salad sandwich and report when he heard voices nearby.

He looked up to see three young men running down the shoreline, but he simply turned back to his work. Soon he became aware that someone was standing nearby and, looking up, he saw the same young men standing next to him. They smiled and asked him for money. When he declined, one of

them produced a club and changed the request to a demand.

Reaching inside his briefcase, the insurance adjuster produced the handgun and directed them to leave. Two of them complied, but the one who held the club indicated that he didn't believe the man would use the gun. As the thug stepped closer, the adjuster raised his revolver and fired one round. The young man dropped his club and started to turn before he fell on his back, dead.

The bullet was recovered from the thug's liver and had a diameter of .69 inch and weighed 214 grains.

• • • • •

He had an interest in the Old West, so he had purchased a single-action Colt Army with a 7 1/2-inch barrel chambered for the .45 Colt. He shot it often and routinely carried it while going about his duties on his large ranch. He had originally loaded it with standard .45 Colt ammo, but when he had to dispatch an injured cow, he found that load inadequate. He then purchased a box of Federal lead hollowpoints.

He was in the process of repairing some fence when he realized that he needed more nails. Going to the barn, he found that he was out of the appropriate size. He told his wife that he had to run into town to buy nails and asked her if she needed anything. She replied in the negative and he jumped in his pickup and headed for town. He was so used to carrying the big Colt he didn't even realize he had it on. It didn't matter, since the western state he lived in had no prohibition against the carrying of an unconcealed handgun.

He parked his truck in front of the hardware store and went inside. After purchasing a box of nails and some other supplies, he returned to the truck but then decided to buy a couple of gallons of the apple cider he loved so much.

He was crossing the street on his way to the market when he heard tires squeal and saw a muscle car speeding down the street. It suddenly swerved to the right and struck the rear of his pickup truck. The driver's side door flew open, and a young man jumped out and immediately fell down. Obviously drunk, he started to curse the dumb cowboy who had parked his truck in such a stupid place. The drunk then ran up and started kicking the truck. The rancher carefully crossed the street and asked the young man to stop, but he responded by pulling a large folding knife and threatening to cut the rancher's throat.

Stepping back, the truck owner pulled his single action and cocked it. He ordered the young man to drop the knife, but instead he lowered his head and charged. The rancher fired one round that struck the young man in the upper chest and drove him to his knees.

He was conveyed to a local hospital where he expired in emergency. The bullet was recovered from the large intestine. It had a recovered diameter of .69 inch and a recovered weight of 219 grains.

16

The Great Subsonic Controversy

What is the "subsonic hollowpoint"? What is the "controversy"? How can the subsonic be improved? How did this all start?

In September 1987, the FBI called together a panel of experts to discuss wound ballistics. This was in response to the April 1986 shootout in Miami, Florida, in which two FBI agents were killed in a shootout with two felons. The Bureau felt the Miami gunfight would have turned out differently if the bullets the agents fired had produced deeper penetration in their opponents.

The 9mm Winchester 115-grain Silvertip fired by Special Agent Jerry Dove penetrated the right biceps of one of the felons, Michael Platt, entered his chest, collapsed his right lung, and came to rest in the lung tissue. Some have speculated that if the bullet had penetrated deeper, it would have taken out his heart and the gunfight would have been over before anyone else was shot.

That sort of wishful thinking is not supported by medical facts, nor has it been the experience of other street cops. Officers with the Montana Highway Patrol, Crisp County, Georgia, Sheriff's Office, and Indianapolis, Indiana, Police Department have reported taking fire after perps took hollowpoint bullets in the heart. Broward County, Florida, medical examiner Dr. Abdullah Fatteh, in his book, *Gunshot Wounds*, documents eight separate cases of amazing physical activity after taking a through-and-through shot to the heart.

The FBI Wound Ballistics Workshop experts could reasonably be expected to know of possible physical activity after a gunshot wound. In spite of the facts, the consensus of the experts was to further investigate the then-new military 147-grain subsonic hollowpoint. This load produced up to twice the penetration of the 115-grain Silvertip hollowpoint.

Actually, the 9mm subsonic was not new at all. In the late 1960s, the original Military Armament Corp. (MAC) loaded 158-grain FMJ subsonic ammo for the U.S. Navy SEALs. The SEALs used this 9mm load in sound-suppressed S&W auto pistols to take out Viet

The Winchester 9mm subsonic hollowpoint was bumped from 140 to 145 grains and again to 147 grains to solve cycle reliability problems. Winchester cautions cops that subsonic hollowpoints may not cycle all guns reliably.

The Hornady 9mm 147-grain JHP at 950 fps is typical of all subsonics that produce too little bullet velocity for reliable expansion and too little slide velocity for reliable weapon functioning.

Even advanced bullet designs like the Black Talon or Ranger SXT cannot make up for low velocities. The 9mm 147-grain subsonic JHP has the worst stopping power of any hollowpoint in that caliber.

Cong guard dogs and sentries at very close range. After Vietnam, the navy emphasis changed to making head and torso shots at 100 yards from submachine guns. First they tried the suppressed open-bolt Uzi, then the suppressed closed-bolt H&K MP5-SD, but the 158-grain hardball was just not accurate enough for 100-yard head shots.

In the late 1970s, Winchester-Olin helped the navy meet its accuracy goals. The first load was a 140-grain jacketed hollowpoint marked "Type B." (When it comes to "match" grade accuracy, the base of a bullet is much more important than its nose. In making jacketed bullets, the ammo companies can control the dimensions on the impact-extruded base of a JHP jacket with much greater precision than the jacket-wrapped base of a FMJ bullet.)

The 140-grain JHP was the first of what would later become the Olin Super Match (OSM). It met the navy standard for 100-yard accuracy, but it would not always cycle the H&K MP5. In the early 1980s, the bullet weight was increased to 145 grains to help functioning. This was still known as "Type B" ammunition.

The 145-grain round improved the functioning in the MP5 and the suppressed MP5-SD, but the short MP5K still needed more bolt momentum, so in the mid-1980s the bullet weight was bumped up again to 147 grains. This subsonic hollowpoint, "Type L," was the military-spec OSM that the FBI workshop experts recommended for police work.

Up until now, match accuracy was the only expectation from the OSM, not stopping power. But the 9mm subsonic had also been

Cor-Bon loads the 9mm 147-grain Gold Dot to +P pressures and 1,000 fps velocities. This improves cycle reliability and tactical penetration and produces a longer, larger, and more debris-tolerant stretch cavity.

plagued by functioning problems ever since it became a hollowpoint.

In the mid-1980s, the navy began using the 9mm subsonic in its worldwide counter-terrorism operations. Further, U.S.-based military police began using the the load in genuine urban police scenarios. For the first time, at least some bullet expansion became a navy requirement in an attempt to avoid overpenetration in urban scenarios. (Again, underexpansion and overpenetration in tissue have *always* been characteristics of the 9mm subsonic.) In the late 1980s, the navy, not the FBI, began a push for reliable bullet expansion from the 9mm subsonic. The Bureau was satisfied with the .498 to .525 inch of expansion in ordnance gelatin, according to its April 1988 report.

Federal Cartridge joined the navy in the design effort. The company made one version for the suppressed H&K MP5-SD that bled bullet velocity down to 777 fps. Since a second version would follow, this Federal load 9 Military Subsonic, 9MS, was designated 9MS-1. The navy then changed its emphasis and required expansion without fragmentation from the MP5K (which produces velocities of 1,009 fps). Federal released a second version with a much narrower hollowpoint cavity, which was unofficially designated 9MS-2. The hollowpoint is almost an exact copy of Winchester's OSM.

In April 1988, and with much fanfare on having solved a tough stopping power problem that they and only they defined, the FBI adopted the military 147-grain Olin Super Match Type L subsonic hollowpoint for police work. The Bureau had done a number of lab tests with gelatin and obstacles like glass, wood, and sheet metal. Of the loads tested, the 9mm subsonic expanded the least and penetrated the most, giving the FBI what it wanted.

Unlike most other federal agencies, the FBI is influential, high profile, and media-oriented. Most police chiefs and sheriffs are shocked to find out the Secret Service, Border Patrol, Customs, and Marshals Service *also* perform bullet tests and that these tests *disagree* with the FBI tests. But it is the Bureau that reaches out to local law enforcement through its National Academy, so it is the Bureau opinion that gets heard.

As a result, *thousands* of city, county, and state police agencies took the FBI testing at face value. They quickly adopted the 9mm subsonic at a time when many agencies were transitioning to auto pistols. Other agencies that had not experienced stopping power, cycling, or penetration problems with their 9mm ammo also dropped whatever duty load they were issuing and fell into line behind the FBI.

Some agencies, however, kept their 115-grain, 124-grain, and 115-grain +P+ ammo. They either did not trust the FBI gelatin testing, were satisfied with their current duty load performance, or were more persuaded by actual gunfight results coming in from agencies like the U.S. Border Patrol, Illinois State Police, and Camden City, New Jersey, Police Department.

This difference of opinion set the stage for the most realistic police ammo performance test ever documented. Metro-Dade, Florida, Police adopted the 147-grain subsonic, while the nearby Miami, Florida, Police kept the 115-grain hollowpoint, and the Florida Marine Patrol opted for the 124-grain +P+ JHP. The FBI had the 147-grain subsonic while the Border Patrol used the 115-grain +P+ hollowpoint, and the Marshal's Service fired the 124-grain +P+ hollowpoint. The Indiana State Police followed along with the 147-grain subsonic, while neighboring Illinois State Police held fast with its 115-grain +P+ JHP, and the Franklin County (Columbus), Ohio, Sheriff issued the 124-grain hollowpoint. Finally, the Los Angeles, California, Sheriff adopted the 147-grain subsonic, while the Los Angeles PD selected the 115-grain +P hollowpoint.

The 9mm subsonic gained in popularity until the facts from the street started to get around in police circles. We now have had eight years of street experience with the 147-grain subsonic compared to other 9mm hollowpoints in the same local or regional police jurisdictions and scenarios. In terms of stopping power, the 115- and 124-grain hollowpoints in both standard- and high-pressure versions have proven to be significantly more effective in a police role than the 147-grain subsonic hollowpoint.

In 1987, no one could prove they had a better answer than the FBI. We now know the problems that the FBI "solution" has caused and can prove it.

The low-velocity, 9mm 147-grain subsonic hollowpoint has four separate and significant problems when it is used as a police duty or personal defense load:

1. It has the lowest stopping power and wound ballistics of any hollowpoint in the 9mm caliber.
2. It offers the least penetration of any 9mm against tactical barriers used as cover, including auto and thermopane glass and car bodies.
3. It has the most excessive penetration in soft tissue of any 9mm hollowpoint.
4. It has the lowest slide velocity of any 9mm load. This has caused cycling failures, both during training and in actual gunfights.

Just because a major police department adopts a particular load, that doesn't make it a good police duty load, and it certainly doesn't make it a good home defense load.

One major (980-man) midwest police department selected the 9mm 147-grain subsonic after performing only accuracy and

The standard-pressure 9mm 124-grain lead and jacketed hollowpoints are better police and defensive loads than any 147-grain JHP. They have more stopping power, are less likely to over-penetrate torsos, are more likely to defeat car bodies, and have better weapon cycling.

muzzle velocity tests. And only on one weight of bullet. No cycle testing was done. No testing against barricades was done. No expansion tests were done. No penetration tests were done.

Police departments aware of their responsibility and liability in ammo selection either conduct their own exhaustive tests or scrutinize test results from other agencies. The problem, however, is that a wide variety of assumptions and test procedures result in very different ammo recommendations, even at the prestigious federal level. As noted, the U.S. Border Patrol researched the 9mm caliber and selected the 115-grain +P+ hollowpoint. The U.S. Marshal's Service researched the 9mm caliber and selected the 124-grain +P+ hollowpoint. The FBI researched the 9mm caliber and selected the 147-grain low-velocity hollowpoint.

CYCLE RELIABILITY PROBLEMS

In ammo selection for an auto pistol, the first responsibility of any load is that it must feed and cycle reliably in the pistol. Cycle reliability is dependent on a number of factors. These include chamber pressure, powder burn rate, bullet weight, bullet velocity, muzzle energy, and muzzle momentum.

The key to cycle reliability is the velocity of the slide as it impacts the frame at its full rearward travel. The design window is typically a minimum of 6 fps and a maximum of 12 fps. Slide velocity, however, is difficult to compute. In fact, gun companies use sophisticated math models, accelerometer instruments, and high-speed photography to accurately obtain it. Both bullet energy and bullet momentum play key roles. The momentum of the bullet must overcome the momentum of the slide. The energy of the bullet must overcome the energy stored in the recoil and trigger springs. (We correctly associate "felt recoil" with bullet momentum. Simplistically, momentum is the product of the bullet weight in grains times the muzzle velocity in fps divided by the constant 225,120.)

Both excessive and insufficient slide velocity cause weapon stoppages. The problem is that poor firearm training and weapon maintenance and certain confrontational factors can work together to actually reduce slide velocity totally independent of the ammo. These include failure to lock the wrist, improper grip (either a grip that is too low or thumb friction against the slide), friction from a barricade used as cover, dirt and debris, improper lubrication (either too much or too little), marginal ammo by design, defective ammo, and shooting before a full stance is achieved.

Every one of these factors steals slide velocity. As a general observation and with equal chamber pressures, heavier bullets have slower, less snappy slide velocities. The result is a failure to eject, failure to engage the slide lock, or failure to strip the top cartridge in the magazine.

A short stroke is the result of too little slide velocity. This means the slide does not have enough rearward travel. Listed in chronologic order are signs of too little rearward slide velocity.

1. Rechamber the fired case.
2. Extract case but have extractor claw pull off case head before ejection; attempt but fail to rechamber the fired case.
3. Extract but fail to eject (stovepipe); empty case caught by slide and barrel.
4. Eject but fail to strip next round; close on empty chamber.
5. Eject but only partially engage top round; friction in magazine prevents upward full travel of top round.
6. Engage top round but fail to push forward with enough force. This includes A) not chambered; live cartridge case put partially in chamber but not under the extractor claw, and B) almost chambered; just short of being in battery.
7. Failure of slide to lock open after last round.

Low-momentum, low-energy ammo like the 9mm 147-grain subsonic is the single

The .40 S&W 165-grain Medium Velocity loads from Federal (shown here) and CCI produce less stopping power and less slide velocity than typical 180-grain loads. These may not cycle all .40 S&W pistols reliably.

greatest cause of what many police trainers call shooter-induced stoppages. But these stoppages are not shooter-induced; they are actually ammo-induced. They go away when cops use low-momentum, high-energy loads like the 9mm standard-pressure 115-grain JHP. In police work, we call that a "clue."

The most intolerable fault of the 9mm 147-grain subsonic hollowpoint is poor cycle reliability. Winchester has known this for years since it helped the navy develop the load. This included bumping the bullet weight twice to help solve the problem.

Winchester specifically cautions subsonic-shooting cops about these jams in its police catalog: *"Due to the slower cycling (slide velocity) of subsonic ammunition, it is critical that your weapon be well-maintained and cleaned regularly. It is important to keep your wrist locked when using subsonic ammo, as the reduced recoil (momentum) may cause your weapon to cycle incorrectly and jam. Subsonic ammunition may not reliably function in all types of firearms."*

The 147-grain subsonic is a low-momentum load. This means it produces a low slide impulse. Smaller stature shooters, shooters with a weak or improper grip, and shooters in a physical struggle where the grip was not rock solid have experienced up to a 30 percent cycle failure. And this has had nothing to do with the make of auto pistol; it has happened with Sigs, Berettas, Glocks, and Smiths alike.

All auto pistols by all gun makers are designed to operate reliably within a certain range of slide impact velocities. However, some factories will indicate which loads within that range have the most margin of safety in terms of cycle reliability. Glock is one such responsible company.

The Glock is specifically designed to cycle all factory ammo, from the fastest lightweights to the most sluggish subsonics. Yet during its certified Armorer's School, the +P, +P+, and "carbine" loads in the 9mm caliber are specifically recommended for the most reliability given the realities of the street.

Any time the shooter is not a perfectly rigid firing platform, the ammo must take up the slack. The best way to identify shooter-related stoppages that are actually ammo-related stoppages is to set up a simple test. Have the smallest person who will use the ammo shoot 200 of the proposed loads one-handed with both the strong and weak hand. Watch for stoppages normally but incorrectly called shooter-induced. Select the auto pistol ammo which produced the least of these cycle failures. Choosing the ammo that has momentum and energy to spare under ideal training conditions such as this means the ammo will still have enough momentum and energy under adverse duty conditions.

One example of how to fix the problem of poor cycle reliability from the subsonic's low slide velocity comes from the Indianapolis, Indiana, Police Department. The IPD issues the Federal 147-grain (9MS-2) JHP load, except it is loaded hotter. As a specific and concerted effort to improve the slide velocity from 9mm subsonic ammo, the IPD requires a load that is 50 fps faster than the standard subsonic loading. This is Federal's special-purpose load, XM9MS, which reaches 1,040 fps from the Glock 17. The extra 50 fps makes a big difference at subsonic velocities that can be the difference between cycling a recoil-operated pistol and a stoppage in the middle of a gunfight.

Cycle Reliability Problems with the .40 S&W

The 9mm is not the only auto pistol caliber with ammo downloaded enough to risk the slide velocity being too slow. It happened to the .40 S&W caliber, too.

At the FBI's request, Federal Cartridge released the first .40 S&W Medium Velocity 165-grain Hydra-Shok. Not wanting to be excluded from bidding on large ammo contracts, CCI-Speer followed suit with a 165-

The Winchester 9mm 147-grain Supreme SXT produces a very controlled 13.7 inches of penetration in gelatin. At 320 ft-lbs. of energy, this improved load still has trouble defeating car bodies and building materials compared to higher energy 9mm JHPs.

grain Medium Velocity Gold Dot. Federal and CCI load their 165-grain hollowpoints down to the 950 fps velocity normally associated with 180-grain JHPs. Instead of 33,000 psi, the Federal load, for example, has a chamber pressure of just 25,000 psi.

The official rationale for such low-pressure, mid-range, medium-velocity .40 S&W loads is that they will produce less weapon wear and less recoil. The FBI wanted a load that was more controllable for its special agents than the then-available 155-, 165-, and 180-grain JHPs. The felt recoil for this 950 fps, 165-grain ammo is similar to that of a 9mm 115-grain +P. These low-recoil, slow-slide-velocity .40 S&W loads certainly do allow faster follow-up shots, and they certainly do produce less wear and tear on the pistols.

In terms of wound ballistics, however, these medium-velocity .40 S&W loads are only good. The 165-grain MV Hydra-Shok expands to .61 caliber and penetrates 13.8 inches. The resulting stretch cavity is no larger than an average .38 Special +P hollowpoint. This load calculates to about 82 percent effective.

The 165-grain MV Gold Dot expands to .66 caliber, penetrates 14.5 inches, and produces a slightly larger crush cavity and a slightly larger stretch cavity than the Hydra-Shok. The predicted wound ballistics, however, are still 82 percent.

The real problem with these two medium-velocity loads is that they each produce 8 percent less energy and 8 percent less impulse than the 180-grain, 950 fps ammo. This also means they produce the least slide velocity of any hollowpoint in the .40 S&W caliber. All .40 S&W auto pistols were originally designed around the slide impulse from 180-grain, 950 fps ammo. To fire a load with less energy and less recoil than the original load risks creating a slide velocity too slow to make these recoil-operated pistols reliable under a wide variety of shooting scenarios.

If the recoil from the standard-velocity .40 S&W ammo is so much for some shooters that they must be issued ammo with 9mm recoil, then they should be issued 9mm auto pistols.

Issuing .40 S&W recoil-operated auto pistols and hoping they will operate with 9mm levels of recoil is a serious risk.

EXPANSION PROBLEMS

Most subsonic hollowpoints all have thresholds of expansion just below their muzzle velocity. The threshold of expansion is the velocity at which the bullet just begins to expand. This is not the velocity necessary to achieve a fully mushroomed diameter but just to start the mechanical movement of the lead core and copper jacket. Below this threshold, the bullet will not expand.

When the muzzle velocity is way above the threshold of expansion, like the 9mm 115-grain +P+, the JHP bullet always expands and sometimes even fragments. However, when the muzzle velocity is just barely above the threshold of expansion, like the 9mm 147-grain, the JHP seldom expands. If it does expand, it is not much.

An extra 50 fps of muzzle velocity so close to the threshold of expansion can make the difference between expanding and failing to expand. The JHP bullet that expands fixes two other problems with the subsonic: it transfers more energy, which increases stopping power, and it produces less excessive soft tissue penetration, which reduces risks associated with overpenetrating bullets.

An extra 50 fps such as required by the Indianapolis PD also begins to solve the fourth problem with subsonic ammo: low tactical penetration. Given the same basic construction and hardness, a bullet with more energy will penetrate hard cover better than a bullet with less energy. Energy is the ability to do work. In this case, the work is penetrating auto and domestic glass, car doors, wood and steel dwelling doors, and other domestic building materials. A bullet with more velocity has more energy and is more likely to defeat these types of tactical cover.

STOPPING POWER PROBLEMS

Poor cycle reliability caused by low slide velocity and dismal expansion from the 9mm 147-grain subsonic hollowpoint are just two of its problems. Another is relatively low stopping power for the caliber.

Based on 588 shooting reports from all 50 states and six foreign countries, the 9mm 147-grain subsonic is 76 percent effective. This compares to 82 percent for the standard-pressure 115-grain hollowpoint and 83 percent

In spite of all the hype about the 9mm subsonic, the (left to right) Remington 115-grain JHP, Federal 115-grain JHP, and Winchester 115-grain STHP each have better street records than any 147-grain JHP.

for the 124-grain hollowpoint. The 115-grain +P+ is effective a magnum-like 90 percent of the time. The 147-grain subsonic is the least effective hollowpoint in the caliber. Every major police department using the 9mm 147-grain subsonic has a list of horror stories with this load, whether it will officially acknowledge them or not.

Actually, many law enforcement agencies are in an advanced stage of denial concerning the stopping power of the 9mm 147-grain subsonic hollowpoint. Some even go so far as to confuse the eventual lethality from the load with its instantaneous stopping power. Of course, lethality and stopping power in police and defensive scenarios are almost totally unrelated.

For example, more people have been killed by the .22 Long Rifle than any other metallic cartridge. Certainly the .22 Long Rifle is incredibly lethal, yet it has the least instantaneous stopping power of any metallic cartridge. At the opposite end of the stopping power scale, we find loads that are instantly incapacitating yet are no more lethal than loads with less stopping power. The issue of lethality is strictly one of shot placement; the issue of stopping power is more one of energy transfer. That is why,

when given the same shot placement, some caliber's bullets incapacitate more rapidly than other caliber's bullets.

PENETRATION PROBLEMS

As if stopping power problems are not bad enough, in general, the 147-grain subsonic produces excessive penetration in soft tissue and too little penetration against bone and vehicles.

Because it does not expand, the subsonic exits on a torso shot between 65 and 75 percent of the time. This was well known to the U.S. Navy, which helped develop the load, but it was not a concern for navy scenarios. However, in an urban police role, over-penetration is a major issue both from civil liability and moral viewpoints.

The fact that the same 9mm 147-grain subsonic ammo can overpenetrate in one scenario and underpenetrate in another can be confusing even to cops who select ammo for a living. The subsonic bullet overpenetrates in soft tissue because it does not expand. It underpenetrates against bone and vehicles because it is a low energy round, and energy gives a projectile the ability to perform work, namely penetrate hard objects. These

The Federal 9mm 115-grain +P+ JHP (left) and Winchester 9mm 115-grain Silvertip (center) do not exit a 14-inch block of gelatin. The Federal 147-grain JHP (right) exits with enough energy to cause a casualty as defined by the U.S. Army.

engineering aspects of bullet penetration are just not that difficult to understand.

In soft tissue, bullets which fail to expand penetrate more than those which do expand. In hard objects, bullets with less energy penetrate less than those with more energy. Higher velocity bullets typically have higher energies. They expand more reliably, have a controlled soft tissue penetration, and are able to reliably defeat most barricades. Sluggish subsonic bullets are just the opposite. With the bullet diameter and construction equal, energy means tactical penetration.

Of the 147-grain JHPs, the Federal Hydra-Shok seems the most able to expand reliably after defeating heavy clothes. The CCI-Speer Gold Dot is the best load against automotive and thermopane glass since it will not shed its copper-plated jacket. The best of the subsonics against building materials and steel car panels, while still achieving expansion in tissue, is the Remington Golden Saber.

A responsible minimum penetration depth in soft tissue is in the 8- to 10-inch range. The success of the off-duty Glaser Safety Slug, which penetrates 6 to 7 inches, and Winchester's Illinois State Police duty 9mm 115-grain +P+ hollowpoint, which penetrates 8 to 10 inches, indicate that the 12-inch minimum quoted by others is incorrect. A realistic minimum penetration distance in calibrated ordnance gelatin for duty ammo is, in fact, 10 inches. See Chapter 28 for an analysis of what the optimum penetration distance, based on a variety of gunfights, really is.

Just in terms of stopping power alone, a maximum penetration depth of 14 inches should be established. However, we have an additional duty to prevent injury from exiting bullets. Beyond 14 inches, as the stopping power decreases, the threat of overpenetration obviously increases.

The risk from exiting bullets can indeed be measured objectively. U.S. Army surgeons determined 58 ft-lbs. of energy was required to cause a casualty. Recently, a major federal police service has confirmed support for this number. A valid definition of dangerous

overpenetration, therefore, is any bullet which has more than 58 ft-lbs. of energy after passing through a certain depth of gelatin.

An estimated 70 percent of the bullets with 15 1/2 inches of penetration in gelatin overpenetrate with solid torso shots on the street. We have selected 14 inches of gelatin as the amount to use when checking for this dangerous overpenetration.

The test is easy. All it takes is one chronograph to get entry velocity, a 14-inch block of 10-percent calibrated gelatin, and another chronograph to get exit velocity.

With 9mm hollowpoints, for example, few if any of the 115-, 124-, or 115-grain +P+ loads that we tested even exited the 14-inch block. These loads pose the least downrange risk. Some of the advanced-design 147-grain hollowpoints and 124-grain +P+ hollowpoints exit the block with up to 48 ft-lbs. of energy. The standard 147-grain hollowpoints exited with up to 93 ft-lbs. of energy.

In today's litigious society, police departments know or should have known about excessive penetration. If they wantonly disregard this aspect of ammo in their research, they could be found deliberately negligent in their duty to protect bystanders.

REPLACING THE 9mm 147-GRAIN SUBSONIC

Clearly, and by all realistic and relevant ways of measuring bullet effectiveness, the 147-grain subsonic produces the least stopping power of any 9mm hollowpoint. This is one of the reasons why police agencies from coast to coast are dropping it in favor of a better bullet or are dropping the 9mm caliber altogether.

Keep in mind that a switch in either bullet or caliber is a tacit admission of an error somewhere in the process. No one wants to admit to this sort of thing, especially police officers who are held to a higher standard. Great credit goes to those departments that have had the guts to switch from the politically correct 9mm 147-grain JHP to a more effective bullet in the same caliber. These agencies include Las Vegas Metro

Police, Jacksonville, Florida, Sheriff's Department, and Waco, Texas, Police.

This change within the 9mm caliber is almost too much to expect from many police departments, as it is a slam directly to the 147-grain subsonic bullet and the entire test methodology that brought it about. But a much more face-saving way exists.

The 9mm 147-grain subsonic is being dropped in huge numbers simply by transitioning from the 9mm to the .40 S&W or .45 Auto. Watch for these "caliber upgrades." Anytime you learn of a police department adopting a new caliber, find out what the old caliber was and what bullet was in use. By a landslide, the caliber being abandoned is the 9mm, and the load being dropped is the 147-grain subsonic hollowpoint. This process of upgrading calibers is, in fact, evidence that the 9mm 147-grain JHP is not suitable for law enforcement. No one will admit this, of course. They do not have to admit it. Their actions speak loudly enough.

The new law restricting civilian auto pistol magazines to 10 rounds has greatly helped police departments looking for an easy and innocent way to dump the 9mm 147-grain subsonic. It works like this. The law has put existing high-capacity 9mm auto pistols used by the police in great demand. This is a large pool of prerestriction auto pistols. Police firearm distributors can make big money in the retail market by getting their hands on these pistols. In fact, many distributors will trade even with a police department to get these guns.

That is right. The police department trades in their "old" high-capacity 9mm pistols for brand new .40 S&W pistols at *no cost*. The cops get new guns. The cops dump the subsonic. The distributor makes money on the civilian market. Civilians get high-capacity pistols that are unavailable any other legal way. Everyone wins.

The politically correct .40 S&W load is the 180-grain JHP. It has none of the drawbacks that the politically correct 9mm 147-grain JHP has. This is a real success story. The cops get more reliable and more effective .40 S&W pistols and don't have to say one word against the 9mm 147-grain subsonic. However, regardless of appearances or press releases, this is still dumping the 9mm 147-grain subsonic at the very first face-saving opportunity.

The very least a police department can do to improve stopping power is to upgrade within the 147-grain bullet weight itself. The Winchester 147-grain OSM JHP has been

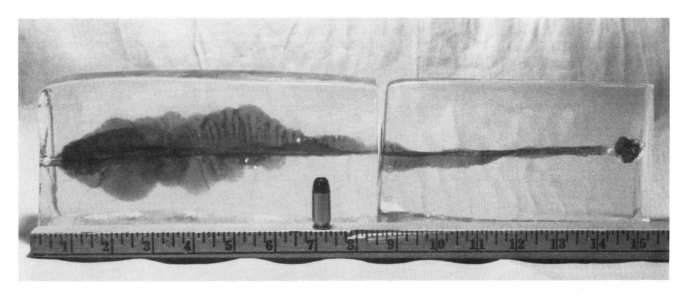

The Winchester .45 Auto 230-grain subsonic JHP was designed to limit expansion and penetrate deeply. As a rule, bullets with poor expansion produce poor stopping power.

proven to be the least effective hollowpoint in this caliber and weight. On the other hand, the Federal 147-grain Hydra-Shok has proven to have the most stopping power among standard-pressure 147-grain hollowpoints. The Winchester 147-grain Supreme SXT, Remington 147-grain Golden Saber, and CCI-Speer 147-grain Gold Dot all appear to be extremely promising based on multimedia gelatin tests.

CONCLUSION

Twenty years ago, the Illinois State Police went through "today's" problems of poor stopping power, over and underpenetration, and poor cycle reliability with 9mm ammo. To solve all these problems, the ISP worked with both Federal Cartridge and Winchester-Olin to develop what we know of today as the 115-grain +P+ ammo. Today, every major ammo company makes a police-only +P+ load. Street experience has proven this to be the single most effective, most reliable ammo to use in a 9mm auto pistol. Civilian shooters can get close to this performance with the 115-grain +P hollowpoint from Remington, Cor-Bon,

TABLE 16-1
9mm TACTICAL PENETRATION ABILITY, MOST TO LEAST

LOAD	ENERGY
115-gr. +P+ JHP	438 ft-lbs.
124-gr. +P+ JHP	410 ft-lbs.
115-gr. +P JHP	406 ft-lbs.
115-gr. Win. STHP	383 ft-lbs.
124-gr. Std. Vel. JHP	345 ft-lbs.
115-gr. Fed./Rem. JHP	340 ft-lbs.
147-gr. Subsonic JHP	295 ft-lbs.

Triton, Black Hills, Georgia Arms, and others.

For sheer accuracy, the best possible choice is the 147-grain subsonic Olin Super Match, as it was specifically and originally designed for tight 100-yard groups. But we now have four good reasons to pick some other 9mm hollowpoint or switch to another caliber like the .40 S&W for police and personal defense. It is time to call off the side-by-side police street tests before more good guys get hurt or killed.

TABLE 16-2
ACTUAL 9mm STOPPING POWER

9mm LOAD	AVERAGE VELOCITY, FPS	AVERAGE ONE-SHOT STOPS, %
115-gr. JHP +P,+P+	1,300	90
124-gr. JHP +P+	1,250	86
124-gr. LHP	1,100	84
115-gr. JHP	1,160	82
124-gr. JHP	1,100	81
147-gr. JHP Subsonic	950	76
115-gr. FMJ	1,160	63

TABLE 16-3
9mm EXCESS PENETRATION

LOAD	MUZZLE ENERGY, FT-LBS.	ENERGY AFTER 14 INCHES OF GELATIN, FT-LBS.
115-gr. +P+ JHP	438	no exit
115-gr. +P JHP	406	no exit
115-gr. Win STHP	383	no exit
124-gr. Std. JHP	345	no exit
115-gr. Fed JHP	340	no exit
147-gr. Hydra-Shok	295	5
124-gr. +P+ JHP	410	35
147-gr. Black Talon	295	35
147-gr. Win JHP	295	51
147-gr. Fed JHP	295	66

58 ft-lbs. causes casualties (U.S. Army)

TABLE 16-4
9mm SLIDE CYCLE VELOCITY, MOST TO LEAST

LOAD	VELOCITY FPS	ENERGY FT-LBS.	MOMENTUM LB-SEC.
115-gr. +P+ JHP	1,310	438	.67
124-gr. +P+ JHP	1,220	410	.67
115-gr. +P JHP	1,260	406	.64
115-gr. Win STHP	1,225	383	.63
124-gr. Std. Vel. JHP	1,120	345	.62
115-gr. Fed/Rem JHP	1,155	340	.59
147-gr. Subsonic JHP	950	285	.62

TABLE 16-5
.40 S&W SLIDE VELOCITY, MOST TO LEAST

LOAD	VELOCITY FPS	ENERGY FT-LBS.	MOMENTUM LB-SEC.
Win 155-gr. Silvertip	1,205	500	.830
Rem 165-gr. Golden Saber	1,150	485	.843
Cor-Bon 135-gr. Sierra JHP	1,325	526	.795
Cor-Bon 150-gr. Sierra JHP	1,200	480	.800
Fed 180-gr. Hydra-Shok	950	361	.760
Fed 165-gr. Hydra-Shok MV	950	331	.696
CCI-Speer 165-gr. Gold Dot MV	950	331	.696

17

Cor-Bon Ammo

Cor-Bon Ammunition has become well known as high-performance, street-reliable ammunition. This relatively new manufacturer has rocked the older, more conservative companies with its high-velocity, reliably expanding handgun ammunition.

The Cor-Bon approach is the result of the fertile mind of Peter Pi. Pi felt that ammunition makers tended to be overly conservative and generally more concerned about exotic names and unusual bullet configurations instead of real performance. He felt that Lee Jurras of Super Vel had been on the right track but that Super Vel failed for reasons other than performance.

Using the same innovative approach he had applied to heavy handgun hunting loads, Pi soon developed a number loads that offered high velocities with excellent accuracy and minimal muzzle flash. One federal agency found the Cor-Bon 115-grain 9mm JHP capable of shooting 25-meter groups of less than 1/2 inch from a test barrel.

There are those, of course, who are skeptical of the light, fast approach. Some "experts" have claimed that Cor-Bon ammo does not penetrate deeply enough in 10-percent gelatin to produce reliable results. But the results from the street have shown that Cor-Bon does extremely well in the real world.

One federal agency decided on an arbitrary minimum of 12 inches in 10-percent gelatin as a performance standard. This agency gave the Cor-Bon 9mm 115-grain JHP—which has a velocity of 1,356 fps out of Evan Marshall's Karl Sokol customized Browning Hi Power—a wounding value of zero. Now the merits of a 115-grain, .355-diameter hollowpoint bullet at 1,356 fps can be argued long and hard, but does any reasonable person really feel it has a wounding value of zero?

In the real world, of course, the Cor-Bon 9mm 115-grain JHP has a stopping power record of 29 stops out of 32 shootings for a percentage of 91 percent. While it fails to penetrate 12 inches of 10-percent gelatin, it routinely penetrates human tissue deeply enough to pierce or damage vital organs and stop people bent on destruction.

Other Cor-Bon loads have also proven to be reliable performers where it counts—on the street. In fact, the company has produced the

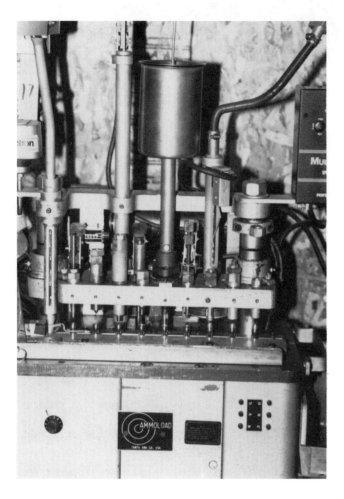

Ammoload machines allow Cor-Bon to keep up with customer demands.

Cor-Bon uses Dillon presses for specialty loads.

number one street stopper in the following calibers: .380 ACP, .38 Special (4-inch or longer barrel), 9mm, .40 S&W, and 10mm. The Cor-Bon .45 ACP 185-grain JHP is the only Cor-Bon load that we have actual shooting data on that is not the number one performer in its respective caliber.

Pi has not ignored those who prefer heavier bullets. His 147-grain 9mm JHP +P offering is the only 147-grain 9mm load that Evan Marshall would carry. With a velocity of 1,087 fps from a Browning Hi Power, it expands to .80 caliber in 10-percent gelatin and penetrates 13 inches.

Pi also loads a serious 165-grain .40 S&W. Unlike other brands in this bullet weight, it

averages 1,134 fps from a Heckler & Koch USP pistol and is very accurate. The Cor-Bon 180-grain .40 S&W JHP averages 1,078 fps from the same H&K pistol with low muzzle flash.

The Cor-Bon 158-grain lead hollowpoint +P+ turns the .38 snub into a significant weapon. It averages 916 fps from Evan Marshall's 2-inch-barreled Smith & Wesson Centennial. It expands well and has excellent accuracy.

The Cor-Bon 10mm 180-grain JHP not only leaves the competition in the dust but is gratifyingly accurate in Marshall's Glock 10mm. For those who prefer this caliber and are leery of the 135-grain Cor-Bon hollowpoint, it offers an attractive alternative.

Cor-Bon president Peter Pi at one of the company's ammunition loading machines.

The Cor-Bon .45 ACP 230-grain hollow-point averages 968 fps from Marshall's Russ Carniak customized Series 70 Colt Goverment model. It produces excellent accuracy and is very controllable. It penetrates 13 inches in 10-percent gelatin and expands to .70 caliber. While we haven't had any shootings with it yet, it looks extremely promising.

Cor-Bon also offers an impressive number of middleweight contenders, including a 9mm 124-grain JHP (1,268 fps), .45 ACP 200-grain JHP (1,034 fps), .357 Magnum 125-grain JHP (1,455 fps), and .45 Colt 200-grain JHP (1,022 fps).

Finally, Cor-Bon offers high-performance loads for some unusual calibers, including 9mm Makarov, 7.62x39mm, and .357 SIG. Cor-Bon's .308 125-grain ballistic point offering has proven to be quite accurate in Evan Marshall's Galil Sniper, outperforming several "match" loads.

The current street results from Cor-Bon are shown in Table 17-1.

Cor-Bon may not be one of the better known ammunition companies, but that's in the process of changing. If you're serious about self-defense, you should carry serious ammunition. As far as the authors are concerned, Cor-Bon is the most serious ammo of all.

TABLE 17-1
COR-BON AMMUNITION ACTUAL RESULTS

LOAD	VELOCITY FPS	TOTAL SHOOTINGS	ONE-SHOT STOPS	PERCENTAGE
.380 90-gr. JHP	1,007	20	14	70
9mm 115-gr. JHP	1,356	32	29	91
.40 S&W 135-gr. JHP	1,329	24	23	96
10mm 150-gr. JHP	1,322	10	9	90
.38 Spec 115-gr. JHP	1,269	29	24	83
.45 ACP 185-gr. JHP	1,135	12	11	92

ABOVE: Cor-Bon's most successful load is its 9mm 115-grain +P JHP at 1,330 fps, which leads the caliber at 91 percent effective. Cor-Bon was the first to produce police-only spec ammo for all shooters.

ABOVE: The wound profile of Cor-Bon's 9mm 115-grain +P JHP shows a rapid energy release and a controlled penetration. Optimal penetration is just 8.4 inches deep.

LEFT: The load with the most stopping power in the fastest growing caliber is this Cor-Bon .40 S&W 135-grain Nosler JHP. At 96 percent, this equals the .357 Magnum 125-grain JHP.

18
MagSafe and Glaser Updates

The book *Handgun Stopping Power* was finalized in mid-1991. At that time, the Glaser Safety Slug was by far the most proven of the frangible, prefragmented designs. The MagSafe frangible loads were a fairly new concept then and were undergoing dramatic design revisions every six months. We wrote:

"Overall, the MagSafe has the potential to be an extremely effective round. In some loads, it is a clear and genuine improvement over the Glaser due to deeper pellet penetration. Like all new designs, however, bugs in some of the MagSafe rounds need to be worked out."

That was then. This is mid-1995, and the MagSafe has been tweaked and perfected. It has indeed surpassed the Glaser Safety Slug in terms of overall wound ballistics.

Since the late 1980s, MagSafe has consolidated bullet designs and standardized on shot sizes. The company used to use birdshot numbers 6, 7 1/2, or 9 in the .355 to .357 caliber projectiles and numbers 2, 6, or 7 1/2 for the big-bore projectiles. With rare excep-

tions, MagSafe now uses numbers 2, 3, or 4 for all bullets.

The number 12 shot in the Glaser Blue penetrates 5 to 6 inches regardless of caliber or striking velocity. The number 6 shot in the Glaser Silver penetrates 7 1/2 to 8 1/2 inches in gelatin. The number 2 and 4 birdshot used in the MagSafe penetrates 9 to 13 inches.

Depending on the load, the MagSafe typically generates a larger temporary stretch cavity than the Glaser. Both designs break up with equal speed and reliability. It is this deeper pellet penetration into the police "duty" range of 10 to 14 inches that gives the MagSafe the technical knockout over the Glaser.

The MagSafe was the clear and obvious winner of the Strasbourg Tests. In most calibers, the Strasbourg researchers fired MagSafe's basic load, the Defender, against Glaser's basic load, the Blue Safety Slug. The Blue Safety Slug beat the MagSafe by .04 second in the .38 Special +P caliber, but that was the only Glaser victory. The Defender caused the most rapid collapse times in .380 Auto,

9mm, .357 Magnum, .40 S&W, 10mm, and .45 Auto. Of the currently available loads, the MagSafe .38 Special 65-grain +P+ Max and the MagSafe .357 Magnum 68-grain Defender tied in producing the fastest individual collapse times of the entire Strasbourg Tests at 1.7 seconds. MagSafe also scored the fastest average collapse time of all loads and calibers with the 10mm 96-grain Defender at 4.48 seconds.

The MagSafe Defender (left) and Glaser Safety Slug (right) won the Strasbourg Tests. Each load fires a copper-jacketed projectile with a birdshot core.

The grand averages from the Strasbourg Tests clearly tell the story. The average incapacitation times (AIT) for all seven handgun calibers were themselves averaged for the MagSafe, the Glaser, and the best conventional JHP regardless of make, weight, or design. They are:

LOAD	AIT
MagSafe Defender	4.99 sec
Glaser Blue Safety Slug	6.08 sec
Best JHP	8.51 sec

Let's take a close look at each load and see what is new over the past five years.

GLASER SAFETY SLUG

In the 1970s and 1980s, the projectile in the Glaser Safety Slug was a copper jacket filled with loose number 12 birdshot, sealed in place with a flat plastic wafer. This gave the Safety Slug a semiwadcutter feed profile.

In early 1987, all Glaser auto pistol caliber bullets were converted to a round-nose feed profile. A spherical ball was crimped in the copper jacket instead of a flat wafer. By mid 1987, all revolver caliber bullets were also switched from semiwadcutter to round-nose profile.

The flat-point Glaser had two legitimate problems. One was feed reliability in the auto pistol calibers; the other was its performance in a human target after penetrating glass. The

The MagSafe .38 Special +P+ 65-grain MAX is loaded with nine pieces of magnum-hard nickel-plated number 3 birdshot embedded in marine epoxy.

feed problem was solved in 1987 with the round-nose Safety Slug—the Glaser took on the exact profile of round-nose hardball, and the feeding question simply disappeared. As a side benefit, the round-nose plug delayed the breakup of the bullet, resulting in the average saturation depth in 9mm increasing from 5.13 to 5.84 inches.

The problem of tissue penetration after passing through glass remained a problem. Glass is incredibly hard on all bullets, but it is the hardest on the higher velocity bullets and

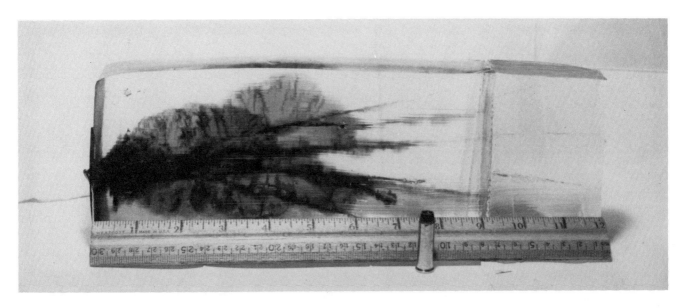

On impact, the MagSafe .38 Special +P+ 65-grain MAX fragments. Nine pieces of birdshot penetrate 12 to 13 inches of gelatin.

bullets designed to expand like the JHP or fragment like the Glaser. This tactical side issue of Glasers, however, did not affect the round's street reputation.

By the late 1980s, "adequate penetration" became the vogue term of the experts. In fact, some of the experts abandoned the idea of expanding bullets altogether, even though the street superiority of the jacketed hollowpoint is one of the most proven facts of wound ballistics. These same experts recommended deeply penetrating FMJ solid-core bullets, even though they have the worst actual street record of any load in a caliber.

The swing of the pendulum from no concern at all about penetration to the demand for excessive penetration was a force felt by everyone producing ammo, including Glaser. All of a sudden, experts were critical of one of the most effective defensive loads ever made because it didn't meet arbitrary ideal penetration depths. Everyone forgot the liability advantages of no overpenetration and no ricochet.

To remain competitive in the ammo industry, Glaser was forced to respond with a new line of ammo, coming out with the Glaser

The MagSafe .44 Special +P 115-grain Urban Defense and 9mm +P 64-grain Stealth are packed with hard nickel-plated number 2 birdshot. Each pellet penetrates 10 to 11 inches of tissue.

Silver in early 1991. The original Safety Slug with its loose core of number 12 shot would become known as the Glaser Blue since the round-nose plastic nosecap is blue. The .25 Auto and .32 Auto would be available as Glaser Blue; all other calibers except the rifle loads were available in both Glaser Blue and Glaser Silver.

The Glaser Silver uses a compressed core of number 6 birdshot. The core is compressed just to the point of removing the airspace from between the pellets. Each pellet now has an octangular shape rather than spherical. This

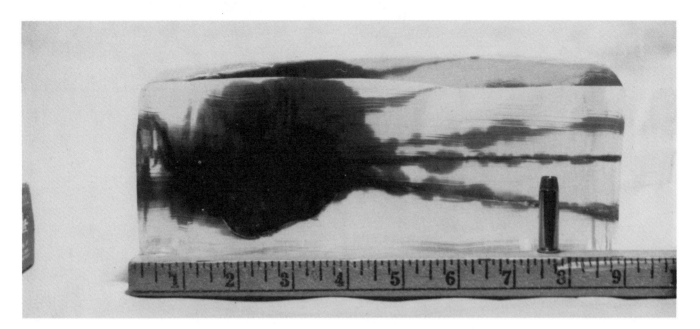

The MagSafe .38 Special non +P 52-grain Defender fragments on impact and saturates 9 inches of tissue with birdshot. This is plenty of penetration for most scenarios.

The devastating .44 Special +P 115-grain Urban Defense dumps 430 ft-lbs. of energy in 10 inches and has an 89 percent rating.

irregular shape causes an even wider distribution of shot in tissue after impact. The faster the shot spreads out after impact, the more likely a vital organ along the bullet path will be punctured.

We performed tests in ordnance gelatin to see the improvement in penetration depth for the 9mm and the .357 Magnum. The heavier Glaser Silver fragmented on impact as designed and formed an extremely large temporary

The low-recoil MagSafe .44 Magnum 115-grain Urban Defense fragments on impact and shreds the first 11 inches of tissue.

stretch cavity, as all Glasers do. Pieces of the jacket were found between 2 and 3 inches deep. By 7 inches, the shot had spread out to saturate an area 5 inches in diameter. The angular pellets of number 6 shot were recovered between 7 1/2 and 9 1/2 inches. We recorded 46 separate .11-caliber pellet paths. The Glaser Blue generated 350 paths with its .05-caliber number 12 pellet. The temporary stretch cavity of the Glaser Silver was larger than the Glaser Blue because the Silver penetrated deeper.

We never believed that shallow penetration depth was a real street issue with the Glaser. The stretch cavity is simply too large, and too much tissue gets perforated then dislodged. Street results from cops were simply too favorable. Remember, it was the experts in the labs and campus offices who got this whole penetration issue going, certainly not a significant number of ammo failures on the street. However, the Glaser Silver does indeed solve one of the age-old problems of the fragmenting bullet—overcoming tactical obstacles.

We fired the 9mm and .357 Magnum Glaser Silver into plywood in front of ordnance gelatin and then repeated this secondary target test using plate glass. It is in these areas where the round displays a realistic design improvement. The Silver punched through the half-inch plywood and penetrated to between 6 and 8 1/2 inches of gelatin. In the acid-test glass scenario, the Silver pulverized the glass and still penetrated to between 5 and 6 inches of gelatin. Most lightweight JHP bullets, even in the big-bore .45 Auto and .40 S&W, do not fare much better than this after glass.

So Glaser offers two soft tissue penetration options. Glaser Blue minimizes the downrange danger from bullets that miss the primary target. Glaser Silver maximizes soft tissue penetration while still avoiding overpenetration. Glaser ammo is available in handgun and rifle calibers from .25 ACP to .45 Colt, including .223 Remington and .30-06. Both the Silver and Blue come only in round-nose profile, meaning they will feed like FMJ hardball and

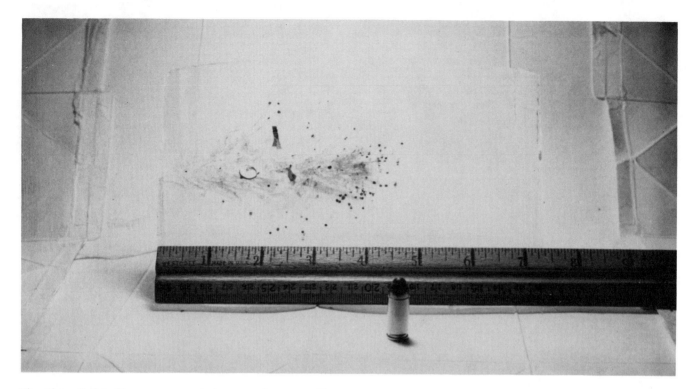

The Glaser Safety Slug was upgraded to round-nose profile in 1987 to improve feed reliability. This load used loose number 12 birdshot in the core.

speedload into a revolver as quickly as lead round-nose ammo.

The advantages of the compressed-core construction were so great that in late 1991, the Glaser Blue Safety Slug was also converted to this process. Its loose-packed core of spherical number 12 shot was replaced with a nearly fused core of number 12 shot. The change was to compress and crush the birdshot pellets in the jacket cup. This made the bullet denser for better accuracy, and it increased the number of pellets in the core for more wounding. Finally, the partially fused core penetrated roughly 10 percent deeper before the bullet fragmented. Today, all Glaser Safety Slugs except the small bores and the rifle calibers use compressed-core projectiles.

We fired a sampling of the Glaser Blue ammo with compressed number 12 shot. The wound ballistics in calibrated gelatin are what we have come to expect from Glaser. The hundreds of pellets cause a cone-shaped wound cavity similar to a shotgun fired in contact with the target. The Glaser totally trashes the first 6 to 7 inches of soft tissue and bone. Pellets perforate the tissue, then the stretch cavity dislodges the tissue.

As was recorded in the National Institute of Justice tests years ago, the Glaser forms about the largest temporary stretch cavity of any bullet design. It breaks up fast and transfers energy rapidly. However, it also produces enormous crush cavities since the birdshot fans out and pulverizes everything in its reach. The Glaser crushes more tissue in 6 inches of penetration than most mushroomed hollow-points do in 14 inches.

Large stretch cavities and large crush cavities always add up to large amounts of stopping power. The new compressed-core Glaser shoots about 12 percent tighter groups, feeds in all auto pistols, and still produces legendary wound ballistics.

MAGSAFE AMMO

MagSafe Ammo outgrew its awkward early years and today stands fully mature as the best of the frangible bullet designs. This is the ammo of choice for scenarios which call for frangible ammunition, including courtroom and VIP security, police backup, civilian concealed carry, carjack defense, and especially home, apartment, and mobile home defense.

The MagSafe product line has been trimmed back from a bewildering cross-section of ammo to just about two basic loads. The MagSafe Defender is the flagship of the line. This is the full-power, no-nonsense load upon which MagSafe built its dominating reputation. All handgun calibers from .25 Auto to .50 Action Express are available in a Defender load.

The Defender's "controlled core" bullet construction contains nickel- or copper-plated numbers 2, 3, or 4 magnum-hard birdshot. These pellets are encapsulated in tough marine epoxy. The epoxy matrix, however, shatters like glass on contact with soft tissue at high velocities, releasing the shot inside the target in a tight pattern of dispersion.

Against tactical materials like wood, the epoxy works just the opposite. It gives the bullet structural integrity to allow the MagSafe to penetrate certain building materials intact to later fragment on impact with soft targets. The exception to this is the SWAT load, which will be discussed later.

A unique feature of the Defender is its ability to generate destructive secondary missiles. As the core breaks up, 6 to 17 pellets, depending on caliber, are released. These continue forward, creating separate bullet paths. Along with adequate penetration, these separate missiles are responsible for the great wounding power of the MagSafe.

The only conventional ammo to launch such destructive missiles independent of the main bullet core are the scallop-serrated magnum revolver bullets from Remington Arms.

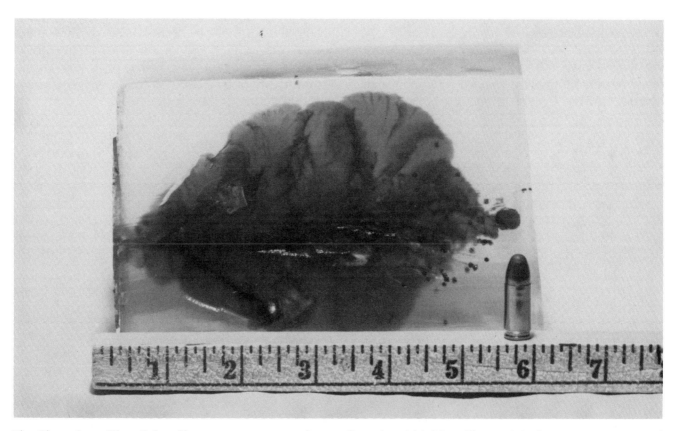

The Glaser 9mm Silver Safety Slug uses a compressed core of number 6 birdshot. The result is deeper penetration and better accuracy.

These generally leave a half dozen wound tracts 4 to 6 inches long in addition to the main bullet. The MagSafe pellets produce wound tracts up to 16 inches long.

The MagSafe puts a relatively small hole in the tissue and organs it strikes, but it has a much greater probability of striking vital tissue for the same shot placement. That is why secondary missiles add so much to a bullet's stopping power. For example, the MagSafe .38 Special MAX launches nine number 2 pellets. The number 2 shot only punches a .15-caliber hole through tissue. However, it contacts as much total tissue as .45 Auto hardball, and it is nine times more likely than the .45 Auto hardball to strike a vital organ.

MagSafe ammo has undergone near constant change since its introduction in the early 1980s, and with each change comes improvement. The loads available in 1995 have better accuracy, more even pellet dispersion, deeper penetration, and especially better feed designs.

Joe Zambone, president of MagSafe, started off testing his ammo in modeling clay, Ductseal, and wet newspaper like so many people still do. Then he went to packaged meat, which he still reverts to when he gets bored. Finally he advanced to 10-percent gelatin for his product testing and design. He now tests in heavily clothed gelatin and occasionally throws in obstacles to simulate ribs and muscle. When you test like that, your product has to be good.

While the ammo testing is quite advanced, the ammo manufacture is painstakingly slow and done all by hand. Zambone starts off with bullets made by companies such as Remington and Winchester. He literally melts the lead out of them to get the jackets to start the MagSafe bullet. These jackets are then filled by hand with the right number of the right kind of shot. For example, the 9mm Stealth load gets nine pieces of nickel-plated number 2 birdshot, while the .44 Special Defender gets eleven pieces of number 2 shot plus six pieces of plated number 4 shot. Once the pellets are in place, epoxy is poured over the shot payload to secure it (the epoxy is put into the .25 Auto Defender bullet with a syringe). From here the projectile is ready to load like any conventional bullet.

Part of the success of MagSafe ammo is its basic design, which offers Glaser performance with three times the penetration. The other part is the company's willingness to make some calibers available in loads with incredibly high chamber pressures.

The potent Glaser .357 Magnum Silver Safety Slug uses a compressed core of number 6 birdshot. This load gets in 9.5 inches deep.

The Glaser revolver calibers (from left to right: .38 Special, .357 Magnum, .44 Special, .44 Magnum, and .45 Colt) use round-nose Safety Slugs for the deepest penetration and the fastest speed loading.

The Glaser auto pistol Safety Slugs (from left to right: .25 ACP, .32 ACP, .380 ACP, 9mm, .38 Super, and .45 ACP) use round-nose bullets for maximum feed reliability. A .40 S&W load is available in both Blue and Silver.

MagSafe ammo is available in standard-pressure, +P, and +P+ loads depending on the caliber. If the load is not specially labelled, it can be fired safely in great quantities with no ill effects on the weapon. The shooter is warned, however, to avoid using +P-labelled ammo in older, weaker, or marginal quality guns. Simply do not shoot this stuff in battle-worn relics, cheaply made, or aluminum-framed guns, as the +P ammo will accelerate the wear even in top quality guns.

Responding to customer requests, MagSafe also loads ammo to what it calls +P+ pressures in its MAX line. This ammo is at or above industry chamber pressure standards, and a much stronger cartridge case is used. A special warning label is enclosed with each +P+ load. Some require stiffer recoil and firing pin springs to reduce the stress on the gun. The hot load in .38 Special, for example, quite clearly says that pressures normally associated with the .357 Magnum are generated.

In addition to the Defender, MagSafe also offers a SWAT load in most calibers. We normally associate the SWAT label with some enhanced ability or special function, and so it is with the MagSafe SWAT. The special purpose here is reduced wall penetration and the fastest possible bullet breakup.

MagSafe SWAT ammunition comes in two basic designs. One is slightly downloaded bullets that use caliber-wide hollowpoint openings for the fastest breakup in walls and other building materials. This SWAT ammo is specifically designed for police details like courtroom and airport security and forced entry. It is also ideal for apartment and mobile home dwellers. In these scenarios, a lot of bullets fly, and most miss. This puts a priority on minimum tactical penetration.

MagSafe SWAT loads in .38 Special, 9mm, and .357 Magnum break up after two layers of drywall or gypsum board. The number 2 pellets still exit this plasterboard, but on their own they only have 10 percent of the penetration energy that the original Defender slug has. Since the SWAT load still uses the number 2 shot, the pellet penetration in soft tissue is still deep, as the gelatin results show.

From a forensics viewpoint, the SWAT loads leave a unique wound signature. The six petals on the Remington scallop-serrated jacket break away from the main bullet after 3/4 inch of penetration to form a perfect six-point star with a diameter of roughly 1 1/2 inches. This positively identifies the projectile as coming from a MagSafe SWAT round.

The other basic SWAT design is a copper jacket filled entirely with marine epoxy and containing no birdshot at all. Available only in .40 S&W and .45 Auto, these loads use 46- and

66-grain bullets, respectively, driven to more than 2,100 fps. These SWAT loads produce massive riflelike temporary stretch cavities with shallow 6-inch penetration depths and the least wall penetration. In fact, the MagSafe SWAT is the least likely of any projectile to cause a downrange injury in the event of either a miss or marginal shot placement.

TABLE 18-1
GLASER "COMPRESSED BLUE" SAFETY SLUG

CALIBER	WT. GR.	MUZZLE VEL. FPS	MUZZLE ENERGY F.-LBS.	RECOIL IMPULSE LB-SEC.	GEL. PEN. INCH	REC. DIA. INCH	CRUSH CAVITY IN3	STRETCH CAVITY IN3	ONE-SHOT STOP EST.
.380 ACP	70	1,350	283	.42	5	290x.05	2.8	15.0	75%
.38 Spl.	80	1,350	324	.48	6	330x.05	3.9	14.2	79%
.38 Spl. +P	80	1,500	400	.53	7	330x.05	4.5	24.8	85%
9mm	80	1,650	484	.59	6	330x.05	3.9	52.1	88%
.357 Mag.	80	1,700	513	.60	6	330x.05	3.9	48.1	89%
.45 ACP	140	1,400	609	.87	6	575x.05	6.8	42.1	93%
.40 S&W	105	1,500	524	.70	6	430x.05	5.0	55.5	90%
10mm	105	1,650	635	.77	6	430x.05	5.0	66.6	92%

TABLE 18-2
GLASER SAFETY SLUG TERMINAL BALLISTICS

	GEL. PEN. DEPTH INCH	PELLET CALIBER	WOUND PATHS	PERM. CRUSH CAVITY IN3	TOTAL PELLET DISPER-SION DIA.	TEMP. STRETCH CAVITY IN3	GEL. AFTER PLATE GLASS
9mm flatpoint (obsolete)	5.13	.05 in.	350	3.5	2.5 in.	25.2	n/a
9mm Blue round-nose	5.84	.05 in.	350	4.0	3.25 in.	27.2	2.0 in.
9mm Silver round-nose	8.50	.11 in.	46	3.7	5.0 in.	39.6	5.5 in.

TABLE 18-3
SELECT MAGSAFE TERMINAL BALLISTICS

CALIBER	LOAD GRAIN	VEL. FPS	ENERGY FT-LBS.	PELLET & COUNT	PEN. RANGE INCH	ONE-SHOT STOP, %
.25 Auto +P	22 Defender	1,610	127	6 pcs. #7 1/2 3 pcs. #9	5.0-7.0	40
.380 Auto +P+	52 MAX	1,720	342	6 pcs. #3	11.0-12.0	81
.38 Special +P+	65 MAX	1,670	402	9 pcs. #3	11.8-13.5	84
.357 Magnum	68 SWAT	1,700	436	9 pcs. #2	11.0-12.0	86
9mm +P	64 Stealth	1,950	540	9 pcs. #3	9.0-11.0	90
10mm	96 Defender	1,800	690	12 pcs. #3	8.8-16.5	92
.44 Special +P+	92 Defender	1,620	535	11 pcs. #3	5.5-12.0	92
.45 Auto +P+	103 MAX	1,900	825	10 pcs. #2, 7 pcs. #4	8.0-13.0	94
.44 Special +P	115 Urban Defense	1,300	431	12 pcs. #2	8.0-10.0	89
.40 S&W	84 Defender	1,800	604	12 pcs. #3	9.0-14.0	92
.40 S&W	46 SWAT	2,100	451	epoxy core only	5.5-6.0	88

TABLE 18-4
MAGSAFE AMMO

CALIBER	LOAD	WEIGHT GRAIN	VELOCITY FPS	ENERGY FT-LBS.
.25 ACP	25D +P Defender	22	1,610	127
7.62x25 Tokarev	7.62 TOK Defender	57	2,120	519
.32 ACP	32U Undercover Load	40	1,400	174
.32 S&W Long	32L Defender	50	1,350	202
.32 H&R Mag	32HD Defender	50	1,700	321
.380 ACP	380D Defender	60	1,500	300
	380 MAX +P+	52	1,720	342
9mm Makarov	9 MAK +P Defender	51	1,700	327
9mm Parabellum	9DX +P+ Delayed Exp	102	1,550	544
	9S +P Stealth Load	64	1,950	540
	9L Lite Load	60	1,800	431
	9W SWAT Load	58	2,000	515
.38 Super Auto	38AD Defender	68	1,850	517
.38 S&W	38SWD Defender	48	1,450	224
.38 Special	38 MAX +P+	65	1,670	402
	38W SWAT Load	68	1,420	304
	38D Defender	52	1,620	303
.357 Magnum	357D Defender	70	1,730	465
	357W SWAT Load	68	1,700	436

TABLE 18-4
MAGSAFE AMMO (CONTINUED)

CALIBER	LOAD	WEIGHT GRAIN	VELOCITY FPS	ENERGY FT-LBS.
.357 Sig	357 SIG Police Load	64	2,150	657
10mm	10D Defender	96	1,800	690
	10W SWAT Load	46	2,400	588
.40 S&W	40D Defender	84	1,800	604
	40W SWAT Load	46	2,100	451
.41 Magnum	41D Defender	99	1,830	736
	41W Urban Defense	85	1,850	646
.44 Special	44SD +P Defender	92	1,620	535
	44UDL +P Urban Defense	115	1,300	431
.44 Magnum	44MD Defender	117	1,860	899
	44MUDL Urban Defense	115	1,620	669
.45 ACP	45D +P Defender	96	1,900	825
	45 MAX +P+	103	2,140	671
	45W SWAT Load	66	2,260	771
	45SS SUPER SWAT	68		
.45 Long Colt	45CD +P Defender	96	1,700	615
.45 Win Mag	45MD Defender	112	1,950	945
	45MW SWAT Load	66	2,650	1,029
.454 Casull	454D Defender	136	2,510	1,903
.50 Action Exp.	50AE Defender	180	2,040	1,665
.30 Carbine	30 Carbine SWAT Load	52	2,400	665
7.62x39 Russian	7.62R SWAT Load	80	2,750	1,343
.30-30 Win	30-30S SWAT Load	94	2,800	1,737
.308 Winchester	308S SWAT Load	94	3,200	2,137
.30-06	30-06S SWAT Load	94	3,300	2,273
.300 Win Mag	300 MS SWAT Load	94	3,500	2,557
.50 BMG	50S Urban Sniper Load	tba	tba	tba

TABLE 18-5
GLASER BLUE (#12) SAFETY SLUG BALLISTICS

CALIBER	WEIGHT GRAIN	VELOCITY FPS	ENERGY FT-LBS.
.25 ACP	35	1,150	103
.32 ACP	55	1,300	206
.380 ACP	70	1,350	283
9mm +P	80	1,650	484
.38 Super	80	1,700	513
.38 Spec. Std.	80	1,500	400
.38 Spec. +P	80	1,650	484
.357 Magnum	80	1,800	575
.40 S&W	115	1,550	613
10mm	115	1,650	695
.44 Special	135	1,350	546
.44 Magnum	135	1,850	1,025
.45 ACP +P	145	1,350	587
.45 Colt	145	1,350	587
.223	45	3,430	1,175
7.62x39	130	2,300	1,527
.308	130	3,000	2,597
.30-06	130	3,100	2,774

TABLE 18-6
GLASER SILVER (#6) SAFETY SLUG BALLISTICS

CALIBER	WEIGHT GRAIN	VELOCITY FPS	ENERGY FT-LBS.
.380 ACP	70	1,350	283
9mm +P	80	1,650	484
.38 Super	80	1,700	513
.38 Spec. Std.	80	1,500	400
.38 Spec. +P	80	1,650	484
.357 Magnum	80	1,800	575
.40 S&W	115	1,550	613
10mm	115	1,650	695
.44 Special	135	1,350	546
.44 Magnum	135	1,850	1,025
.45 ACP +P	145	1,350	587
.45 Colt	145	1,350	587

19

Black Talon and Winchester Supreme SXT

With all expanding bullets, the jacket has always been designed to fold out of the way and let the soft lead bullet core do the work. Not so for Winchester's Black Talon hollowpoint. The Black Talon's jacket plays a very active role in wounding by adding a third mechanism of wounding—cutting. With the Black Talon, for the first time in the history of ammunition, the copper jacket of the bullet had been specifically designed to increase stopping power.

Originally called the Supreme Expansion Talon, SXT, the Black Talon represented the latest step up on hollowpoint bullet performance. It combined the rapid expansion of a Silvertip with the deep penetration of a subsonic load. Yet the Talon added a new dimension of wounding. After expansion, the actual shape of most hollowpoint bullets is that of a round-nose lead. These bullets slip through soft tissue with a minimum of wounding. The Talon, however, expands to expose razor-sharp reinforced jacket petals. These cut tissue in the wake of the penetrating core.

The Black Talon line of ammo was announced at the 1992 SHOT Show. The bullet was taken off the market in November 1993. It was available in four auto pistol calibers (9mm, 10mm Medium Velocity, .40 S&W, and .45 Auto) and two revolver calibers (.357 Magnum and .44 Magnum).

The Black Talon was invented by David Schluckebier when he was with Winchester. Schluckebier later went to work for Remington, where he invented the Golden Saber. These accomplishments rank Schluckebier with Tom Burczynski (inventor of the Hydra-Shok, Starfire, and Quik-Shok) as the two most brilliant bullet designers of our time. After Schluckebier's departure from Winchester, the Black Talon was refined by Winchester's Alan Corzine.

The key to the Talon's wounding is the special alloy, selectively annealed, reversed-taper jacket. The copper-zinc jacket alloy has a higher percent of copper than other JHP jackets. This makes it softer, more ductile, and easier to fold back during expansion. The high copper content in the jacket was also selected to totally eliminate fragmentation or separation of the jacket petals. This produces the razor-sharp "talons."

Many JHP bullets will expand and break off pieces of the jacket. This is not an issue one way or another for an ordinary JHP bullet design. These small jacket pieces do not effect the retained weight by much, nor do they travel outside the wound tract to form separate wound cavities.

With the Black Talon design, these jacket pieces must stay attached to the bullet for maximum effectiveness. The less brittle copper alloy allows this. Every single Black Talon in all six calibers fired into both ordnance gelatin and animal tissue had a 100 percent retention of the jacket petals.

A jacket alloy with a higher percent of copper also allows cleaner and more distinct tears as the jacket talons peel back along the serration lines. The result is a series of sharply defined, equally spaced, and reliably repeatable jacket talons.

The Black Talon bullet is formed in the same steps as the aluminum-jacketed Silvertip hollowpoint. This is, however, quite different from the copper-jacketed, nickel-plated Silvertip and other JHP bullets. At one point in the process, the Black Talon looks exactly like a full-metal-jacket hardball bullet. The FMJ, STHP, and Talon all have an exposed lead bullet base. The Talon, like the STHP, later goes through a piercing operation where a punch forms the hollowpoint cavity.

Winchester selected this style of bullet manufacturing to allow the use of a reversed-taper jacket. In an ordinary JHP with a closed bullet base, the jacket has a thinner wall near the opening and a thicker wall near the bullet base. A normal JHP needs the jacket to be thin near the hollowpoint opening to allow easy expansion.

The Black Talon design, however, needs the strength of a thicker jacket to keep the talon sections rigid after expansion. The Talon uses the same basic jacket as ordinary JHP bullets. The critical difference is that the bullet is formed upside down. The exposed lead and the thin jacket walls are normally at the front of the bullet. This becomes the base of the Talon bullet. The thick walls that normally make up the base of a JHP are now the front of the Talon bullet.

Since the expanded jacket itself adds to the stopping power of the Black Talon, it is important for the jacket to remain with the bullet core. The inverted core, or reversed-taper jacket, locks the core into place, preventing it from sliding forward or the jacket from slipping rearward. The jacket is also locked in at the heel or base of the bullet.

In addition to the thicker jacket near the bullet tip, the process that makes all this work is a very special heat treatment. The jacket is selectively annealed, or softened. This selective anneal takes place before the jacket is wrapped around the core and before the hollowpoint cavity is punched. During the process, the very tip of the jacket is heat treated to become as soft as possible. (This is the part of the jacket that will be driven down inside the bullet to form the hollowpoint cavity. The Black Talon, like the Silvertip, is a fully jacketed hollowpoint. The tip needs to be soft to fold back easily.) The middle of the jacket is partially annealed. The shank, base, and heel of the Talon jacket is fully hard.

The final operation that gives the Black Talon its unique rate of expansion and recovered diameter is the notching or jacket serration process. Of all the steps, this is the most critical. It is where the 90 degree angles that become the talons after expansion are formed. This jacket area needs to be reinforced to prevent the talons from being flattened back along the bullet shank after expansion.

A specially shaped punch is used to form serration notches in the jacket and the hollowpoint cavity in the lead core. This process moves more metal into the area that will form the 90 degree bends, which both reinforces and work-hardens the bends. The built-up 90 degree becomes extremely rigid, which enables the jacket to hold its shape in this area even after the most violent impacts such as with bone.

During this same operation, the jacket is folded inside the hollowpoint cavity. Also, the jacket is cut and prestressed all the way through. Even the lead in the hollowpoint cavity wall is prenotched. As a result, as the Talon expands, the jacket literally pulls the hollowpoint walls open—the lead core does not push against the copper jacket as much as the jacket pulls the lead open.

Because of its softer alloy jacket, deeper jacket serrations, and the expansion action of the jacket itself, the Talon expands much more aggressively than, for example, Winchester's other subsonic-label JHP bullets. This is especially evident in the 9mm 147-grain bullet weight. The 9mm 147-grain OSM or Type L typically expands to a .52 caliber by .58 caliber six-star bullet. The 9mm Black Talon typically expands to a .58 by .66 six-star bullet.

When examing spent bullets, most law enforcement agencies measure the diameter of the recovered core and ignore the recovered diameter of the jacket attached to the core. This has been absolutely correct because until now, the jacket has not added to the recovered diameter. However, the jacket on the Talon does, in fact, establish the crush diameter. The diameter of the rigid petals or talons should be treated as the recovered bullet diameter.

The Black Talon will cut open tissue that may have been stretched but not torn by a normal JHP. It will also cut tissue that the ordinary JHP merely rolled out of the way. Cutting has long been recognized by medical experts as a more effective wounding mechanism than either stretching or crushing tissue.

The most interesting part of the Talon development is the fact that Winchester had built on its own previous bullet designs to reach the Talon level. The aluminum-jacketed Silvertip expanded exactly like the Talon. (The 90 degree petals were actually evident on the vintage .45 Auto Silvertip.) These jacket formations were simply a by-product of the Silvertip crease-fold serrations pioneered by Silvertip designer Henry Halverson. At the time, it was an extremely efficient method to get the jacket peeled back in a hurry to expose

the lead core. The aluminum jacket, however, was so thin that these petals were easily smashed against the bullet shank as the bullet engaged more tissue. Until the Black Talon, no one thought to stiffen the aluminum jacket to add a cutting mechanism to the wounding.

In fact, the very idea that a sharp jacket could add to stopping power by cutting tissue that would otherwise escape injury came from a most unlikely bullet. Believe it or not, this originated with the ineffective 9mm 147-grain Olin Super Match.

Medical personnel who only see perps long after the gunfight is over tried to defend the OSM in a number of feeble ways. One of these ways was to point out how the jacket peeled back to form razor-sharp trailing ribbons. The fact is that the jacket was slammed back against the bullet shank well inside the hollowpoint diameter, so these razor ribbons never engaged any tissue on their own. This was just one of the numerous attempts to talk cops into using a match bullet for police work.

At about this same time, the PMC Ultramag tubular bullet was released. This bullet focused the forensic attention on cutting as a third tissue-wounding mechanism in addition to stretching and crushing. In fact, cutting was ranked superior to crushing (permanent cavity) and far superior to stretching (temporary cavity) by some wound ballistics experts.

Once cutting was recognized as a legitimate wounding mechanism, the rest was just a matter of clever engineering by Winchester. The Winchester OSM produced sharp and ragged jacket ribbons, but they did not stick out to engage tissue. The Winchester Silvertip folded back to produce 90 degree "talons," but they were too flimsy to hold their shape.

The logical combination of these two resulted in the Black Talon. The Talon expands to large diameters like the original Silvertip. It has adequate to deep penetration like other subsonic bullets. And it produces a real cutting action during bullet travel through its razor-sharp and rigidly formed 90 degree talons.

One final observation on the Black Talon wound ballistics is in order. The Talon penetrates somewhat deeper than an ordinary JHP before the jacket starts to expand. The depth of the maximum stretch cavity is an inch or so deeper than a regular JHP and 2 inches deeper than a semiexotic JHP. The Talon will travel deeper at caliber diameter before expansion. This is a late energy-release design.

In cross-torso or quartering scenarios and in shootings where the bullet must penetrate upper arms before engaging the torso, this delay is good. These are common police scenarios. On a direct frontal shot, more rapid expansion may be desired. However, once the Talon starts to expand, it does so rapidly.

The overall Talon expansion is greater than a JHP, and the total depth of penetration is much more controlled than with subsonic ammo. The Talon penetrates and expands but maintains a higher penetrating velocity than an ordinary JHP. This gives maximum effect rather than just slamming into the target, expanding, and losing penetrating momentum immediately.

The Black Talon appeared to be a genuine improvement over conventional JHP ammo in wound ballistics. Using ordnance gelatin, we estimated one-shot stops in the four auto pistol calibers to be in the 77 to 87 percent range. This represented a big improvement in the 9mm 147-grain and 9mm MV 200-grain loads and a small improvement in the .40 S&W 180-grain and .45 Auto 230-grain loads.

Overall, however, the estimated stopping power seemed to fall below our expectations for such a technically advanced bullet. We were unable to factor in the benefits of the cutting mechanism of the petals into the one-shot stop equations. However, we anticipated the Talon loads would do much better than predicted when it came to actual shootings.

The first indication that the gelatin predictions were right after all and the anticipated improvements would not take place occurred during the Strasbourg Tests. These tests immediately discovered the late energy-release characteristics designed into the Talon. Remember, the thickness of the goats, from side-to-side across both lungs, was 11.5 to 12 inches. The penetration distances were a realistic comparison to the human torso overall and certainly exceeded the human torso front-to-rear.

In every caliber, Winchester's own lighter weight Silvertip outperformed the Black Talon

TABLE 19-1
STRASBOURG TEST COMPARISONS

CALIBER	LOAD	COLLAPSE TIME	COMMENTS
9mm	Fed. 115-gr. JHP +P+ (9BPLE)	8.90 sec	best overall JHP
9mm	Fed. 147-gr. Hydra-Shok	9.58 sec	best 147-grain JHP
9mm	Win. 147-gr. Black Talon	9.68 sec	new load
9mm	Win. 147-gr. JHP (OSM)	9.90 sec	control load
.40 S&W	Win. 155-gr. Silvertip	7.86 sec	best overall JHP
.40 S&W	Fed. 180-gr. Hydra-Shok	8.32 sec	best 180-gr. JHP
.40 S&W	Win. 180-gr. Black Talon	8.76 sec	new load
10mm MV	Fed. 180-gr. Hydra-Shok	8.22 sec	best 180-gr. JHP
10mm MV	Win. 200-gr. Black Talon	8.40 sec	best 230-gr. JHP
.45 ACP	Rem. 185-gr. JHP +P	7.98 sec	best overall JHP
.45 ACP	Fed. 230-gr. Hydra-Shok	8.40 sec	best stnd.-press. load
.45 ACP	Win. 230-gr. Black Talon	9.14 sec	new load

The Black Talon is the first bullet ever designed to have the jacket play an active role in wounding.

during the tests. On a weight-for-weight basis, in every caliber, the Federal Hydra-Shok significantly beat the Black Talon. Of the premium hollowpoints, as a rule, the Talon was the least effective. In most calibers, the Talon was at the bottom of the list along with the other hollowpoint intentionally designed to have a late energy release, the Hornady XTP-HP.

The only chance the Black Talon had for success on the street was if the Strasbourg Tests were so specialized and specific that they did not represent reality. But just the opposite happened. Actual street results and the Strasbourg Tests have an extremely high rank correlation.

Street results started to accumulate for the Black Talon, and they confirmed both the gelatin predictions and the Strasbourg rankings. In 9mm, the 147-grain Black Talon came in clearly less effective than the 147-grain Hydra-Shok and both generations of Federal's 147-grain 9MS JHP. They showed the Talon to be tied with Winchester's conventional 147-grain OSM subsonic JHP. In .40 S&W, street results proved the 180-grain Black Talon was far less effective than the 180-grain Hydra-Shok and again tied with the Winchester 180-grain subsonic JHP.

In .45 Auto, the Talon turned out to be tied as one of the least effective hollowpoints. Premium and conventional hollowpoints weighing 185, 200, and 230 grains in both standard and +P pressure levels all were better. In fact, the Winchester 230-grain Black Talon was tied in one-shot stops with the Remington 185-grain JHP. This is the same 185-grain JHP picked by the 1987 FBI Wound Ballistics Symposium simply because it seldom expanded. As a result, this 185-grain JHP gave the Bureau the excessive penetration it was told it needed. It is extremely ironic that the Winchester 185-grain Silvertip, shunned by the FBI panelists, also turned out to be better than the Winchester 230-grain Black Talon.

The harsh reality is that the Talon has the worst street record of any of the reported hollowpoints. Premium and conventional JHPs, even the Hornady XTP hollowpoint, all beat the Black Talon. It seems clear that the talons themselves were not adding to the load's overall wounding and stopping power, in spite of the medical sense it made that they should add to the effectiveness.

A comparison of the actual street results from all hollowpoint bullet designs weighing the same amount proves the point:

9mm

Federal 147-gr. Hydra-Shok	78%
Federal 147-gr. JHP 9MS-2	77%
Federal 147-gr. JHP 9MS-1	76%
Winchester 147-gr. subsonic JHP	74%
Winchester 147-gr. Black Talon	74%

.40 S&W

Federal 180-gr. Hydra-Shok	89%
Cor-Bon 180-gr. Sierra JHP	86%
Black Hills 180-gr. Hornady XTP	85%
PMC/Eldorado 180-gr. Starfire	83%
Winchester 180-gr. subsonic JHP	81%
Winchester 180-gr. Black Talon	80%

.45 AUTO

Federal 230-gr. Hydra-Shok	94%
Winchester 230-gr. Black Talon	81%

The Winchester Black Talon was a unique and credible design. What it lacked in outright bullet performance it more than made up for in product differentiation. Winchester had a premium hollowpoint replacement for the Silvertip that was easily recognized and well-received by all civilians and most police agencies. But this ease of product recognition became a double-edged sword and a marketing nightmare in a few short months.

In mid 1993, high-performance hollow-point ammunition became a political football on the national scene. Under pressure to reduce crime, politicians, activists, and the press focused for the first time on conventional handgun ammo. (This attention must not be confused with the late 1980s ban on the so-called "cop killer" bullets. No police officer anywhere had ever been killed, or even shot, with a "cop killer" bullet. In spite of this fact, the U.S. Congress banned the sale and possession of certain kinds of bullets that were already very expensive, hard to obtain, and genuinely exotic.)

This recent attack on handgun ammo was the first effort against "mainstream" bullets. Taxes of up to 10,000 percent were seriously considered on conventional hollowpoints. The possession of more than 1,000 rounds of any kind of ammo or even the same amount of primers were proposed to constitute an "arsenal" requiring a special license and three visits a year by Bureau of Alcohol, Tobacco, and Firearm (BATF) agents.

In July 1993, a disgruntled client entered a San Francisco law firm with a 9mm handgun and wounded or killed a number of legal aides and lawyers. It was soon revealed that he had used Winchester Black Talon ammunition in his shooting spree. Critics in the media and government seemed unaware that the outcome of this tragic event could have been the same or even worse if nonhollowpoint FMJ hardball ammo was used. Because hardball ammo produces two to three times the penetration of the controlled-expansion Black Talon, the chances of injury to a second person after exiting the first person are much higher.

None of this mattered. The Black Talon was an extremely advanced bullet. It carried a controversial name. It expanded in a way unlike any hollowpoint bullet in history. It

These 9mm 147-grain Black Talons were recovered from animals. The talon exposure is aggressive, even when fired through skull bones.

was a high profile load from its very release. As such, it made a perfect target. The press and politicians demonized the bullet design. They sunk their talons into the Black Talon.

By November 1993, the anti-hollowpoint and anti-Talon hype reached a feverish pitch. Winchester found itself embroiled in a terrible mess through no fault of its own. The Black Talon started to show up on TV news shows and in news segments covering legislative sessions and testimony from victims of the San Francisco tragedy. Excerpts from Ed Sanow's review of the Black Talon published in the November 1992 issue of Petersen's *Handguns* were read into the Congressional Record. The pressure was on Winchester to stop the sale of Black Talon.

In early November 1993, the news magazine *Dateline NBC* interviewed Congressman Daniel Patrick Moynihan, who was leading the assault on the Black Talon. As a backdrop to the program's misleading Black Talon animation, Moynihan decried the bullet "designed to rip your guts out."

The program was scheduled to air on November 23. On November 22, 1993, Winchester withdrew Black Talon ammunition from sale to the general public. Of course, the segment aired anyhow. The same day, the print and electronic media, including *USA*

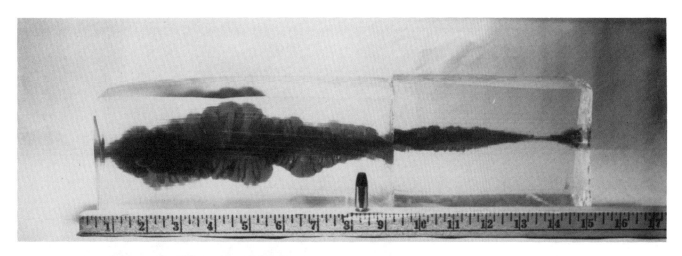

ABOVE: The 9mm 147-grain Black Talon, aka Ranger SXT, produces a late energy release and 77 percent one-shot stops.

LEFT: This .45 Auto 230-grain Black Talon shows .78 caliber expansion and protruding talons. The late-energy-release design limited the one-shot stops to 81 percent.

This .40 S&W 180-grain Black Talon expanded to .72 caliber and stopped in 13 inches. This load has achieved an 80 percent rating.

Today and the *CBS Evening News*, covered the Winchester decision.

The Winchester press release read, in part, "This action is being taken because the Black Talon ammunition is becoming the focal point for broader issues that are well beyond control of Winchester Ammunition. The controversy also threatens the good name of Winchester, which has stood for safe and responsible use of ammunition and firearms for 125 years."

Winchester officials were exactly correct. A larger issue of a prohibitive tax on ammo or an outright ban on hollowpoints was on the agenda. The Black Talon was a lightning rod, a rallying point, a clearly defined target that came to represent all handgun ammunition.

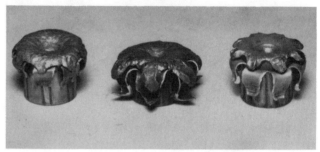

ABOVE: Over the past 20 years, Winchester has changed jacket materials, hollowpoint cavity shapes, and jacket serration designs. From left: aluminum-jacketed Silvertip, copper-jacketed Subsonic, reverse-taper Black Talon, and sump-cavity Supreme SXT.

ABOVE RIGHT: Three generations of Winchester 9mm 147-grain bullets are shown. From left: OSM Type L Subsonic, Black Talon or Ranger SXT, and Supreme SXT. The OSM and Supreme SXT are quite similar.

MIDDLE RIGHT: In .45 Auto, the 230-grain Subsonic (left) and the 230-grain Supreme SXT (right) show little expansion. The 230-grain Black Talon (center) expands to larger diameters.

RIGHT: The Winchester Supreme SXT replaced the Black Talon for civilian shooters. This design features a deep, sump-type hollowpoint cavity to absorb debris.

Winchester hoped that pulling its unique hollowpoint from the market would defuse the rapidly escalating situation before it exploded. It worked. Handgunners everywhere owe a debt of gratitude to Winchester for its action.

As of that press release, the sale of the Supreme Expansion Talon (SXT), known as the Black Talon, in handgun calibers was restricted to police and government sales only. The controversial Black Talon name was replaced by the name Ranger SXT. Winchester's most advanced bullet, which was originally designed for police use, was now officially restricted to police use.

This was the first time in the history of centerfire handgun ammunition that such a product was voluntarily withdrawn from the public. As such, some confusion exists.

Federal law was *not* enacted to ban the sale or possession of Black Talon ammunition. Instead, sale of the Black Talon was restricted by Winchester internal policy. A big difference exists between a business decision made by Winchester and a legislative or executive action taken by the federal government. Restricted ammo is not illegal to buy, possess, or use. It is just very difficult to obtain.

The Black Talon simply became one of the dozens of restricted police-only loads that Winchester calls Q-loads. Q-loads are normally cartridges loaded to pressures exceeding SAAMI industry standards under specific instructions from a police agency. Such a manufacturer's restriction is no big deal.

Although this ammo was not made illegal at the federal level, some cities and counties

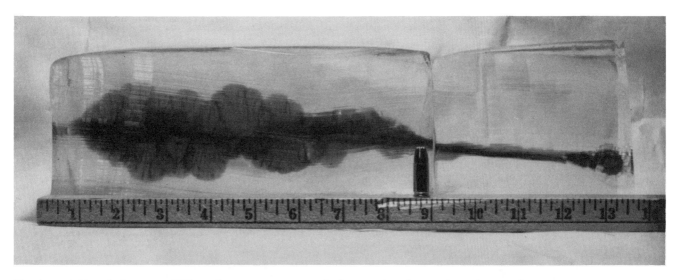

The 9mm 147-grain Supreme SXT produces a more controlled expansion than earlier subsonic designs.

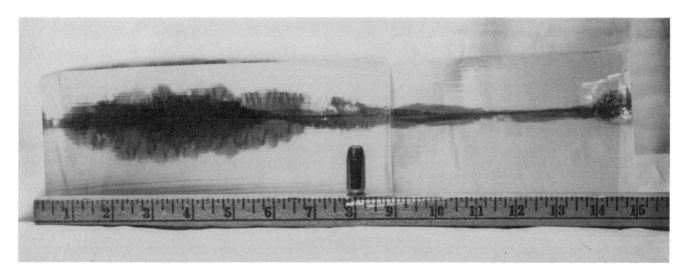

The gradual- and late-energy-release design of the .45 Auto 230-grain Supreme SXT is obvious from this wound profile.

have enacted local ordinances which do ban its sale or possession. Incredibly enough, the burden of proof that the ammo was purchased before the cutoff date rests on the handgunner. Check the local laws.

Twice in less than 10 years, excellent Winchester hollowpoints were made public scapegoats over issues having nothing to do with bullet performance. The first was the 9mm 115-grain Silvertip following the 1986 FBI shootout in Miami. This event has since been widely acknowledged as tactics failure rather than bullet failure. Then the Black Talon fell victim to a political agenda following a tragedy where even more people could have been injured if the Talon was not used.

In early 1994, Winchester engineers went back to the drawing board with one of the toughest possible job assignments—to design a politically correct high-performance hollowpoint. The goal was to create a load that would still perform well under the FBI multibarrier test methodolo-

The darling of the Ranger SXT lineup is this 9mm +P+ 127-grain load. This contender for NYPD use produces adequate but controlled penetration and excellent wound ballistics.

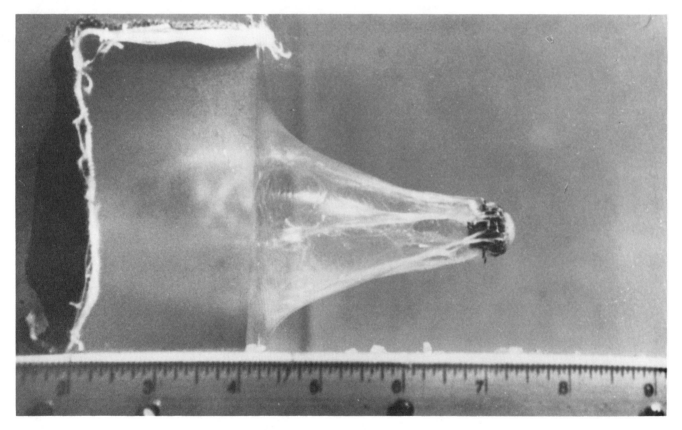

This high-speed photo clearly shows that the jacket tips on the Black Talon are exposed to tissue along the bullet path. (Photo credit: Tom Burczynski)

RIGHT: The Black Talon/Ranger SXT (left) has a reverse-taper jacket that extends from the bullet base into the nose cavity, helping to pull it open. The Subsonic (right) has a closed bullet base and a jacket that ends at the cavity.

BELOW: The long, oval stretch cavity of this .45 Auto 230-grain Ranger SXT shows its late energy release.

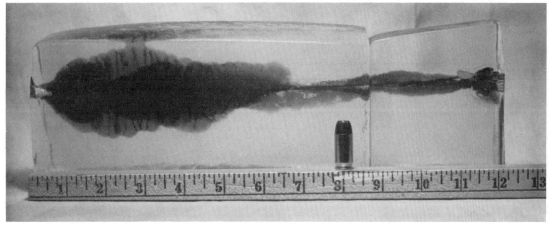

gy. Winchester wanted another accepted law enforcement bullet that would avoid any negative association with the Black Talon. Of course, the civilian defensive, sporting, and hunting ammo market is quite competitive, so in addition to passing the FBI tests, the new load had to perform like a premium hollowpoint bullet.

Winchester defanged the Black Talon design to come up with the civilian version called the Supreme SXT. SXT in the civilian line of ammo stands for Supreme Expansion Technology; in the Ranger police-only line it still stands for Supreme Expansion Talon.

For the Supreme SXT, Winchester totally eliminated the sharp jacket petals. However, it retained two of the engineering advances pioneered with the original Talon—the reverse-taper jacket and the sump-type hollowpoint cavity. A totally new feature of the Supreme SXT is the eight-notch jacket serrations as opposed to the six-notch Talon design.

The jacket alloy of the Supreme SXT still has a higher copper content than other JHP bullets. This makes it softer, more ductile, and easier to fold back during expansion. The higher percent of copper was also selected to eliminate the separation of jacket petals during expansion, which allows for the most retained weight.

The Supreme SXT bullet, like the Silvertip, Ranger SXT, and all FMJ hardball bullets, has an exposed lead bullet base. At one step in the bullet-making process, the Supreme SXT looks exactly like a FMJ bullet. The thicker wall of the jacket cup is near the front of the bullet while the thinner wall is wrapped around the bullet base. This jacket is reversed for most JHP bullets, which must have a closed bullet base and an open bullet nose. This is where Winchester gets the term "reverse-taper" jacket.

In the last bullet-forming operation, the Supreme SXT bullet has the hollowpoint cavi-

The 9mm subsonic 147-grain Ranger SXT expands to .62 caliber and achieves 77 percent one-shot stops.

The 10mm 200-grain Medium Velocity Ranger SXT is among the best of the medium-velocity loads with an 87 percent rating.

ty pierced right through the jacketed bullet nose. The inverted-core (or reversed-taper) jacket locks the core into place. The core is restricted from sliding forward and the jacket is restricted from sliding rearward. Winchester pioneered this form of bullet assembly with the aluminum-jacketed Silvertips. The company perfected it with what is now the Ranger SXT. The technology was simply transferred to the Supreme SXT.

With this design, the jacket almost always stays intact with the core. Some slippage may occur with the more aggressively expanding bullets, but jacket separation from the core is rare.

This is true even when the Supreme SXT first strikes hard barriers like glass, metal, or wood.

The reverse-taper jacket also produces a more accurate JHP bullet than a conventional hollowpoint design. Decades ago, it was proven that a JHP bullet with a precisely formed closed bullet base was more accurate than a FMJ bullet with a jacket folded over the heel of the bullet base. The deep-drawn base of the JHP is easier to make perfectly square than the folded-over base of the FMJ. The Supreme SXT has the same folded heel as the FMJ except the jacket near the heel is much thinner, which makes it easier to fold precisely.

The real advantage of the Supreme SXT over conventional hollowpoints comes in the final form operation where the bullet maker tries to make the rifling bearing area of the shank perfectly straight.

On a conventional JHP, the die pressure exerts the most force near the bullet nose where the jacket is the thinnest. The least pressure is exerted near the bullet base where the jacket is the thickest. When the die pressure is released, the thicker jacket near the base springs back outward more than the thinner jacket near the nose. The result of this uneven springback is a bulge near the base called "heel bulge," making bullet diameter near the nose different than at the base. This means the rifling bearing surface is not straight nor parallel. The result can be poor accuracy.

The Supreme SXT, however, has a thicker jacket where the die pressure is the greatest and a thinner jacket where the die pressure is the least. Thus when the die is released, the Supreme SXT bullet has less springback and a straighter rifling bearing surface.

The other design feature the Supreme SXT shares with the original Black Talon is the sump-type hollowpoint cavity shape. Winchester developed these internal cavity dimensions specifically for the FBI barrier tests.

Most hollowpoints have a V- or Y-shaped cavity that starts out wide and tapers back to a point. Barrier debris like heavy clothes and wood fiber can easily fill these shallow tapered cavities. The plugged bullet will then act like a nonexpanding softpoint rather than a hollowpoint because the point is no longer hollow.

The Supreme SXT has a deep, cylindrical hollowpoint cavity. Debris that enters the cavity is forced to the bottom. Depending on the thickness of the barrier, this still allows the Supreme SXT to impact the primary target with a partially empty hollowpoint cavity. This means the Supreme SXT will expand more reliably and have a more controlled penetration after these test barriers. Of course, any cavity can be plugged if the barrier is thick enough. Deep cavities, like the sump-type cav-ity of the Supreme SXT, are among the least likely to be plugged.

The design feature totally unique to the Supreme SXT is the notch pattern in the jacket serrations. The jacket of the Supreme SXT wraps around the bullet nose and extends slightly into the hollowpoint cavity. The technique, pioneered by Winchester on the original Silvertip bullets, has two advantages.

First, full jacket coverage helps the cycle reliability of auto pistol bullets as they bounce and slide up the feed ramp. The hard and rounded edge of the jacket-protected hollowpoint opening is less likely to catch on the ramp and jam the pistol.

Second, the jacket actually assists in bullet expansion on impact. As the Supreme SXT expands, the jacket inside the hollowpoint cavity actually pulls the lead cavity walls open as the jacket peels back. The lead core does not push against the copper jacket as much as the jacket pulls the lead cavity open.

The Supreme SXT expands at a slightly faster rate than the original Black Talon. However, it is more like the rapidly expanding Silvertip and less like the sluggish-responding subsonic. (The Black Talon/Ranger SXT penetrates deeper before expansion starts than most JHPs. This was originally considered the best design for law enforcement applications.)

The eight-notch jacket serrations developed for the Silvertip are used on the Supreme SXT. Some calibers of the Winchester subsonic also used an eight-notch pattern, but these jackets did not wrap into the hollowpoint cavity. A six-notch pattern was selected for the Black Talon only to provide longer and stronger jacket petals.

The eight-notch pattern produces a more smoothly rounded covered diameter than some JHP bullets with fewer serrations. This design also reduces lopsided or uneven bullet expansion that can in turn cause the bullet to tumble sideways.

As a rule, the expanded Supreme SXT has a smaller recovered diameter than the Black Talon/Ranger SXT but a larger diameter than the subsonic.

The Supreme SXT has an ideally controlled penetration depth. The three subsonic loads averaged 15.7 inches of penetration in calibrated 10-percent Type 250A ordnance gelatin. The Ranger SXT loads in the same calibers and bullet weights averaged 13.9 inches. The new generation Supreme SXT loads averaged 13.5 inches. The best performing street loads, based on documented officer-involved shootings, averaged 13.3 inches. The Supreme SXT is right on target.

The 9mm 147-grain Supreme SXT deserves a special mention. When originally adopted by law enforcement in the dark ages of the 1980s, the 147-grain bullets rarely expanded and perforated the targets on torso shots most of the time. Penetration distances in bare gelatin from 16 to 18 inches were common. As these street failures became common knowledge, the 147-grain hollowpoints were redesigned to expand more reliably, and the penetration distances fell into the 10- to 14-inch range of maximum effectiveness. The 9mm 147-grain Supreme SXT is the most recent improvement in a long line of steady improvements.

The original Black Talon was a radical and controversial change to the conventional jacketed hollowpoint. In comparison, the Supreme SXT is still a conventional hollowpoint but a seriously tweaked one.

TABLE 19-2
WINCHESTER RANGER SXT, SUPREME SXT, & SUBSONIC JHP AMMO

CALIBER	LOAD GRAIN	VEL. FPS	ENERGY FT-LBS.	DIA. INCH	PEN. INCH	CRUSH CAVITY CU.IN.	STRETCH CAVITY CU.IN.	ONE-SHOT STOP %
.380 Auto	95 Supreme SXT	955	192	.60	9.3	2.6	18.2	64 est
9mm	147 Subsonic JHP	990	320	.58	15.9	4.2	19.6	74 act
9mm	147 Ranger SXT (Talon)	990	320	.62	15.8	4.8	28.8	74 act
9mm	147 Supreme SXT	990	320	.57	13.7	3.5	30.7	78 est
.357 Mag	180 Ranger SXT (Talon)	1,150	528	.68	13.3	4.8	41.4	89 est
.40 S&W	180 Subsonic JHP	990	392	.64	14.6	4.6	31.1	81 act
.40 S&W	180 Ranger SXT (Talon)	990	392	.72	13.0	5.3	29.1	80 act
.40 S&W	180 Supreme SXT	990	392	.68	12.0	4.4	34.4	86 est
10mm MV	180 Subsonic JHP	990	392	.66	15.5	5.3	32.0	82 act
10mm MV	200 Ranger SXT (Talon)	990	435	.68	14.3	5.2	29.3	87 est
.45 Auto	230 Subsonic JHP	860	378	.66	15.5	5.3	23.6	86 est
.45 Auto	230 Ranger SXT (Talon)	860	378	.78	13.0	6.2	25.4	81 act
.45 Auto	230 Supreme SXT	860	378	.68	14.8	5.4	20.1	86 est

20
CCI-Speer Gold Dot

The CCI-Speer Gold Dot is one of the most recent developments in law enforcement ammunition. The Gold Dot differs greatly from conventional jacketed hollowpoint ammo, yet it still passes the tough FBI battery of bullet tests.

CCI pioneered the use of copper-plated handgun bullets. Introduced in 1988, the company's totally metal jacketed (TMJ) bullets were originally used to reduce the hazards of airborne lead. In 1990, its plated hollowpoint (PHP) bullets were developed for defensive work using TMJ technology.

Copper-plated hollowpoint bullets have a number of advantages over standard JHPs made with separate jackets. First, the chemical bond between the lead and copper on electroplated bullets eliminates core slippage for improved accuracy. Second, the precise jacket thickness of a plated hollowpoint is easier to control than impact-extruded jackets. The result is better jacket-to-core concentricity, which also improves accuracy. Third, the tight jacket bond prevents the jacket separation common with standard bullet designs at high impact velocities or when hard objects like glass are struck. The secure jacket improves weight retention

and maintains control over bullet expansion. Even after defeating the tough obstacles in the 40-round, eight-media FBI tests, Gold Dot bullets averaged a 95 percent weight retention. Fourth, the base of the TMJ bullet is fully encased in copper, which reduces airborne lead contamination. Fifth, the TMJ and PHP bullets produce the least bounce-back on steel targets, making them equal to the all-lead bullets in terms of shooter safety.

For the record, the PHP and TMJ bullets have genuine copper jackets and not merely a cosmetic copper flash. The jackets are .007- and .010-inch thick. The TMJ Silhouette bullets have a whopping .022-inch thick copper-plated jacket. To put it another way, the lead core on a 9mm 115-grain TMJ weighs 104 grains before plating. The copper plating adds a full 11 grains. The copper plating process produces real jackets.

The jacket in conventional JHP, JSP, and FMJ bullets is made from a copper-zinc "gilding" alloy. The CCI plated jacket is pure copper with a finer grain size than the gilding metal. The concentricity of the jacket to the bullet core is much more uniform. The thick-

The CCI-Speer Gold Dot bullet starts off as a copper-plated slug. It is then pierced by a star-shaped punch, followed by a cone-shaped punch. The Gold Dot peels back following the prestressed lines.

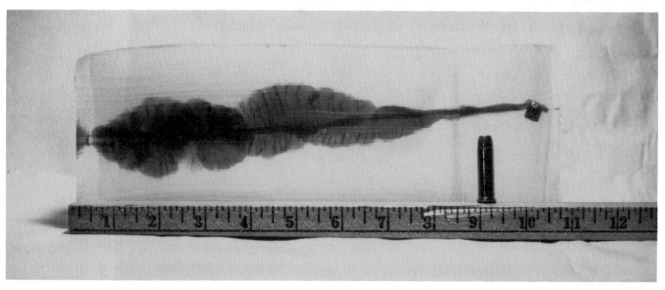

The CCI .38 Special +P 125-grain Gold Dot expands to .60 caliber even from 2-inch snubnose revolvers.

ness is also easier to control precisely—gilding metal jackets are measured in thousandths of an inch, copper plating in millionths.

The CCI copper-plated bullet goes through different steps during the manufacturing process, depending on the caliber and design. All the bullets start off with swaged lead cores. The PHP uses a .85 percent antimony lead core, while the TMJ uses 3 percent antimony and the TMJ Silhouette and TMJ Match slugs get a 5 percent core. Antimony is used to make lead harder. CCI wants the PHP cores hard enough to grab the rifling and to keep the bullet base from deforming. However, it wants them soft enough to expand reliably in tissue. On the other hand, CCI wants the Silhouette core as hard as it can be for the best knockdown power against steel targets.

Copper cannot be plated evenly to a sharp surface such as the shoulder on a Keith-style SWC. For the TMJ Silhouette and TMJ Match

bullets, the sharp shoulder required for accuracy is swaged in place after plating. The crimping cannelure is also rolled in after plating.

The most unusual TMJ bullets are the ones that become PHP hollowpoints. For these, the core is simply a rounded slug of lead. After plating, the core is hit with a star-shaped punch that pierces through the copper plating to form a six-point cavity. In the next operation, a cone-shaped punch finishes off the cavity while the rest of the bullet ogive is formed. The result is the extremely effective PHP bullet.

The chemical bond between the copper and the PHP lead is actually stronger than the integrity of the lead to itself, so the jacket will always "stick" to the lead. The TMJ bullet may break up on a steel target or the PHP may expand violently in tissue, but the jacket does not separate from the lead. The lead tears away from itself before the copper-plated bond is broken.

As a result, the PHP hollowpoint has an incredibly high weight retention even at the highest speeds. The .40 S&W 155-grain PHP smacked the gelatin at 1,160 fps, which is enough to fragment any .40 S&W bullet. The plump .69-diameter recovered slug had a 100 percent weight retention. Bullet designers have been trying to do that ever since Lee Jurras pioneered high-speed bullets in the mid 1960s. CCI has done it.

Copper plating gives hollowpoint bullet designers additional flexibility in that they can easily change the jacket thickness for the best wound ballistics. The "hardness" of a conventional brass jacket can be changed to vary how rapidly the bullet expands, but this is nearly insignificant. The differences in performance from a full work-hardened jacket to a fully annealed soft jacket are minor compared to changing the thickness. CCI engineers found that the thickness of the copper jacket has much more control over expansion than the jacket hardness. The differences in wound ballistics between a work-hardened jacket and a soft-annealed jacket just don't compare to making the jacket thinner. Put another way, a thinner jacket allows more reliable expansion than a softer one.

The size and shape of the hollowpoint cavity will always be the most important part of the bullet design. However, when the cavity size is limited, as it is in auto pistol bullets, the ability to control the jacket thickness one millionth of an inch at a time gives CCI engineers one more way to assure expansion. But that is not the best part.

The best part of the PHP bullet is reliable expansion with large recovered diameters and full weight retention at all impact speeds. It is easy to make a bullet expand; it is tough to keep it from fragmenting and losing the full mushroom. A fragmenting bullet that spins off pieces of lead and jacket to engage tissue missed by the main bullet core *increases* stopping power. These secondary missiles seldom happen.

Most JHP bullets expand, then fragment, leaving little pieces of bullet trailing in the cavity formed by the bullet core. This *decreases* stopping power since the fragmented bullet has a smaller recovered diameter and a smaller crush cavity than the expanded bullet. CCI solved this with a copper jacket chemically bonded to the lead core. As noted, the PHP expands but never sheds its jacket, so the jacket keeps the rest of the bullet together.

In 1992, CCI adopted the name Uni-Core for the process which plates copper jackets over lead cores by electrochemical deposition. These bullets really do act as one unified projectile instead of the jacket and core acting separately.

CCI upgraded its plated hollowpoints for 1993. These bullets now bear the new name

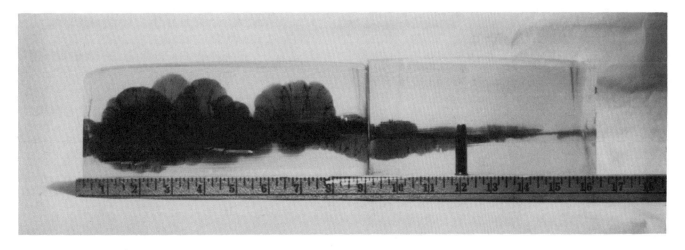

The CCI .357 Magnum 125-grain Gold Dot bullet holds together even when impacting at 1,450 fps. The long stretch cavity is the most street tolerant.

Gold Dot. The name comes from a small circle of copper jacket material swaged into the center of the hollowpoint cavity. This dot of jacket material comes from the hollowpoint piercing operation, when it is simply punched into the bottom of the hollowpoint cavity. Six or eight jacket serrations are also cut at this time. Unlike older JHP designs, the Gold Dot does not expand beyond the bottom of the hollowpoint cavity. After expansion, this dot of material becomes visible, indicating that the Gold Dot bullet has reached optimal expansion yet retained enough weight and length for adequate penetration.

The Gold Dot hollowpoint (GDHP) is formed in two steps. The first is a star-shaped punch that forms flutes, or peaks and valleys, in the cavity. The second is a cone-shaped punch, which forms a standard-appearing hollowpoint cavity. However, the lead core still retains the grain lines, or stress lines, from the first operation. On expansion, the hollowpoint peels back along these prestressed "flute" lines in a way similar to the PMC/Eldorado Starfire.

CCI discovered that the key to both adequate penetration and reliable expansion from all bullet weights and velocities was the retained bullet "length" after expansion. The Gold Dot was specifically designed to expand rapidly, which enhanced the size of the temporary cavity. It was also designed to stop expansion before the mushroom sheared away. The concept of retained length is seldom considered by other ammo manufacturers and wound ballistics experts.

Some lightweight JHP bullets, such as the 9mm 115-grain, shorten up so much after expansion that penetration can suffer. The Uni-Cor TMJ technology permits lighter Gold Dot bullets to penetrate more reliably than other bullets of similar weight. The FBI results confirmed this, especially for the 9mm 115-grain Gold Dot.

Rapid initial expansion up to a controlled diameter produces a large temporary stretch cavity. The retained mushroom diameter and the maximum retained length produces a large permanent crush cavity. Both are impor-

The CCI .40 S&W 155-grain Gold Dot expands and tries to fragment, but the copper plating keeps the bullet together.

tant for maximum bullet effectiveness in police scenarios.

CCI spent 1 1/2 years "tweaking" each PHP bullet specifically to the velocity it would be fired in each specific caliber. The jacket thickness, hollowpoint diameter, depth, and geometry were all modified for the best performance. These tweaks are what made PHP bullets the Gold Dot bullets.

CCI then subjected all its Gold Dot bullets to the famous battery of tests designed by the FBI after its 1986 shootout in Miami. The tests require both adequate penetration and reliable expansion for best results. The Gold Dot was tailored by the company's engineers in each caliber and weight for the maximum overall score in these areas. But the Gold Dot was also designed for rapid expansion so it would generate the largest temporary stretch cavities (which have been repeatedly and statistically linked to stopping power, the Strasbourg Tests being the most recent confirmation of this), even though the FBI tests do not include measurement of this cavity.

A good example of CCI's tweaking is the 9mm 147-grain GDHP. Since expansion reliability has always been a problem with subsonic ammo, CCI built the 147-grain Gold Dot with a massive cavity as large as the original Federal subsonic loaded for the U.S. Navy SEALs. The 147-grain GDHP now produces larger average recovered diameters than even lightweight 115-

ABOVE: The CCI .40 S&W 155-grain Gold Dot shows a controlled energy release. The copper-plated bullet expands to .70 caliber for an 89 percent rating.

LEFT: The CCI .45 Auto 230-grain Gold Dot promises to be an 86 percent load. The massive hollowpoint expands to .70 caliber and maintains both maximum length and weight.

grain hollowpoints. Better yet, the dangerous runaway penetration, so common with subsonic 147-grain ammo, has been eliminated by CCI ammo designers. The subsonic 147-grain Gold Dot now produces *less* average penetration than the 115-grain version.

From strictly a wound ballistics view, the 9mm 147-grain GDHP proves to be an excellent police duty load—and those words come from a vocal and long-time critic of the subsonic loads. As the failures on the street get fed back to ammo designers, bullet performance indeed improves. After eight years, the subsonic is *starting* to act less like a match bullet and more like a police bullet.

The Phoenix, Arizona, Police Department has become the first major department to issue a Gold Dot hollowpoint. The Phoenix PD shot up its early-designed subsonic ammo and are now issuing the 9mm 147-grain Gold Dot subsonic.

The 147-grain GDHP generates a temporary stretch cavity nearly as large as the faster 124-grain GDHP and much larger than the 115-grain GDHP. Taken together, the crush cavity and the stretch cavity from the 147-grain Gold Dot show it to be the CCI 9mm load with the most predicted stopping power. With a one-shot stop rating of 78 percent, the 147-grain GDHP will outperform the original subsonics, which have an effectiveness of just 69 to 72 percent.

The Gold Dot is one of the few bullet designs that produces both reliable expansion

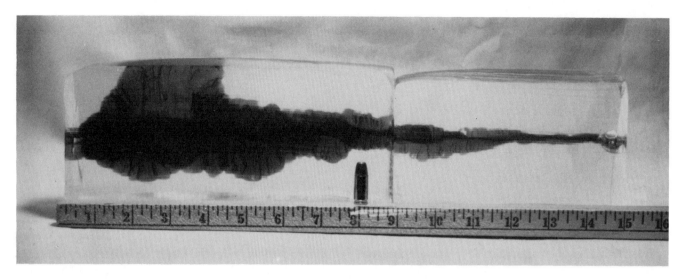

This CCI 9mm +P 124-grain Gold Dot was developed for the New York City Police. It has plenty of penetration and an 83 percent rating.

The CCI .380 Auto 90-grain Gold Dot is tied for the best in the caliber with a 65 percent one-shot stop estimate.

from heavy bullets at subsonic velocities and adequate penetration from light bullets at supersonic velocities. The best examples of this effort are the high-speed .40 S&W 155-grain GDHP and the subsonic .40 S&W 180-grain GDHP and .45 Auto 230-grain GDHP.

The 1,186 fps lightweight .40 S&W penetrated an ideal 12.3 inches of calibrated 10-

percent gelatin. With a large .70 caliber recovered diameter and a moderate stretch cavity, this 155-grain load produced the most stopping power of the Gold Dot big-bore bullets.

The subsonic Gold Dot loads in .40 S&W and .45 Auto did not act like subsonics. The 180-grain GDHP expanded to .68 caliber while the 230-grain GDHP expanded to .70 caliber.

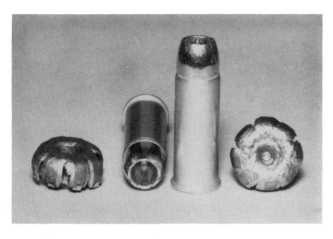

The CCI .44 Special 200-grain Gold Dot is the only standard hollowpoint in the caliber to show true expansion. This load has an 85 percent rating.

Most importantly, both loads produced a limited and controlled penetration. Unlike the deep penetrating subsonics of old, these penetrated just 11.6 and 13.5 inches, respectively. This range is just right for personal defense and police use.

CCI-Speer sells its Gold Dot bullets as reloading components to everyone from individual handloaders to commercial loading companies with millions in sales. Of the commercial loaders, at least two—Cor-Bon and Georgia Arms—have recognized the true nature of the Gold Dot design: it works best when pushed hard. At higher pressures and velocities where other bullets fragment to small recovered weights and diameters, the Gold Dot expands violently but hangs together.

Although Cor-Bon and Georgia Arms have selected the CCI Gold Dot as the bullet for their highest-pressure loads, licensing and sales agreements prevent either company from marketing these rounds as using Gold Dot-brand bullets. Cor-Bon calls them bonded hollowpoints (BHP), and Georgia Arms calls them Shear Power Plus plated hollowpoints. Make no mistake—both are genuine CCI Gold Dot hollowpoints.

Cor-Bon has accurately been compared to the Super Vel Corporation, circa 1965. Super Vel was the first company to produce lightweight, high-velocity hollowpoints. By the mid 1970s, every major ammo maker had them. Cor-Bon reinvented high-performance hollowpoints in the late 1980s by simply pushing conventional jacketed hollowpoints to unconventional velocities.

Cor-Bon was the first company to produce +P pressure ammo without restrictions. Just five years ago, two basic kinds of ammo existed: the standard pressure, including +P, was one, and the +P+ was the other. The standard-pressure ammo was available to all shooters; the .38 Special +P+ and 9mm +P+ were restricted to police agencies like the U.S. Treasury and Illinois State Police that signed a waiver of liability. Cor-Bon bridged this gap with +P and +P+ ammo in a wide variety of calibers. It made "police only" ammo available to all shooters. Small and large ammo makers alike have now followed Cor-Bon's lead.

The bonded-core hollowpoint (BHP) now used in the Cor-Bon 9mm 124-grain +P and 9mm 147-grain +P produces greater expansion and more controlled penetration than the bullet make previously used. A small "gold dot" in the center of the expanded hollowpoint identifies these bullets as the very best CCI-Speer has to offer.

This Cor-Bon 9mm 147-grain BHP is the first 147-grain bullet to achieve a one-shot stop rating of over 80 percent. The reasons for this enhanced bullet performance are its "nonsubsonic" 1,000 fps muzzle velocity and the massive hollowpoint cavity used in the Uni-Cor bullet. Separately, the change to the Uni-Cor bullet for the Cor-Bon .45 ACP 230-grain +P load also results in more controlled penetration, larger wound cavities, and increased stopping power.

Georgia Arms is the shooter-direct outlet for Master Cartridge. The majority of Master Cartridge ammo is sold directly to police departments across the country but especially in the deep South. (Master Cartridge ammo is loaded outside Atlanta.) The rest is split between large distributors and Georgia Arms, which sells the same ammo in smaller packages directly to gun shops and individual shooters.

The CCI .40 S&W 180-grain Gold Dot offers ideal .68 caliber expansion and optimum 11.6 inch penetration. This is one of the highest rated 180-grain loads at 87 percent.

Master Cartridge has been loading police duty and qualifying ammo for 15 years. It buys jacketed bullets but makes its own high-antimony lead bullets. Its ammo has been used by competitors at the Bianchi Cup, Steel Challenge, Masters, IPSC Nationals, and even Camp Perry in addition to hundreds of NRA Action Pistol and police PPC matches.

Georgia Arms recently released Speer Gold Dot bullets all loaded to +P pressures. These Shear Power Plus loads are available in 9mm, .40 S&W, 10mm, and .45 ACP in two different bullet weights per caliber. Shear Power Plus loads weighing 125 grains are in the works for the .38 Special +P and .357 Magnum. The company already sells Remington hollowpoints loaded to +P velocities in 9mm 115-grain +P and .45 ACP 185-grain +P. The Shear Power Plus loads, however, use nickel-plated cases for maximum extraction reliability.

The Georgia Arms .40 S&W 155-grain PHP is the best example of how well the Gold Dot bullet works when pushed very fast. The jacket petals peeled back far enough and form an .80 caliber bullet that looks like a badminton birdie. Most bullets at this velocity would have the mushroom sheared away. The Shear Power Plus load also weighed a full 155 grains, allowing the bullet to retain enough energy to reach the 12-inch-deep mark.

The Gold Dot bullet loaded by Master Cartridge picks up an average of 11 percentage points in one-shot stopping power over standard-velocity Gold Dots. The increase in felt recoil was handled easily, and the accuracy was not affected at all. This is top-grade ammo. A predicted average of 73.6 percent one-shot stops for standard-pressure Gold Dots improves to 84.6 percent with Shear Power Plus loads. That is an impressive increase.

CCI-Speer itself announced a 9mm +P 124-grain Gold Dot loading of its own for 1995. This is the company's *first* and only 9mm +P pressure load, and it has a very special heritage—it was developed specifically for the New York City Police Department.

The jury is still out on which hollowpoint the 38,000-member NYPD will select. They have, however, narrowed the field to three: Federal 9mm +P+ 124-grain Hydra-Shok, Winchester 9mm +P+ 127-grain Ranger SXT, and CCI-Speer 9mm +P 124-grain Gold Dot. The NYPD is focusing on the 124-grain bullet at +P velocities of 1,220 fps to be absolutely sure its auto pistols will cycle in all scenarios. The nation's oldest, most street-savvy police department understands that some stoppages that appear to be shooter-induced are actually ammo-induced, so it is going to give its members a big safety margin when it comes to slide velocity.

Frankly, all three of these +P velocity 9mm 124-grain hollowpoints will make excellent police and defensive loads. Indeed, since the performance is so similar, the NYPD's first general issue hollowpoint may just be decided by low bid. Regardless of the outcome, the CCI-Speer 9mm +P 124-grain Gold Dot will always be the Gold Dot "developed for the New York City Police."

TABLE 20-1
CCI GOLD DOT

CALIBER	BULLET GDHP GR.	VEL. FPS	ENERGY FT-LBS.	REC. DIA. INCH	PEN. DEPTH INCH	CRUSH CAVITY CU. IN.	STRETCH CAVITY CU. IN.	EST. 1-SHOT STOPS %
9mm	115	1,200	341	.48	17.0	3.1	22.4	77
9mm	124	1,150	367	.55	12.8	3.0	35.2	82
9mm	147	985	326	.58	14.5	3.8	33.2	78
.40 S&W	155	1,175	475	.70	12.3	4.7	20.2	89
.40 S&W	180	985	400	.68	11.6	4.2	18.3	87
.44 Spl.	200	875	340	.64	12.5	4.0	14.0	85
.45 Auto	185	1,050	453	.60	12.0	3.4	16.8	90
.45 Auto	230	890	404	.70	13.5	5.2	14.4	88
.38 Spl. +P	125	945	248	.60	11.0	3.1	20.2	72
.357 Mag.	125	1,450	583	.65	15.0	5.0	53.5	89
.357 Mag.	158	1,235	535	.62	15.0	4.5	42.2	88
.380 Auto	90	990	196	.60	8.0	2.3	16.8	65
.357 SIG	125	1,398	543	.68	16.5	6.0	51.7	86
.40 S&W MV	165	970	345	.66	14.5	5.0	20.4	82
9mm +P	124	1,220	410	.57	15.5	3.9	44.4	83

TABLE 20-2
COR-BON & GEORGIA ARMS +P PRESSURE GOLD DOT AMMO

CALIBER	BULLET GR.	VEL. FPS	ENERGY FT-LBS.	PENE-TRATION (INCH)	EXPAN-SION (INCH)	PERM CRUSH CAVITY CU. IN.	TEMP. STRETCH CAVITY CU. IN.	EST. 1-SHOT STOPS %
COR-BON AMMO								
9mm +P	124 BHP	1,250	430	15.5	.57	3.9	44.4	84
9mm +P	147 BHP	1,000	326	16.4	.52 (f)	3.5	43.9	77
.45 ACP +P	230 BHP	950	461	14.0	.70	5.4	37.6	89
GEORGIA ARMS								
9mm +P	115 PHP	1,275	415	15.5	.55	3.7	36.4	83
9mm +P	124 PHP	1,225	413	15.5	.57	3.9	44.4	83
.40 S&W +P	155 PHP	1,200	496	12.0	.80	6.0	52.3	90
.40 S&W +P	180 PHP	1,050	441	15.5	.72	6.3	25.6	86
.45 ACP +P	185 PHP	1,075	475	13.0	.70	5.0	32.8	90

CCI-SPEER GOLD DOT

21
Remington Golden Saber

The Remington Golden Saber is the most recent development in handgun hollow-point ammunition. Led by the original Winchester Black Talon, the ammo industry is increasing the role that the bullet jacket plays in overall wounding. The jacket is no longer used simply to control the rate of core expansion; the most recently designed bullets use the jacket itself to increase tissue damage along the bullet path.

The copper alloy called "gilding metal" has been used to make rifle and handgun bullet jackets for more than 100 years. Nearly all jacketed hollowpoint, jacketed softpoint, and full-metal jacket bullets use this alloy. Gilding metal is 95 percent copper and 5 percent zinc.

In the early 1970s, Winchester stirred up the ammo industry with its aluminum-jacketed Silvertip hollowpoint. This aluminum-alloy jacket has a lower tensile and yield point than gilding metal. CCI-Lawman was the second ammo maker to use some other material in bullet jackets than gilding metal. Its copper-plated Gold Dot uses pure copper, which is also softer than gilding metal.

More recently, Winchester selected a non-traditional, copper-rich alloy for its original Black Talon hollowpoint. The selectively heat-treated Talon jacket has a higher copper content than gilding metal. This softer jacket allows the petals to peel back easily and makes them less likely to break off after impact. This bullet is now available in the police-only Ranger SXT ammo.

Remington Arms was next to stir the ammo industry with its Golden Saber high-performance jacket (HPJ) hollowpoint bullet, which uses a jacket made from hard cartridge brass. Cartridge brass is the same copper alloy used to make brass cartridge cases, hence the name. Containing 70 percent copper and 30 percent zinc, it is much stiffer than gilding metal and has a higher yield and tensile strength, according to Golden Saber design engineer Dave Schluckebier. Formerly with Winchester, Schluckebier is the original patent owner of the Black Talon design and is currently with Remington. For even greater strength, the HPJ bullets also use thicker-than-normal bullet jackets.

RIGHT: The newest Golden Saber is the .380 Auto 102-grain BJHP. This heaviest .380 Auto load still expands to .60 caliber.

BELOW: The .380 Auto 102-grain Golden Saber penetrates 9.4 inches of gelatin and has a 64 percent rating.

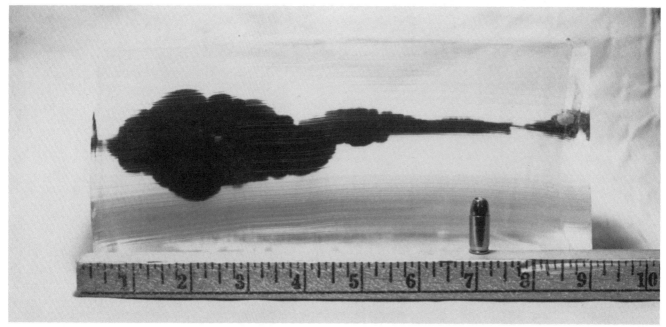

The logic behind the Remington Golden Saber HPJ is exactly the same as the Winchester Black Talon—Remington has shifted some of the wounding ability from the bullet core to the bullet jacket. With the Golden Saber, the brass jacket expands outward to form a mushroom shape while the lead core expands very little.

Remington used a stiff cartridge because it wanted a jacket that would stand out from the bullet shank after expansion. The result is the same as the 90 degree bends used in the Black Talon: both designs get their final recovered bullet diameter from the jacket, not the core.

Just like the exposed tip of the Black Talon jacket petals, the exposed ragged edges of the Golden Saber do indeed cut tissue along the bullet path. The Golden Saber is the fourth bullet after the PMC Ultramag, Winchester Black Talon, and PMC/Eldorado Starfire to use cutting in addition to crushing and stretching as a wounding mechanism.

Unlike conventional JHP bullets, the Golden Saber HPJ is designed to expand to a larger diameter than the lead core. Its shallow hollowpoint cavity actually limits the amount of core expansion. With minimal core expansion, the Golden Saber retains the maximum weight and thus produces the most reliable penetration. Just like the Black Talon, measurement of the recovered bullet diameter for the Golden Saber must be over the expanded jacket area to get the true crush diameter of the bullet.

The Golden Saber produces a larger measured recovered diameter while actually having a smaller frontal area. This allows both large

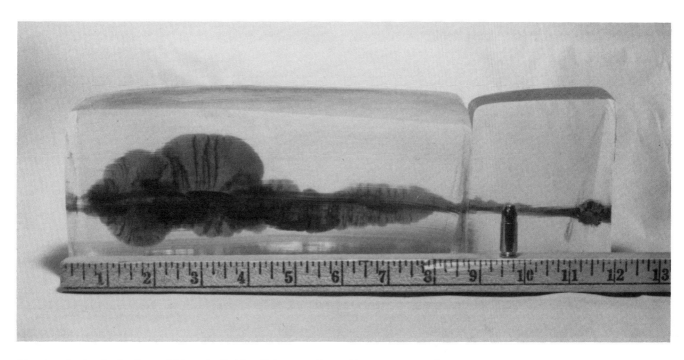

The standard-velocity 9mm 124-grain Golden Saber produces 81 percent one-shot stops.

crush cavities and deeper penetration. Usually, the bullet can only give one or the other.

The first-generation Golden Saber HPJ bullet was designed with a very wide but shallow hollowpoint cavity. The cavity is as wide as the jacket opening allows, and the serrations in the brass jacket are cut all the way through. Both features are required to generate enough expansion force to peel back the stiff brass jacket. Ammo tests in calibrated ordnance gelatin and in game animals struck by motorists confirm that the Golden Saber HPJ does indeed expand reliably to 145 percent or more of the caliber.

Expansion of the HPJ brass jacket petals is slower than gilding metal-, aluminum-, or pure copper-jacketed bullets. This speeds the rate of energy transfer and forms a very long temporary stretch cavity. The long-release, football-shaped stretch cavity is the most tolerant of intermediate obstacles and cross-torso shooting scenarios.

Remington calculates the speed of energy transfer by measuring the length of the radial cracks after each inch of penetration in calibrated ordnance gelatin. The Golden Saber starts to

transfer energy as fast as the best hollowpoint designs. However, it continues to transfer its peak amount of energy over a longer distance.

Due to its higher weight retention, the Golden Saber maintains a higher than average speed during its passage. It slows down at a slower rate and still transfers energy at a greater rate. It does all this because the jacket punches a bigger hole than its true calculated surface area would first indicate.

Unlike some bullets that were developed by firing them into wax, water, or bare gelatin, Remington used heavily clothed gelatin as a test media. The Golden Saber was designed for optimum performance in FBI ammo tests 2 and 7, which are the close-range and 20-yard shots at heavily clothed gelatin.

(Remington did no testing at all in water with the Golden Saber. The company felt that water simulates nothing. It does not recommend test firing for expansion in water, as water causes jackets to separate from cores when in real gunfights that does not often happen. Generally, bullets which expand perfectly in bare gelatin and water are too strong for good expansion in humans.)

The Golden Saber design uses what Remington calls a "driving band." On most small arms bullets, the rifling of the firearm engages or engraves the entire length of the bullet shank. Not so with the Golden Saber. The forward part of the HPJ is .008 inch smaller in diameter than the rear part. The forward part is almost the same diameter as the rifling "lands," while the rear part is almost the same diameter as the rifling "grooves."

The larger diameter rear driving band reduces friction between the stiff cartridge brass jacket and the rifling. The HPJ jacket is stiff enough, so only a short length of rifling engagement is needed to spin stabilize the bullet. The short driving band on the jacket resists slipping or stripping out in the rifling and avoids full rifling engagement with the softer gilding metal jacket.

The bearing surface area of the Golden Saber was actually scaled to be proportional in tensile strength with gilding metal jackets. As a result, the friction and barrel wear with the stiff-jacketed Golden Saber is the same as or less than conventional JHP bullets.

On conventional JHP bullets, the fully expanded core serves to lock the jacket to the core. On the Golden Saber, the jacket expands but the core does not, or at least not much. This causes great pressure to pull the jacket off the core. Remington designed the Golden Saber core to expand as little as possible while at the same time expanding enough to prevent jacket separation from lack of expansion. The rest was up to the driving band.

The small-diameter forward section of the HPJ jacket mechanically locks the jacket to the bullet core for better retained weight. The reduced nose diameter also allows the Golden Saber bullet to align precisely with the bore before the rifling lands dig into the driving band. Precise bullet alignment in the bore produces the maximum accuracy.

The stiffer jacket alloy and the HPJ jacket positively locked in place by the driving band makes the Golden Saber an ideal tactical police bullet. Glass and sheet metal are extremely destructive to high-performance

As originally released, the Golden Saber used large hollowpoint cavities and straight-cut serrations. The brass-jacketed .38 Special +P 125-grain Saber was promising.

The .45 Auto 230-grain load forced the change from straight-cut to spiral-cut serrations. These Golden Sabers expand like the aperture of a camera opening.

hollowpoints, but the Golden Saber has the jacket rigidity and core construction to defeat auto and thermopane glass and auto body panels much more reliably than all conventional JHP bullets and nearly all premium, semiexotic JHPs.

After the .38 Special +P, .357 Magnum Medium Velocity, 9mm, and .40 S&W Golden Saber brass-jacketed hollowpoint (BJHP) bullets were developed, Remington made a significant improvement in the serration design by changing from a straight-cut to a spiral-cut serration. All Golden Sabers produced from 1994 on used the new design. The original four cal-

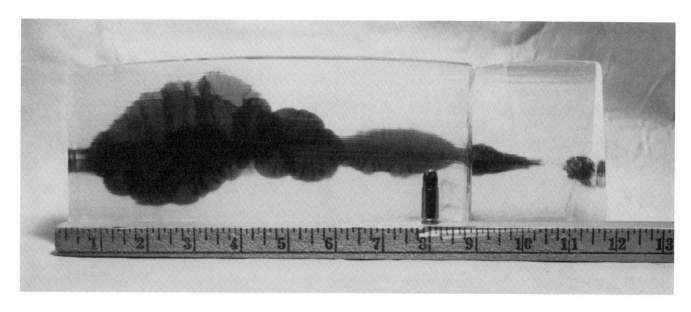

The 9mm +P 124-grain Golden Saber penetrates 12 inches of gelatin and expands to .65 caliber. This is an 83 percent load.

The 9mm 147-grain spiral-cut Golden Saber penetrates a more controlled 14.5 inches of gelatin. This is one of the very best subsonics, with a 77 percent effectiveness.

ibers were upgraded to the spiral serration, and the first release of the .45 Auto had them.

With the spiral-cut jacket, one edge of the jacket petal is cut completely through and folded 90 degrees inward toward the center of the hollowpoint cavity. In fact, this folded edge is just visible in cutting through the lead core to the inside of the cavity. The outer edge, which remains straight cut, is folded over the adjacent jacket petal. The result is a series of serrations that looks like an overlapping camera lens aperture.

The jacket petals on the spiral-cut Sabers overlap one another in a clockwise direction as viewed from the front. The really alert handgunner will wonder if this new bullet

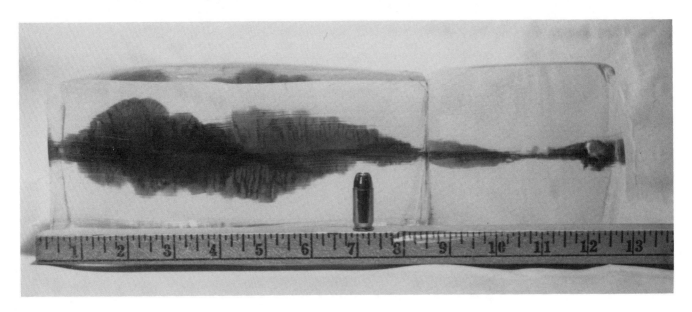

The .45 Auto 185-grain Golden Saber expands to .70 caliber and produces an impressive 89 percent one-shot stops.

design will expand faster from a left-hand rifling twist gun than from a right-hand twist. Remington engineers wondered, too.

They loaded one .40-caliber spiral-cut 180-grain BJHP in a .40 S&W case and fired it at 1,015 fps from a right-hand twist barrel. They loaded another .40-caliber spiral-cut 180-grain BJHP in a 10mm case and fired it at 1,015 fps from a left-hand twist barrel. Both bullets produced the same penetration depths and had the same recovered bullet diameters. They concluded that barrel twist does not effect spiral-cut Sabers.

The spiral-cut jacket design has an advantage over the Remington straight-cut serration because the jacket is cut completely through, so it does not need to tear any more to allow the bullet to expand. All it needs to do is bend. Of course, the jacket does tear as the expansion continues, but it does not need to tear to allow the expansion to start.

The length of the jacket serrations varies by the bullet weight. For example, the heavier and slower Sabers have serrations as long as the hollowpoint cavity is deep. The lighter and faster rounds have serrations about half as long as the cavity is deep.

As with the original straight-cut Sabers, the spiral design goal was to deform the lead core as little as possible during expansion for the most reliable penetration depths. The jacket alone becomes the mechanism of expansion and energy transfer on a Golden Saber, so the jacket expansion must be measured to get the true recovered diameter.

The jacket petals that protrude deeply into the hollowpoint cavity forced a redesign of the interior cavity dimensions. The cavity was reshaped using thick-wall-pressure vessel engineering concepts. The result was a smaller cavity with an entirely unique inner profile.

The prefailed jacket also allows a smaller hollowpoint with the same or better expansion reliability. Smaller cavities allow more rounded auto pistol bullets for better feed reliability. They also clear out heavy clothes, wood, and wallboard debris easier. This means the new Golden Saber is even more likely to expand in gelatin during the FBI barrier tests.

The first auto pistol Golden Sabers were the subsonic-class loads thrust on law enforcement by the FBI despite street results to the contrary. The second round of Sabers use the medium-weight, higher-velocity bullets that have proven time and again to be more effective in every caliber except .45 Auto.

The .45 Auto 230-grain spiral-cut Golden Saber produces the second best wound ballistics in the caliber, nearly tied with the 230-grain Hydra-Shok.

The spiral-cut jacket serrations lowered the threshold of expansion on this .40 S&W 180-grain Golden Saber to just 575 fps. (Photo credit: Remington Arms)

Like the original Sabers, these new, lighter, spiral-cut Sabers also produce long temporary stretch cavities because the stiffer cartridge brass used in the jacket peels back at a slower rate. The energy transfer is thus spread out over a longer distance, making the bullet the most tolerant of intermediate obstacles like upper arms.

Extremely detailed wound ballistics data is available about the straight-cut Saber design versus the spiral-cut design for two loads: the 9mm 147-grain BJHP and the .40 S&W 180-grain BJHP.

For starters, the spiral-cut jacket lowers the threshold of expansion. (This is *not* the velocity required to fully mushroom the hollowpoint. It is the velocity at which the mushrooming *starts* to occur in bare ordnance gelatin.) For the 9mm 147-grain BJHP, the original straight-cut brass jacket has a minimum velocity threshold of 790 fps. The new spiral-cut version of this same subsonic hollowpoint has a minimum velocity threshold of just 620 fps. This is a big margin of safety in a load that starts off at only 990 fps. Simply put, the spiral-cut 9mm 147-grain Saber is more likely to expand and to expand under a wider variety of scenarios than the straight-cut version.

This is even more evident with the .40 S&W 180-grain BJHP. The original straight-cut versions had a threshold of expansion at 700 fps. The spiral-cut design and the newly engineered hollowpoint cavity lower this to merely 575 fps. This load starts off at 1,015 fps, which is nearly twice the minimum required velocity to expand.

Other performance differences between the old and new serration design showed up as Remington conducted the FBI barrier tests. The spiral-cut rounds were superior in nearly every test category of gelatin after some sort of tactical obstacle, producing larger recovered diameters and penetration closer to the 10 to 14 inch depths. They were especially effective after passing through wallboard and plywood. The smaller hollowpoint cavity really does clear itself of debris better than the original design.

After passing through wallboard and plywood, the straight-cut Saber frequently plugged up and failed to expand in gelatin, resulting in gelatin penetration between 18.5 and 25.5 inches. This kind of penetration is clearly excessive and an obvious civil liability. The spiral-cut jacket serrations allowed the bullets to expand up to .65 caliber after these two barriers, reducing the penetration to between 13.9 and 16.3 inches.

During the 40-round barrier test, the weighted average bullet expansion for the 9mm 147-grain BJHP increased from .506 inch for the straight-cut to .574 inch for the spiral-cut. The average penetration depth dropped from an excessive 16.5 inches to an ideal 13.0 inches. The same held true for the change from straight-cut to spiral-cut serrations on the .40 S&W 180-grain BJHP. The recovered diameter grew from .568 inch to .636 inch, and overall penetration decreased from 16.4 inches to 13.8 inches. Excellent.

The new spiral-cut Golden Sabers are also dramatically better bullets than Remington's conventional hollowpoints in the same caliber and weight. The best direct comparison is the .45 Auto 185-grain JHP versus the 185-grain Golden Saber.

The Remington .45 Auto standard-pressure 185-grain JHP has become a benchmark of performance not because it has good wound ballistics but because the group of deeper-is-better experts "thinks" it has good wound ballistics. The facts are, the load is only marginal compared to others in this big-bore caliber. The 185-grain Golden Saber has much better performance after steel, wallboard, and plywood barriers. The average expansion in a 40-round, eight-barrier test for the conventional JHP is .598 inch with an excessive 16.9 inches of penetration. The Golden Saber has an average expansion of .647 inch, with an ideally controlled average penetration depth of 13.1

inches. The best of the proven street loads in all calibers average 13.3 inches of penetration in gelatin.

The most impressive of the new Sabers is the .40 S&W 165-grain BJHP. Unlike the new Federal 165-grain Hydra-Shok, the 165-grain Golden Saber is a full-power, 485 ft-lb. load. Its plump .68-caliber recovered diameter, ideal 12-inch depth of penetration, and massive stretch cavity have earned this load an impressive 94-percent one-shot stops in actual gunfights. This is nearly the best in the .40 S&W caliber, behind only the Cor-Bon 135-grain Nosler JHP and tied with the Federal 155-grain JHP.

The Remington .40 S&W 165-grain Golden Saber is better than even the best 9mm +P+ hollowpoints' and is actually tied with the incredible Federal .45 Auto 230-grain Hydra-Shok, which is the most effective big-bore load in history. The Arkansas State Police, wanting to take advantage of the greater tactical penetration made possible by the hard brass jacket, are the latest to investigate this 165-grain BJHP. It is also the duty load by choice of author Ed Sanow for the Glock 22 he uses on patrol with the Benton County, Indiana, Sheriff.

The newest Golden Saber is the .380 Auto 102-grain BJHP. At 102 grains, it is the heaviest .380 Auto bullet ever loaded. With a 925 fps velocity, this load generates among the snappiest slide velocities. The smallest Saber expands reliably to .60 caliber and penetrates to a depth of 9.4 inches.

This is excellent penetration from a .380 Auto hollowpoint that actually expands. Most .380 Auto JHPs either expand reliably or penetrate adequately, but not both. The Golden Saber is one of the very few .380 Auto JHPs to do both. Actually, the Remington Golden Saber itself is one of the few bullet designs to expand reliably after penetrating barriers like gypsum and heavy clothing.

TABLE 21-1
REMINGTON GOLDEN SABER AMMUNITION

CALIBER	LOAD BJHP GRAIN	VEL. FPS	ENERBY FT-LBS.	EXPAN-SION INCH	PEN. INCH	CRUSH CAVITY CU. IN.	STRETCH CAVITY CU. IN.	ONE-SHOT STOP %
.380 Auto	102 spiral	940	200	.60	9.4	2.7	13.8	65 est
.38 Spl. +P	125 straight	975	264	.59	12.4	3.4	19.8	73 est
9mm	124 spiral	1,125	349	.59	12.0	3.3	26.4	81 est
9mm	147 straight	990	320	.62	14.5	4.4	31.8	78 est
9mm	147 spiral	990	320	.66	12.8	4.4	25.4	79 est
9mm +P	124 spiral	1,180	417	.65	12.0	4.0	28.1	85 est
.357 Mag. MV	125 straight	1,220	413	.60	13.0	3.7	30.4	85 est
.40 S&W	165 spiral	1,150	485	.68	12.0	4.4	41.1	94 act
.40 S&W	180 straight	1,015	412	.83	12.9	7.0	27.9	87 est
.45 Auto	185 spiral	1,015	423	.70	13.0	5.0	24.6	89 est
.45 Auto	230 spiral	875	391	.75	14.3	6.3	25.4	87 est

TABLE 21-2
STRAIGHT-CUT VS. SPIRAL-CUT 9mm GOLDEN SABER

BARRIER	ORIGINAL STRAIGHT-CUT 9mm 147-GRAIN BJHP		NEW SPIRAL-CUT 9mm 147-GRAIN BJHP	
	PENETRATION	EXPANSION	PENETRATION	EXPANSION
bare gelatin	14.3 in	.64 in	12.8 in	.66 in
heavy clothes @ 10 ft.	16.1 in	.62 in	14.2 in	.66 in
sheet steel	18.5 in	.45 in	14.3 in	.47 in
wallboard	25.2 in	.36 in	13.9 in	.62 in
plywood	19.8 in	.36 in	14.4 in	.59 in
auto glass @ 10 ft.	10.9 in	.52 in	9.2 in	.47 in
light clothes @ 20 yds.	15.4 in	.64 in	13.2 in	.66 in
auto glass @ 20 yds.	11.2 in	.48 in	11.6 in	.46 in
averages	16.45 in	.506 in	12.95 in	.574 in

22

The History of Hydra-Shok, Starfire, and Quik-Shok Ammunition

by Tom Burczynski

I designed the first Hydra-Shok prototype in the mid 1970s after becoming thoroughly disenchanted with the hollowpoints of that era. Regardless of the manufacturer, the bullets in those days simply wouldn't expand well (if at all) at low velocity. I concluded that the only way to force a hollowpoint bullet to expand consistently faster was to incorporate a simple machine into its cavity, which was lacking in conventional hollowpoints. I surmised that the main problem with a conical or frusto-conical hollowpoint was that as fluidic material entered the cavity, it was redirected toward the axis of the bullet right toward the thick, harder-to-expand shank area.

Typical hollowpoints clearly had (and still have) inherent limitations. Even for a modern hollowpoint to be consistently efficient, it must have exposed lead or a pronounced skive pattern in conjunction with an aggressive cavity. It also has to be fired at relatively high velocity. In the bad old days, hollowpoints were clearly self-limiting. They had small, relatively short conical or frusto-conical cavities

and hard cores. To exacerbate the problem, factory ammunition yielded low velocities. Viewed collectively, this was a recipe for failure, and these bullets cost many law enforcement officers their lives.

Simple machines make work easier. In this case, the "work" I was trying to achieve dealt with expanding the ogive portion of the bullet. Due to the constraints of cavity size, the only logical choice was the wedge. Since the cone is a form of the wedge and possesses omnidirectional potential, I was convinced that its presence would promote rapid, uniform expansion. With manufacturing economics in mind, I finally settled on a tapered "post" that would be formed from the bullet core itself.

I theorized that if the post height and angle were optimized, incoming fluidic material would be redirected and momentarily focused on the interior wall of the cavity near the meplat of the bullet. This fluid "deflection" would create a brief but intense radial impulse which would initiate expansion hydraulically by way of high-pressure force vectors. This

This is a .38 Special Scorpion bullet. This 146-grain lead-alloy Hydra-Shok bullet was the first bullet commercially loaded at the Hydra-Shok manufacturing facility. Scorpion bullets were manufactured exclusively by the Alberts Corporation.

This 158-grain .38/.357 bullet was the first cold-swaged bullet using the old cylindrical die and nose punch system. The 125-grain version of this bullet performed extremely well on a 190 pound European Boar. Note the tapered hemispherical post that extends slightly beyond the bullet nose. Later bullets utilized a recessed post.

This 158-grain bullet was made using a cylindrical die and has a smaller, conical post very similar to Federal's current factory Hydra-Shok.

This 158-grain prototype made for the Hydra-Shok Corporation by the Sierra Bullet Company utilized a flat-ended recessed post. This bullet was never commercially produced because the flat post caused excessive penetration.

impulse would occur even before peak pressure within the annular cavity was achieved. As the bullet continued to penetrate, overall pressure within the annular cavity would be amplified as the post pierced new tissue. My rationale was that this hydrodynamic action would substantially expedite expansion. I could only guess at just how much faster the bullet would expand. But from a terminal standpoint, I knew that the more rapid the expansion, the sooner a large, flat surface would be exposed to vital organs—a key element in inducing shock.

In order to reduce the theory to practice, I made drawings of a cylindrical die and a nose-forming/post-forming punch and delivered it to my uncle, master machinist Stan Burczy-

nski. Two days later the dies were installed in an Echo Press and bullets were being swaged. Two hundred bullets later, the nose punch was broken. The breakage problem stemmed from the cylindrical die set. In order to form a decent ogive without a pronounced shoulder, the nose punch required a very thin leading edge. This edge broke down under the extreme pressure generated during the cold-swaging process. I was forced to redesign the nose punch several times. The hardness and interior angle of the punch both were modified again and again. These efforts met with limited success, and I finally abandoned the cylindrical die concept altogether.

However, while testing these first ogival prototypes, it became evident that Hydra-Shok

This 125-grain State Department Loading (SDL) in .38 and .357 Magnum was the first bullet made using the newer profile die system. SDL rounds utilized the hemisperical post. Factory-loaded SDL cartridges with rare "H-S Proto" stamped on the bullet base are valued at $60 to $90 each. There are fewer than 200 of these cartridges in existence.

This solid brass Hydra-Shok bullet with a conical post was made using the profile die system. This lightweight 9mm prototype expanded well even when using standard-pressure loadings.

bullets didn't require a large cavity or high velocity to expand dramatically, even when fired through clothing. There was no doubt about it—the efficiency differential that existed between the two designs was a direct result of the angle of internal tissue deflection, caused by a powerful, post-prompted radial impulse. It became increasingly apparent that while the conventional hollowpoint caused *inward* deflection, the Hydra-Shok design deflected tissue *outwardly*, away from the cone, in the precise direction I wanted to bend the tip of the bullet's ogive.

After almost six years of research and development and testing many variations of the bullet, patents were applied for and issued. It was about this time that we were directed to Jerry Alberts of the Alberts Corporation. Jerry was a lead bullet guru of national renown. He owned a bullet company, made his own bullet-making machinery, and purportedly was the most resourceful tool and die maker around. There was nothing he couldn't do. We drove out to New Jersey and met with him.

After explaining that we needed a Hydra-Shok bullet with an ogive, Jerry said that it wouldn't be a problem. He was amiable enough, but he struck me as somewhat condescending. He thought it was rather amusing that anyone could be so concerned over such a minor problem. Jerry told us that he'd send us samples in a couple of weeks.

A couple of weeks turned into a couple of months. Finally, Jerry contacted us and was forced to admit that he couldn't make the bullet with an ogive because the punches broke too often *and* the lead locked itself around the post-forming punch so tightly that he couldn't get the bullets to strip free. I was disappointed but found some solace in the fact that I wasn't the only one who had failed.

Jerry suggested an alternative product—a full wadcutter incorporating the patented post. I was against the idea. Even I had accomplished making full wadcutters using a cylindrical die system, which was what he was proposing. But lead bullets could only be driven at modest velocities. The new speedloaders that had just hit the market were all but worthless loaded with full wadcutters. Wadcutters would also be unstable at a hundred yards. I hated everything about the idea. But stepping back and looking at the situation pragmatically, from a business standpoint, I figured that if this was all that could be made . . . and if the ammo sold . . .

I finally relented to logic. An agreement was entered into. Alberts made the bullets. The new ammunition was loaded near the Hydra-Shok headquarters in upstate New York.

The 146-grain .38 Special wadcutter was named the Hydra-Shok Scorpion. It shot quite well, expanded well, and, surprisingly, it sold very well. But I was never really content

The 110-grain Copperhead .38 Special round expands almost instantly due to its conical post and higher velocity.

with this single, ballistically limited product. Every time I looked at it, I was reminded of my failure to develop a system to produce an ogival version.

Finally, I got serious. I took a couple days off and began sketching dies and punches. I ultimately designed a 7/8 x 14 profile die with a web area separating the die bore from a larger upper chamber. This allowed a shouldered, post-forming punch to slide up and down through a concentric hole in the web area.

Using an RCBS Rockchucker press, the prototype bullet-swaging process was now a straightforward procedure. A bullet was placed on top of a base punch and swaged. The base punch was withdrawn from the die as the handle of the press was swung upward. Then a small leather mallet was used to tap the top of the post-forming punch to eject the bullet. Once the punch was tapped to the full *down* position, the bullet was no longer confined within the die. However, it was still very much attached to the forming punch. This is where the punch's shoulder came into play. From here, a simple upward nudge on the bullet seated its lower ogive area in the mouth of the die so that slight friction held the punch with attached bullet in a partial *up* position. Then, a sharp blow to the top of the punch drove the punch and bullet downward until the shoulder of the punch

stopped abruptly as it impacted the internal web area of the die. At this point, inertia took over and stripped the bullet from the punch, where it was caught in a hand. Finally, the die and punch were both viable entities and relatively durable. This was a major milestone. Without this basic die system, Hydra-Shok ammo utilizing ogival form bullets would never have been commercially available.

This full-manual inertial system worked well for making prototypes, but the process was rather slow and laborious. The base system had to be engineered to incorporate some type of automatic ejection feature before mass-production of Hydra-Shok bullets could become a reality. I pondered this on and off for about a week and struck upon the idea of a double-yoke ejection system. This system comprised a 5-inch-long upper yoke that threaded over the top of the post-forming punch and a bottom yoke that clamped around the ram of the press. The lower yoke had tapped holes in either end into which threaded rods were secured. The upper yoke had two matching holes which allowed the rods to slide freely for several inches as the handle of the press was moved up and down.

Positioned atop the upper yoke were two powerful die springs. Each spring contained two shouldered bushings, and atop these bushings were two hex locknuts. The bushings allowed hard contact engagement after the springs were fully compressed. After swaging a bullet, the handle of the press was moved upward. This action fully compressed the die springs. The bushings contacted one another and the bullet was forced downward toward the opening of the die. Once the bullet escaped the confines of the die, the springs released their energy, driving the shouldered post-forming punch into the web area and stripping the bullet from the punch. This inertial ejection system took advantage of the compound leverage which RCBS built into its press so that hundreds of prototypes could be swaged and ejected with a minimum of effort. About 30 prototypes per minute could be swaged using this system, but although this was a vast

This early 160-grain .38 Hydra-Shok bullet shows classic "ringing" that occurred during expansion if enough resistance was met. The bullet shank section continued to penetrate after punching through the expanded bullet ogive. Note how the hemispherical post was flattened slightly during penetration. This bullet was reformed from a Speer 3/4 jacketed softpoint.

improvement over the full-manual concept, it was still only a "semiautomatic" mechanism.

From here, I designed a stronger yoke assembly, had it machined, and attached it to a hydraulic press. This press was relatively small and could barely duplicate the force generated by the RCBS Rockchucker hand press. It was powerful enough for mass production, though, and the Hydra-Shok Corporation was finally in high gear.

As it turned out, this mass-production capability was developed in the nick of time, as we had previously sent .38 and .357 ammo containing jacketed prototypes to the U.S. Department of State for testing and had just received a very favorable response. For several months prior to this, the State Department had been in the process of testing every brand of ammunition manufactured. The tests, which were carried out using 20-percent gelatin, were so stringent that none of the ammo submitted by other manufacturers even came close. They wanted a .38 round that would deliver 7 1/2 to 8 1/2 inches of penetration in gelatin and not a fraction more or less. Typical ammo of that era launched bullets that penetrated 13 to 24 inches.

Hydra-Shok was the last round to be tested—and it was almost a State Department afterthought. Being last definitely worked to our advantage, however, because they had already obtained extremely disappointing results with everything else. During the initial tests, even the Hydra-Shok 125-grain jacketed bullet overpenetrated to a depth of 9 inches. Despite this, the department was so elated that they asked us to fine tune it and immediately scheduled another test. We increased the powder charge slightly, which raised the velocity about 30 fps. This caused the bullet to expand even faster and resulted in a penetration depth that was right on the money.

The State Department also wanted a .357 Magnum round that generated less than 30,000 psi, expanded to between .55 and .60 caliber, and penetrated no more than 8 1/2 inches. Keeping within these parameters was impossible using bullets of the day at normal .357 velocities. Our solution resulted in the first reduced loading offered by any manufacturer. It did everything they wanted it to do at reduced flash, blast, and recoil levels. This load was dubbed SDL, an acronym which really stood for two things: Super Defense Load and State Department Loading. The Department ultimately adopted the .38 Scorpion and the 125-grain jacketed loadings in .38 and .357 Magnum. The first order was for three-quarters of a million rounds, and much to the agency's delight, higher qualification scores were immediately reported.

It was during this government contract period that the FBI contacted us and asked if we could produce six million Hydra-Shok rounds for them, to their specs. We had to turn them down. We simply didn't have the production capacity to service the police market, the dealer market, and two government agencies. One of the FBI officials suggested that we license the patent rights to one of the major manufacturers. This way they could get large

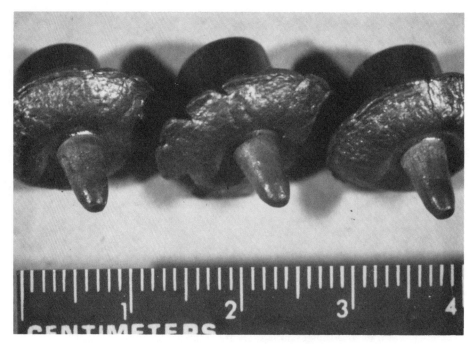

Three .38 Special Hydra-Shok bullets of early design fired from a short-barrelled revolver. Note the uniform expansion and large, hemispherical post. (Photo credit: Shep Kelly)

quantities of Hydra-Shok ammo built to their specs, and we wouldn't have to put up with the hassle of producing bullets and ammo.

A while later, shortly after successfully completing our thirteenth State Department contract, Federal Cartridge Company began to show a keen interest in Hydra-Shok. It appeared that word had gotten around that the FBI had taken a hard look at our ammo. Federal needed a new product to compete with Winchester's Silvertip round. From all police reports, Hydra-Shok was working well on the street. Everything appeared to be falling into place. Federal set up an initial meeting. In 1987, after about three months of negotiations, we granted an exclusive manufacturing license to Federal and sold our remaining inventory.

The exclusive license called for dies, punches, presses, prototype bullets, drawings, and a degree of technical assistance. I supplied Federal with a quantity of written material explaining the functions of the different post styles, their specific actions, and their various applications. It was important that Federal understand the reasons for the different post shapes. This would save them untold hours of extra R&D.

I pointed out to them that most of the early Hydra-Shoks utilized a tapered post which ter-

minated in a hemispherical tip. Later on, the conical post was added to the lead .45 Auto bullet and a couple of 158-grain bullets in .38 and .357. The tapered "hemi-post" was used where somewhat deeper penetration was desired. This post design caused a more localized tissue deflection very close to the tip of the bullet, but since the wall of the annular cavity was very close to the radius of the hemispherical surface, there wasn't as much area involved to accept incoming material. The end result was a slightly slower expansion rate that netted extra penetration. It was pointed out that even though the hemi-post provided a slower rate of expansion, the expansion was *much* faster at any given speed than any bullet on the market at that time.

I further explained that the cone-shaped post was used to increase the rate of expansion in the heavier, slower moving bullets. A good example was the 230-grain Hydra-Shok in .45 Auto. This was a lead-antimony bullet. The harder, thicker bullet needed all the help it could get as far as expansion was concerned. The conical post provided a sharper, more effective working angle and increased volume in the annular cavity at the same time. This conical post also deflected tissue like the

Classic high-speed photo of Federal 230-grain .45 Auto Hydra-Shok fully expanded in 2 inches of 10-percent gelatin. A 1/2,000,000th second flash froze the action. (Photo credit: Tom Burczynski)

hemi-post but focused it over a wider band on the cavity wall. The conical post was used in all the heavier bullets (except the .44 Magnum), since heavy bullets had a natural tendency to overpenetrate. This post style effectively increased the rate of expansion and decreased penetration. I pointed out that most of the original Hydra-Shok bullets contained the hemi-post because the meplat area was relatively wide, which allowed more room in the cavity to accommodate a larger post.

Samples of all the prototypes made over the years were sent to Federal. There were a total of 21 prototypes designed over a period of about six years. Ironically, the first prototype was very similar to the final design, with one exception. It utilized the tapered hemi-post, but the tip of the post protruded slightly beyond the bullet nose. This bullet was ogival in form and even though it had a good ballistic coefficient, it required considerably more

swaging force to form the longer post, which was eventually abandoned in favor of the recessed version.

In 1973, I used the long post prototype to dispatch a 190-pound European Boar, with excellent results. These animals are extremely tough and hard to disable, even using a rifle. The boar was shot through the lungs at a distance of about 35 yards and collapsed instantly. Although he made it to his feet, I knew I had invented a viable defense bullet. A quick shot through the neck killed the animal. The bullet was a 125-grainer that left the muzzle of a 5-inch Model 27 at 1,250 fps. This was a rather mild load for a .357, but an impromptu field autopsy revealed a great deal of lung damage and about a quart and a half of blood in the chest cavity.

Since then, I've personally been made aware of 35 or more local deer having been taken with first- and second-generation Hydra-

Shok rounds in 9mm, .357, and .44. Heart and lung shots almost always produced the same result—a great deal of hemorrhage and the deer dropping within 15 to 30 yards.

Trial and error testing of these early prototypes was time-consuming. If the annular cavity was too shallow or too large, premature "ringing" could occur because the post caused the ogive area to expand far too quickly. (Ringing is a terminal condition in which the expanded ogive shears away after having penetrated a distance into the target.) In the quest for peak performance, scores of forming punches were machined. Internal bullet dimensions had to be tailored specifically for each caliber and velocity range. A good many post/cavity combinations were tried, from very deep cavities with short posts to dual-angled posts having shallow cavities. Thousands of test firings were an integral part of the research. Fortunately, careful analysis of the test media eliminated less effective geometry within a reasonable time frame.

Without the patience and machining expertise my Uncle Stan provided, the R&D would have taken a great deal longer. He was great. He had to literally invent new ways of machining these strange dies and punches. We could always count on him to machine the difficult parts immediately; the impossible took him a little longer. Each time I brought in some far-out cryptic drawing, he'd just smile and shake his head. I owe him a lot for service above and beyond the call of duty.

Once the ball was in its court, Federal quickly geared up for production. Its engineering team did a great job of designing (and redesigning) the second-generation Hydra-Shok. It was evident that they had paid attention to the written material I supplied that covered the functions of the two post styles. Ultimately, Federal incorporated the conical post into its entire line with the exception of the 129-grain .38 load. The .38 revolver bullet worked well with the larger hemi-post. With the inherently wider nose, this bullet expanded very quickly because the annular cavity had greater volume. If a conical post had been

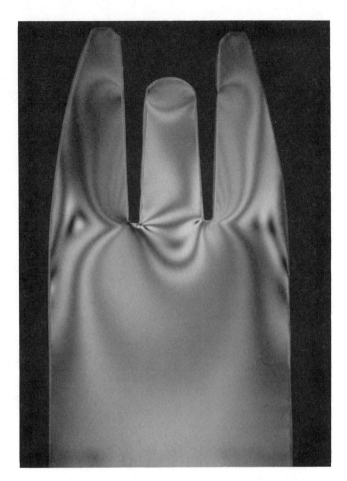

This birefringent image of a Plexiglas model reveals stress patterns that develop in the Federal 9mm Hydra-Shok bullet. Crowded lines indicate areas of greatest stress. (Photo credit: Tom Burczynski)

used here, penetration would have suffered because expansion would have occurred far too quickly. A good analogy of this penetration-defeating deceleration is the effect produced when a parachute abruptly opens behind a dragster.

As mentioned in the other calibers, Federal went with the conical post to expedite expansion. Essentially they reduced the post size, decreased the size of the meplat, extended the jacket to the radius of the nose, and added skives. From a production standpoint, the conical post was a logical choice because the sharper post angle facilitated stripping the bullet from the punch. From a cartridge-feeding

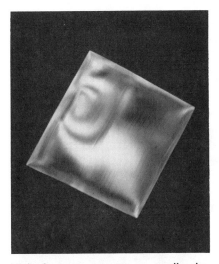

Light finger pressure on a small cube of 10-percent gelatin shows iso-elastic stresses produced well in front of the contact point. This proves that a pressure front travels ahead of a bullet as the crush cavity and temporary cavity are being formed. (Photo credit: Tom Burczynski)

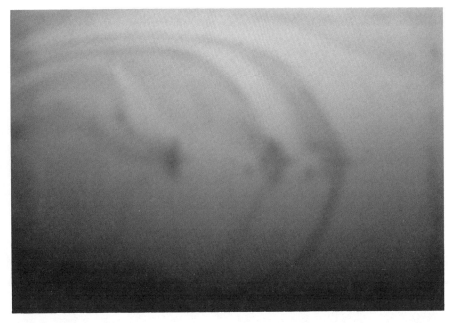

This triple-flash strobe photo taken at 1/100,000th second produces a fuzzy but useful image of a 10mm Hydra-Shok bullet penetrating gelatin. This slow flash speed clearly defines the shape of the semitransparent temporary cavity and the changing shape of the bullet. Note the "flat" face of the expanded bullet in its early travel (first exposure). The flatter and more rapid the expansion, the greater the stopping power. (Photo credit: Tom Burczynski)

standpoint, it made total sense because it allowed their engineers the latitude to design a bullet profile with a smaller meplat. From a terminal ballistic standpoint, because the meplat dictated wall thickness and cavity diameter, the conical post was the only choice. The smaller cavity demanded a smaller post, and the conical post expedited expansion in spite of the reduced cavity volume. Federal engineers designed the post so that it could bend after it had outlived its usefulness during target penetration. When the post bends, it causes the core to yaw inside the target, which safeguards against overpenetration. The conical post allowed Federal the flexibility to make a Hydra-Shok bullet do almost anything.

A good example of this flexibility is found in Federal's current 147-grain 9mm Hydra-Shok round. Due to the subsonic velocity involved, this bullet absolutely needs all the expansion assistance it can get. This assistance is fully provided by the coni-cal post. Most 9mm bullets in this weight expand only marginally, even under ideal conditions. Sometimes bullets supplied by other manufacturers don't expand at all, especially after penetrating a clothing barri-er. Unlike typical hollowpoints, Hydra-Shok's conical post allows this slow bullet to expand quickly and to a large diameter, even after penetrating clothing.

During penetration through clothing, con-ventional hollowpoint bullets immediately become clogged with dry fabric—and without fluid present, they often fail to expand at all. When fabric enters the Hydra-Shok cavity, it is pierced by the post and shoved toward the base of the cavity. This leaves the tip of the post exposed to accept incoming fluid. It's business as usual. The conical post doesn't care if the material is wet or dry; the simple machine principle works regardless.

The FBI went to a great deal of time and expense to prove this by removing the posts.

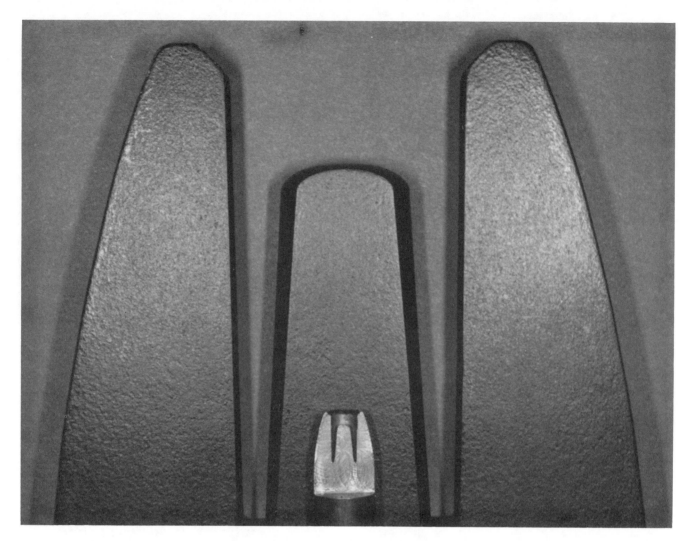

An aluminum model of a 147-grain 9mm Hydra-Shok bullet was used in neutrally buoyant helium bubble tests. As high-speed helium bubbles flowed around the post, they accumulated just behind its tip and against the sides of the cavity wall, then flowed back out of the cavity. These tests reconfirmed the accuracy of the birefringent image experiments.

The result was that Hydra-Shok was much more effective throughout their tests with the post than without. A simple machine must be present to do extra work. Conventional, smooth-walled hollowpoints lack a simple machine. Hydra-Shok's anti-clogging ability gives law enforcement officers a great advantage on the street. And in light of recent Hydra-Shok improvement patents issued to Federal, they will continue to have a great advantage over their competition for years to come.

Federal engineers did a great job of balancing expansion and penetration. What impressed me most was the fact that they were willing to continue their R&D and did so by incorporating subtle design changes into the various calibers in order to give the FBI exactly what it wanted. Remington and Winchester elected not to do this, and it is my understanding that they told the FBI's John Hall that they weren't interested in doing any special development work for them. It was a take-what-we've-got-or-leave-it situation. This was a grave

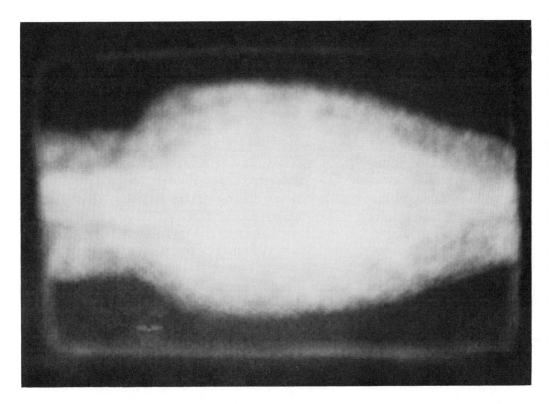

This photo of a monitor image shows the infrared heat pattern in a gelatin block after being struck by 9mm Hydra-Shok bullet. The bullet entered at the left. The wide entrance neck and abrupt shoulder area indicate a friction-produced heat pattern caused by extremely rapid expansion/energy transfer. Maximum "heat-pattern growth" occurred approximately 15 seconds after impact. (Photo credit: Tom Burczynski)

mistake, and Federal took advantage of it. Federal gave them exactly what they wanted—bullets that could make it through the gauntlet of incredibly rigorous tests the Bureau had developed. Now that the Hydra-Shok line has been perfected, other major law enforcement agencies can feel totally confident in adopting the end product that satisfied the FBI.

Federal also built outstanding accuracy into its version of Hydra-Shok. Depending on the weapon, accuracy ranges from very good to astounding. To law enforcement groups, this is vitally important. If your duty ammo prevents accurate bullet placement, bullet efficiency becomes almost meaningless. Today, you can pick up just about any gun magazine and find more than one table showing Hydra-Shok leading the competition in the accuracy department.

Federal reduced cartridge feeding to a fine science as well. Its Hydra-Shok ammo feeds flawlessly in almost every weapon known. A great deal of research went into this. If you're a cop, it's comforting to know that if you carry Hydra-Shok ammo you won't die because of a cartridge jam or a bullet that doesn't expand.

The entire Hydra-Shok experience has been one long learning curve. I was forced to increase my knowledge of analytical tools by using high-speed flash equipment, neutrally buoyant helium bubble generators, isoelastic stress techniques, and infrared scanning technology in order to prove, beyond a shadow of a doubt, that Hydra-Shok was a superefficient design. In the final analysis, the most enduring proof of Hydra-Shok's superiority lies in its performance on the street. These statistics speak for themselves.

In retrospect, we hadn't done too badly. Ideas had been converted to patents. Impossible manufacturing techniques had been developed. Over an eight-year period, an array of lead and jacketed bullets and ammo in all the popular calibers had been developed (in spite of an outrageous 21 percent interest rate that prevailed during that time). Hydra-Shok was solvent, a substantial amount of money had been made, and the patents had been licensed to Federal. The experience has been a good one.

The interaction with Federal Cartridge has

been good too, and in my opinion, Federal is still the most progressive-thinking company of the Big Three. This is due in part to the fact that they do not suffer from the NIH (not invented here) Syndrome. This foresight and openmindedness can be attributed to sharp minds in key positions, namely Ron Mason, President of Federal, Dave Longren, Director of Product Engineering, and Bob Kramer, Product Engineering Manager. Mason's prudent delegation of authority to certain individuals and the latitude they have in making judgment calls has certainly paid off for Federal. The company also has the ability to adapt, and it has several new products on the back burner—not just run-of-the-mill products but radically new designs that will cause major concern for every manufacturer out there and will extend the lead Federal already enjoys.

No man is an island, and I owe debts of gratitude to many people for helping to make Hydra-Shok the most phenomenal success story in modern ammunition history. Just within the family there's quite a list: my brother, Mike, who got me involved in reloading ammunition many years ago; my Uncle Stan, for doing impossible machining over the years; my brothers Frank and Dan for making extremely complex CAD drawings for me when they didn't really have the time; my dad, Joe Burczynski, who proved to be a good sounding board; and my wife, Lori, for preparing tons of gelatin and putting up with bullets and gun magazines scattered throughout the house.

Within the industry, my thanks go to people at Federal Cartridge like Alan Newcomb, who was instrumental in convincing Federal that Hydra-Shok was a viable product; Hugh Reed, who was responsible for negotiating the terms of the licensing agreement; Dave Longren and Bob Kramer, for developing Hydra-Shok in new calibers; and Mike Bussard, who was instrumental in cultivating early Hydra-Shok sales. A special thanks goes to Shep Kelly, who acted as liaison between the FBI and Federal and dramatically increased law enforcement and government sales of Hydra-Shok ammunition.

• • • • •

I actually invented the Starfire back in the 1970s. The design lay dormant for several years because we had our hands full trying to get Hydra-Shok up and running. It wasn't until the late 1980s, after the first patent was issued, that I did any serious development work with it.

Starfire and Hydra-Shok share a conceptual similarity. Both incorporate a variation of the wedge in the cavity to bring about rapid expansion. Hydra-Shok utilizes a cone situated concentrically. Starfire utilizes apically curving, eccentrically situated wedges. Like Hydra-Shok's post, the Starfire ribs are an integral part of the core material.

All the early Starfire prototypes utilized a deep cavity comprising a series of wedge-shaped ribs and flutes similar to the factory ammo being sold today. This cavity was very different from the smooth-walled cavity found in a common hollowpoint. The Starfire cavity was very intricate. The ribs had relatively sharp, longitudinal edges close to the axis of the bullet (and to one another). They widened as they neared the mouth of the cavity, then narrowed again, diminishing in area and terminating in "points." The ribs were separated by an equal number of tapered, curving flutes that widened as they approached the mouth of the cavity. These flutes were actually formed by the general frusto-conical shape of the forming punch. The ribs were formed by the tapered grooves that were machined into the punch.

Starfire's internal wedges split incoming

The Starfire has compound internal angles and a hollowpoint cavity nearly as deep as the bullet is long.

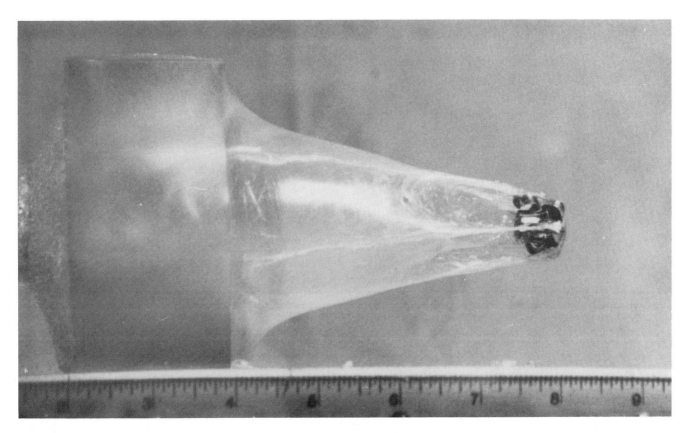

This .45 Auto 230-grain Starfire has expanded to .68 caliber in just 2 inches of gelatin. It eventually penetrates 13.8 inches of gelatin and has an 86 percent rating.

The .357 Magnum 150-grain Starfire transfers 484 ft-lbs. of energy in just 12 inches.

tissue and redirect it radially under amplified pressure into the flute areas. Each flute is forced to accept fluidic material from two bordering ribs, effectively doubling the pressure within the flute. Again, as in the case with Hydra-Shok, it is this fluid "deflection" that creates a brief but intense radial impulse which initiates expansion hydraulically by way of high-pressure force vectors. Simply put, the wedges make the work of stretching and tearing the core material outside the flute areas easier. The end result is accelerated expansion.

Just like the Hydra-Shok post, the Starfire ribs serve a three-fold purpose: they provide the central mass needed for stable flight, they accelerate expansion, and, after expansion, the sharp ribs assist in penetration.

A Starfire bullet actually possesses the inherent potential to expand to a larger diame-

The 9mm 124-grain Starfire produces controlled penetration and expands to .68 caliber in ordnance gelatin. It expands all the way to the bullet base and gives 81 percent one-shot stops.

ter than Hydra-Shok because the cavity is nearly as deep as the bullet is long. By the same token, Hydra-Shok can be designed to penetrate very deeply. Life consists of trade-offs, and ballistics is no exception. As designed, however, Starfire consistently delivers optimum penetration.

Designing the "release angles" required for the very first forming punch was not an easy task. There were *three* angles involved in the geometry of the punch, one of which terminated in a radius. I managed to make a drawing and immediately realized that this punch was truly a machinist's nightmare. I had succeeded in creating a monster. This was definitely a job for Superman.

I hand-carried the sketch to Uncle Stan. Normally, Stan took my wild drawings in stride. But when I didn't see his usual smile, I knew he had entered into his deep thought mode. He told me that some of the dimensions may have to be compromised in order to keep the ribs as wide as I had indicated and still have the bullet

release from the punch. He was concerned over creating a "locking angle" situation.

He machined the first punch with six ribs and flutes as requested. The ribs formed, but the bullets weren't stripping from the punch as readily as had been anticipated. Either the x-axis angles had to be changed or the apical height of the ribs had to be reduced. As I wanted to maintain the rib height, I asked him to machine a new punch with five ribs. This gave him the machining latitude he needed and increased the height of the rib at the same time, which brought the center of mass in closer to the bullet's axis. This punch formed nice-looking ribs and the bullets stripped well. In the months that followed, Stan experimented with various angles until he was satisfied that the bullets would strip from the punch as easily as they were ever going to.

These punch angles worked fine for that one caliber (.38 Special). But naturally, each time we changed the diameter of the punch for a new caliber, all the angles changed. This was

The 10mm Medium Velocity 180-grain Starfire expands more than most MV hollowpoints and has a higher 84 percent rating.

The .44 Magnum 240-grain Starfire penetrates the least gelatin of any JHP in this caliber at 14.8 inches, achieving an impressive 91 percent rating.

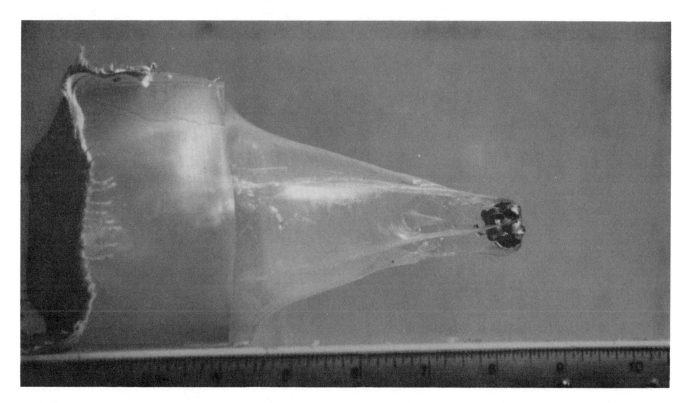

A 155-grain .40 S&W Starfire bullet penetrating three layers of fabric (denim, flannel, T-shirt material) and 2 inches of 10-percent gelatin. Clothing has minimal effect on its expansion due to its sharp ribs. Small pieces of shredded denim can be seen in the stretch bubble. During expansion, the sharp rib edges lacerate material directly ahead of bullet, assisting in penetration. Starfire produces a flat expanded profile of large diameter. (Photo credit: Tom Burczynski)

A sectioned .38 Starfire bullets reveals that the rib and flute cavity is nearly as deep as the bullet is long. This assures maximum expansion regardless of caliber.

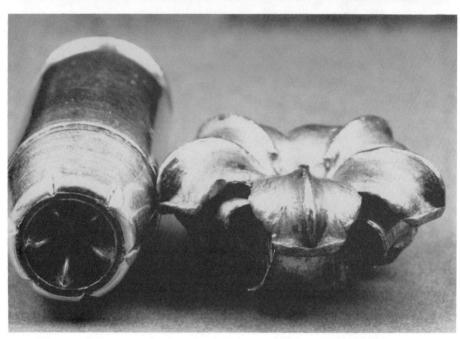

A .45 Auto cartridge and expanded 230-grain Starfire bullet. This was the first .45 prototype sent to PMC/Eldorado. This skived bullet was reformed from an existing, commercially available hollowpoint.

slow work, but in spite of all the changes, Stan never complained.

Fortunately, the inertial ejection system I designed for Hydra-Shok worked perfectly for making Starfire prototypes as well. We tested prototypes in five calibers in 10-percent and 8-percent gelatin and on a good many deer in New York and Pennsylvania. The tissue dam-age created in deer of all sizes was, to say the least, severe, and they never traveled far, if at all. After developing accurate, high-velocity loads in 9mm, .38, .357, .44, and .45, we let Starfire simmer on the back burner for a while.

Prior to actual negotiations with Federal for the Hydra-Shok rights, the merits of the Starfire design were discussed. Interestingly,

TABLE 22-1
PMC/ELDORADO CARTRIDGE STARFIRE AMMUNITION

CALIBER	SFHP LOAD	VEL. FPS	ENERGY FT-LBS.	EXPAN-SION INCH	PENE-TRATION INCH	CRUSH CAVITY CU. IN.	STRETCH CAVITY CU. IN.	ONE-SHOT STOP %
.380 Auto	95 gr.	925	180	.56	8.9	2.2	10.2	62 est
.38 Spl. +P	125 gr.	950	251	.61	9.3	2.7	15.4	73 est
9mm	115 gr.	1,120	320	.68	10.5	3.8	42.3	79 est
9mm	124 gr.	1,090	327	.68	11.0	4.0	31.1	80 est
.357 Mag.	150 gr.	1,205	484	.68	12.0	4.4	57.7	88 est
.40 S&W	155 gr.	1,160	463	.75	10.8	4.8	37.7	89 est
.40 S&W	180 gr.	985	388	.75	12.0	5.3	42.4	86 act
.45 Auto	230 gr.	850	369	.68	13.8	5.0	23.2	86 est
10mm MV	180 gr.	950	361	.70	13.0	5.0	38.5	84 est
.44 Mag.	240 gr.	1,300	900	.84	14.8	8.2	75.3	92 est

Federal liked both designs and didn't appear to have a preference. Fortunately for them (with the FBI's penchant for deeper penetration), they chose Hydra-Shok.

After Hydra-Shok was licensed to Federal, a major decision had to be made—whether to continue in the ammunition business or license the Starfire manufacturing rights to an existing company. It was decided that we would find a company in need of a great bullet design. Winchester had its Silvertip and Remington didn't respond well to outside inventions. One day we decided to place a call to Speer. I think we talked to someone in the guardhouse. Apparently they were working four 10-hour days and the plant was closed that day.

We tossed a coin. Hornady or PMC? The lot fell to PMC.

PMC had just formed a new company, Eldorado Cartridge Corporation (ECC). It had built a new plant in Boulder City, Nevada, and, incredibly, it was looking for a new product to market! We couldn't believe our good fortune. It appeared that the hand of providence was involved. We talked to Dan Flaherty, who was then head of marketing for Eldorado. Dan seemed genuinely interested in our proposal. He also seemed relieved that he wouldn't have to go out looking for a new product. The timing of the call was perfect.

We sent prototypes and drawings to ECC and waited. There were a few calls back and forth for a couple of weeks. There seemed to be some hesitation on their part after having examined the bullets and doing some initial test firing. They were concerned about not being able to strip the bullets off the punch! I thought, not *this* again! Dan grilled us about the manufacturing technique used to strip the bullets. We explained the heretofore unheard-of inertial ejection system. Apparently, this was too bizarre for their chief engineer to believe. He wanted Dan and Ron Reiber (ECC's ballistician) to fly out to the Hydra-Shok plant to see with their own eyes if such a system actually existed.

They arrived a couple days later and we talked for a half an hour or so, but it was obvious that they were anxious to see this "thing" in action. We ran some .38 bullets, then some 9s, then some .44s, and finally some .45s. All one heard was a snap every second and a half as the springs released their energy. They marveled at this strange sight. Every bullet stripped from its punch perfectly. Every bullet was perfectly formed. Dan and Ron were happy and appeared relieved to learn that

Two blocks of 10-percent ordnance gelatin show temporary cavity fractures caused by 180-grain 10mm Starfire bullets at different velocities. Note the upper fracture (left) has split completely through the top of the block. Bullets with large expanded diameters produce large temporary cavities/crush cavities. When bullet diameter doubles, the expanded area of the bullet surface squares.

there was a system and that it actually worked. They could fly home with a positive report, and they wouldn't have to search all over Hades for a new product.

Negotiations dragged on for about two months. Personnel involved in the negotiations and ECC's then president, Chung Ryu, were very careful. Every word was scrutinized. The agreement was amended several times. Concessions were made on both sides, and finally a contract was signed. As in the case with Federal, the exclusive license agreement called for dies, punches, presses, prototype bullets, drawings, and one year of technical assistance.

Even though the material items and technical assistance were supplied as per the letter of the contract, I voluntarily continued to furnish a great deal of additional materials and assistance, including Starfire punch drawings in several calibers, and later, new punch designs and new bullet manufacturing techniques. I also offered a good many suggestions regarding bullet weights, core tempers, muzzle velocities, and new products in general. Additional suggestions came from the head of advertising, Larry McGhee, and later from the new vice president of marketing, Dick Graham. Some of our suggestions were considered by engineer-

ing, but unfortunately most were not. Initially, joint decisions were few and far between. ECC could have entered into the premium ammo arena with greater leverage had more people been involved in the decision-making process concerning new products.

In spite of a slow start, once the bullet and ammunition equipment was functional, the Starfire products that were made were made quickly and produced in large quantities. In addition to 125-grain .38 Special ammo, ECC successfully catered to law enforcement and private citizens at the same time by wisely introducing 115- and 124-grain 9mm ammunition in standard-pressure loadings. It then added 180-grain rounds in 10mm and .40 S&W, a 185-grain .45 Auto, a 150-grain .357 Magnum, and a 240-grain .44 Magnum round.

Experimentation continued regarding core tempers and dimensional changes, and a full line of ammunition in popular bullet weights now exists.

Under the direction of Dick Graham, the marketing of Starfire ammunition went well. Dick set up a network of effective distributors and, working closely with Larry McGhee in advertising, sales flourished. Since the license agreement was signed, however, many things have changed. Mi Ryu Ahn took her brother's place and is now president and owner of the company. Several people have come and gone. Dick Graham moved on and took a position with another firm. Peter Hofmann is now involved in marketing. Fortunately, Larry McGhee has remained with the company, is still head of advertising, and is, without question, their most valuable player due to his expertise in many areas and his innumerable contacts in the industry. Probably the most profound change is that the head of engineering is gone. This means that many of the new products and manufacturing techniques that I and others have suggested over the years will more than likely be implemented. If implemented, these can do nothing but help ECC.

New ground has recently been broken in producing the first all-copper .30-30 bullet in Starfire configuration. This round owes its existence to Larry McGhee. Larry called in late 1993 and asked me about the production feasibility of such a product. I told him that it was possible but not using the standard jacketed bullet manufacturing process. I explained that the current punches would never hold up to the stresses imposed on them by pure copper. I assured him that I would try to design a punch and develop an alternative manufacturing process.

A few weeks later, I had two punches machined to my specs and sent a CAD drawing (supplied by my brother, Dan) to ECC's draftsman, Paul Fricovsky. Some of my most basic recommendations were ignored by engineering's old guard, and the simple four-step process I had advocated grew into a process much more complex than it had to be. The development of this process took several months, but eventually bullets were being made. The new engineering department has fully perfected the annealing process, and this bullet is very accurate and expands beautifully, even when fired from a Contender pistol. The development of the .30-30 Starfire was a milestone for the company and has opened the door to a whole new realm of products.

In addition, Mi Ryu Ahn is taking the company in a new direction by having recently implemented a team-based philosophy wherein various personnel form teams that interact with one another to expedite short term projects and achieve long range goals. Using this approach, many things in different areas will be accomplished at the same time. Mi Ahn's insight in establishing multiple team involvement will, without question, pay big dividends to her company in the long run. As a result of this new system, ECC is currently developing several new products simultaneously, some of which will set new standards of quality and innovation in the industry.

As in the case with Hydra-Shok, I owe a great deal to a number of people for making Starfire a success. Again, thanks goes to my brothers, Frank and Dan, for CAD work and metallurgical input, and of course to Stan Burczynski for the many hours he invested in analyzing and machining Starfire punches. Within the industry, my thanks goes to people who are or were at one time connected with ECC: Dan Flaherty for convincing ECC that Starfire was a product with a future; Chung Ryu and Mi Ryu Ahn for investing in and believing in the product; Ron Reiber for doing the early load development; Paul Fricovsky and Al Van Abbema, who sometimes acted as interpreters between the head of engineering's old guard and myself; ECC's present ballistician, Lane Ponich, who tirelessly develops safe and accurate loads; and J.J. Robinson for his most recent marketing efforts. Special thanks goes to Dick Graham, Charlie Hays, and Larry McGhee for putting Starfire ammunition on the map and keeping it there.

• • • • •

Quik-Shok is a unique fragmenting bullet designed primarily for law enforcement use in hostage situations or special situations where extremely rapid incapacitation is paramount.

I began the early design work on the first variation of Quik-Shok in 1988. As I wanted to nail down the design with patents on both the bullet and the manufacturing process as soon as possible, I crammed a huge amount of preliminary research and development into the following months.

Again, brother Dan supplied CAD drawings, and my uncle machined the punches and dies. We experimented with various approaches to swaging and ejecting lead bullet cores, lead alloy bullet bodies, and later, solid copper and brass bullet bodies.

The first Quik-Shok design (Q-S1) used a "core intrusion" process. The now patented swaging process formed a series of internal radial cuts within the bullet core (or bullet body, in the case of a lead-alloy or copper bullet) which terminated inside its outer periphery. The cuts were deep. This process left web areas in line with the cuts near the outside of the core. The purpose of the web areas was to control the degree and rapidity of expansion/fragmentation (in the case of an unjacketed lead-alloy bullet it also served to prevent the bullet nose from opening up in flight). Once the split core was seated in a jacket or when a lead-alloy bullet body was longitudinally compressed in another die, the triangular-shaped portions of the core were forced together and the spaces between them were eliminated. This left a series of "parting lines" which delineated opposing surfaces. The bullet was then formed in a profile die and became nearly indistinguishable from a normal softpoint or hollowpoint bullet. Depending on the depth and number of internal parting lines and the thickness of the web areas, the Quik-Shok round could be designed to fragment completely into three, four, five, or six sections (depending on the number of cuts present) or to fragment into three, four, five, or six frontal sections, leaving a solid base portion which continued to penetrate.

Once I was convinced of the effectiveness of the design, I applied for patents on both the manufacturing process and the bullet design itself. The patents were issued and I erroneously assumed I could slow down a little.

Shortly after this, I invented a similar design (Q-S2) which I thought could virtually render the same terminal results while employing an entirely different manufacturing technique. This time, brother Frank supplied CAD drawings, and Stan, as usual, skillfully machined the intricate dies. This Quik-Shok variant used a unique "core extrusion" process. And again, I was forced to hurry through R&D and testing in order to get the patent applications moving as quickly as possible.

This manufacturing approach utilized an extrusion process which formed a series of external radial slots running the entire length of the bullet core (or bullet body) when it was forced through a die having a series of radially extending fins which stopped short of its central axis. This process left a common "hub area" at the center of the core which fanned out into a series of "lobes." The purpose of this hub area was to control the degree and rapidity of expansion/fragmentation. If the hub was penetrated by a hollowpoint punch during the profile forming stage, an internal web was created which not only controlled the rate of expansion and fragmentation but also ensured that the nose of a lead-alloy bullet wouldn't spread open during flight. Once the extruded core was seated in a jacket or when the bullet body was longitudinally compressed in another die, the lobes were forced together and the spaces between the lobes were eliminated. This left a series of "parting lines" which, again, delineated opposing surfaces.

The bullet was then formed in a profile die and, as was the case with QS-1, became nearly indistinguishable from a normal softpoint or hollowpoint bullet. Depending on the depth and number of parting lines and the thickness of the hub or web area, the Q-S2 bullet could be designed to fragment completely into three, four, five, or six sections. Patent protection relative to Q-S2 was obtained in less than a year and a half.

In testing the Q-S 1 design, it was immediately evident that I was dealing with something that was tremendously devastating. Right from the start, the very first three-segment hollowpoint prototype created extraordinary damage to gelatin targets. A 125-grain Quik-Shok bullet fired from a .357 at 1,400 fps would literally shred a 4" x 4" x 12" gelatin block into three ragged strips. The damage was

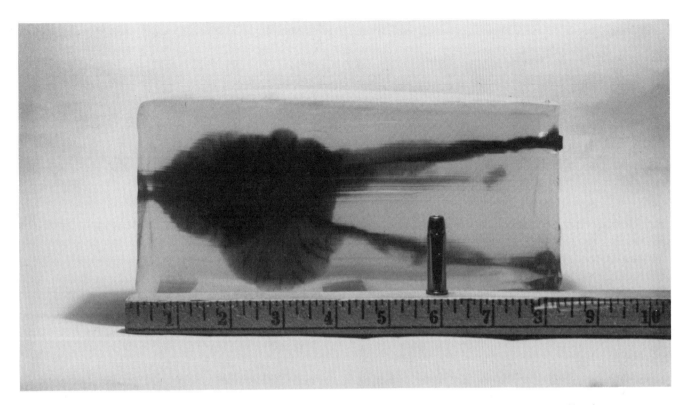

The .38 Special 125-grain Quik-Shok prototype expands and then fragments into three massive pieces of lead.

so much greater than any conventional hollowpoint made that there was really nothing to compare it with.

When I did comparison tests against Glaser, the Q-S1 created more damage in the first 6 inches *and* penetrated much deeper. The damage obtained with Quik-Shok equaled MagSafe, except that the Q-S1 bullet segments exited the sides of the block after 6 inches of penetration, while the expanded bullet base penetrated in a straight line to about 10 inches. By comparison, the MagSafe pellets were clustered about the centerline of the target, and several of them had exited the rear of the block. I had to use a larger block in order to capture the Q-S1 segments in the gelatin and to accurately compare the two. Using the larger block, the Quik-Shok segments penetrated another inch. Just like before, the base continued on to the 10-inch mark. MagSafe is a very destructive round by anyone's standards, and at that time I was content with the performance of this early Quik-Shok prototype.

The QS-1 was being tested right around the time the FBI published its views on deeper penetration, and I became intent on increasing the penetration of the new round. I developed a softpoint version which delayed fragmentation and brought penetration up to 12 inches. The softpoint version was almost as devastating as the hollowpoint except that maximum target damage occurred a little later in its transit. This was far from the 12-inch *average* that the FBI was recommending, but I had formerly proven to my own satisfaction that 11 inches in gelatin was an optimum penetration distance, even for a conventional hollowpoint. Anything greater and most bullets wouldn't open up reliably, especially if fired through clothing. Of course in this regard, Quik-Shok had a huge advantage over a conventional bullet. Its structure was so dramatically weakened by the deep, wide cuts in the core that it would shuck the jacket like so much paper and fragment violently even after penetrating clothing, with or without a hollowpoint. After

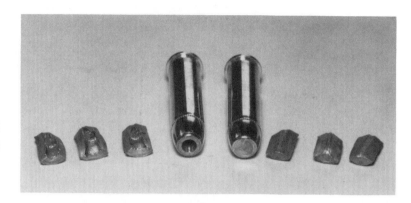

The .357 Magnum 125-grain Quik-Shok HP (left) and Quik-Shok SP (right) both break into three large fragments for maximum effectiveness.

developing the softpoint, I stopped trying to make the bullet *less* efficient and focused on tuning it to create maximum darnage and to deliver maximum shock. This was the kind of bullet SWAT teams needed for serious, life-threatening work.

From a production standpoint, the Q-S2 was a much easier bullet to make. The cores extruded like butter by the thousands. Every core was perfectly uniform. Ballistically, the Q-S2 design did everything Q-S1 did except that after fragmentation there was no bullet base involved at all. The entire bullet core sheared into three pieces and, just like its earlier cousin, these sections traveled away from the initial axis of entry in three different directions in an ever-widening pattern.

In either version, Quik-Shok's unique geometry can yield infinite degrees of a desired effect. There are several different ways to make it do just about anything. If more penetration is needed prior to fragmentation, the thickness of the web area can be increased in the Q-S1 design or the diameter of the hub area can be increased in the Q-S2 version. Conversely, if a more rapid fragmentation and less penetration is required, this can be accomplished by thinning the web and shrinking the hub diameter. The same effect can also be brought about by increasing the number of segments (i.e., penetration is decreased by decreasing the mass of each segment). To go *either* way, the core can be hardened or softened. The jacket can be thickened or thinned. The hollowpoint can be narrowed, deepened, widened, or omitted. I knew this kind of "dial-

a-result" flexibility would make this bullet design a valuable commodity in law enforcement circles.

To verify its overall efficiency, 9mm, .357, and .44 Magnum Quik-Shok ammunition was taken afield in New York and Pennsylvania. Many deer were killed. Often, the deer crumpled without running at all. The ones that fell and got up were down again in only a few yards. Tissue damage was extraordinary in every case, regardless of where they were shot.

One whitetail buck taken with a .357 (Q-S2) round was quartering away at about 40 yards. The bullet hit at an angle well behind the shoulder and fragmented. One of the segments pierced the heart, one penetrated a lung and stopped beneath the skin of the chest, and the third one angled upwardly, penetrated the spine near the base of the neck, and actually traveled right up the spinal cord itself for about 5 inches. The jacket had also fragmented, and small pieces of it were found in the chest cavity. This deer weighed 120 pounds and died instantly. The 125-grain Q-S2 bullet had a muzzle velocity of 1,400 fps.

Another 130-pound buck was hit in the neck near the base of the skull with this same load at about 55 yards. The deer was running straight away and was almost decapitated. The bullet blew the Atlas and the second cervical vertebrae completely out of the body along with the upper larynx and a huge section of muscle tissue. Of course, this deer died instantly as well.

Another deer, weighing about 150 pounds, was hit broadside at approximately 65 yards with the 180-grain .44 Magnum load. The Q-S2 bullet center-punched a 3/4-inch maple branch about 6 feet in front of the deer. It expanded on the branch and still fragmented as it passed through the shoulder and into the boiler room, just like it was supposed to. The deer jumped straight in the air, did a 270 degree pirouette, and appeared to stagger sideways over a knoll and out of sight. We found it in a heap about 30 yards away from the maple branch. There was a triangular-shaped entrance hole 7/8 inch in diameter through the shoulder and ribs. The bullet segments never exited the deer. The lungs were a mess, and there was about a gallon of blood in the chest cavity.

Most of the other deer were taken with traditional "shoulder shots" (heart and/or lung shots) that penetrated at various angles. Tremendous tissue damage and massive hemorrhage always resulted. Several of these deer dropped and stayed down, but most of them floundered for 10 to 15 yards before going down for good. Four of these deer were shot with the 115-grain 9mm Q-S2 load (1,300 fps). Every solid shoulder hit with this cartridge proved very effective. Some of these deer weighed as much as 175 pounds. About 60 percent of all the deer shot were shot with the 1,400 fps .357 bullet. There didn't appear to be a huge difference in stopping power between the .357 and the .44 Magnum Quik-Shok rounds. What this indicates to me is that the .357 Magnum cartridge *is* a potent deer cartridge when the right ammunition is used.

The hyper-stressed, rapid-fragmenting Quik-Shok bullet definitely produces the most devastating terminal effect. In laboratory-controlled tests (Strasbourg) involving the humane termination of 611 large animals, .357 Magnum and 9mm prototypes of this design scored a first and a second place, respectively. These two Quik-Shok loads were tested along with all the popular brands of ammunition at that time, including Glaser and MagSafe. The Quik-Shok design produced the shortest Average Incapacitation Time (AIT) in .357 Magnum and the second shortest AIT in 9mm, second only to MagSafe. I was somewhat dis-

appointed that the 9mm was edged out of first place by the MagSafe round (by .08 seconds), but this version of Quik-Shok utilized an unskived jacket. Since then, I've developed a skived version which fragments even faster.

In addition to handgun bullets, Quik-Shok bullets work remarkably well in rifle applications. Because the Quik-Shok has all the standard properties of a "solid" bullet in its passage through the bore of the rifle, bench rest accuracy can and has been obtained in both the .222 Remington and .308 Winchester cartridges. Target damage on game is so great that it has to be seen to be appreciated. During field tests using 150-grain Q-S2 bullets fired from .30-06 rifles, most deer were killed instantly in their tracks or in midjump. Organ damage was so horrendous that I won't describe it here lest some witless "liberal presser" use it as fuel to condemn guns and hunting (inevitably, this bullet will someday save the life of a liberal reporter taken hostage by a terrorist group). Suffice it to say that Quik-Shok rifle ammunition will gain a reputation as being the most accurate, most effective police sniper round on Earth.

There are many advantages associated with Quik-Shok. The bullets (in either rifle or pistol) comprise standard weights, and, unlike very lightweight, high-velocity projectiles, are extremely accurate and shoot to point of aim. The bullets are so effective that standard chamber pressures can be used. Standard chamber pressures will produce standard muzzle flash, blast, and recoil. The full-weight bullets possess the mass to easily punch through heavy bones prior to fragmentation. The bullets fragment violently even after penetrating thick clothing. Multiple wound paths, compound pressure fronts, and overlapping temporary cavities increase both hemorrhage and motor interruption simultaneously. The cone-shaped segment pattern which develops brings about a much greater increase in the odds of striking or affecting one or more vital organs, even in the event of a poorly placed bullet.

Since the first prototype, many different configurations have been tried. I've experimented extensively with solid copper and brass Quik-Shok bullets. Although substantially greater force is required to form them, these bullets work just like their lead counterparts and deliver extra penetration because the segments themselves do not expand to any appreciable degree.

As of this writing, negotiations are currently underway regarding the licensing of the Quik-Shok patent rights (centerfire and .22 rimfire). It looks as if Triton Cartridge of Wappinger Falls, New York, will be the exclusive producer of Quik-Shok. Since Triton already markets extremely accurate high-velocity hollowpoint ammunition, the union should be a good one. Hopefully, this ammunition will be available in large quantities to law enforcement groups and others by the end of 1995.

23

New Ammo: Rhino/Razor, Quik-Shok, and Omega Star

ozens of new bullets are "invented" each year. On closer examination, however, most turn out to be either rehashes of previous designs or, worse yet, fail miserably to meet the claims of their designer.

The three new loads covered in this chapter, developed and released to the public in 1994 and 1995, are new. Most importantly, they are a true departure from previous bullet designs, and they actually work exactly as they are supposed to.

The frangible Rhino/Razor is covered here because of the controversy it raised upon its introduction. The Triton Quik-Shok and D&D Omega Star are true hybrids between the hollowpoint and frangible bullet. The Quik-Shok is a little closer to the frangible, while the Omega Star is a little closer to the hollowpoint.

RHINO/RAZOR AMMO

In just three short weeks in 1994, two new bullet designs went from total obscurity to the subject of every talk radio show in America and every congressional press conference in Washington, D.C. The bullets, called Rhino-

Ammo and Black-Rhino by Signature Products, were described as *the* magic bullets to a hoax to a political conspiracy as fast as the modern media could process the information.

The bullets' inventor was accused of conspiring with Handgun Control Inc. to give the organization a rallying point. A long list of antigun politicians, led by Congressman Charles Schumer (D-NY), and Senators Bill Bradley (D-NJ), Dianne Feinstein (D-CA), and Daniel Patrick Moynihan (D-NY) banded together to ban them. On the other hand, many in the gun press tried to defuse the hype by calling the new bullets either a hoax, ordinary fragmenting bullets, or something even less effective than hardball.

The Secretary of Treasury was involved, and so was the director of the Bureau of Alcohol, Tobacco, and Firearms. One editorial cartoon pictured the Grim Reaper in his lab asking, "What's a poor, starving, out-of-work, totally amoral defense industry research chemist to do?" Another cartoon depicted police officers used as clay pigeons during the bullet development process. CompuServe's "Gun Politics" on-line discussion group was alive with rumor, innuendo, misinformation, accusations, questions, confusion, and character assassination.

Despite all of this public and political fervor, *no one* had been shot with Rhino-Ammo, and *no* independent lab had fired even a single round of production Rhino-Ammo ammunition. And *no one* in the press or government had even so much as seen a prototype of the armor-piercing Black-Rhino load. Every bit of the reaction, from local letters to the editor to the comments of President Bill Clinton's treasury secretary, was based on advertising claims from the manufacturer and the test firing of three prototype rounds used during the load development process.

What began as the latest technology in kinetic energy transfer became the lightning rod for the social issues and morality of lethal force.

David Keen is the innovator behind Rhino-Ammo and Black-Rhino. He is new to wound ballistics and the gun industry. A bona fide research chemist, Keen is the CEO of Signature Products in Huntsville, Alabama. As a U.S. Army officer, his specialty was nuclear ordnance. He left the military to start a polymer manufacturing business.

In the mid 1980s, Keen tried to develop a plastic adhesive that would conduct electricity. To do this, he successfully cracked the carbon-60 molecule and inserted metal ions.

Keen wanted to dry the space-age glue by microwave, but he noticed that the glue got hot in the microwave but would not solidify. This meant the polymer was trapping and absorbing microwave energy and converting it to heat. From his military days, Keen knew that this was exactly what stealth materials do to radar waves. He had accidentally developed a radar-absorbing material. His company, Signature Products, got its name from the radar-bounced return signal, or radar signature, of a target.

Keen had become intrigued with the concept of plastic bullets for military and covert uses. The most advanced end use of this tech-

The Razor-Rhino is available in every popular defensive caliber, including (from left) .380 Auto, 9mm Makarov, 9mm, .40 S&W, .38 Special non +P, and .38 Special +P+.

nology is the development of a small arms projectile that can pass through enemy radar without being detected. (High-tech military devices can actually pinpoint a hidden shooter's exact location by tracking the trajectory of a bullet in flight.) Signature Products was a natural to bid on military contracts involving this technology. It had already developed hardened coatings for aircraft leading edges and helicopter rotors. Now it had a plastic that absorbed radar waves.

In May 1994, Signature contacted MagSafe Ammo to discuss a joint venture on a 7.62mm NATO lead-free indoor training round. MagSafe had pioneered the use of frangible bullets with lead birdshot embedded in marine epoxy in its Defender line of bullets. While testing his indoor training rounds in gelatin, Keen discovered the true fragmenting nature of his polymer-filled bullets. The loads had up to 90 percent fragmentation, while high-performance hollowpoints exhibited 20 to 50 percent fragmentation. Subsonic hollowpoints and nonhollowpoints did not fragment at all.

The temporary wound cavities from the Rhino-Ammo loads were both larger in diameter and in total volume than any regular hollowpoint in the same caliber. The Rhino-Ammo prototypes packed more energy and transferred more of it than conventional JHPs. Because of these characteristics, Keen was encouraged by fellow scientists and military friends to pursue a frangible handgun load.

The Signature .45 Auto 125-grain Razor has a 1,560 fps velocity and 675 ft-lbs. of energy. It shatters on impact and releases birdshot and shards of polymer, which are as hard as metal. This is a 94 percent load.

Keen developed his own bullet design using Signaflux polymer in the core. Signaflux is as light as plastic but as hard as metal. On impact with a tissue simulant, the polymer does indeed fragment into shards of sharp plastic. However, these shards do not contribute much to stopping power.

By design, Keen intended to rely on the separate crush paths formed by the plastic shards and on penetration of the jacket itself to cause wounding. He was determined to have the jacket hold together longer than other fragmenting loads to produce deeper penetration. Jackets from MagSafe and Glaser Safety Slug fragment into small pieces of copper alloy as soon as the first inch of penetration in gelatin, and these pieces rarely penetrate deeper than 3 inches.

The first Keen design was similar to the MagSafe SWAT bullet with one large difference. The SWAT bullet used in .40 S&W and .45 ACP is an empty copper jacket filled with epoxy. The first Rhino-Ammo bullet had a wall of lead inside the jacket forming a thin-walled hollowpoint cavity. This was filled with polymer.

The Rhino-Ammo .45 ACP round starts off as a CCI-Speer 225-grain hollowpoint. The bullet is chucked in a lathe and the hollowpoint cavity drilled down to nearly the bullet base and out to a diameter nearly as large as the jacket opening. After drilling, the hollowed-out bullet is put in a fluid energy mill. Here it is tumbled in media that removes a bit more lead, smooths out the cavity walls, and polishes the jacket.

On the original loads, the polymer was poured into this drilled-out cavity. However, Keen found that the bullet was too rear heavy to be stable in air and thus was not accurate enough. The solution was to add weight forward of the center of gravity. This led to the second generation loads, which grouped into 5 inches at 50 feet. The polymer on these second generation bullets was poured into the cavity almost to the top and the plastic was cured. Then seven number 4 birdshot pellets were placed on top of this cured core and additional polymer was added to secure the birdshot.

This generation of the .45 ACP Rhino-Ammo bullet weighed 125 grains while the 9mm version weighed 98 grains. With this design, the jacket peels back, then the plastic core fragments, then the birdshot pellets are released.

But the Rhino-Ammo load described above was almost totally lost in the controversy over the Black-Rhino, designed to defeat soft body armor.

It is not "news" that a fragmenting bullet can defeat armor. The late 1980s Glaser Black Tip Safety Slug and the early 1990s MagSafe Kevlar-defeating Agent load were both armor piercing. Both are out of production.

Nor does this concept defy any laws of physics, as some critics asserted. In fact, these frangible bullets depend on the laws of physics to work. Simply put, energy is the ability to perform work. The more energy a bullet has, the more it is able to penetrate any surface. The old Black Tip and Agent loads proved that even a fragile capsule of birdshot could defeat armor if driven fast enough.

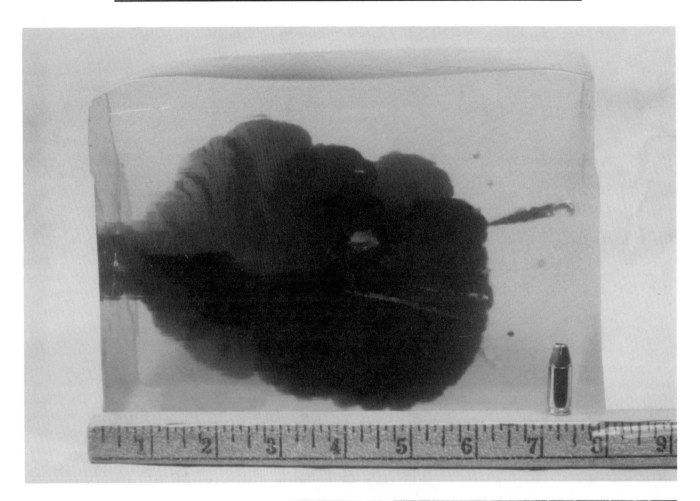

ABOVE: The Signature 9mm 98-grain Razor has a 1,650 fps velocity and 590 ft-lbs. of energy. It penetrates a controlled 7.8 inches of gelatin and produces a stretch cavity larger than any +P+ hollowpoint. This is a 93 percent load.

RIGHT: This is what the controversy was all about—the armor-piercing Black Rhino. The bullet has a polymer core with a carbon fiber center post. This ammo was never released.

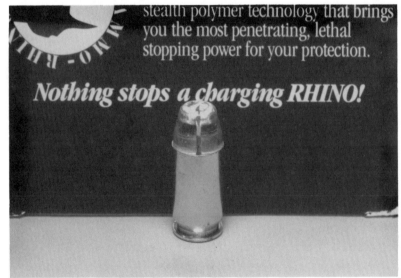

Signature Products adopted a military solution to achieve its goal. Using age-old armor-piercing, fin-stabilized, discarding-sabot technology, it developed the Black-Rhino. Keen's design involved composite reinforced carbon fibers instead of a metal insert. At 50 grains of bullet weight and driven to easily attainable hypervelocities, this bullet would have worked exactly as designed. The critics who claim that a projectile cannot be armor-piercing and fragmenting at the same time have not been exposed to much small arms design or history.

Keen intended to market the Black-Rhino only to the good guys to shoot only the bad guys wearing soft body armor. Of course, it is impossible to restrict any such ammunition in that way. And when Keen stated he would sell the Black-Rhino to law enforcement agencies or individuals with a federal firearms license only, he demonstrated how new to the gun industry he really was, as every single gun-shop owner in America has just such an FFL.

With all this in mind, Keen applied for a license to manufacture and sell both the Rhino-Ammo and Black-Rhino. In early December 1994, his local paper, *The Huntsville Times*, ran the first story on the two new bullets. The piece included some enthusiastic statements from Keen, a very graphic description of the wounding effects as he saw it, and a lengthy discussion of the armor-piercing Black-Rhino.

The December 19, 1994, issue of *Newsweek* ran a tiny blurb about the two new loads, excerpting three sentences from the backside of the packaging. After the small mention in *Newsweek*, an Associated Press national writer was assigned to look into the story. His piece went over the wire for the Tuesday after Christmas. A reporter for 26 years, Robert Dvorchak would later say he never had that much response on a single story in his entire career.

Keen was quoted as saying, "When Rhino-Ammo hits somebody, they're going to die. It causes a horrific wound. That's not by accident. It's engineered by design. The round disintegrates as it hits. There's no way to stop the

bleeding," and, "The beauty behind it is that it makes an incredible wound. There's no way to stop the bleeding. I don't care where it hits. They're going down for good."

The politicians and mainstream press went berserk. The controversy caught the gun press off guard, which in turn reacted defensively to both Keen and the media. His choice of words made instant opponents out of many politicians, forensic and medical folks, and members of both the gun and antigun press.

No one in the wound ballistics community had ever heard of the Rhino-Ammo rounds, let alone independently tested them. In fact, no production samples were available to anyone. Since no one outside Signature Products had any test ammo, rumors of a hoax surfaced, then accusations of a publicity stunt and even an antigun conspiracy.

However, some Rhino-Ammo loads were indeed available. Keen had sent some development loads to *Newsweek* earlier in the month. During the media frenzy, these were given to ABC-TV's *Nightline*, which in turn gave them to H.P. White Labs, our nation's most prestigious independent test lab. H.P. White chronographed three Rhino-Ammo loads and fired at least one into gelatin.

H.P. White accurately recorded very erratic muzzle velocities of 794 fps, 1,218 fps, and 1,488 fps. It also documented a temporary stretch cavity just 3.5 inches deep with a maximum diameter of only 2 inches across. The official conclusion was that the Rhino-Ammo was less than half as powerful as Keen had claimed, and that the Rhino-Ammo makes about the same size wound as other fragmenting bullets already on the market. The H.P. White ballistician stated that such a wound would not kill someone instantaneously. As a result, *Nightline* was satisfied that it had exposed a scam.

Unknown to H.P. White Labs or anyone else, the ammo it had fired were samples taken from a group of work-up loads. In any load development process, the powder charge is increased in steps. After firing loads from each step, the cartridge case is examined for signs of excess pressure such as primer flattening, enlarged primer pockets, and case head bulges.

Keen performed this measured gradient methodology to arrive at maximum pressures and then backed off 15 percent. This is, in fact, exactly the development procedure that eventually results in submittal to an outfit like H.P. White for certified pressure tests. Yet it was various samples from this step-up analysis that Keen forwarded to *Newsweek*, and they were to be for photo purposes only. They were not production loads like the Rhino-Ammo fired for a *Handguns* magazine review, which chronographed 1,500 to 1,600 fps velocities on both calibers.

The other problem with the *Nightline* test involved the continued use of two different gelatin ratios. The U.S. Army pioneered the use of 20-percent gelatin in the 1940s. The infamous NIJ/LEAA tests from the 1970s also used 20 percent. The Secret Service favors this ratio, too. However, nearly all of law enforcement, including the FBI, and all ammo makers, have standardized on 10-percent gelatin.

Keen developed the Rhino-Ammo in the more popular but uncalibrated 10-percent gelatin. Keen claimed the wound cavity would be 4 to 5 inches in diameter and 9 inches deep. In calibrated 10-percent gelatin, *Handguns* got 5.3-inch cavity diameters and a penetration depth of 7.5 inches. The average adult male torso is only 9.4 inches, front to back. Because H.P. White was reported on *Nightline* as using 20-percent gelatin, of course its cavity diameters and depths were smaller.

Keen unknowingly got caught up in the great gelatin ratio debate, but the press simply reported it as yet another exaggerated claim. This one was not. Using full-power production ammo, the cavity sizes and depths claimed by Keen have been essentially confirmed.

On Wednesday of that week, Keen showed the press a block of gelatin into which he had fired a production Rhino-Ammo load. No one would remember this. On Thursday morning, he withdrew plans to market the armor-piercing Black-Rhino on NBC's *Today* show. On Thursday night, ABC ran the *Nightline* program, and Keen was denounced as a charlatan by Representative Schumer. The biggest news story of the Christmas week, and the biggest ammo controversy ever, was old news by New Year's Day.

We tested production Rhino-Ammo loads in 9mm and .45 ACP. The bullet construction is very different from the Glaser Safety Slug but very similar to MagSafe bullets. It is a cross between the epoxy-only SWAT load and the epoxy-embedded birdshot Defender load.

We found that the Rhino-Ammo loads fragmented instantly in gelatin even after heavy clothes. The bullet has no hollowpoint cavity to plug up with debris, and the birdshot pellets at the nose of the bullet do indeed penetrate independently of the main stretch cavity. So do fragments from the lead lining that was once the lead core.

We did not find any independent penetration from the plastic shards after the polymer core fragmented. Keen depended on these shards to contribute to the overall wounding, but they do not. They merely line the inside of the temporary cavity, which is caused by the bullet breakup.

Unlike earlier claims, these sharp pieces of polymer could be removed from the gelatin by probing with bare fingers and could be irrigated from the gelatin with a stream of water. The plastic fragments are sharp and hard but do not have enough weight to penetrate on their own. Nor do they readily cut skin or latex gloves.

We also compared the Rhino-Ammo with the conventional hollowpoint in each caliber with the highest recorded street effectiveness based on actual officer- and civilian-involved shootings. We reviewed other loads in the same caliber that are popular in spite of low stopping power. Finally, we listed other calibers and loads in the same muzzle energy range as the Rhino-Ammo that generate similar stretch cavity sizes. This analysis makes it very easy to size up the Rhino-Ammo—it is extremely powerful and effective personal defense ammunition.

In both 9mm and .45 Auto, Rhino-Ammo proved to be as good as the best frangible load in each caliber. It was clearly more effective

TABLE 23-1
RHINO-AMMO WOUND BALLISTICS COMPARISON

CALIBER	DESCRIPTION	WT. GR.	VEL. FPS	ENERGY FT-LBS.	PENE- TRATION INCHES	TEMP. STRETCH CAVITY IN3	ONE- SHOT STOP %
.45 Auto	Rhino-Ammo	125	1,560	676	7.5	78.1	94% est
.45 Auto	MagSafe Defender	96	1,660	588	10.0	75.5	94% est
.45 Auto	Glaser Blue	140	1,400	610	7.5	44.3	93% est
.45 Auto	MagSafe SWAT	66	2,140	671	6.0	73.5	93% est
.45 Auto	Rem JHP (+P)	185	1,140	534	12.3	58.2	90% act
.45 Auto	Win FMJ Ball	230	820	343	27.0	9.0	62% act
9mm	Rhino-Ammo	98	1,650	593	7.8	74.3	93% est
9mm	MagSafe Stealth	64	1,950	540	10.9	46.3	93% est
9mm	Fed JHP (+P+)	115	1,304	434	12.0	44.5	90% act
9mm	Glaser Blue	80	1,650	484	6.0	52.1	88% est
9mm	Win Subsonic JHP	147	887	257	15.9	19.6	75% act
.357 Mag	Federal JHP	125	1,450	584	12.0	79.8	96% act
.40 S&W	Cor-Bon Nosler JHP	135	1,300	507	9.8	69.1	95% act
.44 Mag	Win Silvertip	210	1,250	729	15.1	78.2	89% act
.41 Mag	Win Silvertip	175	1,250	608	14.0	83.2	88% act

TABLE 23-2
RAZOR-AMMO

CALIBER	WEIGHT	VELOCITY/BARREL	ENERGY	STRETCH CAVITY
.380 ACP +P+	68 gr.	1,550 fps/3″	363	58 in3
.38 Special	100 gr.	1,100 fps/2″	269	41 in3
.38 Spl. +P+	100 gr.	1,650 fps/6″	605	72 in3
9mm +P+	95 gr.	1,650 fps/6″	593	74 in3
9 Makarov +P	80 gr.	1,365 fps/5″	331	49 in3
.357 Magnum	100 gr.	1,800 fps/6″	720	81 in3
.40 S&W +P+	115 gr.	1,675 fps/5″	716	78 in3
.44 Mag. +P+	130 gr.	1,865 fps/5″	1,005	97 in3
10mm +P+	115 gr.	1,775 fps/5″	805	78 in3
.45 ACP +P+	125 gr.	1,720 fps/6″	676	78 in3

than the best hollowpoints in the calibers and produced far and away more stopping power than subsonic and nonhollowpoint loads.

Like the Glaser Safety Slug, MagSafe SWAT, and, to a lesser degree, MagSafe Defender, Rhino-Ammo will be the most effective with a frontal, upper-torso shot placement. These loads can all be considered less effective on lower-torso and cross-torso shots and in bullet placements involving upper arms as intermediate targets. In an unobstructed upper torso shot, even the most bitter opponents of frangible bullets will reluctantly admit that Rhino-Ammo is indeed most likely to cause an instantly incapacitating and rapidly lethal injury.

As a fragmenting bullet, Rhino-Ammo is safer than any subsonic hollowpoint or nonhollowpoint for inside home defense. It is among the least likely of any bullet to penetrate building material and exit a dwelling. On the street, Rhino-Ammo is among the least likely to ricochet or enter a dwelling.

Finally, like the other frangible bullets, Rhino-Ammo is the least likely bullet to exit a soft tissue target. This means it will not overpenetrate to become a downrange threat. It is indeed a "safety" round.

By March 1995, the government was forced to act upon Keen's license to produce and sell ammunition. Every print and electronic media organization in the country called both the BATF and Signature Products on a weekly basis until a decision was made. In a final effort to stop the license, Senator Moynihan met with BATF Director John Magaw and Treasury Secretary Robert Ruben. The license was granted anyhow, and no one has made a peep since.

Just before the full release of Rhino-Ammo to the marketplace, another wrinkle developed. Fiocchi of America claimed it had legal rights to the name "Rhino." It had used the terms "rino" and "little rhino" in conjunction with its line of shotshells imported from Italy. The company had not copyrighted the terms but had established their "first use" in the gun industry. As a result, Signature was forced to change its product's name from Rhino-Ammo, which had become a household word, to Razor-Ammo.

The 9mm and .45 Auto versions were just the first loads to be developed by Signature Products. The company plans to make Razor-Ammo in all defensive handgun calibers from .32 Auto to .44 Magnum. Dealers can also order a "starters pack"—a 12-inch-deep plastic pitcher with a preweighed package of gelatin and complete directions on how to mix the gelatin and run bullet performance demos.

The Associated Press did a six-month follow-up on its blockbuster Rhino story. As part of the segment, it provided H.P. White Labs with a larger quantity of genuine production ammo to rerun velocity and wounding tests using 10 percent gelatin. This time, H.P. White confirmed the results originally reported by Ed Sanow. The nation's most mistrusted and misunderstood personal defense ammo continued to sell newspapers in its search for credibility.

Critics of Razor-Ammo would be much less vocal if they fully understood how difficult it is to get any handgun load to produce 93 to 94 percent one-shot stops. Keen has developed one of the few bullets in the history of handguns to achieve this lofty level of stopping power. It is easy to see why a newcomer to the ammo industry would want to boast a little and could get a little carried away with his claims.

No, these are not magic manstopping bullets that produce 100 percent stops regardless of where they hit an attacker. However, in a defensive scenario, gelatin tests indicate that they will be an incredible 93 to 94 percent effective. That is as good as the best.

As we go to press, we have learned that the career of Rhino-Razor ammo has ended as abruptly as it started. In October 1995, an NRA writer tested the chamber pressure on a number of Rhino calibers. He found many to be over pressure and in violation of SAAMI standards. Keen was advised of the results and conducted a recall of his ammo. In November 1995, Keen made the surprising announcement that Signature Products was withdrawing from the ammunition business.

QUIK-SHOK AMMO

One of the most promising new bullet designs is the Quik-Shok from Triton Cartridge. This is the fourth major design by the upstate New York bullet genius, Tom Burczynski, arguably the best bullet designer of all time. The four bullets include the Neutralizer Tunnel Point, Federal Hydra-Shok, Eldorado Starfire, and now the Quik-Shok. (See Chapter 22 for the histories of the Hydra-Shok, Starfire, and Quik-Shok written by Tom Burczynski himself.)

The Quik-Shok is totally unlike Burczynski's earlier designs. It bridges the gap between conventional hollowpoints and fragmenting bullets.

The round first gained prominence in 1992 during the Strasbourg Tests (see Chapter 4) when two loads were tested by the Strasbourg researchers. The 9mm 115-grain +P+ Quik-Shok came in second in that caliber out of 24 hollowpoint and frangible loads. Only the MagSafe beat it and by only .1 second. In .357 Magnum, the 125-grain Quik-Shok hollowpoint came in best in the caliber out of 22 police and defensive loads.

The Strasbourg tests involved a total of 114 different high-performance bullets in calibers from .380 Auto to .45 Auto, including the potent .40 S&W and full-power 10mm. Of all these loads, the .357 Magnum Quik-Shok hollowpoint had the fastest incapacitation time.

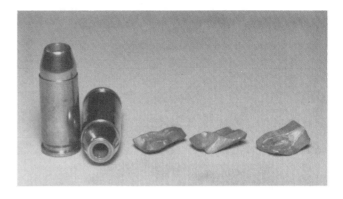

The Triton 9mm 115-grain Quik-Shok fragments on impact into three massive pieces of lead. Each frag veers off in a separate crush cavity.

Again, and for the record, the .357 Magnum 125-grain Quik-Shok produced the most rapid incapacitation of any load in any caliber. It worked a full 3 seconds faster than the .357 Magnum 125-grain JHPs from Remington and Federal.

Based only on the 9mm and .357 Magnum calibers, the Quik-Shok produced an average incapacitation *more* rapid than either the MagSafe and especially the Glaser. It far outperformed even the best of the high energy JHPs. The latest Burczynski bullet was one of only eight loads out of 114 fired to produce a collapse in less than 2 seconds.

The Quik-Shok bullet uses a preweakened or prestressed lead core inside a conventional copper-alloy jacket. The key to the Quik-Shok's rapid incapacitation is its bullet fragmentation. On impact, the bullet expands and then breaks into three pieces. These three huge fragments each weigh 34 grains and look like a military frag simulator. Each piece veers off in a different direction after 2 1/2 inches of depth and penetrates independently up to 9 1/2 inches.

The Quik-Shok was developed in both hollowpoint and softpoint versions. The biggest difference between the two is the rate of bullet breakup and the resulting penetration depth. The hollowpoint frags penetrate rough-

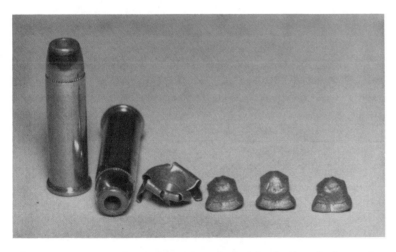

The Triton .38 Special +P 125-grain Quik-Shok looks like a hollowpoint but acts like a frangible. Each frag weighs a hefty 34 grains each.

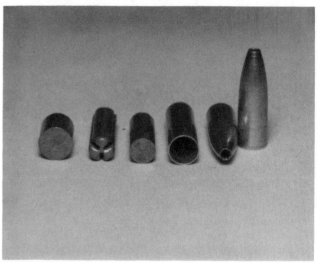

ABOVE: The single most effective load during the Strasbourg Tests was the (now Triton) .357 Magnum 125-grain Quik-Shok. This is a hybrid between a hollowpoint and a frangible.

ABOVE RIGHT: The basic Quik-Shok design works as well as a softpoint as it does as a hollowpoint. The penetration is a little deeper and the frag dispersion is a little tighter.

RIGHT: Triton has selected the Quik-Shok Revision Two bullet for production. The steps to make this bullet are to cut off solid wire, externally flute the wire, compress the wire again, insert into the jacket cup, and form the final shape.

ly 8 to 9 inches while the softpoint-based frags go in 9.5 inches deep.

All of the bullets used during the Strasbourg Tests and tested for this chapter had a dead-soft, zero-antimony, pure lead core and a nonserrated Corbin jacket. A harder core or a less aggressive hollowpoint cavity would slow down the rate of expansion, delay the frag separation, and increase the penetration depth.

Quik-Shok Revision One is the result of a patented bullet swaging process which forms a series of internal radial cuts within the bullet core. These cuts stop just inside the outside diameter of the bullet. This process leaves web areas in line with the internal cuts near the outside of the core. The purpose of the web

areas is to control the degree and rapidity of the expansion or fragmentation.

Once the split core is seated in the jacket, or when the core is compressed in another die, the triangular-shaped portions of the core are forced together. The airspaces between the segments are eliminated, leaving a series of parting lines. The Quik-Shok bullet is formed in a profile and becomes visually identical to and indistinguishable from a normal hollowpoint or softpoint.

Quik-Shok Revision Two uses the same concept of deep, longitudinal cuts into the bullet core, except from the outside in. The remaining web of lead is along the centerline of the bullet. The parting lines are along the outside of the

The original version of the Quik-Shok had internal flutes which were formed in the wire. The wire was then collapsed, inserted into the jacket cup, and then formed into a hollowpoint bullet.

core. Again, the airspaces are eliminated by compressing the core back to its original shape during the final swaging operation.

Like Quik-Shok One, the completed Quik-Shok Two is impossible to tell from a conventional JSP or JHP. And again, the amount of web, and the length and number of cuts, determine how the Quik-Shok Two will react on impact.

Yet another design option exists with the Quik-Shok—it can be made to expand but not fragment. This is done by limiting the length of the cuts in the core. In this event, the Quik-Shok would expand much like the Barnes X-bullet and produce deeper penetration.

In the preproduction ammo loaded by Burczynski, the .38 Special Quik-Shok hollowpoint fragments fan out 1 1/2 inches from the centerline of the bullet path. The .357 Magnum softpoint frags veer 2 inches from the theoretical bullet path, while the .357 Magnum hollowpoint pieces pattern 2 1/2 inches each from the centerline.

Obviously, the odds of striking a vital organ or vessel are greatly increased with three large and deeply penetrating fragments. The multiple bullet paths and overlapping stretch cavities increase stopping power by way of increased bleeding and increased neural shock. This is not just theory; it is the reality from the blood-and-guts Strasbourg tests.

The softpoint version of the .357 Magnum Quik-Shok is most impressive. Most conventional softpoints do not expand at all, let alone fragment. This innocent appearing bullet is a

good choice for departments and locales that ban the use of hollowpoints. The Quik-Shok softpoint is a genuine softpoint; it just acts differently.

Compared to the Quik-Shok hollowpoint, the angle of dispersion, or pattern of the fragments, from the Quik-Shok softpoint is narrower. The penetration is slightly deeper on the development loads we tested. However, the use of a harder core or a thicker jacket could increase the penetration depth further if desired.

The Quik-Shok is so fundamentally different from other frangible loads that it has a list of characteristics all its own.

First, it has better accuracy. The Quik-Shok uses standard bullet weights and velocities that are a match for standard handgun rifling twist rates. The bullet has a true solid core with no airspaces or differences in density across the core.

Second, because of these standard weights and velocities, the Quik-Shok shoots to the point of aim. Most frangible loads have half the standard bullet weight and half again as much velocity. This causes them to have a point of impact well below the point of aim.

Third, the Quik-Shok has a normal muzzle flash, which in most calibers is not visible. Standard bullet weights allow the use of conventional flash-suppressed powder and allows

Triton has the design flexibility to flute the lead core only partially down the bullet length instead of all the way. Partially fluted Quik-Shoks expand as shown but do not fragment.

A Quik-Shok bullet just emerging from a slice of gelatin. Three bullet sections angle away from the initial axis of entry, while the base of the bullet continues to penetrate in a straight line. One millisecond later, a major exit blast was recorded. (Photo credit: Tom Burczynski)

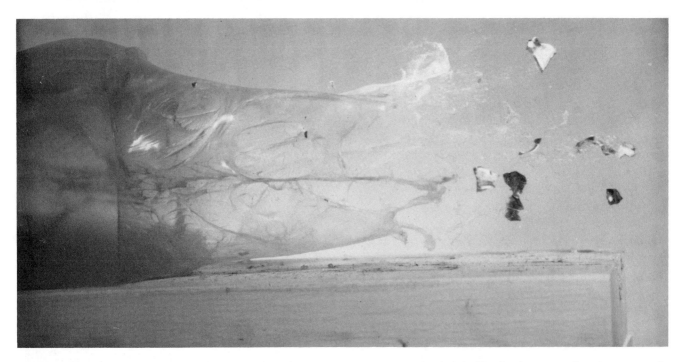

Absolute stopping power. Tremendous exit blast from a 125-grain .357 Quik-Shok bullet fired at 1,325 fps. An extremely accurate 1,400 fps version was used during the Strasbourg Tests. Unlike Glaser, heavy bone and clothing have no adverse effects on this full-weight bullet. Note the incredible width of the stretch bubble (as wide as the block itself). Only MagSafe produces a pressure front of this magnitude. (Photo credit: Tom Burczynski)

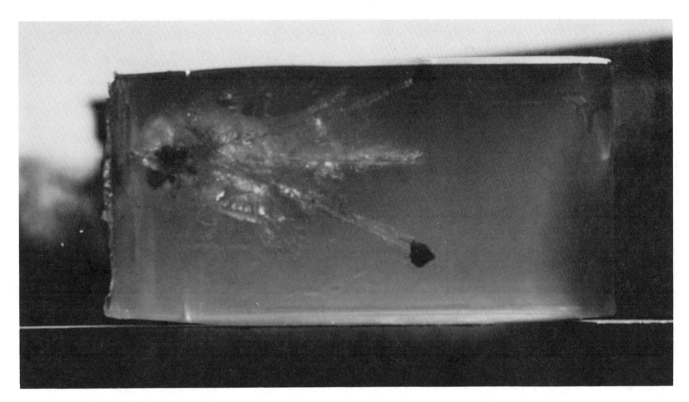

This full-length gelatin block was struck by a .357 Quik-Shok (Q-S2) hollowpoint. Note the wide radial dispersion of the core segments. The far center segment has exited the side of the block. Penetration depth can be increased or decreased in a number of ways.

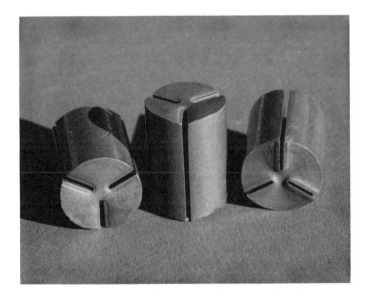

Three extruded Q-S2 cores showing front, side, and base. Note the extremely straight channels. Uniformity and channel depth of this degree guarantee rapid, consistent fragmentation on impact. The geometry of the Q-S1 core is just the opposite—channels extend from the center out.

it to burn more completely than the lighter weight frangibles.

Fourth, the Quik-Shok produces adequate soft tissue penetration. Some of the frangible loads have maximum depths of just 5 to 6 inches. The Quik-Shok hollowpoint produces penetration in the 8-inch range, while the softpoint goes in 9.5 inches deep. (Read the comments on optimal penetration depth in Chapters 27 and 28.)

Fifth, the Quik-Shok breaks through bones without exploding prematurely. It uses all of its bullet weight to break through the "shell" of the target. The same goes for striking a fleshy upper extremity before entering the torso. Even if the Quik-Shok expands and separates in an upper arm, the exiting frags headed to the torso are much more potent.

The Quik-Shok fragments weigh 34 grains each. That is about what a number 1 buckshot pellet weighs. The number 2 birdshot used by MagSafe weighs 5 grains, while the number 12 birdshot used in the Glaser Blue weighs .2 grains. The size of the frags are also very different. The Quik-Shok frag is a .28 caliber slug measuring .48 inch long. The number 2 birdshot is .15 caliber, while the number 12 birdshot is .05 inch in diameter.

Sixth, the Quik-Shok reacts like a conventional hollowpoint and not a frangible when it strikes sheet metal. The bullet nose folds in on itself. The same goes for its reaction to building materials like wallboard and plywood. The Quik-Shok expands and produces slightly less tactical penetration than a hollowpoint but more reliable penetration than a typical frangible.

Seventh, the Quik-Shok penetrates auto glass like a conventional hollowpoint—it expands rather than fragments. Due to its conventional bullet weight, the Quik-Shok has a better bullet flight integrity than the lighter frangibles, which are easily deflected or simply broken up by glass. The round will, however, fragment or expand when contacting a soft tissue medium after being fired through glass.

The Quik-Shok has an advantage over conventional hollowpoints and frangible bullets alike. It unleashes three huge pieces of lead inside the target. In this regard it is similar to a close-range multiple bullet load. Placement of Quik-Shok bullets is less critical than that of conventional hollowpoints because of its cone-shaped pattern of lead that begins shortly after impact. The three segments of the bullet

Two .357 Magnum Q-S1 cartridges. In either softpoint or hollowpoint form, Quik-Shok delivers maximum shock.

separate and begin three separate crush cavities, which increases the chances of striking or affecting one or more vital organs. The Quik-Shok can be most effective even in the event of a poorly placed shot.

As this book goes to press in late 1995, Burczynskis's company, Experimental Research, reached a licensing agreement with the New York-based Triton Cartridge to produce the Quik-Shok. Triton has already gained fame by being the first direct, head-to-head competitor to Cor-Bon.

TABLE 23-3
QUIK-SHOK "PREMIUM PLUS" AMMUNITION

CALIBER	LOAD	MUZ-ZLE VEL. FPS	MUZ-ZLE ENGY. FT-LBS.	GEL. PEN. INCH	NO. OF FRAGS	CRUSH CAVITY INCH3	STRETCH CAVITY INCH3	SEPAR-ATION DEPTH INCH	RADIAL PATTERN INCH	FULLER INDEX %
.38 Spl. +P	125-gr. HP	986	270	8	3	2.4	37.0	2	3	75
9mm	115-gr. HP	1,311	439	8	3	2.4	51.5	1.5	3	87
.357 Mag.	125-gr. HP	1,403	546	9	3	2.7	47.5	2	5	90
.357 Mag	125-gr. SP	1,403	546	9.5	3	2.9	43.9	2.5	4	90

Triton has selected the Quik-Shok Revision Two bullet design to begin production. This is the version with exterior cuts and the single, internal web along the centerline of the bullet. The company will produce the Quik-Shok in hollowpoint form at the start but may later produce the softpoint.

The exact velocities have not yet been finalized, but the initial bullet weights have been released. They are:

.380 ACP	90 grains
9mm	115 grains
.38 Special +P	125 grains
.357 Magnum	125 grains
.40 S&W	135 grains
10mm	165 grains
.44 Special	180 grains
.44 Magnum	180 grains
.45 ACP	185 grains

OMEGA STAR

One of the most interesting new loads is D&D Bullet's Omega Star. Developed in 1994 by Rick Dixon, the Omega Star is another true hybrid bullet. But while the Triton Quik-Shok is a hybrid closer to the frangible side, the Omega Star is a hybrid closer to a jacketed hollowpoint.

The Omega Star looks like a jacketed hollowpoint, but half of the bullet core is made up of fused numbers 2 and 4 birdshot. The remainder of the core is a lead slug like all conventional jacketed hollowpoints.

A similar hybrid bullet was produced by Chappie Genet in the early 1990s. His Core-Shot was a frangible and fragmenting bullet that had some features of the Glaser Safety Slug and some features of a jacketed hollowpoint. Like all frangible designs, the Core-Shot started off with a copper jacket. Genet's company, Genco, put deep, full-length serrations in the jacket and partially loaded it with number 12 birdshot. It then placed a few pieces of much larger number 4 or 2 shot over the finer shot. The large and small birdshot was fused together to form a solid core with a conventional hollowpoint cavity. The finished bullet

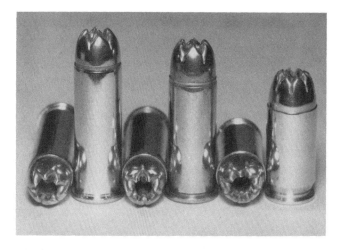

The Dixon Omega Star is available in (from left) .44 Magnum 210-grain, .44 Special 170- and 210-grain, and .45 Auto 160-, 200-, and 230-grain versions. More are coming.

The .44 Special 210-grain Omega Star releases a payload of birdshot on impact, but the main core remains intact. This load has an 81 percent rating.

looks like a deeply serrated but otherwise conventional JHP.

The Omega Star was developed to take advantage of the stopping power demonstrated by the frangible bullets during the Strasbourg Tests. Yet it was also designed to overcome the disadvantages of most frangible bullets, i.e., relatively shallow penetration, low point of impact, and mediocre accuracy.

The Omega Star looks like a Kaswer Pin Grabber, expands like a Winchester Black Talon, disperses birdshot like a MagSafe Defender, and penetrates like a Federal Hydra-Shok. The .45 Auto 230-grain Omega Star is shown.

The Omega Star is a true hybrid between hollowpoints and frangibles. It has the same point of impact as conventional ammo and better performance against barriers than the frangibles.

The Omega Star was developed using water testing only. It was originally designed with the front core composed of numbers 6 and 8 birdshot, capped with a lead disk. The disk was intended to protect the compressed lead birdshot and help reduce bullet breakup on intermediate targets. Later testing in gelatin proved this lead disk could be eliminated. This testing also indicated that the birdshot size should be increased from numbers 6 and 8 to numbers 2 and 4. The result was an all-around better bullet.

The Omega Star starts off with a standard-length gilding metal jacket from Corbin. A lead cylinder is cut off from lead wire, headed to the correct diameter, and chemically bonded to the copper jacket. On top of this lead core, Dixon adds some number 4 but mostly number 2 birdshot pellets. These pellets are fused together by a punch that also forms a conventional-appearing hollowpoint cavity.

The Omega Star also has a pronounced "visual" impact. The jacket is pinched sharply in six areas at the bullet mouth, forming an aggressive serrated edge. The round has a saw-tooth appearance like the Kaswer Pin Grabber and Law Grabber. However, the actual jacket formation is much more similar to the original Black Talon. With the Talon, the pinched jacket edges were sheathed in the hollowpoint cavity; with the Omega Star, the pinched edges are openly exposed. This is one of the least likely JHP bullets to ricochet off bone, period.

As the Omega Star expands, the very pointed jacket serrations peel back along the bullet shank. They remain exposed to tissue for some length of passage, much like the Black Talon. But while the Talon tips remain at a 90 degree angle to the bullet shank, the Omega Star jacket eventually folds in flat.

On impact, the Omega Star expands like a JHP. This releases the large shot pellets from the front of the dual core. These pellets penetrate up to 5 inches deep and form a 3-inch shot pattern. The rest of the bullet expands

TABLE 23-4
DIXON OMEGA STAR BALLISTICS
(PROTOTYPE AMMUNITION)

CALIBER	BULLET GRAIN	VELOCITY FPS	ENERGY FT-LBS.	REC'D INCH	PENE. INCH	CRUSH CAVITY CU. IN.	STRETCH CAVITY CU. IN.	ONE SHOT STOP %
.44 Spl.	210	800	299	.65 f	13.5	4.5	32.5	81 est
.45 ACP	200	965	414	.60 f	11.8	3.3	36.5	89 est
.45 ACP	230	885	400	.65 f	14.5	5.1	33.4	87 est

Note: Numbers 2 and 4 birdshot penetrated 5-inches deep and had a 3-inch pattern by 5-inches. All of the birdshot was dispersed from each of the bullets.

exactly like a JHP and produces exactly the range of penetration expected from an expanded JHP. For example, the .45 Auto 200-grain Omega Star expanded to .60 caliber and penetrated 12 inches of gelatin. This does not even include the separate five to eight .11 caliber frag paths. All of the shot was totally released and evenly dispersed in the three test calibers. In every case, the chemically bonded rear core remained fully intact with the jacket.

To sum it up, the Omega Star looks like a Pin Grabber, expands like a Black Talon, disperses birdshot like a MagSafe, and penetrates like a jacketed hollowpoint. It appears to be the best of both worlds in that it produces the large stretch cavities, multiple bullet paths, and rapid energy transfer of a frangible bullet yet also has the accuracy, range, point of impact, cycle reliability, and penetration of a conventional weight JHP.

As we go to press, the Omega Star has been licensed to the Red River Cartridge Company of Texas. Red River will be making the bullets and loading the ammo. The current loads are 160, 200, and 230 grains for .45 ACP, 210 grains for .44 Special, and 210 grains for .44 Magnum. A 170-grain .44 Special is in the works, along with Omega Stars in other calibers.

24
Effects of Multiple Bullet Impacts

For years, defensive pistol craft instructors have taught the value of the double tap—the firing of two shots as quickly together as possible to increase the effect of pistols shots on the human body. Evan Marshall taught this techniuque too, until he went back through his shooting results and compared those instances where two or three shots impacted on the thoracic cavity instead of one. Those instances are listed in Table 24-1.

As readers can see, the results show that the double tap is an overhyped technique that has little effect in the real world. Yes, I used to teach it, but like good friend and superb weapons instructor John Farnam, I've dropped it. These days, I tell my students to continue to fire until their attacker is no longer in their sight picture. Frankly, I'm convinced that no intelligent man or woman should ever take a handgun to a gunfight with any degree of enthusiasm.

TABLE 24-1
DOUBLE TAP RESULTS

LOAD	TOTAL SHOOTINGS	ONE-SHOT STOPS	PERCENTAGE
.22 LONG RIFLE			
1. CCI Stinger	395	134	34
CCI Stinger	723	249	34 (2 hits)
2. Fed LHP	612	184	30
Fed LHP	924	286	31 (2 hits)
3. Win LHP	567	164	29
Win LHP	814	244	30 (2 hits)
.25 ACP			
1. Win 45-gr. exp. point	119	30	25
Win 45-gr. exp. point	44	11	25 (2 hits)
2. Fed 50-gr. FMJ	1,864	410	22
Fed 50-gr. FMJ	678	156	23 (3 hits)
3. Rem 50-gr. FMJ	1,977	435	22
Rem 50-gr. FMJ	466	103	22 (2 hits)
.380 ACP			
1. Cor-Bon 90-gr. JHP	20	14	70
Cor-Bon 90-gr. JHP	38	27	71 (2 hits)
2. Fed 90-gr. JHP	109	75	69
Fed 90-gr. JHP	194	134	69 (2 hits)
3. Fed FMJ	131	67	51
Fed FMJ	184	94	51 (3 hits)
.38 SPECIAL—2"			
1. Win 158-gr. LHP	106	71	67
Win 158-gr. LHP	293	196	67 (2 hits)
2. Rem 125-gr. JHP	91	59	65
Rem 125-gr. JHP	178	116	65 (2 hits)

LOAD	TOTAL SHOOTINGS	ONE-SHOT STOPS	PERCENTAGE
3. Fed 158-gr. RNL	319	157	49
Fed 158-gr. RNL	504	253	50 (2 hits)

.38 SPECIAL—4"

LOAD	TOTAL SHOOTINGS	ONE-SHOT STOPS	PERCENTAGE
1. Cor-Bon 115-gr. JHP +P+	29	24	83
Cor-Bon 115-gr. JHP +P+	19	16	84 (2 hits)
2. Fed 158-gr. LHP +P	209	161	77
Fed 158-gr. LHP +P	349	272	78 (2 hits)
3. Rem 95-gr. JHP +P	119	78	66
Rem 95-gr. JHP +P	344	231	67 (2 hits)

9mm

LOAD	TOTAL SHOOTINGS	ONE-SHOT STOPS	PERCENTAGE
1. Cor-Bon 115-gr. JHP +P	32	29	91
Cor-Bon 115-gr. JHP +P	16	15	94 (2 hits)
2. Fed 124-gr. JHP +P+ HS	63	54	86
Fed 124-gr. JHP +P+ HS	114	100	88 (2 hits)
3. Win 115-gr. JHP ST	304	252	83
Win 115-gr. JHP ST	488	410	84 (2 hits)

.357 MAGNUM

LOAD	TOTAL SHOOTINGS	ONE-SHOT STOPS	PERCENTAGE
1. Fed 125-gr. JHP	523	501	96
Fed 125-gr. JHP	829	804	97 (2 hits)
2. Fed 110-gr. JHP	204	184	90
Fed 110-gr. JHP	394	359	91 (2 hits)
3. Rem 158-gr. JHP	38	31	82
Rem 158-gr. JHP	76	65	86 (2 hits)

.40 S&W

LOAD	TOTAL SHOOTINGS	ONE-SHOT STOPS	PERCENTAGE
1. Cor-Bon 135-gr. JHP	24	23	96
Cor-Bon 135-gr. JHP	10	10	100 (2 hits)
2. Fed 155-gr. JHP	34	32	94
Fed 155-gr. JHP	102	99	97 (2 hits)
3. Black Hills 180-gr. JHP	46	39	85
Black Hills 180-gr. JHP	94	81	86 (2 hits)

EFFECTS OF MULTIPLE BULLET IMPACTS

LOAD	TOTAL SHOOTINGS	ONE-SHOT STOPS	PERCENTAGE
10mm			
1. Fed 180-gr. JHP	27	22	81
Fed 180-gr. JHP	35	29	83 (2 hits)
2. Win 180-gr. JHP	44	36	82
Win 180-gr. JHP	63	53	84 (2 hits)
3. Rem 180-gr. JHP	31	25	81
Rem 180-gr. JHP	12	10	83 (2 hits)
.41 MAGNUM			
1. Win 170 -gr. JHP	53	47	89
Win 170 -gr. JHP	97	90	93 (2 hits)
2. Win 210-gr. JHP	34	28	82
Win 210-gr. JHP	47	39	83 (2 hits)
3. Rem 210-gr. SWC	57	43	75
Rem 210-gr. SWC	29	22	76 (2 hits)
.44 SPECIAL			
1. Fed 200-gr. LHP	49	36	73
Fed 200-gr. LHP	68	51	75 (2 hits)
2. Win 200-gr. JHP ST	60	45	75
Win 200-gr. JHP ST	78	60	77 (2 hits)
3. Rem 240-gr. SWC	17	11	65
Rem 240-gr. SWC	24	16	67 (2 hits)
.44 MAGNUM			
1. Win 210-gr. JHP	50	45	90
Win 210-gr. JHP	92	84	91 (2 hits)
2. Fed 180-gr. JHP	37	33	89
Fed 180-gr. JHP	77	70	91 (2 hits)
3. Rem 240-gr. JHP	34	30	88
Rem 240-gr. JHP	56	50	89 (2 hits)

LOAD	TOTAL SHOOTINGS	ONE-SHOT STOPS	PERCENTAGE
.45 ACP			
1. Fed 230-gr. JHP HS	71	67	94
Fed 230-gr. JHP HS	114	109	96 (2 hits)
2. Rem 185-gr. JHP +P	44	40	91
Rem 185-gr. JHP +P	88	81	92 (2 hits)
3. Win 230-gr. FMJ	179	112	63
Win 230-gr. FMJ	293	185	63 (2 hits)
.45 COLT			
1. Fed 225-gr. LHP	69	54	78
Fed 225-gr. LHP	22	18	81 (2 hits)
2. Win 225-gr. JHP ST	53	39	74
Win 225-gr. JHP ST	94	71	76 (2 hits)
3. Rem 255-gr. RNL	19	12	63
Rem 255-gr. RNL	45	29	64 (2 hits)

25
Shotgun and Rifle Results

The 12-gauge shotgun has been the traditional long gun in U.S. law enforcement circles for decades. Its reliable stopping power has been proven time after time in real incidents. Unfortunately, its heavy recoil and multiple projecticle capability has caused concern among today's urban cops. Also, federal court rulings have eliminated height and gender restrictions when hiring police officers, so law enforcement use of the 12-gauge shotgun is being re-evaluated.

One of the problems with the 12-gauge shotgun in law enforcement circles is that ignorant people have deployed it improperly and given it a black eye. It is not an appropriate weapon for crowd control unless used as a chemical agent launcher. Additionally, people need to understand its limitations and realize that buckshot is a 25 meter weapon in the hands of the *average* officer, while slugs are 35

meter rounds in the same situation. Reduced recoil or "tactical loads" have been developed to make the weapon more viable for today's police personnel.

12-GAUGE SHOTGUN

The 12-gauge shotgun is a favorite weapon of both authors. Unlike many handgun loads, 12-gauge buckshot and slug loads offer decisive stopping power. Evan Marshall witnessed the shooting of two felons with 12-gauge slugs, and the results were instantaneous and gruesome.

Only 00 and #4 buckshot are reported, as other buckshot and birdshot loads offered erratic results. The choice of a specific minimum number of pellets was an arbitrary one made by Evan Marshall, but he felt rather strongly that the collector of the data should be the establisher of the criteria.

TABLE 25-1
00 BUCKSHOT ACTUAL RESULTS

LOAD	TOTAL	ONE-SHOT SHOOTINGS	PERCENTAGE STOPS
1. Win 2 3/4″	293	275	94
2. Fed 2 3/4″	235	210	89
3. Rem 2 3/4″	419	370	88
4. Fed 2 3/4″*	89	85	96
5. Rem 3″ MAG	34	32	94

* "Tactical buckshot"—reduced recoil load for law enforcement.
NOTE: Thoracic cavity hits include at least 6 out of 9 pellets in 2 3/4″ loads impacted, and 9 out of 12 hit with 3″ loads impacted.

TABLE 25-2
#4 BUCKSHOT ACTUAL RESULTS

LOAD	TOTAL	ONE-SHOT SHOOTINGS	PERCENTAGE STOPS
1. Win 2 3/4″	114	95	83
2. Rem 2 3/4″	223	180	81

NOTE: Thoracic cavity hits with at least 18 out of 27 pellets impacted.

Federal 12-gauge tactical 00 buckshot produces the most one-shot stops of any shotgun load at 96 percent.

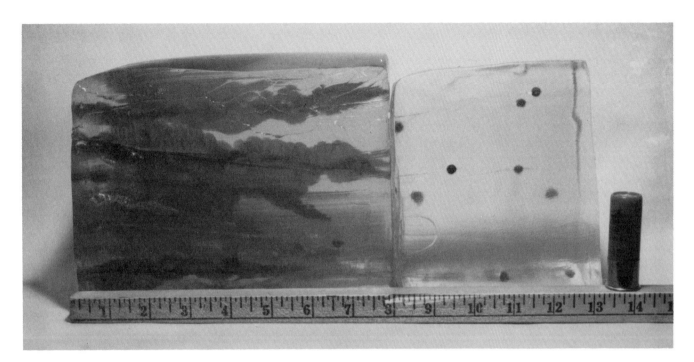

Number 4 buckshot produces just 81 to 83 percent one-shot stops. This 12-gauge load is acceptable for home defense but not law enforcement.

Pellet size, not shotgun gauge, determines the penetration distance in gelatin. Number 4 birdshot penetrates 4 to 9 inches.

Individual buckshot pellets are not very powerful. Left to right: number 4 buck is about like the .22 Short; number 1 buck equals .32 ACP ball; number 0 buck is similar to the old .38 S&W; and even number 00 buck is only comparable to .380 Auto ball.

The 12-gauge number 7 1/2 birdshot penetrates 3 to 6 inches of gelatin. This load is easily defeated by heavy clothes.

12-GAUGE SHOTGUN SLUGS

The 12-gauge slug is an excellent defensive choice despite heavy recoil and muzzle blast. The standard slug is of rather soft construction and doesn't overpenetrate the human torso as often as one might think. At the same time, the slug does relatively well against commonly encountered barricades.

Hard sabot slugs were not included in the data, but they do even better when serious penetration is needed.

RIFLES

While the authors are aware that rifles of all calibers have been used in defense of life, the results of only two calibers are included in this work: .223 and .308. It should be noted that while the .223 results include a wide variety of loads, the .308s included are match offerings used in police and military sniper situations.

TABLE 25-3
SHOTGUN SLUG ACTUAL RESULTS

LOAD	TOTAL	ONE-SHOT SHOOTINGS	PERCENTAGE STOPS
1. Win 2 3/4"	119	116	98
2. Fed 2 3/4"	78	76	98
3. Rem 2 3/4"	99	96	98

NOTE: These are thoracic cavity hits only.

TABLE 25-4
.223 RIFLE ACTUAL RESULTS

LOAD	TOTAL	ONE-SHOT SHOOTINGS	PERCENTAGE STOPS
1. Rem 60-gr. JHP	11	11	100
2. Win 69-gr. Match	12	12	100
3. SS109 FMJ	199	197	99
4. Fed 40-gr. JHP	126	125	99
5. Win 55-gr. JSP	26	25	96
6. Win 55-gr. FMJ	167	161	96
7. Fed 55-gr. JHP	95	90	95
8. Rem 55-gr. FMJ	39	37	95
9. Fed 62-gr. JHP	34	32	94
10. Rem 55-gr. JSP	18	17	94
11. Fed 55-gr. FMJ	88	82	93

NOTE: All these shootings took place at distances less than 100 meters. Beyond this distance, .223 results become erratic.

ABOVE: The Federal .223 Rem 40-grain Blitz JHP fragments on impact and produces 99 percent one-shot stops. It penetrates just 6.5 to 9 inches of gelatin and produces a massive stretch cavity.

RIGHT: The Federal .223 Rem 69-grain Sierra hollowpoint boat-tail Match bullet fragments in gelatin. So far, this police countersniper load produces 100 percent one-shot stops. It penetrates about 12 inches of gelatin and produces the largest stretch cavity of the caliber.

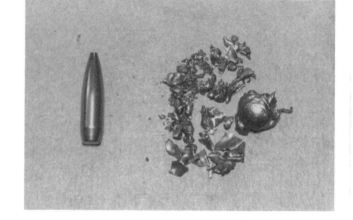

.223

This has become a popular law enforcement caliber due in great part to its adoption by the U.S. military. It has proven to be a superb stopper at ranges of 100 meters or less. Beyond that range, we found that it became erratic.

The authors are fully aware that the two top offerings results of 100 percent are troubling. Nothing, of course, is 100 percent in the real world. We're convinced that as we get more results, we will come across failures. However, we feel committed to report accurately on the data we have. We, like all collectors of data, are dependent on our sources.

.308

The .308 has become the premier sniper rifle in the United States and other countries.

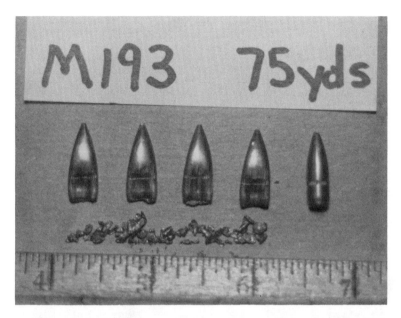

At very close ranges, the M193 .223 Rem 55-grain FMJ-BT breaks in half and fragments. However at 75 yards, the bullet tumbles on impact but only bends. This is the least effective .223 Rem load.

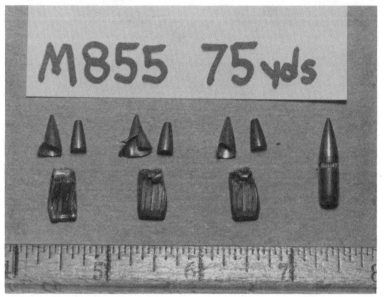

The M855/SS109 .223 Rem 62-grain FMJ-BT breaks in two even at extended ranges. The resulting multiple bullet paths explain its 99 percent effectiveness.

The .308 Match offering from a wide variety of sources relies on the same bullet—the Sierra Match King. It is superbly accurate and intensely lethal. All the shootings included here were at distances of less than 500 meters.

Over 60 percent of the time, they produced through and through wounds regardless of the distance. Only thoracic cavity hits were included in this data base.

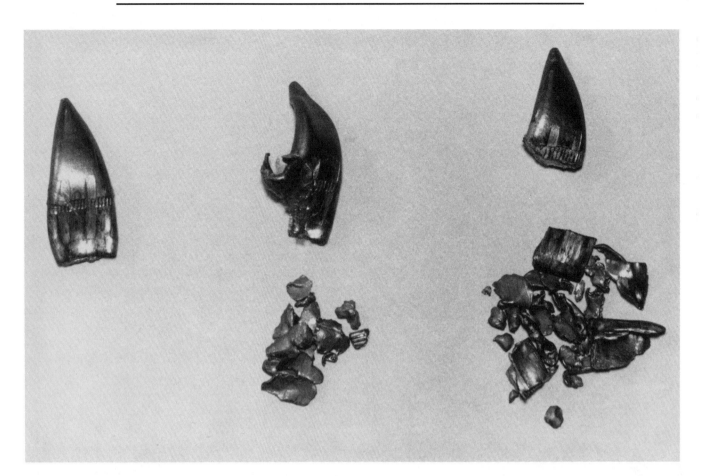

The .223 Rem 55-grain M193 is shown recovered from gelatin at (left to right) 75, 50, and 25 yards. This may explain the differences in effectiveness reported for this FMJ load.

The Federal .308 Win 168-grain Sierra hollowpoint boat-tail Match is the definite police countersniper load. The hollowpoint section snaps off on impact and the bullet fragments. It produces the same stretch cavity as a hunting softpoint. Two separate frag paths help explain a 99 percent one-shot stop rating. Total penetration is 16.7 inches of gelatin.

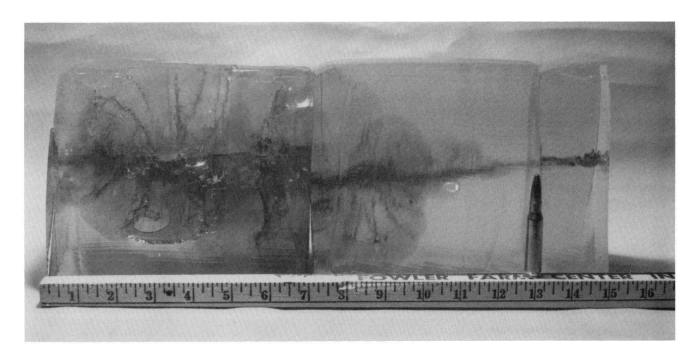

The Rem .308 Win 150-grain PSP Core-Lokt produces just 15.5 inches of penetration in 10-percent gelatin. This has police applications.

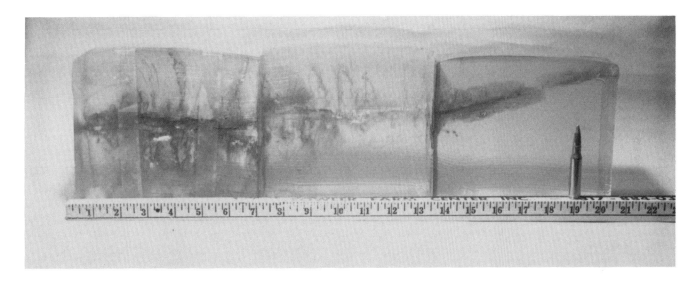

The Win .308 180-grain Supreme PSP-BT penetrates 21.5 inches of gelatin. This is typical performance from .30 caliber softpoints.

TABLE 25-5
.308 RIFLE ACTUAL RESULTS

LOAD	TOTAL	ONE-SHOT SHOOTINGS	PERCENTAGE STOPS
1. Rem 168-gr. Match	19	19	100
2. Mil 168-gr. Match	199	197	99
3. Fed 168-gr. Match	73	72	99
4. IMI 168-gr. Match	306	300	98
5. Win 168-gr. Match	34	33	97

TABLE 25-6
SHOTGUN BALLISTICS

LOAD	GAUGE	PELLET SIZE & CHARGE	VELOCITY FPS	RECOIL LB-SEC.	HEAVY CLOTHES & GEL. INCH	1/2 IN. PLASTER BOARD LAYERS
Fed Tactical	12	00 Buck, 9 pellet	1,145	2.47	16.5-19	6 1/2
Win Super-X	12	4 Buck, 27 pellet	1,325	3.19	8.5-13	4
Win Game	12	2 Bird, 1 1/4 oz.	1,330	3.23	6-11	3
Win Pigeon	12	7 1/2 Bird, 1 1/4 oz.	1,220	2.96	3-6	2
Fed Hi-Power	.410	4 Bird, 1 1/16 oz.	1,135	1.52	4-9	2 1/2

TABLE 25-7
CLOSE-RANGE SHOTGUN PATTERN

SHOTGUN	10 FT.	20 FT.	30 FT.	40 FT.	50 FT.
Federal 12-ga. 2.75 inch Tactical, 00 Buck 9 pellet	2.5 in	5.0 in	6.5 in	8.5 in	11.0 in
Winchester 12-ga. 2.75 inch Super-X, 4 Buck 27 pellet	4.0 in	8.5 in	13.0 in	15.0 in	24.0 in
Winchester 12-ga. 2.75 inch Game, 2 Bird 1 1/4 ounces	5.5 in	11.0 in	17.0 in	23.0 in	28.0 in
Winchester 12-ga. 2.75 inch Pigeon, 7 1/2 Bird, 1 1/4 ounces	6.0 in	14.0 in	21.0 in	28.0 in	32.0 in
Federal .410 Bore 3 inch Hi-Power, 4 Bird, 1 1/16 ounces	4.5 in	8.0 in	9.0 in	17.0 in	22.0 in

TABLE 25-8
LEAD BUCKSHOT AND BIRDSHOT

SHOT SIZE	PELLET DIAMETER	PELLET WEIGHT GR.
000 Buck	.36	70
00 Buck	.33	54
0 Buck	.32	48
1 Buck	.30	40
3 Buck	.25	23
4 Buck	.24	20
BB	.18	8.8
2 Bird	.15	4.9
5 Bird	.12	2.6
6 Bird	.11	1.9
7 1/2 Bird	.095	1.3
8 Bird	.09	1.1
8 1/2 Bird	.085	.90
9 Bird	.08	.75
10 Bird	.07	.50
11 Bird	.06	.31
12 Bird	.05	.18

TABLE 25-9
.223 WOUND BALLISTICS

AMMO GRAIN	TOTAL PEN. INCH	REC'D DIA. INCH	% FRAG.	MAXIMUM STRETCH DIA. INCH	DEPTH OF MAXIMUM INCH	STRETCH CAVITY CU. IN
69 HP	12.0	.43	53	6.16	6	138.4
64 PSP	11.5	.32	49	5.9	6	130.3
55 HP-BT	9.5	.37	63	6.25	4	120.1
55 PSP	9.5	.38	56	5.7	3.5	106.8
40 HP	6.5	frag	88	5.9	5	92.3
42 Glaser	6.5	frag	85	4.5	3.5	64.9
62 FMJ-BT	17	.41	52	3.75	7.2	46.1
55 FMJ-BT	17	.24	18	3.3	7.2	36.6

TABLE 25-10
.308 WOUND BALLISTICS

AMMO GRAIN	TOTAL PEN. INCH	REC'D DIA. INCH	% FRAG.	MAXIMUM STRETCH DIA. INCH	DEPTH OF MAXIMUM INCH	STRETCH CAVITY CU. IN
Fed MatchKing 168-gr. HP-BT	19.3	.59 f	55	6.4	7	273.2
Rem Core-Lokt 150-gr. PSP	15.5	.73	21	7.6	4	n/a
Fed Hi-Power 165-gr. HP-BT	16.7	.66	26	6.6	3	n/a
Win Supreme 180-gr. PSP-BT	21.5	.78	20	7	4	n/a

26
Submachine Gun Results

The last few years have seen a dramatic increase in the use of submachine guns by American law enforcement. Unfortunately, training generally has not been sufficient to allow accurate, controlled use of these weapons on full-auto fire. As a result, many SWAT teams use them as semiautomatic carbines, forbidding the use of full-auto fire unless the most extreme conditions exist.

Unfortunately, many police submachine guns users think the nominally longer barrel offers dramatically increased stopping power levels. In 9mm at least, they, of course, do not. Evan Marshall chronographed the below-listed loads out of a Heckler & Koch MP5 submachine gun. The velocities are included.

TEST REPORT

9mm Ammunition Performance
   in Suppressed Submachine Guns
Prepared by Vince McMullen
Senior Quality Engineer
Federal Cartridge Company

Due to the increasing use of suppressed submachine guns by law enforcement agencies, Federal Cartridge Company has compiled the following report reflecting projectile performance and penetration in 10-percent ordnance gelatin using H&K MP5SD and H&K MP5K (suppressed) submachine guns.

The H&K MP5SD uses what is referred to as an "integral suppressor," i.e. the barrel is ported to bleed propellant gases into the suppressor chamber in order to reduce the projectile's velocity from the supersonic range into the subsonic range. This lower velocity and gas trapping causes a reduction in the sound of the weapon during firing and eliminates the need to use special low-velocity ammunition. The H&K MP5K is a version of the MP5 currently used by the Navy Special Operations community and had a detachable suppressor that attaches to the end of the barrel. This suppressor captures the propellant gases and projectile at full velocity, causing a reduction in sound, but not to the extent caused by the "integral suppressor" and ported barrel of the

TABLE 26-1
9MM SMG ACTUAL RESULTS

LOAD	VELOCITY FPS	TOTAL	ONE-SHOT SHOOTINGS	PERCENTAGE STOPS
1. Fed 115-gr. JHP	1,304	39	33	85
2. Win 115-gr. ST	1,316	42	36	86
3. Rem 115-gr. JHP	1,289	24	20	83
4. Fed 124-gr. HS	1,205	22	19	86
5. Fed 124-gr. HS *	1,347	37	33	89
6. Fed 124-gr. Nyclad	1,301	56	50	80
7. Fed 147-gr. JHP	1,037	168	132	78
8. Fed 147-gr. HS	1,068	112	90	80
9. Win 147-gr. JHP	1,024	82	65	79

* This is the +P+ version of the Federal 124-grain Hydra-Shok hollowpoint.
NOTE: In each of the above shootings, at least two and no more than four rounds struck each victim in the thoracic cavity. Over 92 percent of these "stops" were fatal shootings.

TABLE 26-2
.45 ACP SMG ACTUAL RESULTS

LOAD	VELOCITY FPS	TOTAL	ONE-SHOT SHOOTINGS	PERCENTAGE STOPS
1. Win 230-gr. FMJ	986	122	101	83
2. Rem 230-gr. FMJ	956	78	64	82
3. Fed 230-gr. FMJ	933	39	32	82

NOTE: These shootings are with Thompson submachine guns and were at least 10 years old when Evan Marshall acquired them in 1972. At least two and no more than four rounds struck the victim in the thoracic cavity. Over 97 percent of these "stops" were fatal shootings. Interestingly enough, the .45 ACP offers significant improvements over the same round fired from pistols. Why? Well, the authors could offer a number of theories, but the most honest answer is simply that we don't know.

MP5SD or similar weapons. The suppressor used on the MP5K and other similar detachable suppressors are designed to provide a balance between noise attenuation and projectile velocity, that latter remaining at a higher level to facilitate bullet penetration/expansion.

As shown in the accompanying report, significant projectile performance differences exist when rounds are fired through the two suppressed weapons. Agencies should use this report as a guide in selecting ammunition for use in suppressed 9mm submachine guns and are encouraged to conduct their own tests.

This was a test of a H&K MP5 with an integral H&K suppressor. This variant uses a ported barrel in order to vent propellant gas as a means of reducing the velocity of a standard NATO spec 9mm round into the subsonic range without having to resort to special ammunition. During the test, rounds were fired in full automatic mode for function with no malfunctions noted. Velocity was taken

SUPPRESSED MP5 VELOCITY & EXPANSION TEST RESULTS (9MM)

PRODUCT STYLE	9AP FMJ	9MS JHP	9BPLEP +P+	9HS2 H-S	P9HS3 H-S +P+	P9HS1 H-S	9BP JHP	P9BP NYCL.	9MS JHP
Weight	124	147	115	147	124	124	115	124	147
Velocity	1,120	975	1,300	975	1,200	1,120	1,160	1,120	975
Sup. Vel.	837	785	1,086	777	997	924	967	957	1,009
Vel. Loss	284	191	214	199	203	196	193	163	-34
% Vel. Loss	25	19	16	20	16	17	16	14	-3
Expansion	.40	.40	.620	.40	.622	.531	.574	.482	.642
Penetration "	18+	14	12	13.5	11	14	11	14	12

with screens at 15 feet apart with the muzzle 3 feet behind the first screen. Blocks of 10-percent ballistic gelatin were used as the expansion medium and they were placed 2 feet behind the second screen (20 feet from the muzzle). For comparison, a group of 9MS was fired from a suppressed Navy MP5K, which does not use a vented barrel, the results being given in the last column.

Editor note: Federal Cartridge emphasizes that this report is based on ammunition designs circa 1991. The overall performance of all the projectiles in terms of expansion, penetration, and weight retention from both 9mm firearms has improved. This is especially true of the 9mm "P9HS3" 124-grain Hydra-Shok +P+. This projectile was redesigned in late 1995 with a thicker jacket, lower center post, and revised hollowpoint cavity for optimal performance across a broad range of impact velocities. Similar improvements have been and are continuing to be made on all Federal Cartridge ammunition.

27
Changing Ammo Test Standards

Right is right. It shouldn't matter who identifies the truth, as long as the word gets out. On the topic of bullet penetration, a big city police sergeant and a small county corporal faced off against the FBI and a dozen other organizations trained by a group that trained the FBI.

What is the ideal range of bullet penetration in calibrated 10-percent ordnance gelatin?

Should penetration beyond that range disqualify a bullet for police duty use?

Are the eight-media barrier tests realistic for most law enforcement?

Is bullet fragmentation after expansion in calibrated 10-percent ordnance gelatin a sign of good performance or poor performance?

The position spelled out in the book *Handgun Stopping Power* and subsequent magazine articles is:

1. The ideal range of penetration is 10 to 14 inches.

2. Bullets that penetrate beyond 14 inches should not be used for police duty nor home defense.

3. The use of tactical barriers in front of gelatin is interesting, perhaps important. However, the results should not be weighted equally.

Instead of the bare gelatin phase getting one-eighth weighting and the barriers getting seven-eighths weightings, it should be more balanced.

Wallboard (FBI test 4) and plywood (FBI test 5) are essentially duplicate tests. Auto glass at 10 feet (FBI test 6) and auto glass at 20 yards (FBI test 8) are also redundant. Heavy clothes at 10 feet (FBI test 2) and heavy clothes at 20 yards (FBI test 7) are clearly duplications of the same test.

The use of redundant tests in the average weighting process forces ammo designers to develop bullets that work better against tactical objects than people. The Hornady XTP-HP bullet is a perfect example. Hornady was the first to design a bullet with these tests in mind. To succeed in the tests, the hollowpoint bullet must not expand. Hornady therefore designed its XTP hollowpoint to suppress expansion and totally avoid fragmentation.

Consequently, the XTP worked well against barriers. Unfortunately, the bullet does not work well against flesh and blood. It was clearly the loser during the Strasbourg Tests, and the officer-involved shootings in this book rank it in the bottom half of the results. (We typically tell officers and civilians to pick *anything* in the top third.)

Our position has been to reduce the eight tests to just four: bare gelatin, steel, glass, and heavy clothes. The results should still favor performance in bare gelatin, giving it a 40 to 50 percent weighting.

4. Bullets that expand and then fragment in calibrated 10-percent ordnance gelatin have been found to at least expand in combinations of living tissue of various densities. Fragmentation is a sign the bullet will work under the widest variety of shooting scenarios.

The opposing position, circa 1987, is:

1. The ideal range of penetration, according to FBI guidelines, is 12 to 18 inches. Penetration less than 12 inches disqualifies the load.

2. Bullets that penetrate beyond 18 inches are acceptable. In fact, Dr. Carroll Peters, one of the 1987 FBI Wound Ballistic Workshop panelists, stated:

". . . I suggest that any bullet that will not penetrate at least 30 cm (11.8 inches) into typical soft tissue should not be considered suitable for law enforcement use, and that capability to penetrate 45-50 cm (17.7 to 19.7 inches) is desirable."

The FBI's early summaries of its ammo tests stated, "Penetration of 18 inches is even better." Penetration beyond 18 inches is not discounted nor discouraged in any way under the Bureau's concepts, but only the permanent cavity formed in the first 18 inches is used in its calculations.

In 1987, Dr. Martin Fackler, another one of the Wound Ballistic Workshop panelists, stated:

"The blood vessels of the abdomen are 6 inches from the front abdominal skin even in a slender person. In the upper chest, they are at least that deep when approached from the other side. Adding to this a possible 4 inches for the thickness of an arm or a large abdomen and it becomes obvious that 10 inches must be the absolute minimum penetration depth capability of any bullet that could be considered acceptable."

The official Summary from the 1987 FBI Workshop read:

"Any bullet that will not reliably penetrate a minimum of 10 to 12 inches of soft tissue is inadequate."

However, in the September 1992 issue of the police magazine *Law and Order*, in a debate forum against Ed Sanow, Dr. Fackler wrote:

"Ideal bullet penetration depth in the body is between 12 and 20 inches. Penetration beyond 20 inches is preferable to penetration under 12 inches, but it wastes bullet potential."

What is all this squabbling over 2 inches— 10-inch minimum versus 12-inch, minimum? Ammo that does not meet the 12-inch mark but clearly works in the street should not be disqualified!

Some examples will make this flawed minimum standard quite clear:

TABLE 27-1

LOAD	PENETRATION	STREET RESULTS
9mm Cor-Bon 115-gr. JHP +P	9.0″	91% in 32 shootings
9mm Winchester 115-gr. JHP +P	7.9″	90% in 98 shootings
9mm Federal 124-gr. Nyclad-HP	11.5″	84% in 239 shootings
9mm Federal 115-gr. JHP 9BP	10.0″	82% in 208 shootings
9mm Winchester 115-gr. Silvertip	8.0″	83% in 304 shootings
.357 Mag. Federal 110-gr. JHP	10.0″	90% in 204 shootings
.357 Mag. Remington 110-gr. JHP	10.8″	89% in 53 shootings
.45 Auto CCI 200-gr. JHP	9.4″	88% in 111 shootings
.45 Auto Cor-Bon 185-gr. JHP +P	11.3″	92% in 12 shootings
.40 S&W Cor-Bon 135-gr. JHP	9.8″	96% in 24 shootings
.38 Spl. Winchester 110-gr. JHP +P	7.0″	81% in 31 shootings
Average	9.5″	88% in 120 shootings

Now let's review the "deep penetrator" hollowpoints:

TABLE 27-2

LOAD	PENETRATION	STREET RESULTS
9mm Federal 147-gr. JHP 9MS-2	18.0″	77% in 27 shootings
9mm Winchester 147-gr. JHP OSM	15.9″	74% in 232 shootings
.357 Mag. Remington 158-gr. JHP	19.0″	82% in 38 shootings
.357 Mag. Federal 158-gr. Nyclad	16.5″	81% in 42 shootings
.45 Auto Remington 185-gr. JHP	23.0″	81% in 114 shootings
10mm MV Winchester 180-gr. JHP	15.5″	82% in 44 shootings
.40 S&W Hornady 180-gr. XTP-HP	16.4″	85% in 46 shootings
.45 Colt Federal 225-gr. LHP	19.5″	78% in 69 shootings
Average	17.9″	80% in 77 shootings

And now let's review the nonexpanding hardball, round-nose lead, and semiwadcutters:

TABLE 27-3

LOAD	PENETRATION	STREET RESULTS
.38 Spl. Federal 158-gr. SWC	23.5″	52% in 278 shootings
.38 Spl. Federal 158-gr. RNL	28.0″	51% in 456 shootings
9mm Winchester 115-gr. FMJ	24.5″	63% in 256 shootings
.357 Mag. Winchester 158-gr. SWC	26.9″	72% in 98 shootings
.44 Spl. Winchester 246-gr. RNL	23.0″	65% in 71 shootings
.45 Auto Rem., Fed., Win. 230-gr. FMJ	27.0″	63% in 469 shootings
.40 S&W Winchester 180-gr. FMJ	25.0″	71% in 17 shootings
.45 Colt Winchester 255-gr. SWC	28.5″	69% in 59 shootings
Average	25.8″	63% in 213 shootings

Clearly, the more penetration the bullet produced, the less energy it transferred to the target and the lower the stopping power. Since the minimum penetration also achieves the maximum stopping power, again, how much penetration is a realistic minimum for the police duty scenario?

Gary Roberts, DDS, provided some helpful insights in his published review of 9mm, .40 S&W, and .45 Auto hollowpoints:

"Vital anatomic structures are located deep within the body, protected by various layers of tissue. The average thickness of an adult human torso is 9.4 inches (measured front to back). The major blood vessels in the torso of even a slender adult are located approximately 6.0 inches from the ventral (front) skin surface. From oblique and transverse angles, the heart and major blood vessels of the torso can be over 7.9 inches deep."

It is easy to see why the original recommendation made to the FBI was that 10 inches be considered the minimum. But 10 inches is deeper than the average adult male is thick.

We, of course, feel that the original recommendations made to the FBI of 10 inches as a minimum were correct. The minimum depth of 12 inches is simply a hedge, with no street

Many police agencies are starting to disqualify bullets that exceed 18 inches of gelatin to reduce the risk of overpenetration.

Experts who once pushed for 18 to 20 inches of penetration now indicate that 15 inches should be the maximum.

results to back up the need for this deeper minimum. In fact, the street results and the powerful formulas developed by Steve Fuller in Chapter 28 indicate that even a 10-inch minimum is a bit deep.

While a 12-inch minimum is the dogma of the opposing view, some dissention is starting to surface in light of these street results.

The original recommendation made by Dr. Fackler was 10 inches, minimum. He later changed his mind, and the minds of his followers, to 12 inches, minimum. The standards are continuing to change. The latest position is "11.5 inches is the minimum, but this depends on the load."

The street-results-based recommendations

Many police agencies are starting to agree that 12 inches is not necessarily a realistic minimum for police ammo. Most 9mm 115-grain JHPs produce less than 12 inches of penetration but the most stopping power in actual police-action shootings.

have, however, not changed. A depth of 8 inches appears to be acceptable in many police-action shootings, although a 10-inch minimum depth remains our design criteria.

From a civil liability viewpoint, the most promising of the changing official standards is the maximum penetration depth.

In 1987, the maximum depth of 18 inches was adopted by most FBI panelists, with 20 inches being perfectly acceptable. In 1992, Dr. Fackler sided with Dr. Peters in setting 20 inches as the outer marker. Fortunately for responding police officers and innocent bystanders, all of that has changed dramatically.

In the late 1980s, penetration in excess of 18 inches simply wasn't considered in the overall wounding calculation. After we pointed out how dangerous this was, some serious backpedalling took place. Today, overpenetration is discussed openly and is given equal time and equal consideration when discussing adequate penetration.

The opposing view is still internally divid-

ed, but two very definite concessions have been made in published reports.

First, from an article published by Alex Jason and Evan Thompson: "A penetration beyond 18 inches is generally considered excessive."

Second, from an article published by Gary Roberts, which almost totally agrees with our view: "Bullets which penetrate beyond 18 inches are wasting tissue disruption potential which could be used to make a larger hole *in the ideal 12- to 15-inch range* of penetration required for handgun bullets intended for law enforcement and military special operations use." [Emphasis added.]

That is right—the ideal range, published in the *Wound Ballistics Review*, is 12 to 15 inches. That is a lot different than 12 to 18 inches or 12 to 20 inches! When the bottom limit is lowered to 11.5 inches, as it has been at least in verbal presentations, the two opposing views are not very far apart at all. We favor, and have always favored, 10 to 14 inches. Street results have forced "them" down to an arguable 11.5 to 15 inches. With that concession, and an "excessive" label attached to ammo that exceeds the ideal range, both camps can be considered to be in agreement. The handgun ammo with the most proven successful street records work inside these ranges.

Part of the concession that 15 inches is a more realistic maximum than either 18 or 20 inches is the realization that handgun bullets must expand to be the most effective. Bullets that expand do not penetrate 18 inches.

It took a while to realize the significance of the crush cavity volume being much more effected by bullet diameter than by penetration depth. Crush volume, the basis of the opposing view, goes up linearly with increased penetration but it increases with the square of the recovered diameter. Once this sunk in, bullet expansion came back into play among the deeper-is-better proponents.

Our standards for expansion were published in the book *Handgun Stopping Power*. For years, the opposing view had no standards for expansion since such standards would disqualify all deep-penetrating, subsonic hollowpoints. This, too, has changed. They now agree with us.

TABLE 27-4
MINIMUM EXPANSION

CALIBER	CPL. SANOW	ROBERTS, DDS
9mm	.60 cal	.60 cal
.40 S&W	.67 cal	.65 cal
.45 Auto	.75 cal	.70 cal

3. According to the FBI, the use of the eight-barrier protocol makes the tests practical and indicative of a cartridge's suitability over a wide range of conditions in which law enforcement officers engage in shootings. That was in the late 1980s and early 1990s. In the meantime, the FBI had come under so much fire from *both* sides—each objected to the emphasis on barriers instead of tissue simulants as not being realistic or practical—that it made a major retraction.

The Bureau is now citing that its protocol is for the likely scenarios that *its agents* face, and that it may not necessarily reflect the likely scenarios of other law enforcement officers. Thank you. We only hope that as many officers hear the retraction as had heard the first claims.

The other major concession concerned the FBI protocol "Wound Value, W." Here is exactly how the Bureau itself defined its Wound Value:

"'W' is the index of actual wounding effectiveness, not potential, as measured by the FBI Ammunition Test results. W is the critical value for comparative purposes. As W increases, the more effective and reliable the wound that round will inflict. Given identically located hits, a round with twice the W value should have twice the potential for incapacitation of the subject."

Unfortunately, when we statistically compared the FBI Wound Value W to actual street reports for ten FBI loads in *Handgun Stopping Power*, the correlation coefficient was a dismal 0.53. That was the worst correlation of any method ever offered to predict effectiveness.

As a change, the FBI no longer calculates and reports a Wound Value in its published data. It found that police officers in flyover country were actually taking the Wound Value at face value—they were actually expecting a load with twice the Wound Value to be twice as effective, exactly as it was defined by the Bureau. This data is no longer published to keep police officers from making that "mistake." Thank you.

4. The last major area of dispute is the issue of bullet fragmentation. Frankly, this is becoming less of an issue since the most recent bullet designs *will not* fragment. These include the Remington Golden Saber, CCI-Speer Gold Dot, Winchester Ranger SXT (Talon) and Supreme SXT, and Eldorado Starfire. Even the JHP designs in new calibers like the .357 SIG are made with thicker jackets and higher antimony lead cores.

However, some bullet designs do indeed fragment, including most of the Federal Hydra-Shoks and nearly all of the so-called "high-velocity" hollowpoints. So, the topic is still open to some debate, although as we go to

This Federal 9mm 124-grain Hydra-Shok has a better street record than any 147-grain subsonic hollowpoint. This kind of fragmentation in gelatin confuses some people. It is a sign of reliable expansion in actual shootings.

press, Federal is increasing the jacket thickness and core hardness on all its Hydra-Shoks to reduce fragmentation.

Bullet fragmentation after expansion is a sign that the ammo will work under the widest range of scenarios. Police ammo that expands violently and fragments turns in the very best actual street performance. Bullets that expand and then fragment in gelatin at least expand reliably in the various densities of living tissue.

We compared the recovered bullet diameter in gelatin to the number of one-shot stops for the same ammo in 1,800 officer-involved shootings. In general, bullets with large recovered diameters had more stopping power than bullets with small recovered diameters. This should not surprise anyone.

For example, the 9mm hardball recovered at .36 inch works about 62 percent of the time. Big-bore .45 Auto ball which measures .45 inch when recovered works about 64 percent of the time. The 9mm Nyclad hollowpoint expands to .68 caliber and has an 81 percent one-shot record. The .45 Auto Hydra-Shok opens to .76 caliber and has a 90 percent record.

However, the problems of accurately predicting stopping power go way beyond such a simplistic bigger-is-better analysis. First, bullets that fragment have a better street record than their recovered diameter would indicate. Second, bullets that expand in gelatin to sometimes twice their caliber don't always expand in tissue on the street. (However, bullets that fragment in gelatin nearly always expand in tissue.) Third, sometimes a bullet will spin off a fragment of lead that will hit vital tissue missed by the main core. This, of course, greatly increases stopping power.

Check out the recovered diameters of the 9mm 115-grain +P+ JHP, .357 Magnum 125-grain JHP, .40 S&W 135- and 155-grain JHPs, and .45 Auto 185-grain +P JHP. Each load expands and fragments back to just about caliber diameter. The loss of the plump mushroom on the 9mm +P+ and .357 Magnum results in .40- to .50-inch diameter slugs instead of .68 to .70 calibers of the slower loads. The .40 S&W hollowpoints erode back to .55 caliber. The .45 Auto is recovered from gelatin measuring just .50 to .55 caliber instead of the common .80 caliber.

Yet each of these loads has an extremely good stopping power record. In fact, the fragmenting 9mm +P+, .357 Magnum, and .40 S&W loads produce the most documented stopping power in their calibers. The fragmenting .45 Auto +P loads are third and fourth overall of all .45 Autos.

We compared loads that fragment and leave a smaller recovered diameter to the exact same bullets that go slower but retain plump mushrooms. According to 458 officer-involved shootings, the loads that fragment when tested in gelatin actually have an 11 percent better street record than loads that do not fragment. That increase in stopping power is extremely significant if for no other reason than it is an increase and not a decrease, as some would think.

Statistician Dan Watters from the University of South Carolina took a similar, logical approach. He analyzed 2,315 shooting results from two different groups of bullets. One group was made up of bullets that had a 100 percent recovered weight retention when fired into gelatin. This was the no fragmentation group. The second group was made up of bullets which had some degree of weight loss when fired in gelatin. This varied from a few percent fragmentation typical of the medium-velocity hollowpoints to the 40 percent fragmentation typical of many high-velocity hollowpoints.

In this analysis, "fragmentation" simply meant a recovered bullet diameter from gelatin less than 100 percent of the original weight. It did not mean hollowpoints that spun off fragments of lead that exited the main bullet path. In fact, for most bullets in this group, the expanded mushroom was scrubbed off or worn away back to a smaller bullet diameter. In these cases, the fragments did not contribute directly to wounding. Instead, they were simply recovered along the primary crush cavity in the trail of the main bullet core.

Watters found that the bullets that exhibited fragmentation in gelatin had a success ratio

This Cor-Bon .38 Special +P+ 115-grain Sierra JHP fragments violently in gelatin. This means it expands reliably under the widest variety of shooting scenarios. Proof of this is the best street record of any .38 Special load.

in actual gunfights of 88 percent. This was based on 1,364 shootings. Bullets which exhibited *no* fragmentation in gelatin had a success ratio of just 74 percent. This was based on a sample size of 951 shootings.

The flip-side of this analysis is equally informative. Bullets that fragment in gelatin have a 12-percent failure rate with one shot to the torso. Bullets that do *not* fragment in gelatin have a 26-percent failure rate. Bullets with a 100 percent weight retention are more than twice as likely to *fail* in actual shootings as bullets which show at least a little breakup in gelatin.

Bullets with fragmentation in gelatin have a better street record than bullets that merely expand! Part of the reason for the superior street experience is explained by a comparison of two very similar .40 S&W loads.

Cor-Bon has two lightweight loads for the .40 S&W. The production load uses a 150-grain Sierra driven to 1,200 fps. Available as a special-order-only is a 155-grain Hornady XTP with a velocity of 1,175 fps. It is designed to suppress expansion and totally avoid fragmentation. These two loads make an

This Cor-Bon 9mm +P+ 115-grain Sierra JHP fragments on impact with gelatin. This means it will be the most tolerant of heavy clothing. This expanding and fragmenting JHP has a better actual street record than any other 9mm load.

LEFT: The Cor-Bon and Triton .40 S&W 135-grain JHPs using either Nosler or Sierra bullets expand and fragment in gelatin. A bullet that fragments in gelatin will at least expand in combinations of soft and hard tissue. This load has the best wound ballistics in the caliber.

BELOW: Just because a hollowpoint expands in gelatin does not mean it will always expand on the street. This is true for even the .45 Auto 200-grain JHP that expands to .81 caliber in gelatin.

excellent study into the effects of shearing off the mushroom after expansion.

The concept is that a bullet that fragments in gelatin will at least expand in tissue. Sometimes it is tough to get some hollowpoints to even expand in tissue.

We fired both Cor-Bon loads into T-shirt-covered gelatin. The 150-grain JHP bullet expanded and fragmented to a recovered diameter of "only" .55 inch. The 155-grain XTP bullet penetrated the exact same depth but kept a .68 inch mushroom. With the same energy and depth of penetration, the stopping power advantage goes to the larger recovered bullet, the XTP in this example.

Next we fired the same two .40 S&W loads into gelatin clothed with eight layers of denim. Nothing magic about that—we just wanted enough clothing to plug up the hollowpoint cavity and act as an obstacle that cops may face. The 150-grain JHP bullet that fragmented before still expanded to .65 caliber. The 155-grain XTP bullet that merely expanded to .68 caliber in bare gelatin now expanded to only .51 caliber.

The stretch and crush cavity still favors the

Based on 985 police-action shootings, the expanding and then fragmenting .357 Magnum 125-grain JHP (left) has the best street record ever recorded for any caliber. The fragmenting 9mm +P+ 115-grain JHP (right) leads that caliber.

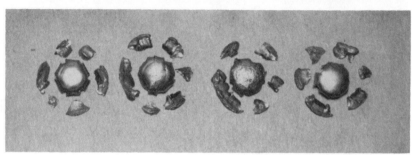

The top four .357 Magnum loads, based on actual shootings, are shown recovered from gelatin. From left: Rem 125-grain S-JHP, Fed 125-grain JHP, CCI 125-grain JHP, and Fed 110-grain JHP. The most proven street stoppers expand and then fragment.

larger recovered bullet, except this time the larger recovered bullet is the one that mushroomed then fragmented last time. The real significance is the estimated stopping power under each test. The expanding and then fragmenting 150-grain JHP design produced about 83 percent stops regardless of obstacle. The 155-grain XTP that expanded in one test but not much in the other crashed from 87 percent to 71 percent just because of the obstacle.

The rule is: a bullet that fragments under ideal conditions will always at least expand even under adverse conditions.

The real shock comes when examining bullets recovered at autopsy. Bullets that normally expand to twice their caliber in gelatin sometimes do not expand at all in tissue. The CCI .45 Auto 200-grain JHP "flying ash can" is an example. (Despite this example, keep in mind that this CCI hollowpoint is an excellent load and is fifth overall in actual .45 Auto stopping power results, with an 88 percent rating.)

The 200-grain Speer hollowpoint expands to between .78 and .90 inch in 10-percent gelatin. No other handgun load expands to these kinds of diameters, period. Yet despite enormous recovered diameters in gelatin, this load would sometimes fail to expand at all when used by Los Angeles Police Department SWAT officers (the first major agency to make wide use of this load). The perps still went down due to surgical shot placement, but the bullet did not expand.

Now, think about bullets like the 9mm 147-grain JHP that barely expand to .58 caliber in gelatin. If bullets that expand easily in gelatin frequently do not expand in tissue, the hard-to-expand bullets will obviously never expand in tissue.

Ten-percent gelatin was designed and developed to duplicate a bullet's penetration, expansion, and fragmentation in living muscle. Depending on the impact velocity and the design of the bullet, it does just that. However, humans obviously are not all muscle. An upper torso shot involves an inch or two of skin, muscle, and fat and then air-filled lungs the rest of the way. It takes an extremely fragment-prone bullet to expand in this combination of tissue.

This logic holds true even for the 9mm 147-grain hollowpoints, which are the worst bullets

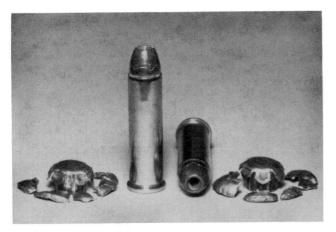

The Remington .357 Magnum 125-grain S-JHP is shown.

If deep penetration is one of the keys to stopping power, why does this .38 Special 158-grain RNL have a 51 percent one-shot stop? Note the calibration BBs.

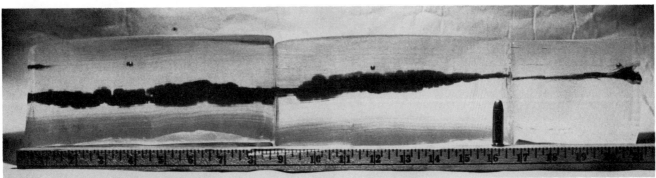

Here is the logic: find the very best load based on actual street results and record how it reacts in gelatin. That will define success.

RIGHT: One of the oddest new standards is that some experts now expect hollowpoint bullets to expand. The 9mm 115-grain JHP (left) and 124-grain Hydra-Shok (center) have always expanded. The 147-grain JHP no longer meets anyone's standards for expansion.

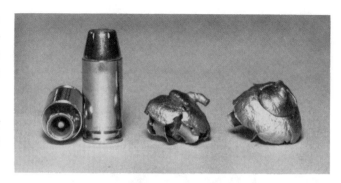

BELOW: Bullets that expand and then either break up or fragment like this Federal .40 S&W 180-grain Hydra-Shok have the most stopping power.

The MagSafe Defender, like this .38 Special +P+ 65-grain MAX, is the best example that fragmentation causes stopping power. Fragmenting bullets completely dominated the blood-and-lungs Strasbourg Tests.

One of the most encouraging new developments is that more people test ammo in gelatin than ever before. According to Remington Arms, testing in water gives misleading results.

of our time. The Federal 147-grain Hydra-Shok has been criticized for fragmenting in gelatin. In 278 shootings, it has a stopping power record of 78 percent one-shot torso shots. The Winchester 147-grain OSM JHP never fragments in gelatin. Based on 232 shootings, its record is 74 percent. Fragmentation in gelatin is a good thing. It shows street tolerance.

Fragmentation inside the torso is also a good thing. Occasionally a hollowpoint will spin off 5- to 10-grain pieces of lead that will exit the main bullet path (as opposed to leaving pieces of lead harmlessly in the wake of the bullet). Secondary missiles like that can travel through 4 to 6 inches of tissue by themselves.

These fragments can do two things. First, they can put holes in vital tissue that was missed by the bullet. Some experts make a big deal out of one shape of bullet pushing a major vessel aside while another bullet cuts it. And that is a big deal. But it is even a bigger deal if the bullet core puts a hole in one vessel while one of its frags puts a hole in another. Medical examiners have documented significant secondary injury from handgun ammo fragmentation.

Second, fragments can put holes in tissue and then set the tissue up for further damage from the temporary stretch cavity that instantly follows. The frags perforate and then the stretch tears. This can in fact dislodge entire sections of tissue. This too has been documented. It is rare for hollowpoints to cause this kind of damage but extremely common for exotic frangible bullets that totally fragment.

As more police departments do their own testing in gelatin, we need to change our thinking about what fragmentation and recovered bullet diameters really mean. Bullets that barely expand in gelatin will not expand on the street. Bullets that easily expand in gelatin to large recovered diameters will probably expand a little on the street. Bullets that violently expand and then fragment will at least expand on the street. Once again, bullet fragmentation is a sign that the bullet will be its most effective even under the worst scenarios.

Bullets that expand and then fragment in gelatin have a better street record than those that merely expand.

TABLE 27-5
HOLLOWPOINT FRAGMENTATION IN GELATIN

	SUCCESS	FAILURE	TOTAL
Fragmentation (under 100% retained weight)	1,194 88%	170 12%	1,364
No Fragmentation (100% weight retention)	706 74%	245 26%	951

28

Predicting Stopping Power

by Steve Fuller

I will probably never need to use a gun to protect myself or my family against any two-legged predators. I am more likely to need to fend off a big, furry, four-legged critter, but that is also not very probable. Still, it was the latter possibility that prompted me to acquire my first handgun several years ago. The choice of ammunition for the .44 Magnum for bears was limited and therefore relatively easy. The choice of a handgun and ammunition for two-legged predators is not so easy.

My interest in the topic initially was piqued by the many magazine articles published regarding "stopping power," so I embarked on a seemingly endless research project on my computer. I soon found out that there are many theories on why a particular cartridge may produce a more destructive wound or be a more effective fight stopper. Some theories assume that increased tissue destruction correlates with increased stopping power. I believe, however, that it may not be necessary to understand the medical aspects of wound ballistics to evaluate a particular type of cartridge.

I began to examine the tremendous volume of street data collected by Evan Marshall and published in association with Edwin Sanow in the book *Handgun Stopping Power: The Definitive Study*. After my early work and preliminary results, I contacted Sanow and Marshall and added their new data to my studies. My underlying assumption is that there are measurable ammunition characteristics that allow reasonable predictions of stopping power. The problem is to determine the most relevant characteristics and develop a relationship or model that best relates to street performance.

Obviously, humans are not homogeneous targets. The effect of a single bullet is a function of many parameters aside from the type of bullet, including point of impact, angle of impact, clothing, and the size of the individual. It is imperative to use the largest number of data points possible to minimize the effect of these nonammunition factors. For this work I used Marshall's updated data from a total of 13,541 shootings.

Since Marshall's data set does not have

equally large data samples for all types of ammunition, the data analysis process must weight the percentage of observed one-shot stops from a cartridge used in several hundred shootings more heavily than one used in only a dozen shootings. In order to consider the different numbers of shootings for each type of ammunition, I used regression analyses of the various ballistic parameters against the percentage of one-shot stops weighted by the number of shootings with the respective cartridges.

When I started this work in 1992, I tested hollowpoint bullets and later applied the same techniques to solid point bullets. To my surprise, the best single predictor of stopping power turned out to be muzzle energy alone. This held true for both hollowpoint and solid point bullets. As I will show later, the inclusion of certain gelatin test data improves the predictive value of energy even further.

METHOD AND CRITERIA FOR MODEL

Using time-honored statistics techniques, I took some educated guesses and tested them mathematically. I considered external ballistic factors first. The results of some tests suggested other combinations of parameters or other model forms to test. Among the parameter combinations I tested were those used by Hatcher, Lott, and Taylor.

Of the many models I tested, some looked good initially but had flaws that caused me to discard them. In my view, a major flaw in a model is the possibility that it could predict effectiveness greater than 100 percent or a negative effectiveness with any ammunition that might be used in a handgun. In other words, the shootee should not be predicted as being stopped before the shot is fired, and the shootee should not be predicted to be in better shape after being shot than before.

The model should also have a minimal number of terms. If it has a great number of terms, it may explain past data well but be unsuitable for predicting the performance of new ammunition. Additionally, the model should seem reasonable. For example, if the model considered only depth

of penetration in gelatin and showed that the optimal depth of penetration was 1 inch, I would consider it suspect.

MUZZLE ENERGY

Figure 1 is a graph of the final weighted mathematical model of hollowpoint bullet performance as a function of energy. The data do not include calibers smaller than .32 ACP because I did not have the small caliber data initially. (Later I will show how the model was expanded to consider the smaller calibers.) The circles represent the individual types of ammunition and the areas of the circles represent the number of shootings (weighting) with that ammunition. The bigger circles contribute more to the shape of the curve than do the smaller circles. It is clear that, with the range of data available, there is little to be gained by energy above some level. I would suggest that 675 ft-lbs. is a practical upper boundary. The relationship between energy and stopping power is exponential, so no finite energy level will produce a predicted 100 percent one-shot stop level.

It should be noted that the statistical process inherently has tolerances and deviations from expectations, or scatter. If two cartridges differ in energy by a small amount, the difference may not be significant or even in the expected direction. Predictions based on muzzle energy do not distinguish between a Silvertip and a Hydra-Shok of the same weight and velocity. The analyses based on Marshall's data suggest that, *on average*, hollowpoint bullets of .32 ACP and larger tended to be similar enough to make some remarkably good predictions.

Obviously, if we consider very disparate rifle loads such as the .25-06 caliber 80-grain hollowpoint varmint load and the .45-70 caliber 300-grain hollowpoint, we see comparable energy levels but radically different performance on game. However, we will not be considering cartridges with equal muzzle energies but where the bullet weights and diameters differ by such a large factor.

Figure 2 is a graph of the final model of solid point bullet performance done the same

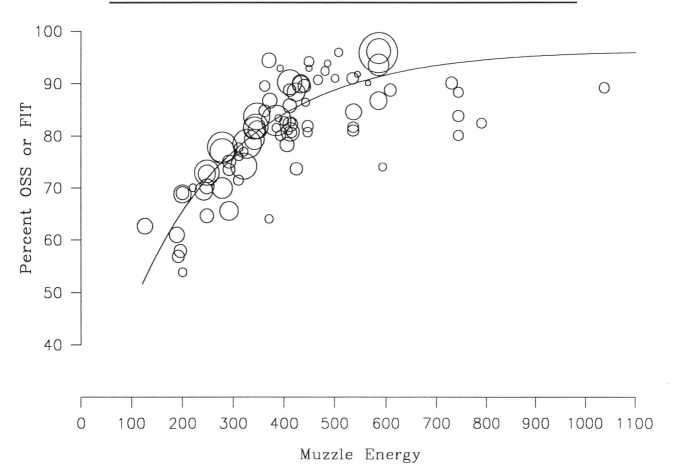

Figure 1: Hollowpoint bullets.

way as was done for hollowpoint bullets but with different coefficients in the same type of relation. As can be seen, solid point bullets require about twice as much energy to produce an 80 percent one-shot stop level as do hollowpoint bullets. Again, there is no finite energy level that will produce a predicted 100 percent one-shot stop level.

For want of a better label, I will give the acronym FIT to the calculated results. Some of my correspondents on this topic have called my result the Fuller Index, but I only lay claim to the technique, the fitting of which has given me fits, so the fitting acronym of Fuller Index Technique, or FIT, is fitting. The FIT number produced by the model is only an index of the projected level of performance and can be considered to be numerically parallel to the street-derived percentage of one-shot stops with the same constraints used by Marshall in collect-ing his data. This allows the FIT model to be plotted on the same graph with the street data.

For hollowpoints:

$$\text{Energy FIT} = 96.34 - 78.24 \times e^{\frac{-\text{Energy}}{215}}$$

For solid points:

$$\text{Energy FIT} = 89.41 - 59.95 \times e^{\frac{-\text{Energy}}{412}}$$

The equations use the number "e" or 2.71828 as the base of the exponential term. "e" is base of the "natural" or Napierian loga-rithm and it often characterizes natural pro-cesses and phenomena. If we examine the data that produced these two basic models, we find that the "fit" of the data to the model is out-

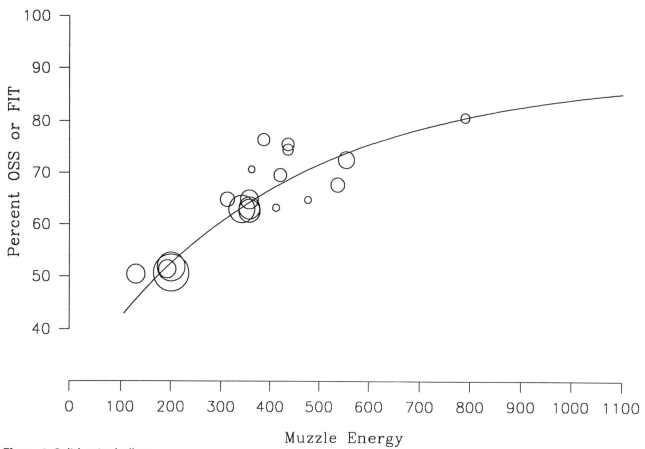

Figure 2: Solid point bullets.

standing for the solid point bullets, with a standard error of 3.03 percent. The practical result of this standard error is that the model predicts effectiveness as well as if data were collected from more than 270 shootings with a particular cartridge. Since only two cartridges can boast that level of street data, the model used for the graph is likely to yield a better prediction for street performance than the raw data. This energy model also yields a coefficient of determination of 0.88. That is, the model can explain 88 percent of the variance between energy as a predictor and the street data. The square root of the coefficient of determination is called the correlation coefficient, which helps to describe the fit of the model to the data. In this case it is 0.94. The closer both of these numbers are to one, the better the fit.

The fit of the performance of these hollow-point bullets to the model is not as good as for the solid point bullets, but it still produces a standard error of 4.89 percent. One would need street data for 105 shootings with a specific cartridge to be likely to give a better prediction of street effectiveness. The coefficient of determination is 0.73 and the correlation coefficient is 0.86.

Taken together, these results show that, with similar bullets, energy is an outstanding predictor of effectiveness. The graphs shown in Figures 1 and 2 are similar in shape, and even the coefficients in the respective models are similar except for the exponential term. Since hollowpoint bullets are not as similar from type to type as are solid point bullets, additional information is needed to improve the model so it can be applied to virtually any bullet type. The most likely source of information that can quantitatively differentiate between various bullet type seems to be gelatin tests.

GELATIN TESTS

As explained elsewhere in this book, gelatin testing has long been used to quantify ammunition performance. Gelatin test results can be very useful, but the data must be used carefully and the tests done precisely.

Let's first look at the "calibration" of gelatin blocks. It is often assumed that the uniformity of depth of penetration of a small air gun projectile in gelatin is sufficient to "calibrate" the test media. Implicit within that assumption are further assumptions that the results from large, massive, high-velocity projectiles will simulate damage to human tissue and the results will also be comparable to those at other test facilities. There is some evi-

dence to show that, with defense rounds, this latter assumption is not valid. Some researchers have found that results can differ if one long block of gelation of a given cross section is replaced by two shorter blocks of the same cross section and of the same total length placed in contact, end to end. Other researchers have found that restraining a block of gelatin will produce different results from an unrestrained block of the same size. Some facilities have even gone so far as to use blocks of a size and weight similar to an adult male. To be on the safe side I feel that comparisons are best made between data from the same facility.

A basic premise of gelatin testing is that it gives results that, unlike the energy models, should be relatively independent of the exact projectile type. In these analyses, I have included all of the calibers for which Marshall

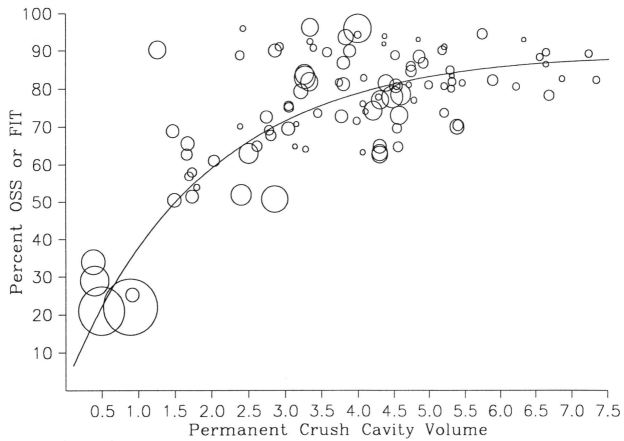

Figure 3: Gelatin crush cavity.

and Sanow have provided data. The cartridges range from .22 Long Rifle to .44 Magnum.

The easiest parameter to measure with accuracy and precision is depth of penetration. Final bullet diameter is easy to measure in the cases where the bullet remains intact. The "permanent" or "crush" cavity would appear to be easy to measure, but this is not the case. If high technology techniques were used to measure the bullet diameter continuously during penetration, then the crush cavity could be calculated accurately. The present method of using the recovered frontal area of the bullet and the length of the penetration to calculate a cylindrical volume is valid only for solid point bullets. Hollowpoint bullets expand to final diameter continuously and at different rates during penetration. If we consider a .45 caliber bullet, for example, that penetrates 12 inches and expands linearly to 3/4 inch diameter in the first 2 inches of penetration like the Hydra-Shok, the crush volume will be 4.9 cubic inches. If another .45 caliber bullet expands linearly to the same final diameter, but in 8 inches like the Ranger SXT, the crush cavity will be 4.1 cubic inches for 12 inches of penetration. The present method of calculation where the constant cavity diameter is assumed to be equal to the final diameter of the bullet would produce a crush volume result of 5.3 cubic inches. This example shows that careful calculations with imprecisely obtained numbers can produce results which could easily be in error by 20 percent.

Because of this imprecision, I feel the crush cavity volume is not a good primary indicator of bullet performance. Indeed, both the quadratic and exponential weighted regression analyses of crush cavity volume with all loads and calibers in Marshall's data gave an unacceptably high standard error of 12.3 percent. The graph of predicted performance vs. crush cavity volume is shown in Figure 3.

The temporary stretch cavity data seem to be a significantly better predictor with the exponential analysis giving a standard error of 7.2 percent. The graph of predicted performance vs. stretch cavity volume is shown in

Figure 4. The relations for calculating effectiveness for the two types of cavities are:

For the crush cavity:

$$\text{Jello FIT} = 89.30 - 87.26 \times e^{\frac{-\text{crush volume}}{1.888}}$$

For the stretch cavity:

$$\text{Jello FIT} = 90.68 - 90.80 \times e^{\frac{-\text{stretch volume}}{10.139}}$$

If we consider the stretch and crush cavities together, we get much better results. Using Sanow's gelatin data for all bullet types and Marshall's street data, I created a relationship using both cavity volumes that describes the performance of a bullet better than either cavity alone. The relationship is exponential with respect to both cavities and gives a standard error of 5.36 percent, a coefficient of determination of 0.96, and a correlation coefficient of 0.98. This means that the gelatin test results alone can explain the street results very well but with a predictive value that is not quite up to that of energy with the appropriate energy model.

The equation derived for both cavities together is:

$$\text{Jello FIT} = 91.38 - 34.38 \times e^{\frac{-\text{crush volume}}{0.851}} - 68.71 \times e^{\frac{-\text{stretch volume}}{11.65}}$$

As can be seen from the coefficients of the exponential terms, the stretch cavity plays almost twice as prominent a role in determining the performance prediction as the crush cavity. The fact that gelatin data allow comparison of different bullet types suggests that gelatin data can facilitate merging the various bullet types into a single model.

MUZZLE ENERGY AND GELATIN

At this point we see that the energy models of both hollowpoint bullets and solid point

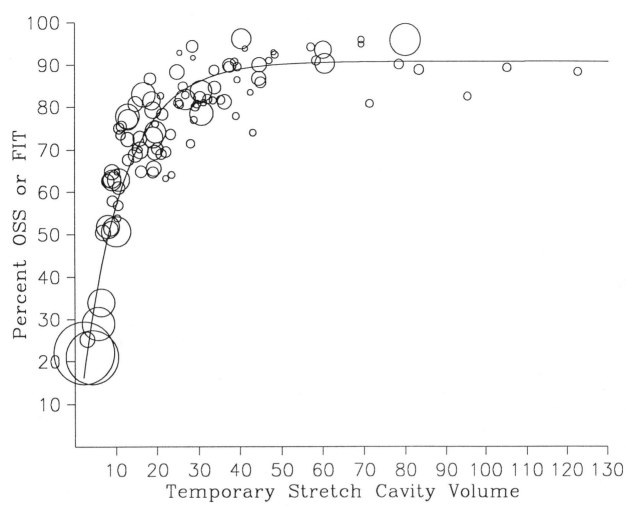

Figure 4: Gelatin stretch cavity.

bullets provide a better fit than the gelatin model, but the gelatin model accounts better for different bullet types. All we need now is a way of combining the two methods into a refined single model with a means of mathematically describing how the bullets differ. The most obvious difference between these two classes of bullets is the easily and accurately measurable depth of penetration—the solid point bullets penetrate much further than do hollowpoints bullets of the same caliber and energy.

Depth of penetration by itself, however, gives virtually no correlation to demonstrated bullet performance.

The hypothesis is that depth of penetration is a nonlinear function of bullet performance.

If depth of penetration adequately differentiates between solid point bullets and hollowpoint bullets, it will likely differentiate between different designs of hollowpoint bullets. To test this hypothesis, I expanded the energy model by including two terms involving depth of penetration. The new model was thus exponential in energy and quadratic in depth of penetration. As hoped, this new model successfully combined the energy and gelatin models into a single new model. When the data were confined to bullets of .32 caliber and larger, the standard error was 4.47 percent, the coefficient of determination was 0.88, and the correlation coefficient was 0.94. This model means that it would take 125 shootings with a given type of ammunition to give a performance prediction as good as that produced by the model. This is very good indeed!

As I came to the end of my analyses of the data, Marshall provided new data on .25 and .22 caliber handgun shootings. There were enough of these shootings to show that the model I just described failed for the very small calibers. Since the model based on energy and depth of penetration overestimated the performance of the very small calibers, I felt certain that inclusion of the initial bullet diameter probably would improve the model and produce good predictions for small calibers as well as the larger calibers. After several tests, I found that the product of energy and diameter in the exponential term gave the best results. The standard error was 4.79 percent, meaning it would take 109 shootings with a given cartridge to give predictions as good as the revised model. The coefficient of determination was 0.97, and the correlation coefficient was 0.98. The significance of the coefficient of determination is that this combination of diameter, depth of penetration, and energy explain 97 percent of the variance between the fit and the street data. Thus, expanding the versatility of the model to encompass a wide range of ammunition resulted in a small sacrifice of precision.

The resulting relationship is:

$$\text{Best FIT} = 90.52 + 0.896 \times \text{depth} - 0.0534 \times \text{depth}^2 - 87.65 \times e^{\frac{\text{dia.} \times \text{energy}}{63.93}}$$

In this relationship, depth refers to bullet depth of penetration (inches) in 10-percent ballistic gelatin, dia refers to initial bullet diameter (inches), and energy refers to bullet muzzle energy in foot pounds. A couple of bits of information can be gleaned from the relationship. Those readers familiar with calculus will see that we can calculate the depth of penetration in gelatin yielding "optimum" performance in the defense scenario, and that it is 8.4 inches. Also, increasing bullet initial diameter or energy or both will improve performance. Unlike the energy models, this relationship works for any of the current projectiles in defensive handgun calibers. We

need to recognize here that we only have data for bullets up to .45 caliber and that if we had a greater range of bullet diameters, the results might be different.

What we now have is a relationship that uses only external ballistic data and easily and precisely measurable gelatin data to produce the most reliable predictions of ammunition performance available to date. The model involves a number of calculations, but none is beyond the average scientific hand calculator or home computer spreadsheet program.

I was able to create an even closer fit using quadratic diameter and depth of penetration terms and an exponential energy term. It gave outstanding results, with a coefficient of determination of 0.98, a correlation coefficient of 0.99, and a standard error of 4.04 percent. Unfortunately this model was unruly, giving unreasonable results when used with hypothetical loads whose parameters were not within the range of the existing data set. At this point, I felt I had thrashed the data well into submission, if not beyond. I am not comfortable with that particular model and will continue to use the former.

Figure 5 shows how a range of .40 caliber cartridges would perform as a function of penetration in gelatin and energy. As a specific example, if we assume 450 ft-lbs. of muzzle energy and 8.4 inches depth of penetration in gelatin, we see a predicted effectiveness of 89 percent. If we change the depth of penetration by 4 inches to either 4.4 inches or 12.4 inches, the effectiveness drops only one percentage point. However, if we increase the depth of penetration an additional 4 inches to 16.4 inches, we see the effectiveness drop to 86 percent. The front left edge of the graph surface illustrates how small changes from optimal have little effect but a significantly greater depth of penetration will quickly reduce the predicted effectiveness. If we look at muzzle energy, we see that to get a decrease of one percentage point, we need only drop the energy from 450 to 425 ft-lbs. Reducing the muzzle energy to 370 ft-lbs. drops the effectiveness to 86 percent.

.40 Caliber Example

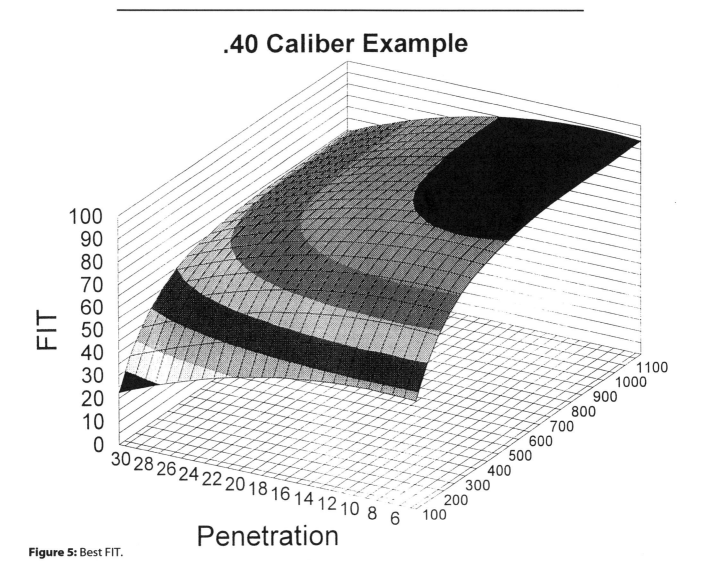

Figure 5: Best FIT.

The effect of energy changes is readily seen in the front right edge of the graph surface.

STRASBOURG TESTS

The Strasbourg goat tests were described in Chapter 4. It has been reported that, in those tests, instrumented goats were shot under controlled conditions and the elapsed time to clinical incapacitation was measured. I take no position on the study or the data except to say that the data may be reliable with respect to the precision of the tests but relatively few loads were tested. There is only one parameter readily available upon which to study the results and that is the Average Incapacitation Time, or AIT.

Clearly this type of parameter calls for a different model since better performance is indicated by reduced AITs. Because of the nature of the test and the limited number of cartridges, I had to put "reasonable" constraints on the models. I suspect that there is some minimum value of AIT such that nothing lower can be achieved, even by total thoracic cavity destruction. I arbitrarily selected the limiting value of 2.5 seconds because it made the results statistically reasonable. I also limited the constant term to a maximum of 100 so that the data would not give predictions greater than 100 percent. At this point it may seem that these two rather arbitrary constraints may simply conjure up good results in

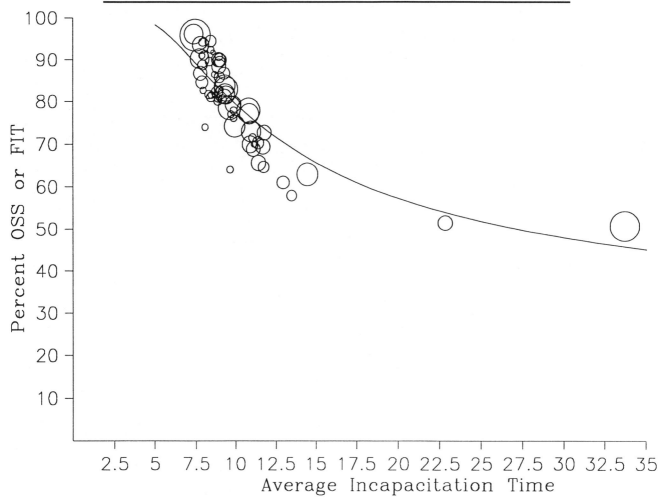

Figure 6: Weighted Strasbourg results.

the face of too little data. Perhaps, but the graph of the derived function of AIT vs. weighted one-shot stops shown in Figure 6 tends to support the reasonableness of this model. The coefficient of determination of 0.85, the correlation coefficient of 0.92, and the standard error of 4.82 percent tend to support the uniformity of the data.

The relationship is:

$$\text{Goat FIT} = 100 - 73.52 \times e^{-\frac{9.461}{\text{AIT} - 2.5}}$$

DISCUSSION

Table 1 shows the loads for which data for the Strasbourg tests, gelatin tests, and Marshall's street data were available. As can be seen, the models yield generally good results. The lone exception, as expected, is the Jello FIT using only the crush cavity.

Among the loads listed, the .45 ACP 230-grain Hydra-Shok is notable in that it performs better than all of the models predict. It is interesting that all of the models, including the crush cavity Jello FIT, give essentially the same results. This may be due to one or more of several factors. The fact that the crush cavity fit is in line with the other predictions suggests that the projectile is expected to be statistically average. That is, the model expects it to behave like any other projectile that achieved the same crush cavity volume as determined by conventional methods. If, however, this bullet expands to its final diameter much earlier than average, that could explain its apparent enhanced street performance. In other words, it may just expand much more quickly than the bullets that determined the model. In fact, this bullet is known to expand in 2 inches of gelatin. Another factor could be that there are only 71 total shootings with this load. That could make the street data less persuasive than the model. Another factor could be that the law enforcement agencies using this round were simply better trained and better marksmen. Fourth, and only slightly tongue-in-cheek, the shooter could have missed with the follow-up shots, giving the assailant time to reconsider the wisdom of continued resistance.

If there was a surprise in the complete data set, it was the .45 ACP Rhino. This highly publicized round was in a virtual tie with the .45 ACP Glaser Blue for the best predicted effectiveness. Caution should be exercised here because such frangible projectiles are not represented in Marshall's collection of data. There are, however, two links that tend to support the reasonableness of the model for such projectiles. The first is that the model supports well those more conventional projectiles that do fragment. Second, the goat tests on these new frangible loads yield results that parallel the model.

Just before the publication deadline, I received some rifle gelatin and one-shot stop data from Sanow and Marshall. Because the data include shootings at ranges of up to 500 yards and the gelatin data were taken at close range, I will comment only that the data seem to follow the Best FIT model very well. The .308 had deeper gelatin penetration than the .223, and it proved less effective as the model would suggest. The energy for both calibers was great enough to make the two bullet diameters of little consequence in the model. In both calibers, the energy was well in excess of the 675 ft-lbs. I suggested earlier as a practical upper bound. Also, the rifle stretch cavity volumes are well in excess of the point at which Figure 4 shows the curve leveling off.

SUMMARY AND CONCLUSIONS

The most important point to be made in

this study is that defensive decisions should not be made on the basis of one round being one or two percentage points better than another round. Other factors such as controllability and muzzle flash should be considered also.

What we have learned is that there is no Magic Bullet, nor is there any certainty that reliance upon a particular cartridge will assure a one-shot stop. There is, however, enough statistical data to allow one to make an informed selection of a caliber/cartridge combination. It is important to recognize that the FIT calculations used statistical techniques that do not consider nonballistic factors that may have been instrumental in some of the observed one-shot stops in Marshall's data.

This relationship does not define a direct causal connection between energy and tissue damage, nor does it say that impact energy was the causal factor in the one-shot stops. The quality of the statistical relationships, coupled with the reasonableness of energy being a causal factor, lead me to believe that a causal relation does exist. Until gelatin tests can be made more accurate, the Best FIT model appears to be the best predictor of defensive ammunition performance.

New techniques can allow the refinement of the gelatin composition to more accurately reflect tissue. Ultrasonic imaging as used in medicine could easily determine if gelatin is a good tissue simulant and, if so, exactly what concentration and temperature would provide the closest approximation to a human torso. Ultrasonic imaging could also yield more precise cavity measurements. Even the old stand-by of high-speed photography could be used to determine how a bullet expands, thus giving more precise measurements of the crush cavity. I firmly believe that uniform and precise gelatin testing, particularly with respect to the crush cavity, will allow the models I have proposed to be tweaked and refined.

At this point the analyses suggest that a large-diameter, high-energy projectile that is brought to a stop in 8.4 inches of gelatin will yield the best street performance, but the optimal range is wide enough to encompass the best of the revolver and semiauto ammunition in a range of popular calibers.

This is a refinement, not a definitive study. Every shooting incident in the future will become part of the past and further modify the data set, thus allowing us to predict the future beyond that shooting with greater confidence. Will we ever get perfect predictions? I hope that there will not be that many shootings. I am reminded of an illustration used by one of my calculus professors. If you put a young man on one side of the room and a young woman on the other side and each one walks half the remaining distance to the center of the room every 30 seconds, will they ever get to the center? No, but they will get close enough for all practical purposes. Hopefully this work and the work done by the current and past researchers in this field is close enough for all practical purposes.

CALIBER	LOAD	WT.	VEL	PENE. DEPTH	FINAL DIA.	CRUSH CAVITY	STRETCH CAVITY	MUZZLE ENERGY	AIT	TOTAL	OSS	OSS%	BEST FIT	GOAT FIT	ENERGY FIT	JELLO FIT	PERM J-FIT	TSC J-FIT
.357 Mag.	Rem 125 gr JHP	125	1450	14.0	0.55	3.33	40.2	584	7.34	204	196	96	89	90	91	89	74	89
.357 Mag.	Fed 125 gr JHP	125	1450	12.0	0.65	3.98	79.8	584	7.44	523	501	96	90	89	91	91	79	91
.357 Mag.	CCI 125 gr JHP	125	1450	15.5	0.56	3.82	59.9	584	7.78	153	143	93	88	88	91	91	78	90
.357 Mag.	Fed 110 gr JHP	110	1295	10.0	0.40	1.26	60.3	410	7.72	204	184	90	85	88	85	83	44	90
.357 Mag.	Rem 110 gr SJHP	110	1295	10.8	0.53	2.37	33.6	410	7.90	53	47	89	85	87	85	85	64	87
.357 Mag.	Win 125 gr JHP	125	1450	13.4	0.60	3.79	44.4	584	7.76	105	91	87	90	88	91	89	78	90
.357 Mag.	Win 145 gr Silvertip	145	1290	14.3	0.65	4.73	33.7	536	7.86	84	71	85	88	87	90	87	82	87
.357 Mag.	Rem 125 gr SJHP mv	125	1220	15.5	0.75	6.85	20.9	413	7.94	23	19	83	83	87	85	80	87	79
.357 Mag.	Rem 158 gr SJHP	158	1235	19.0	0.50	3.73	35.2	535	8.30	38	31	82	84	86	90	88	77	88
.357 Mag.	Fed 158 gr NYLHP	158	1235	16.5	0.62	4.98	25.1	535	8.42	42	34	81	86	85	90	83	83	83
.357 Mag.	CCI 140 gr JHP	140	1380	15.5	0.58	4.10	43.0	592	8.06	23	17	74	88	87	91	89	79	89
.40 S&W	Fed 155 gr JHP	155	1140	12.0	0.65	3.98	56.9	448	7.90	34	32	94	88	87	87	91	79	90
.40 S&W	C-B 150 gr JHP	150	1200	14.0	0.55	3.33	48.2	480	8.42	26	24	92	88	85	88	90	74	90
.40 S&W	Win 155 gr Silvertip	155	1205	13.5	0.70	5.20	46.8	500	7.86	22	20	91	89	87	89	90	84	90
.40 S&W	Fed 180 gr HS	180	950	15.0	0.75	6.63	39.2	361	8.32	38	34	89	83	86	82	89	87	89
.40 S&W	C-B 180 gr JHP +P	180	1050	15.0	0.75	6.63	39.2	441	8.66	22	19	86	86	84	86	89	87	89
.40 S&W	Win 180 gr R-SXT	180	990	13.0	0.72	5.29	29.1	392	8.86	35	28	80	86	83	84	86	84	86
10mm MV	Fed 180 gr JHP	180	980	15.0	0.68	5.45	33.3	384	8.46	27	22	81	84	85	83	87	84	87
10mm MV	Rem 180 gr JHP	180	1055	15.0	0.62	4.53	29.5	445	8.88	31	25	81	87	83	87	86	81	86
.45 ACP	Fed 230 gr HS	230	850	12.0	0.78	5.73	28.4	369	8.40	71	67	94	87	85	82	85	85	85
.45 ACP	C-B 185 gr JHP	185	1150	11.3	0.70	4.35	28.6	544	8.56	12	11	92	92	85	90	85	81	85
.45 ACP	Rem 185 gr JHP +P	185	1140	12.3	0.55	2.91	58.2	534	7.98	44	40	91	91	87	90	90	71	90
.45 ACP	CCI 200 gr JHP	200	975	9.4	0.81	4.84	24.8	422	8.92	111	98	88	90	83	85	83	83	83
.45 ACP	Fed 185 gr JHP	185	950	13.5	0.68	4.90	18.3	371	9.24	75	65	87	86	82	82	77	83	76
.45 ACP	Win 185 gr Silvertip	185	1000	12.0	0.79	5.88	30.2	411	8.82	73	60	82	89	84	85	86	85	86
.45 ACP	Win 230 gr R-SXT	230	900	13.0	0.78	6.21	25.4	414	9.14	36	29	81	88	82	85	84	86	83

CALIBER	LOAD	WT.	VEL	PENE. DEPTH	FINAL DIA.	CRUSH CAVITY	STRETCH CAVITY	MUZZLE ENERGY	AIT	TOTAL	OSS	OSS %	BEST FIT	GOAT FIT	ENERGY FIT	JELLO FIT	PERM J-FIT	TSC J-FIT
.380	C-B 90 gr JHP +P	90	1050	9.0	0.58	2.38	15.7	220	11.12	20	14	70	68	75	68	71	65	71
.380	Fed 90 gr JHP	90	1000	14.4	0.36	1.47	14.7	200	11.06	109	75	69	63	76	66	66	49	69
.380	Win 85 gr Silvertip	85	1000	6.5	0.63	2.03	10.6	189	12.88	82	50	61	63	70	64	61	59	59
.380	CCI 88 gr JHP	88	1000	17.0	0.36	1.73	9.1	196	13.40	57	33	58	61	69	65	55	54	54
.380	Fed 95gr FMJ	95	955	17.0	0.36	1.73	8.7	193	22.80	109	56	51	60	54	52	54	54	52
.38 Sp.	C-B 115 gr +P+	115	1250	15.4	0.58	4.07	26.8	399	8.98	29	24	83	82	83	84	84	79	84
.38 Sp.	Win 158 gr LHP +P	158	890	14.8	0.62	4.47	12.8	278	10.76	302	235	78	74	77	75	68	81	65
.38 Sp.	Fed 158 gr LHP +P	158	890	15.2	0.60	4.30	12.9	278	10.80	209	161	77	73	76	75	68	80	65
.38 Sp.	Fed 125 gr JHP +P	125	945	12.2	0.69	4.56	19.0	248	10.92	214	156	73	72	76	72	78	82	77
.38 Sp.	Rem 125 gr SJHP +P	125	945	11.7	0.64	3.76	15.8	248	11.74	106	77	73	72	74	72	73	77	72
.38 Sp.	Win 110 gr JHP +P+	110	1155	7.0	0.85	3.97	28.0	326	11.02	35	25	71	80	76	79	85	79	85
.38 Sp.	CCI 125 gr JHP +P	125	945	14.0	0.70	5.39	20.1	248	11.36	74	52	70	71	75	72	79	84	78
.38 Sp.	Rem 158 gr LHP +P	158	890	14.8	0.68	5.37	15.9	278	10.86	143	100	70	74	76	75	74	84	72
.38 Sp.	Win 110 gr Silvertip +P	110	995	8.6	0.67	3.03	19.4	242	11.66	111	77	69	72	74	71	77	72	77
.38 Sp.	Rem 95 gr SJHP +P	95	1175	10.5	0.45	1.67	19.2	291	11.38	119	78	66	77	75	76	73	53	77
.38 Sp.	Win 125 gr JHP +P	125	945	12.9	0.67	4.55	19.0	248	11.70	65	42	65	71	74	72	78	81	77
.38 Sp.	Fed 158gr RNL	158	755	28.0	0.36	2.85	10.0	200	33.68	456	231	51	45	46	53	61	70	57
9mm	C-B 115 gr JHP	115	1350	14.2	0.55	3.37	38.5	466	8.92	32	29	91	86	83	87	88	75	89
9mm	Fed 115 gr JHP +P+	115	1300	12.0	0.55	2.85	44.5	432	8.90	109	98	90	86	83	86	89	70	90
9mm	Win 115 gr JHP +P+	115	1305	7.9	0.79	3.87	37.3	435	8.98	98	88	90	86	83	86	88	78	88
9mm	Rem 115 gr JHP +P+	115	1310	12.2	0.61	3.57	37.2	439	8.98	57	51	89	86	83	86	88	76	88
9mm	Fed 124 gr HS +P+	124	1220	13.4	0.67	4.72	44.8	410	8.96	63	54	86	84	83	85	90	82	90
9mm	Fed 124 gr NYLHP	124	1120	11.5	0.60	3.25	30.5	346	9.28	239	200	84	81	82	81	86	74	86
9mm	Win 115 gr Silvertip	115	1225	8.0	0.72	3.26	16.7	383	9.36	304	252	83	84	81	83	74	74	73
9mm	Fed 115 gr JHP	115	1160	10.0	0.65	3.32	26.8	344	9.30	208	170	82	81	82	81	84	74	84
9mm	Rem 115 gr JHP	115	1155	14.5	0.62	4.38	18.7	341	9.36	167	136	81	79	81	80	77	81	76
9mm	Fed 124 gr HS	124	1120	13.4	0.60	3.79	36.1	346	9.28	106	86	81	80	82	81	88	78	88
9mm	CCI 115 gr JHP	115	1155	13.0	0.56	3.20	19.0	341	9.80	135	107	79	80	80	80	77	73	77
9mm	Fed 147 gr HS	147	1000	14.3	0.64	4.58	30.6	327	9.58	278	218	78	78	81	79	86	82	86
9mm	Fed 147 gr JHP (9MS-2)	147	975	18.0	0.55	4.28	38.9	310	9.84	27	21	78	74	80	78	89	80	89
9mm	Win 147 gr R-SXT	147	990	15.8	0.62	4.77	28.8	320	9.68	26	20	77	77	80	79	85	82	85
9mm	Fed 147 gr JHP (9MS-1)	147	975	15.9	0.57	4.06	19.6	310	9.84	25	19	76	76	80	78	78	79	78
9mm	Win 147 gr JHP	147	990	15.9	0.58	4.20	19.6	320	9.90	232	172	74	76	80	79	78	80	78
9mm	Horn 90 gr JHP	90	1360	9.0	0.68	3.27	23.5	370	9.62	25	16	64	83	81	82	82	74	82
9mm	Win 115gr FMJ	115	1155	24.5	0.36	2.49	10.6	341	14.40	256	161	63	67	67	63	62	66	59

NOTE: Jello Fit refers to the gelatin model using both crush and stretch cavity volumes. Perm J-Fit refers to the gelatin model using only crush cavity volume. TSC J-Fit refers to the gelatin model using only temporary stretch cavity volume.

A
Summary
of Results

CALIBER	LOAD	WT.	VEL.	PENE. DEPTH	FINAL DIA.	CRUSH CAVITY	STRETCH CAVITY	MUZZLE ENERGY	TOTAL	OSS	OSS %	BEST FIT
.22LR	CCI Stinger	32	1255	9.8	0.22	0.37	6.3	112	395	134	34	35
.22LR	Fed 38 gr LHP	38	975					80	612	184	30	
.22LR	Win 37 gr LHP	37	975	10.3	0.22	0.39	5.6	78	567	164	29	27
.22LR	Rem 36 gr LHP	36	975					76	879	237	27	
.22LR	Win 40 gr RNL	40	955	12.8	0.22	0.49	4.1	81	1469	308	21	27
.22 Mag.	Win 40 gr JHP	40	1330	13.0	0.32	1.05	13.7	157				42
.22 Mag.	CCI 30 gr +V	30	1450	9.2	0.34	0.84	8.9	140				40
.25 ACP	Win 45 gr XP	45	815	13.8	0.29	0.91	2.9	66	119	30	25	25
.25 ACP	Win 50 gr FMJ	50	760					64	2406	553	23	
.25 ACP	Rem 50 gr FMJ	50	710	18.0	0.25	0.88	2.1	56	1977	435	22	19
.25 ACP	Fed 50 gr FMJ	50	760					64	1864	410	22	
.25 ACP	MagSafe Defender	29	1400	9.0		0.87	11.1	126				41
.25 ACP	MagSafe Defender +P	22	1610	6.0		0.40	7.2	127				41
.25 ACP	Glaser 36 gr Safety Slug	36	1065	7.0		2.00	6.9	91				33
.25 ACP	CCI 45 gr PHP	45	785	12.0	0.25	0.59	5.0	62				25
.32 ACP	Win 60 gr Silvertip	60	970	6.5	0.57	1.66	8.0	125	83	52	63	47
.32 ACP	Win 71gr FMJ	71	905	18.5	0.32	1.49	6.8	129	123	62	50	42
.32 ACP	MagSafe 50 gr Defender	50	1250	7.8		2.40	15.7	174				57
.32 ACP	Glaser 50 gr Safety Slug	50	1065	5.0		2.10	10.7	126				46

CALIBER	LOAD	WT.	VEL.	PENE. DEPTH	FINAL DIA.	CRUSH CAVITY	STRETCH CAVITY	MUZZLE ENERGY	TOTAL	OSS	OSS %	BEST FIT
.32 Long	MagSafe 50 gr Defender	50	1350	8.2		1.00	21.9	202				62
.32 Long	Master 100 gr JHP	100	700	18.0	0.32	1.45	5.0	109				38
.32 Mag.	Master 100 gr JHP	100	965	17.0	0.40	2.14	28.0	207				58
.32 Mag.	Horn 85 gr XTP	85	1040	16.0	0.38	1.81	14.4	204				59
.32 Mag.	MagSafe 50 gr Defender	50	1480	9.5		1.00	24.3	243				67
.380	C-B 90 gr JHP +P	90	1050	9.0	0.58	2.38	15.7	220	20	14	70	68
.380	Fed 90 gr HS	90	1000	10.5	0.58	2.77	21.0	200	58	40	69	65
.380	Fed 90 gr JHP	90	1000	14.4	0.36	1.47	14.7	200	109	75	69	63
.380	Win 85 gr Silvertip	85	1000	6.5	0.63	2.03	10.6	189	82	50	61	63
.380	CCI 88 gr JHP	88	1000	17.0	0.36	1.73	9.1	196	57	33	58	61
.380	Rem 88 gr JHP (old ver)	88	990	12.8	0.41	1.69	10.5	192	51	29	57	63
.380	Horn 90 gr XTP HP	90	1000	11.8	0.44	1.79	10.3	200	26	14	54	65
.380	Fed 95gr FMJ	95	955	17.0	0.36	1.73	8.7	193	109	56	51	60
.380	MagSafe Maximum +P+	52	1720	11.0			27.9	342				81
.380	Glaser Blue	70	1350	5.0		2.80	15.0	283				75
.380	Glaser Silver	70	1295	6.5			28.8	261				73
.380	MagSafe Defender	60	1340	7.5			22.1	239				71
.380	MagSafe Fast Hardball	55	1500	17.5		1.80	14.7	275				71
.380	CCI 90 gr Gold Dot	90	1030	8.0	0.60	2.26	16.8	212				67
.380	Tri 90 gr JHP +P	90	1000	8.5	0.60	2.40	16.9	200				65
.380	Rem 102 gr Golden Saber	102	925	9.4	0.60	2.66	13.8	194				64
.380	Rem 88 gr JHP (new ver)	88	990	9.0	0.54	2.06	15.2	192				64
.380	Eld 95 gr StarFire	95	925	8.9	0.56	2.19	10.2	181				62
9mm	C-B 115 gr JHP	115	1350	14.2	0.55	3.37	38.5	466	32	29	91	86
9mm	Fed 115 gr JHP +P+	115	1300	12.0	0.55	2.85	44.5	432	109	98	90	86
9mm	Win 115 gr JHP +P+	115	1305	7.9	0.79	3.87	37.3	435	98	88	90	86
9mm	Rem 115 gr JHP +P+	115	1310	12.2	0.61	3.57	37.2	439	57	51	89	86
9mm	Fed 124 gr HS +P+	124	1220	13.4	0.67	4.72	44.8	410	63	54	86	84
9mm	Fed 124 gr NYLHP	124	1120	11.5	0.60	3.25	30.5	346	239	200	84	81
9mm	Win 115 gr Silvertip	115	1225	8.0	0.72	3.26	16.7	383	304	252	83	84
9mm	Fed 115 gr JHP	115	1160	10.0	0.65	3.32	26.8	344	208	170	82	81
9mm	Rem 115 gr JHP	115	1155	14.5	0.62	4.38	18.7	341	167	136	81	79
9mm	Fed 124 gr HS	124	1120	13.4	0.60	3.79	36.1	346	106	86	81	80
9mm	CCI 115 gr JHP	115	1155	13.0	0.56	3.20	19.0	341	135	107	79	80
9mm	Fed 147 gr HS	147	1000	14.3	0.64	4.58	30.6	327	278	218	78	78
9mm	Fed 147 gr JHP (9MS-2)	147	975	18.0	0.55	4.28	38.9	310	27	21	78	74
9mm	Win 147 gr R-SXT	147	990	15.8	0.62	4.77	28.8	320	26	20	77	77
9mm	Fed 147 gr JHP (9MS-1)	147	975	15.9	0.57	4.06	19.6	310	25	19	76	76
9mm	Win 147 gr JHP	147	990	15.9	0.58	4.20	19.6	320	232	172	74	76
9mm	Horn 90 gr JHP	90	1360	9.0	0.68	3.27	23.5	370	25	16	64	83
9mm	Win 115gr FMJ	115	1155	24.5	0.36	2.49	10.6	341	256	161	63	67
9mm	Rhino	98	1650	7.8			74.3	593				91

CALIBER	LOAD	WT.	VEL.	PENE. DEPTH	FINAL DIA.	CRUSH CAVITY	STRETCH CAVITY	MUZZLE ENERGY	TOTAL	OSS	OSS %	BEST FIT
9mm	MagSafe Stealth +P	64	1950	10.0			54.6	541				90
9mm	Glaser Blue	80	1650	6.0		3.90	52.1	484				88
9mm	B-H 115 gr JHP	115	1300	14.0	0.47	2.43	41.6	432				85
9mm	Rem 115 gr JHP +P	115	1250	12.1	0.62	3.65	33.2	399				84
9mm	Tri 124 gr XTP HP +P	124	1250	15.5	0.56	3.82	33.1	431				84
9mm	C-B 124 gr BJP +P	124	1250	15.5	0.57	3.96	44.4	431				84
9mm	C-B 125 gr XTP	125	1250	15.8	0.58	4.17	30.5	434				83
9mm	Rem 124 gr Golden Saber +P	124	1180	12.0	0.65	3.98	28.1	384				83
9mm	G-A 115 gr PHP +P	115	1275	15.5	0.55	3.68	36.4	415				83
9mm	G-A 124 gr PHP +P	124	1225	15.5	0.57	3.96	44.4	413				83
9mm	A-A 115 gr ADE-HP	115	1220	13.4	0.55	3.18	29.0	380				82
9mm	CCI 124 gr Gold Dot	124	1150	12.8	0.55	3.04	35.2	364				82
9mm	Eld 115 gr StarFire (NA)	115	1167	10.5	0.68	3.81	42.3	348				81
9mm	Rem 124 gr Golden Saber	124	1125	12.0	0.59	3.28	26.4	349				81
9mm	Eld 124 gr StarFire	124	1090	11.0	0.68	3.99	31.1	327				80
9mm	C-B 147 gr XTP	147	1100	18.0	0.54	4.12	35.6	395				80
9mm	CCI 115 gr Gold Dot	115	1200	17.0	0.48	3.08	22.4	368				79
9mm	MagSafe Fast Hardball	60	1920	22.0		1.80	58.5	491				79
9mm	Win 147 gr S-SXT	147	990	13.7	0.57	3.50	30.7	320				78
9mm	Rem 147 gr Golden Saber	147	990	14.5	0.62	4.38	31.8	320				77
9mm	CCI 147 gr Gold Dot	147	985	14.5	0.58	3.83	33.2	317				77
9mm	Rem 124 gr JHP	124	1070	14.8	0.52	3.14	20.7	315				77
9mm	C-B 147 gr BHP +P	147	1000	16.4	0.52	3.48	43.9	327				77
.38 Sp.	C-B 115 gr +P+	115	1250	15.4	0.58	4.07	26.8	399	29	24	83	82
.38 Sp.	Win 158 gr LHP +P	158	890	14.8	0.62	4.47	12.8	278	302	235	78	74
.38 Sp.	Fed 158 gr LHP +P	158	890	15.2	0.60	4.30	12.9	278	209	161	77	73
.38 Sp.	Fed 125 gr JHP +P	125	945	12.2	0.69	4.56	19.0	248	214	156	73	72
.38 Sp.	Rem 125 gr SJHP +P	125	945	11.7	0.64	3.76	15.8	248	106	77	73	72
.38 Sp.	Win 110 gr JHP +P+	110	1155	7.0	0.85	3.97	28.0	326	35	25	71	80
.38 Sp.	CCI 125 gr JHP +P	125	945	14.0	0.70	5.39	20.1	248	74	52	70	71
.38 Sp.	Rem 158 gr LHP +P	158	890	14.8	0.68	5.37	15.9	278	143	100	70	74
.38 Sp.	Win 110 gr Silvertip +P	110	995	8.6	0.67	3.03	19.4	242	111	77	69	72
.38 Sp.	Rem 95 gr SJHP +P	95	1175	10.5	0.45	1.67	19.2	291	119	78	66	77
.38 Sp.	Win 125 gr JHP +P	125	945	12.9	0.67	4.55	19.0	248	65	42	65	71
.38 Sp.	Fed 158gr SWC	158	755	23.5	0.36	2.39	8.0	200	278	144	52	53
.38 Sp.	Fed 158gr RNL	158	755	28.0	0.36	2.85	10.0	200	456	231	51	45
.38 Sp.	MagSafe Maximum	65	1800	11.0			29.1	468				87
.38 Sp.	Glaser Blue +P	80	1500	7.0		4.50	24.8	400				85
.38 Sp.	MagSafe Fast Hardball +P	49	1820	15.0		1.50	24.1	361				80
.38 Sp.	Glaser Blue	80	1350	6.0		3.90	14.2	324				80
.38 Sp.	Tri 110 gr JHP +P+	110	1230	17.0	0.43	2.47	15.0	370				79
.38 Sp.	Rem 125 gr Golden Saber	125	975	12.4	0.59	3.39	19.8	264				73
.38 Sp.	Tri 158 gr JHP +P+	158	925	18.0	0.60	5.09	27.4	300				73
.38 Sp.	Eld 125 gr StarFire	125	950	9.3	0.61	2.70	15.4	251				73

CALIBER	LOAD	WT.	VEL.	PENE. DEPTH	FINAL DIA.	CRUSH CAVITY	STRETCH CAVITY	MUZZLE ENERGY	TOTAL	OSS	OSS %	BEST FIT
.357 Mag.	Rem 125 gr JHP	125	1450	14.0	0.55	3.33	40.2	584	204	196	96	89
.357 Mag.	Fed 125 gr JHP	125	1450	12.0	0.65	3.98	79.8	584	523	501	96	90
.357 Mag.	CCI 125 gr JHP	125	1450	15.5	0.56	3.82	59.9	584	153	143	93	88
.357 Mag.	Fed 110 gr JHP	110	1295	10.0	0.40	1.26	60.3	410	204	184	90	85
.357 Mag.	Rem 110 gr SJHP	110	1295	10.8	0.53	2.37	33.6	410	53	47	89	85
.357 Mag.	Win 125 gr JHP	125	1450	13.4	0.60	3.79	44.4	584	105	91	87	90
.357 Mag.	Win 145 gr Silvertip	145	1290	14.3	0.65	4.73	33.7	536	84	71	85	88
.357 Mag.	Rem 125 gr SJHP mv	125	1220	15.5	0.75	6.85	20.9	413	23	19	83	83
.357 Mag.	Rem 158 gr SJHP	158	1235	19.0	0.50	3.73	35.2	535	38	31	82	84
.357 Mag.	Fed 158 gr NYLHP	158	1235	16.5	0.62	4.98	25.1	535	42	34	81	86
.357 Mag.	CCI 140 gr JHP	140	1380	15.5	0.58	4.10	43.0	592	23	17	74	88
.357 Mag.	Win 158 gr SWC	158	1255	26.9	0.36	2.74	12.8	553	98	71	72	72
.357 Mag.	Rem 158gr SWC	158	1235	27.5	0.36	2.80	12.9	535	71	48	68	70
.357 Mag.	Glaser Blue	80	1700	6.0		3.90	48.1	514				89
.357 Mag.	Eld 150 gr StarFire	150	1205	12.0	0.68	4.36	57.7	484				88
.357 Mag.	Rem MV 110 gr SJHP	110	1295	9.3	0.53	2.05	25.9	410				85
.357 Mag.	MagSafe Fast Hardball	49	1960	5.0		0.50	31.9	418				85
.357 Mag.	C-B 125 gr XTP	125	1450	19.0	0.54	4.35	26.8	584				85
.357 Mag.	Rem 125 gr Golden Saber	125	1220	13.0	0.60	3.68	30.4	413				84
.40 S&W	C-B 135 gr JHP Nosler	135	1300	9.8	0.56	2.41	69.1	507	24	23	96	90
.40 S&W	Fed 155 gr JHP	155	1140	12.0	0.65	3.98	56.9	448	34	32	94	88
.40 S&W	Rem 165 gr Golden Saber	165	1150	12.0	0.68	4.36	41.1	485	16	15	94	89
.40 S&W	Fed 155 gr HS	155	1140	13.3	0.68	4.83	47.9	448	14	13	93	88
.40 S&W	C-B 150 gr JHP	150	1200	14.0	0.55	3.33	48.2	480	26	24	92	88
.40 S&W	Win 155 gr Silvertip	155	1205	13.5	0.70	5.20	46.8	500	22	20	91	89
.40 S&W	Fed 180 gr HS	180	950	15.0	0.75	6.63	39.2	361	38	34	89	83
.40 S&W	C-B 180 gr JHP +P	180	1050	15.0	0.75	6.63	39.2	441	22	19	86	86
.40 S&W	B-H 180 gr XTP	180	950	16.4	0.64	5.28	26.2	361	46	39	85	82
.40 S&W	Eld 180 gr StarFire	180	985	12.0	0.75	5.30	42.4	388	18	15	83	86
.40 S&W	Win 180 gr JHP	180	1010	14.6	0.64	4.70	31.1	408	21	17	81	85
.40 S&W	Win 180 gr R-SXT	180	990	13.0	0.72	5.29	29.1	392	35	28	80	86
.40 S&W	Win 180 gr FMJ	180	950	25.0	0.40	3.14	14.6	361	17	12	71	70
.40 S&W	Glaser Blue	105	1500	6.0		5.00	55.5	525				91
.40 S&W	C-B 135 gr JHP Sierra	135	1300	10.4	0.59	2.84	59.0	507				90
.40 S&W	MagSafe Fast Hardball	67	1870	12.5		2.30	42.9	521				90
.40 S&W	G-A 155 gr PHP +P	155	1200	12.0	0.80	6.03	52.3	496				90
.40 S&W	CCI 155 gr Gold Dot	155	1186	12.3	0.70	4.73	20.2	484				89
.40 S&W	Eld 155 gr StarFire	155	1160	10.8	0.75	4.77	37.7	463				89
.40 S&W	Horn 155 gr XTP	155	1180	14.0	0.68	5.08	44.6	480				88
.40 S&W	C-B 155 gr XTP	155	1175	14.0	0.68	5.08	44.6	475				88
.40 S&W	C-B 165 gr JHP	165	1125	13.8	0.66	4.72	50.5	464				88
.40 S&W	P-L 150 gr JHP	150	1190	14.5	0.53	3.20	48.4	472				88
.40 S&W	G-A 180 gr PHP +P	180	1050	13.0	0.70	5.00	32.8	441				88
.40 S&W	Tri 165 JHP	165	1125	14.7	0.55	3.49	34.5	464				87

CALIBER	LOAD	WT.	VEL.	PENE. DEPTH	FINAL DIA.	CRUSH CAVITY	STRETCH CAVITY	MUZZLE ENERGY	TOTAL	OSS	OSS %	BEST FIT
.40 S&W	Rem 180 gr Golden Saber	180	1015	12.9	0.83	6.98	27.9	412				87
.40 S&W	Win 180 gr S-SXT	180	990	12.0	0.68	4.36	34.4	392				86
.40 S&W	Rem 155 gr JHP	155	1140	16.5	0.61	4.82	41.2	448				85
.40 S&W	P-L 180 gr JHP Hi-Perf	180	1070	17.0	0.64	5.47	32.6	458				85
.40 S&W	Master 150 gr JHP	150	1100	14.5	0.73	6.07	47.6	403				85
.40 S&W	CCI 180 gr Gold Dot	180	958	11.6	0.68	4.21	18.3	367				85
.40 S&W	A-A 180 gr ADE-HP	180	990	15.5	0.67	5.46	31.6	392				84
.40 S&W	Horn 180 gr XTP	180	950	16.4	0.64	5.28	26.2	361				82
.40 S&W	Fed 165 gr HS	165	950	13.8	0.61	4.03	18.3	331				82
.40 S&W	P-L 180 gr JHP	180	950	16.5	0.60	4.67	29.1	361				82
.40 S&W	Fed 180 gr JHP	180	950	17.0	0.64	5.47	32.6	361				81
.40 S&W	Rem 180 gr JHP	180	950	18.0	0.61	5.26	32.2	361				80
.40 S&W	Master 180 gr PHP	180	950	18.5	0.68	6.72	24.8	361				80
.40 S&W	Win 155 gr FMJ	155	1125	22.0	0.40	2.76	12.8	436				79
.40 S&W	Fed 180 gr SWC	180	950	22.0	0.40	2.76	14.5	361				75
.40 S&W	Master 170 gr SWC	170	925	22.0	0.40	2.76	14.5	323				73
.40 S&W	CCI 180 TMJ	180	950	25.0	0.40	3.14	14.6	361				70
.40 S&W	B-P 180 gr FMJ-FP	180	950	25.0	0.40	3.14	14.6	361				70
10mm MV	Win 180 gr JHP	180	1055	15.5	0.66	5.30	32.0	445	44	36	82	86
10mm MV	Fed 180 gr JHP	180	980	15.0	0.68	5.45	33.3	384	27	22	81	84
10mm MV	Rem 180 gr JHP	180	1055	15.0	0.62	4.53	29.5	445	31	25	81	87
10mm MV	Win 200 gr R-SXT	200	990	14.3	0.68	5.19	29.3	436				87
10mm MV	Fed 180 gr HS	180	1030	13.8	0.67	4.87	33.6	424				87
10mm MV	Eld 180 gr StarFire	180	950	12.0	0.68	4.36	57.7	361				84
10mm	C-B 150 gr JHP	150	1300					563	10	9	90	
10mm	Glaser Blue	105	1650	6.0		5.00	66.6	635				92
10mm	Win 175 gr Silvertip	175	1290	12.5	0.81	6.44	40.1	647				92
10mm	Master 150 gr JHP	150	1334	12.0	0.68	4.36	29.5	593				91
10mm	Tri 135 gr JHP	135	1400	11.9	0.56	2.93	63.1	588				91
10mm	MagSafe Defender	96	1780	14.0			88.3	676				91
10mm	Rem 170 gr JHP	170	1262	16.8	0.65	5.56	31.5	602				88
10mm	FFV Norma 200 gr FMJ	200	1181	29.3	0.40	3.68	15.6	620				69
.41 Mag.	Win 175 gr Silvertip	175	1250	14.0	0.64	4.50	83.2	608	53	47	89	91
.41 Mag.	Win 210 gr JHP	210	1300	17.5	0.73	7.32	95.2	789	34	28	82	89
.41 Mag.	Rem 210 gr JSP	210	1300	19.0	0.59	5.19	71.2	789	31	25	81	88
.41 Mag.	Win 210gr SWC	210	965	23.0	0.41	3.04	11.3	435	57	43	75	77
.41 Mag.	Rem 210 gr SWC	210	965					435	43	32	74	
.44 Sp.	Win 200 gr Silvertip	200	810	10.4	0.61	3.04	10.7	292	60	45	75	82
.44 Sp.	Fed 200 gr LHP	200	810	19.0	0.48	3.44	11.1	292	49	36	73	76
.44 Sp.	Win 246gr RNL	246	755	18.0	0.43	2.61	16.1	312	71	46	65	79
.44 Sp.	Rem 200 gr SWC	200	1035	21.5	0.43	3.12	10.2	476	17	11	65	81
.44 Sp.	MagSafe Defender	92	1620	9.5			39.2	536				92

SUMMARY OF RESULTS

CALIBER	LOAD	WT.	VEL.	PENE. DEPTH	FINAL DIA.	CRUSH CAVITY	STRETCH CAVITY	MUZZLE ENERGY	TOTAL	OSS	OSS %	BEST FIT
.44 Sp.	MagSafe Urban Defender	115	1300	9.0			23.3	432				89
.44 Sp.	C-B 180 gr XTP	180	1000	14.2	0.60	4.01	32.1	400				86
.44 Sp.	CCI 200 gr Gold Dot	200	875	12.5	0.64	4.02	14.0	340				84
.44 Mag	Win 210 gr Silvertip	210	1250	15.1	0.66	5.17	78.2	729	50	45	90	91
.44 Mag	Fed 180 gr JHP	180	1610	15.5	0.77	7.22	104.9	1037	37	33	89	91
.44 Mag	Rem 240 gr SJHP	240	1180	17.0	0.70	6.54	122.4	743	34	30	88	90
.44 Mag	Win 240 gr JHP	240	1180					743	43	36	84	
.44 Mag	Fed 240 gr JHP	240	1180					743	35	28	80	
.44 Mag	Rem 240 gr SWC MV	240	850					385	55	42	76	
.44 Mag	MagSafe Urban Defender	115	1620	11.0			86.7	671				93
.44 Mag	Eld 240 gr StarFire	240	1180	14.8	0.84	8.20	75.3	743				91
.44 Mag	CCI 200 gr JHP	200	1200	16.0	0.75	7.07	71.4	640				90
.44 Mag	C-B 180 gr XTP	180	1200	15.3	0.70	5.89	66.2	576				90
.44 Mag	Fed 240 gr HS	240	1180	20.4	0.55	4.85	100.1	743				86
.44 Mag	CCI 240 gr SWC MV	240	850	29.0	0.43	4.20	23.8	385				65
.45 ACP	Fed 230 gr HS	230	850	12.0	0.78	5.73	28.4	369	71	67	94	87
.45 ACP	Rem 230 gr Golden Saber	230	875	14.3	0.75	6.32	25.4	391	14	13	93	87
.45 ACP	C-B 185 gr JHP	185	1150	11.3	0.70	4.35	28.6	544	12	11	92	92
.45 ACP	Rem 185 gr JHP +P	185	1140	12.3	0.55	2.91	58.2	534	44	40	91	91
.45 ACP	CCI 200 gr JHP	200	975	9.4	0.81	4.84	24.8	422	111	98	88	90
.45 ACP	Fed 185 gr JHP	185	950	13.5	0.68	4.90	18.3	371	75	65	87	86
.45 ACP	Win 185 gr Silvertip	185	1000	12.0	0.79	5.88	30.2	411	73	60	82	89
.45 ACP	Rem 185 gr JHP	185	1000	23.0	0.50	4.52	14.7	411	114	92	81	78
.45 ACP	Win 230 gr R-SXT	230	900	13.0	0.78	6.21	25.4	414	36	29	81	88
.45 ACP	R-P 230gr FMJ	230	835	27.0	0.45	4.29	9.0	356	122	79	65	69
.45 ACP	Fed 230gr FMJ	230	835	27.0	0.45	4.29	9.0	356	168	106	63	69
.45 ACP	Win 230gr FMJ	230	835	27.0	0.45	4.29	9.0	356	179	112	63	69
.45 ACP	Rhino	125	1560	7.5			78.1	676				93
.45 ACP	MagSafe Maximum	103	1900	12.0			104.5	826				93
.45 ACP	MagSafe Swat	66	2140	6.0			73.5	672				93
.45 ACP	Glaser Blue	140	1400	7.5		6.80	42.1	610				93
.45 ACP	MagSafe Defender	96	1660	10.0			75.7	588				93
.45 ACP	Tri 185 gr JHP +P	185	1150	10.2	0.80	5.13	32.5	544				92
.45 ACP	MagSafe Fast Hardball	72	2120	14.5		2.30	57.5	719				92
.45 ACP	Fed 185 gr HS +P	185	1140	12.9	0.69	4.82	31.5	534				91
.45 ACP	C-B 230gr JHP +P	230	950	12.3	0.77	5.73	26.4	461				90
.45 ACP	G-A 185 gr PHP +P	185	1075	13.0	0.70	5.00	32.8	475				90
.45 ACP	CCI 185 gr Gold Dot	185	1050	12.0	0.60	3.39	16.8	453				90
.45 ACP	CCI 185 gr Gold Dot	185	1050	12.0	0.60	3.39	16.8	453				90
.45 ACP	A-A 185 gr ADE HP	185	1000	9.6	0.82	5.07	25.5	411				89
.45 ACP	C-B 230 gr BHP +P	230	950	14.0	0.70	5.39	37.6	461				89
.45 ACP	Rem 185 gr Golden Saber	185	1015	13.0	0.70	5.00	24.6	423				89
.45 ACP	Horn 230 gr JHP+P	230	950	15.0	0.68	5.45	31.8	461				89

CALIBER	LOAD	WT.	VEL.	PENE. DEPTH	FINAL DIA.	CRUSH CAVITY	STRETCH CAVITY	MUZZLE ENERGY	TOTAL	OSS	OSS %	BEST FIT
.45 ACP	Horn 200 gr JHP+P	200	1050	16.5	0.63	5.14	46.8	490				88
.45 ACP	C-B 200 gr JHP	200	1050	16.7	0.64	5.37	27.7	490				88
.45 ACP	Win 230 gr SubSonic	230	925	15.5	0.66	5.30	23.6	437				88
.45 ACP	Eld 230 gr StarFire	230	850	13.8	0.68	5.01	23.2	369				86
.45 ACP	Win 230 gr S-SXT	230	860	14.8	0.68	5.37	20.1	378				86
.45 ACP	CCI 230 gr Gold Dot	230	830	13.5	0.70	5.20	14.4	352				86
.45 ACP	IMI-UZI 185 gr FMJ	185	1046	24.5	0.45	3.90	14.1	450				77
.45 Colt	Fed 225 gr LHP	225	900	19.5	0.66	6.67	21.3	405	69	54	78	83
.45 Colt	Win 225 gr Silvertip	225	920	13.5	0.70	5.20	23.3	423	53	39	74	88
.45 Colt	Win 255 gr RNL	255	860	28.5	0.45	4.53	22.1	419	59	41	69	68
.45 Colt	Rem 250 gr RNL	250	860	25.5	0.45	4.06	22.1	411	19	12	63	74
.45 Colt	CCI 200 gr JHP	200	850	10.7	0.75	4.73	24.7	321				85
.45 Colt	Handload 255 gr SWC	255	825	25.5	0.45	4.06	14.2	386				73

LEGEND FOR APPENDIX 1

C-B	Cor-Bon	Horn	Hornady	P-L	Pro-Load
Fed	Federal	Tri	Triton	B-P	Barber Power
Win	Winchester	Eld	Eldorado	A-A	American Ammo
Rem	Remington	B-H	Black Hills		

STOPPING POWER DECREASES AS PENETRATION INCREASES
EXAMPLE: .40 S&W 180-GR. JHP @ 950 FPS

PENETRATION DEPTH, INCHES	FULLER INDEX ONE-SHOT STOP, PERCENT
8.4	85.1
9.4	85.0
10.4	84.9
11.4	84.6
12.4	84.3
13.4	83.8
14.4	83.2
15.4	82.5
16.4	81.7
17.4	80.8
18.4	79.8
19.4	78.7
20.4	77.4
21.4	76.1
22.4	74.6

SUMMARY OF RESULTS

STOPPING POWER INCREASES AS BULLET DIAMETER INCREASES
EXAMPLE: 12.4 INCHES OF PENETRATION WITH CONSTANT 400 FT-LBS. OF ENERGY

INITIAL BULLET DIAMETER INCH	FULLER INDEX ONE-SHOT STOP, PERCENT
.355	83.9
.400	86.2
.429	87.4
.451	88.2

STOPPING POWER INCREASES AS MUZZLE ENERGY INCREASES
EXAMPLE: .40 S&W 165-GR. BULLET PENETRATING 12.4 INCHES

MUZZLE VELOCITY FPS	MUZZLE ENERGY FT-LBS.	FULLER INDEX ONE-SHOT STOP, PERCENT
950	330	82.3
990	360	84.2
1,030	390	85.8
1,075	420	87.1
1,110	450	88.2
1,145	480	89.1
1,180	510	89.8

B

Autopsy from Triple Gunshot Victim

OFFICE OF THE MEDICAL EXAMINER

| REPORT OF AUTOPSY |
| Toxicology Findings |

Case#   *Name:*   *Age:*   30 yrs

Date of Death: Mar 5, 1994   *Date/Time of Autopsy:*   Mar 6, 1994   08:00 hrs.

Prosector: Assistant Medical Examiner

Drug Screen Results:

Hospital **Blood** Drug Screen {GC-ABN} was NEGATIVE.

Hospital **Blood** Drug Screen {GC-Volatiles} was NEGATIVE.

Hospital **Blood** Drug Screen {RIA-Amph, Methamph} was NEGATIVE.

Urine **Drug** Screen {RIA-Op,Bz,Be} was NEGATIVE.

Drug **Quantitation** Results:

Medical Examiner. The hands are diffusely smeared with dried blood. Gunpowder residue is not identified visually. The hands are tested for the presence of gunpowder residue.

Three gunshot wounds are present. For purposes of description in this report a number will be assigned to each gunshot wound. These number designations are not intended to indicate the sequence in which the injuries were inflicted.

The left pleural cavity contains approximately 1000 ml of fluid and clotted blood.

GUNSHOT WOUND #1: Gunshot Wound #1 is a penetrating gunshot wound of the left chest.

The gunshot wound of entrance, of the distance/indeterminate range type, is located on the anterior surface of the left chest, immediately below the left clavicle. It is centered 32.5 cm inferior to the vertex and 12.5 cm to the left of the midline. It is 15.5 cm directly above the left nipple. The entrance wound consists of an oval cutaneous defect, 1.2 cm wide and 0.9 cm high. The long axis is horizontal. The margins of the entrance wound are surrounded by a symmetric rim of dried abrasion, 0.2 cm wide. There is no visible gunpowder tattooing or soot deposition around the entrance wound. The soft tissues deep to the entrance wound are bright red and have no visible soot deposition.

The injury tract passes through the skin and pectoral muscles of the left chest. The subclavian vein is transected. The injury tract passes through the 1st rib and causes multiple comminuted fractures of the rib. The tract passes through the apex of the left upper lobe of the lung, entering anteriorly and exiting posteriorly.

The injury tract exits the back of the thorax, passing through the neck of the 5th rib posteriorly.

Recovered from the paraspinus muscles of the left back is a partially jacketed projectile and one detached fragment of dark gray metal. The copper jacket has a 1 cm in diameter circular base. The lead core is mushroomed, and shows remnants of a "Hydrashock" central post. The loose fragment of gray metal is an irregularly shaped, flat sheet, approximately 0.5 cm in greatest dimension.

The location of the projectile in the paraspinus muscles is immediately above the exit wound of Gunshot Wound #2 (see below).

The entire injury tract is hemorrhagic.

In **summary**, the trajectory of Gunshot Wound #1 is front to back, left to right, and **down**ward.

GUNSHOT WOUND #2: Gunshot Wound #2 is a perforating gunshot wound of the **left** chest.

The gunshot wound of entrance, of the distant/indeterminate range type, is located on **the** anterior surface of the left chest, centered 40 cm inferior to the vertex and 13 cm to **the** left of the midline. It is 1 cm lateral to and 8.5 cm above the left nipple. The **entrance** wound consists of an oval cutaneous defect, 1.2 cm wide and 1 cm high. The **long** axis is horizontal. The margins of the entrance wound are surrounded by a **symmetric** rim of dried abrasion, 0.2 cm wide. There is no visible soot deposition or **gunpowder** tattooing around the entrance wound. The soft tissues deep to the entrance **wound** are bright red, and have no visible gunpowder deposition.

The injury tract passes through the skin and pectoral muscles, and enters the thorax **through** the muscles of the 2nd intercostal space. The injury trace grazes the upper **margin** of the 3rd rib. The injury tract passes through the lower segment of the left **upper** lobe of the lung, and the upper segment of the left lower lobe of the lung.

The injury tract exits the back of the thorax by passing through the neck of the 6th rib, **posteriorly.**

The gunshot exit wound is located on the left back, centered 40 cm inferior to the **vertex,** and 7 cm to the left of the midline. The exit wound consists of an inverted Y-**shaped** cutaneous slit, 1 X 0.4 X 0.4 cm. The margins of the skin can be opposed and **there is** no net loss of tissue.

The entire injury tract is hemorrhagic.

In summary, the trajectory of Gunshot Wound #2 is front to back, horizontal, and left **to** right.

GUNSHOT WOUND #3: Gunshot Wound #3 is a perforating gunshot wound of the **right** hand, with a terminal impact injury located on the left chest.

The gunshot wound of entrance, of the distance/indeterminate range type, is located on **the** dorsal surface of the right hand, overlying the interspace between the 4th and 5th **metacarpals.** It is immediately proximal to the digital web. The entrance wound consists **of an** oval cutaneous defect, 1.2 cm long (proximal to distal) and 0.9 cm wide. The **entrance** wound is surrounded by a symmetric rim of abrasion, 0.2 cm wide.

The injury tract passes through the 5th metacarpal, the hypothenar muscles, and the flexor surface of the wrist. The 5th metacarpal is fractured.

The gunshot wound of exit is located on the flexor surface of the right wrist, 3 cm proximal to the flexor crease. The exit wound consists of an irregularly linear slit, approximately 2.5 cm long.

The injury tract can be probed, and multiple radiodense projectile fragments are located along the injury tract. The projectile fragments consist of one leaf of a copper jacket and multiple, irregularly shaped pieces of dark gray material consistent with lead core.

The injury tract through the hand is hemorrhagic.

When the right arm is flexed, the gunshot exit wound on the wrist overlies an "impact injury" on the anterior surface of the left chest. This impact injury is located 47.5 cm inferior to the vertex, and 6 cm to the left of the midline. It is in the nipple line, 5 cm medial to the left nipple. The injury consists of an approximately circular, superficial cutaneous laceration, 0.7 cm in diameter, that is surrounded by an irregularly oval rim of abrasion, maximally 1 cm wide at the 2:00 margin and 0.3 cm wide at the 7:00 margin.

Internal examination of the pectoral tissues underneath this impact injury reveals no subcutaneous or intramuscular hemorrhage. The cutaneous laceration leads to a short subcutaneous tract which terminates in the fat and does not penetrate into the pectoral muscles. No radiodense foreign materials are identified in association with this injury.

In summary, the trajectory of the gunshot wound through the hand, when the hand is in anatomic position, is distal to proximal, and posterior to anterior.

INTERNAL EXAMINATION

Injuries have been described.

There is no accumulation of fluid in the right pleural cavity. The pleural surfaces are smooth and glistening. The thoracic viscera have their normal anatomic locations and relationships.

The pericardial sac has been incised and is empty. The pericardial surfaces are smooth and glistening. The great vessels and chambers of the heart appear to have their normal anatomic configuration and relationships.

There is no accumulation of fluid within the peritoneal cavity. The peritoneal surfaces are smooth and glistening. The abdominal viscera have their normal shapes, locations, and relationships.

After removal of the organs from the body, inspection of the cavities reveals no evidence of fractures of the sternum, clavicles, vertebral column, or pelvic bones. The subcutaneous fat on the anterior abdominal wall is 1.2 cm thick.

GROSS EXAMINATION OF THE ORGANS:

ORGANS OF THE NECK: The tongue is atraumatic. There is no hemorrhage present in the soft tissues of the neck. The thyroid gland is symmetrical and on cut section is composed of firm, homogeneous, red-tan tissue. The hyoid bone and laryngeal cartilages are not fractured. No obstruction of the upper respiratory tract is found. The mucosa of the hypopharynx, larynx, and trachea is intact and appears normal. Cervical lymph nodes are not greatly enlarged. No fractures and/or dislocations of the cervical vertebrae are detected.

THYMUS: The thymus is involuted and replaced by adipose tissue.

HEART: The weight of the heart is 370 gm. The organ has its normal anatomic shape. The epicardium is smooth and glistening. The coronary arteries have normal origins and anatomic distributions. On multiple cross sections, no significant atherosclerotic plaques are identified. The posterior circulation is balanced from the right and left. No significant abnormalities are found in the valve leaflets, chordae, or mural endocardium. There are no interatrial or interventricular septal defects. The myocardium is red-brown and firm. There is no gross evidence of recent or remote myocardial infarct.

AORTA: The aorta and its main branches show no significant atherosclerosis.

LUNGS: The weight of the right lung is 320 gm, and the weight of the left lung is 290 gm. The lungs have their normal anatomic shape and lobation. The pleura is smooth, glistening, and minimally anthracotic. On cut section, the parenchyma is atelectatic. No obstruction of the tracheobronchial tree is found. No thrombi and/or emboli are found within the pulmonary vessels. The hilar lymph nodes are not unusual.

LIVER: The weight of the liver is 1400 gm. The organ has its normal anatomic shape. The capsular surface is smooth and glistening. On cut section, the parenchyma is red-brown and has a lobular architecture. There is no increase in consistency. No traumatic lesions are found.

GALLBLADDER AND BILE DUCTS: The gallbladder contains approximately 20 cc of green viscid bile. The mucosa is grossly normal. No stones are present. The bile ducts are not obstructed.

SPLEEN AND LYMPH NODES: The weight of the spleen is 120 gm. The organ has its normal anatomic shape. On cut section, it is composed of red-purple parenchyma. Lymph nodes are composed of firm tan tissue. The sizes are unremarkable.

PANCREAS: The organ has its normal anatomic shape. On cut section it is composed of tan lobular parenchyma.

ALIMENTARY TRACT: No mucosal or mural lesions are found in the alimentary tract. The stomach is empty. Brown fecal material is present in the colon. The appendix is present.

ADRENAL GLANDS: The adrenal glands are approximately equal in size. On cut section, the cortices are bright yellow, and the medullae are gray.

URINARY TRACT: The weight of the right kidney is 140 gm and the weight of the left kidney is 140 gm. They have their normal anatomic shapes. The capsules strip with ease, and the underlying cortical surfaces are smooth. On cut section of each, the cortex and medulla appear normal. No abnormalities are found in the calyces, pelves, and ureters. The urinary bladder is unremarkable and contains approximately 300 ml of pale yellow urine.

GENITAL TRACT: The prostate is not enlarged. No nodules are present.

CENTRAL NERVOUS SYSTEM: There is no hemorrhage within the scalp or galea. There is no epidural, subdural, or subarachnoid hemorrhage. The weight of the unfixed brain is 1520 gm. The cerebral and cerebellar hemispheres are symmetrical. The leptomeninges are clear and glistening. The cerebral vasculature has a normal anatomic distribution. No atherosclerosis is present within the arteries. Venous vessels and sinuses contain only postmortem clot. On multiple coronal sections, no internal hemorrhage or other abnormality is found within the brain or brainstem. The cerebrospinal fluid is clear. No skull fractures are present.

MICROSCOPIC DESCRIPTION

Representative portions of the organs are preserved. No tissues are submitted for microscopic examination.

Autopsy from Headshot Victim

HISTORY:
This 38-year-old white male was found dead at his residence at approximately 12:30 a.m. Saturday April 24, 1993. For further details please consult the ▮▮▮▮▮ State Police scene report and that of the medical examiner's investigator.

PERSONAL EFFECTS: The decedents clothing includes a white T shirt with an auto racing design which has been previously cut up the middle. The shirt is a Winston Nascar Series T Shirt from the Michigan International Speedway with various racing cars on the front and back. The shirt has abundant dried, partially dried, and liquid bright red to reddish-purple material. There are brown corduroy pants and green underwear. White cotton socks are also present. On the left wrist there is a Timex alarm chronograph digital wrist watch, and a plain yellow metal band on the left ring finger. In the pants left front pocket is a small pocket knife with a brown and yellow shell-like pattern on the sides, and one penny. The right front pants pocket has $400.00 (four hundred dollars) in paper money. There are 5 $20.00 bills in one group, and 12 $20.00 bills, 5 $10.00 bills, and 2 $5.00 bills in another group, each group folded in half. The count is verified by Mr. ▮▮▮▮▮ and the State Police personnel.

EXTERNAL DESCRIPTION:
The body is that of a well-developed, well-nourished white male appearing approximately the stated age of 38. The scalp hair is brown and of moderate length with a few gray hairs around the temples. In the left occipital region of the scalp 1 cm above and 5 cm behind the top of the left ear is a single somewhat irregular defect approximately 3/16th of an inch in diameter. There is blackening of the immediate edge of the defect. On inspection no additional defects or foreign material are evident in the surrounding skin. When the hair is shaved from this region the only abnormality of the skin is the previously noted narrow black rim at the edge of the defect. This is approximately 1 to perhaps focally 2 mm in width. Reddish-purple fluid exudes from the defect with small fragments of soft grayish tissue. The eyebrows are brown. There is dried reddish material and brownish material over both eyelids. The irides are blue. The pupils are equal and 4 mm in diameter. There is bright reddish-purple mucoid material exuding from both nostrils. There is a short mustache and a short growth of dark brownish beard around the chin and cheeks. There is semi-solid material coating most of the right side of the lips. There is grayish particulate material and brownish liquid. The ears are not unusual. There is moderate post mortem lividity in the dependent portions. The neck is not unusual. There is a piece of adhesive tape over the left lower neck region, apparently overlying a recent needle puncture-type wound. The anterior chest

has ovoid linear reddish focally abraded markings over the mid-sternum consistent with the marks of a defibrillator paddle. Similar markings are seen in the left lateral lower chest in the anterior to mid-axillary line region. The abdomen is slightly distended and firm. The inguinal regions are not unusual. There are a few small lymph nodes palpable. The external genitalia are those of a circumcised adult male with both testes present in the scrotum. There are no major scars or other markings on the legs. The feet are not unusual. The right arm had dried reddish material over much of its lateral aspect, and moderate post mortem lividity. The dorsum of the hand has a few small linear abrasions. There is a transverse, recent, healing laceration or incised wound on the flexor surface of the wrist. This is diagonally oriented, and 1.6 cm in length. At its mid point it is 1 cm above the heal on the hand. There is some slight blackening of the fingertips of the right hand with a dark purple spot at the tip of the middle finger, 0.3 to 0.4 cm in diameter with some slight splintering of the finger nail. This nail is also concave. The tip of the index finger is substantially broader than that of the left index finger with nodular deformities possibly due to callous formation near the tip. The left arm has the previously noted ring and wrist watch. Small linear abrasions are present upon the dorsum on the hand with a recent deep abrasion-type mark over the fifth MP joint. This is 0.5 x 0.5 cm in greatest dimension. The tips of the fingers are similar with some splitting of the cuticles, and slight concavity of the middle finger nail. There is also a well healed linear scar over the middle phalanx of little finger. The back is not unusual other than reddish material about the shoulders in varying stages of drying. Post mortem lividity is moderate and partially fixed in the dependent portions of the body. Post mortem rigidity is marked throughout. The length of the body is 68 inches. The estimated weight is 175 pounds.

MAIN INCISION:
Skeletal muscles dark red and well developed. Subcutaneous fat midline at the level of the umbilicus 1.5 cm in thickness.

THORAX:
There are no unusual features other than a few delicate adhesions in the interlobar fissure of the left lung.

Heart:
The pericardial sac contains an estimated 15 cc of pale yellow watery fluid. The heart has a normal configuration and an estimated weight of 350 gm. On sectioning there are no abnormalities of the ventricular myocardium. The maximum thickness of the left ventricle is 2.2 cm, the maximum thickness of the right ventricle is 0.6 cm.

PAGE - 5

Coronary arteries:
Focal mild atherosclerotic change, otherwise not unusual.

Lungs:
Estimated weight right 650 gm, left 600 gm. The lungs have mild to moderate anthracosis in a reticular pattern, and on sectioning have moderate congestion and edema. There are no mass lesions.

Trachea and main-stem bronchi:
Contain a small amount of thick brown mucinous material.

Mediastinal lymph nodes:
Up to about 1.2 cm in greatest dimension, soft and blackened.

Aorta:
Patchy mild atherosclerotic change in the distal abdominal aorta.

Esophagus:
The lumen contains a small amount of grayish semi-solid material. No unusual features are present.

ABDOMEN:
The abdominal viscera are normally positioned.

Liver:
Estimated weight 1,800 gm. There is a single small bluish subserosal region about 0.2 cm in greatest dimension in the medial portion of the right lobe. On sectioning of the liver there is mild to moderate congestion. No other unusual features are noted.

Gallbladder:
Partially contracted. It contains a small amount of yellow-brown bile. No unusual features are noted.

Pancreas:
An estimated 150 gm of pancreatic tissue are present. No unusual features are noted.

Spleen:
Estimated weight 250 gm. Spleen is firm and slightly congested. No mass lesions are present.

Adrenal glands:
Estimated weight of each 8 gm. No unusual features noted.

Kidneys:
Estimated weight of each 150 gm. The renal capsule strip with minimal resistance from essentially smooth cortical surfaces.

PAGE - 6

Urinary bladder:
Contains a moderate to large amount of pale yellow urine. No
unusual features are noted. Left in situ.

Prostate gland:
Not apparently enlarged. Left in situ.

Gastrointestinal tract:
The stomach contains a large amount of partially digested semi-
solid gray-brown material. None of the components of this can be
definitely identified. The small and large intestines have no
unusual features. The appendix vermiformis is present.

HEAD:
When the scalp is reflected there is an essentially regular 5 to 6
mm defect in the skull bone underlying the defect in the scalp.
There is no evidence of foreign material, in or around the edges of
this defect. When the skull is opened the bony defect has inward
beveling. The bone has a small to moderate amount of subarachnoid
hemorrhage and subdural hematoma formation. There is a defect in
the cerebral parenchyma in continuity with the defect in the scalp
and skull bone. Fragments of bone are recovered from the left
occipital pole of the brain, and small fragments of metal recovered
from the right frontal pole. On sectioning the brain there is a
tract of destruction of the parenchyma extending from the defect in
the occipital pole to the right frontal region. There is
associated hemorrhage. Of the metal fragments recovered one is
grossly consistent with a portion of copper jacket from a bullet,
and of the gray metal fragments recovered one had a somewhat
cylindrical configuration with the base indented and the opposite
pole irregularly flattened. Faint linear markings are present
along the sides of the structure. After removal of the dura
multiple non-displaced linear fractures of the skull bone are
present. The largest of these radiates from the region of the bony
defect. The most pronounced fractures are through the base of the
skull. Other than these traumatic injuries no unusual features are
noted. The brain has a normal configuration and an estimated
weight of 1,500 gm.

During the course of the autopsy blood and urine samples are
obtained for toxicologic analysis. Portions of these specimens are
given to Trooper Cruise. Other portions are saved. The metallic
fragments recovered from the brain are also given to Trooper
The decedents T shirt is also kept by Trooper

Original -
  Copies -

CENTRAL NERVOUS SYSTEM:
Sections of brainstem have no major abnormalities. A section of cerebellum has regions of subarachnoid and focal intraparenchymal hemorrhage. Sections of the cerebral hemispheres have regions of subarachnoid hemorrhage and tissue disruption with intraparenchymal hemorrhage. Small bone fragments are noted. In one section (#3) there is an irregular dark fragment which corresponds to the location of a small gray metallic fragment in the tissue block.

SKIN:
A section through the skin defect of the scalp has a region of epidermal abrasion and fragmentation with an underlying, almost funnel-shaped region of disruption of the dermis. Some of the dermal collagen is smudged in appearance with dermal and subcutaneous hemorrhage. Along the edges of the dermal defect small fragments of bone and finely granular black material are present.

HEART:
Not unusual.

CORONARY ARTERIES:
Not unusual

LUNGS:
Mild anthracosis with varying degrees of congestion, edema, and intra-alveolar hemorrhage.

TRACHEA:
Not unusual.

MEDIASTINAL LYMPH NODES:
Mild anthracosis.

THYMUS GLAND:
Not unusual.

AORTA:
Mild atherosclerosis.

LIVER:
One section has a cluster of thin walled blood vessels in a subcapsular location. Otherwise not unusual.

GALLBLADDER:
Post mortem mucosal autolysis.

PAGE - 8

ADRENAL GLANDS:
Not unusual.

KIDNEYS:
Not unusual.

GASTROINTESTINAL TRACT:
Not unusual.

About the Authors and Contributors

Evan Marshall retired from the Detroit Police Department with the rank of sergeant after 20 years of service. His assignments included Tactical Unit, Crime Scene Investigation, Special Response Team, Precinct Detective, and Homicide.

Marshall holds a bachelor's degree in history and a master's in criminal justice. He has been published extensively in the firearms and law enforcement press and is widely recognized as a hostage rescue and executive protection trainer, having trained groups as diverse as the Federal Air Marshals and the U.S. Army Special Reaction Teams. He is currently employed in the firearms industry.

Evan Marshall

Marshall and his wife Maryann are the parents of seven children. They live in Midland, Michigan.

Edwin J. Sanow is a 10-year veteran of the Benton County, Indiana, Sheriff's Department. He is currently a fully sworn, single-unit-status reserve deputy sheriff holding the rank of Corporal and routinely rides on duty with fellow officers in jurisdictions ranging from the New York City Police Department to the Los Angeles County Sheriff to the Crisp County, Georgia, Sheriff. He is certified as a firearms and continuing education police instructor by the Indiana Law Enforcement Training Board and serves as a chemical agents and oleoresin capsicum instructor. He was a staff instructor on the topics of wound ballistics and police ammunition selection at the 1993 ASLET International Training Conference. He holds a Distinguished Expert firearms rating and is a certified Glock armorer.

Sanow received his Bachelor of Science degree in Industrial Management (major) and Industrial Engineering (minor) from Purdue University. He has been using ordnance gelatin to analyze handgun, shotgun, and rifle bullet performance for 15 years. He has attended factory tours and technical seminars at Remington Arms, Hydra-Shok Corp., Winchester-Olin, Federal Cartridge, Master Cartridge, CCI-Speer, and Leupold-Stevens.

Sanow has had more than 500 articles published on the topics of ammunition performance, wound ballistics, and firearms training in such magazines as *Law & Order*, *Police*, *Law Enforcement Technology*, *Hoosier Policeman*, *Kansas Trooper*, *SWAT*, *Law Enforcement Times*, *NTOA Tactical Edge*, *Firepower*, *Combat Handguns*, *Gung-Ho*, *New Breed*, *Eagle*, *Handguns Illustrated*, *Sigarms Quarterly*, *AutoWeek*, *Police Marksman*, and *Petersen's Handguns*. He was the coauthor of the book *Handgun Stopping Power: The Definitive Study* with Evan Marshall.

Sanow has been an expert witness on the topics of ammo selection and wound ballistics in both criminal and civil proceedings. He has served as an ammunition consultant to Federal Cartridge Co., the New York City Police Department, and numerous other police departments across the country.

.....

Tom Burczynski grew up in the rolling hills southwest of Watkins Glen, New York, an area which abounds with game and where shooting was almost a daily activity. He first became interested in ballistics at age 17 after being introduced to handloading by his brother, Mike. After attending Mohawk Valley College, he took a position with Westinghouse Electric Corporation as a cathode ray tube technician. It was during his employment there, while studying mechanical engineering and metal fabrication techniques, that he invented the Hydra-Shok bullet. Six years later, he became involved in a water well drilling company, during which time he invented a self-actuating drilling bit, perfected Hydra-Shok, and invented the Starfire bullet.

After obtaining patents on the Hydra-Shok design, Tom collaborated with a local businessman and formed the Hydra-Shok Corpor-

Ed Sanow

ation, serving as vice president. He invented an automatic ejection system to mass produce the bullet and, soon after, Hydra-Shok ammunition was marketed as a rapid-expanding, semiexotic round sold directly to dealers and police departments. Less than a year later, Hydra-Shok had become the official duty round of the U.S. Department of State in .38 Special and .357 Magnum. Seven years later, the patent rights were licensed exclusively to Federal Cartridge. The Starfire patents followed, which were licensed exclusively to PMC/Eldorado in 1990.

Since then, several patents have been issued covering various forms of his latest design, Quik-Shok. Exclusive manufacturing rights to this design are currently being negotiated.

Burczynski has developed 44 bullet designs from his home-based company, Experimental Research, along with more than 80 nonballistic inventions. He currently resides in Montour Falls, New York, is still actively involved in ballistic research and development and patent development, does consulting work, and is always seeking sharp investors to share in the inevitable profits that will be made from his inventions.

· · · · ·

Steven B. Fuller received his Bachelor of Science degree in Electrical Engineering from Washington University. Upon graduation, he worked as a research associate in the WU Center for Biology of Natural Systems and then in the Mechanical Engineering Department. Later, he served as a research engineer in space physics at the WU McDonnell Center for Space Science. In those positions, he designed and built research instrumentation. He has also served as an adjunct lecturer at the WU School of Electrical Engineering.

As director of management services at Environment Measurements, Inc., Fuller began developing flight planning software. He became vice president of Engineering Management Information, Inc., where he continued the development of aviation software, including mathematical models of aircraft performance. He testified before the House Committee on Appropriations on the topic of computer access to weather and flight information.

Fuller was a founding officer of the National Avcomps Council, a trade association of firms providing computer services to the aviation industry. As president of EMI Aerocorp, Inc., he was instrumental in the design and implementation of the first fully automated private-sector flight plan data link, which was between CompuServe and FAA air route traffic control centers.

Fuller has recently left the business world and returned to the Electrical Engineering Department at Washington University, where he handles the technological aspects of the Center for Imaging Science.

Fuller's primary computer strengths are in interactive scientific and data analysis computation, and he has published a number of technical papers. While Fuller holds an instrument-rated private pilot license, he recently hung up his white scarf and goggles.

· · · · ·

Keith Jones is a 25 year veteran of law enforcement. He has a highly diversified police and security background. He has served as a police officer with the medium-sized Newark, Ohio, Police. As a member of their pistol team, Jones was a two-time competitor at the Police PPC Nationals held annually in Jackson, MS. He also served with the large, urban Indianapolis, Indiana, Police Department. Jones was one of IPD's first five Field Training Officers at the beginning of that landmark program, circa 1976.

Jones has been a road deputy with a small, rural sheriffs department and a security officer with a large, metro sheriffs department. He has also served as the town marshal in a small Hoosier community, a police position which carries the broadest statutory and enforcement powers under Indiana law. Jones has received meritorious commendations from each police department he has served.

Jones is a survivor of four police-action gunfights, three while armed with a revolver and one when deployed with a shotgun. Significantly, the ammo used by Jones in two of these scenarios was .38 Special non +P 158-grain round-nose lead, the least effective load in the least powerful duty caliber. The other handgun load was a softpoint. Jones thus speaks with profound authority when it comes to surviving a gunfight by controlling the variables before and during the fight and not by the pursuit of a magic bullet.

Jones is one of very few officers to become an Indiana Law Enforcement Academy-certified "survival tactics instructor." He is currently a deputy sheriff with the Marion County, Indiana, Sheriffs Department. He is a frequent speaker to police and civic groups on the topics of survival tactics, chemical agents, domestic violence intervention, and law enforcement history and heritage.

·····

Dave Pully is a computer scientist and data administrator with ITT Defense & Electronics, where he designs and develops enterprise data systems. He is a gun enthusiast and has experimented with ballistics and terminal performance as a hobby for more than 15 years. Proficient in C++, List, Fourth, objectPal, and SQL, Pully is the creator of Expert Systems and many computer simulations and data analysis programs, including one designed to assist in the selection of handgun loads based on performance specifications. On the hardware side, Pully has designed and built a number of electronic devices and circuits for use in ballistic research, including strobes and triggers for ultrahigh-speed photography.

·····

W. Dennis Tobin, M.D., P.A., is a medical neurologist who has had a lifelong interest in firearms and police survival tactics. He served as a reserve police officer in Illinois for 10 years and is currently involved in city and county police firearm and officer survival training in Texas. He continues to attend various police-related firearms and survival tactics courses.